Research Monograph No. 30

ALCOHOL AND TOBACCO: FROM BASIC SCIENCE TO CLINICAL PRACTICE

Edited by
Joanne B. Fertig, Ph.D.
John P. Allen, Ph.D.

NATIONAL INSTITUTES OF HEALTH
National Institute on Alcohol Abuse and Alcoholism
Bethesda, MD

This monograph is based on the workshop "Alcohol and Tobacco: From Basic Science to Policy" sponsored by the National Institute on Alcohol Abuse and Alcoholism (NIAAA) and held in San Diego, California, on November 7–9, 1994.

About the Editors: Joanne Fertig, Ph.D., is a psychologist with the Treatment Research Branch, Division of Clinical and Prevention Research, NIAAA, and John P. Allen, Ph.D., is chief of the Treatment Research Branch, Division of Clinical and Prevention Research, NIAAA.

NIH Publication No. 95–3931
Printed 1995

For sale by the U.S. Government Printing Office
Superintendent of Documents, Mail Stop: SSOP, Washington, DC 20402-9328
ISBN 0-16-048374-3

CONTENTS

FOREWORD

Despite the frequent co-occurrence of alcohol and tobacco addiction, until recently relatively little was known about the relationship between ethanol and nicotine. During the past decade various lines of evidence have converged suggesting possible mechanisms underlying concurrent use of the two substances as well as suggesting potential treatment strategies.

This volume represents a major effort by the National Institute on Alcohol Abuse and Alcoholism (NIAAA) to expand scientific knowledge of the linkage between alcohol and tobacco use. The chapters were initially presented at the symposium "Alcohol and Tobacco: From Basic Science to Policy" sponsored by NIAAA in San Diego, California, in November 1994. The meeting was designed to explore progress on cross-cutting issues in alcohol and tobacco use disorders and to identify promising directions for future research. The exciting, multidisciplinary interchange focused on integrating genetic, neuropharmacologic, behavioral, and policy domains.

More than 80 eminent researchers participated in the symposium. Although not all of their contributions are included in this volume, NIAAA applauds their work and values their participation. Chapter authors devoted many hours to the writing, revising, and editing of their chapters. NIAAA and the research community deeply appreciate the commitment that this effort represents.

The Treatment Research Branch deserves special recognition for organizing a most successful workshop that allowed researchers in many areas to exchange information, share ideas, and stimulate research. The fruits of this conference will ultimately be manifested both in the quality of future research in this critical topic as well as through more effective treatment of individuals who suffer problems with both alcohol and nicotine.

Enoch Gordis, M.D.
Director
National Institute on Alcohol Abuse and Alcoholism

PREFACE

Abuse of alcohol and tobacco both exact tremendous societal and personal costs because of the increased morbidity and mortality they cause. Concurrent dependence on alcohol and nicotine escalates these tolls synergistically rather than additively. Unfortunately, the two abuse problems frequently occur together.

The relationship between smoking and excessive use of alcohol appears to be far more than a statistical phenomenon, and the two behaviors are related in a variety of ways. Tolerance and reinforcement related to the two substances may be mediated by similar neural mechanisms, and each habit may respond to and be maintained by related interoceptive and exteroceptive cues. So too, predispositional genetic, personality, developmental, and demographic factors may be common to the two problems.

This monograph, *Alcohol and Tobacco: From Basic Science to Clinical Practice*, is a compendium based on presentations at a major symposium on alcohol and tobacco held in San Diego, California, on November 7–9, 1994. Scientists at the conference were senior researchers concerned with co-occurrence of alcohol and tobacco dependence. They were asked to both summarize the state of knowledge on a specific topic in their assigned domains and identify issues most in need of further investigation. A number of the presenters also offered original findings of research projects that they had recently conducted. The current monograph thus serves as an initial report of research findings, a compilation of current knowledge on alcohol and tobacco dependence, and a guide for future research endeavors.

Chapters included in this monograph encompass a particularly broad and rich spectrum, spanning topics from basic science to clinical research. The volume is organized into two major sections. The first section (chapters 1–9) covers sociocultural and genetic influences as well as underlying neurobiologic mechanisms. The first chapter, by Abrams, presents a conceptual framework for the monograph. This is followed by the chapter by Shiffman and Balabanis detailing the associations between alcohol and tobacco use. The next four chapters deal with the contribution of genetic, developmental, and environmental factors to alcohol and tobacco abuse. The following two chapters speculate on biochemical and neurophysiological substrates of consumption of and dependence on alcohol and tobacco. Niaura and Shiffman then provide an overview of the multiple and complex linkages between alcohol and tobacco use that summarizes this section.

The chapters in the second section of the monograph reflect the second day of the symposium and focus heavily on applied issues. These chapters include reports by Hughes, Monti and colleagues, and Bobo and colleagues on treatment for the two problems as well as strategies to maintain abstinence from each. Sobel and coworkers examine the natural recovery data. The chapter by Swan and colleagues discusses the application of tree-structured survival analysis to the prediction of alcohol relapse. Several chapters then deal with the management of smoking and abusive drinking in academic (Baer) and medical settings (Ockene and Adams; Curry and Ludman). The section concludes with an integrative overview of the findings related to treatment, early intervention, and policy.

The symposium not only stimulated a very thought-provoking interchange among researchers with widely different areas of expertise and interest but also nurtured a cross-disciplinary perspective on critical topics. Equally important, the conference allowed scientists and program officials of the Treatment Research Branch of the National Institute on Alcohol Abuse and Alcoholism (NIAAA) to suggest important directions for further research. A variety of research projects will both advance the science on this topic as well as yield findings that have significant impact on national health. The conference and monograph on smoking and alcohol dependence together serve as a foundation for a new and promising program element by NIAAA. Participants and speakers at the symposium richly merit our appreciation and gratitude. We would also like to acknowledge the dedicated help of Diana O'Donovan in the Office of Scientific Affairs, NIAAA, and Eve Shapiro and her colleagues at CSR, Incorporated. Their remarkable attention to detail and pursuit of excellence are highly appreciated.

Joanne Fertig, Ph.D.
John Allen, Ph.D.
National Institute on Alcohol Abuse and Alcoholism

ABBREVIATIONS AND ACRONYMS

AA	Alcoholics Anonymous
ADS	Alcohol Dependence Scale
ANOVA	analysis of variance
AOD	alcohol and other drugs
ATOD	alcohol, tobacco, and other drugs
AVP	arginine vasopressin
BAC	blood alcohol concentration
BMI	body mass index
bpm	beats per minute
CES–D	Center for Epidemiologic Studies–Depression Scale
cm	centimeter
CNS	central nervous system
d	day
df	degrees of freedom
dL	deciliter
DSM–III–R	Diagnostic and Statistical Manual of Mental Disorders, Third Edition, Revised
DSM–IV	Diagnostic and Statistical Manual of Mental Disorders, Fourth Edition
DZ	dizygotic
EAU	experimental alcohol use
ED	estimates of parameters
EEA	equal environment assumption
ETU	experimental tobacco use
FHN	family history negative
FHP	family history positive
FTND	Fagerstrom Test for Nicotine Dependence
FTQ	Fagerstrom Tolerance Questionnaire
g	gram
µg	microgram
GEE	generalized estimating equation
GFI	goodness-of-fit index
h	hour
HAS	high alcohol sensitivity
HIV	human immunodeficiency virus
HMO	health maintenance organization
IOM	Institute of Medicine
JCAHO	Joint Commission on Accreditation of Health Care Organizations
kcal	kilocalorie

kg	kilogram
L	liter
LAS	low alcohol sensitivity
LS	long-sleep
m	meter
M	mean
MAST	Michigan Alcoholism Screening Test
MEOS	microsomal ethanol-oxidizing system
mg	milligram
min	minute
mL	milliliter
mo	month
MRFIT	Multiple Risk Factor Intervention Trial
mRNA	messenger ribonucleic acid
MZ	monozygotic
NADS	National Alcohol and Other Drugs Survey
NAS	National Academy of Sciences
ng	nanogram
NHANES I	National Health and Nutrition Examination Survey
NIAAA	National Institute on Alcohol Abuse and Alcoholism
NRC	National Research Council
ns	nonsignificant
PDSIP	physician-delivered smoking intervention project
pg	picogram
ppm	parts per million
QTL	quantitative trait loci
RAPI	Rutgers Alcohol Problem Inventory
RI	recombinant inbred
s	second
SAAST	Self-Administered Alcohol Screening Testing
SC	subcutaneously
SD	standard deviation
SE	standard error
SEM	standard error of the mean
SS	short-sleep
TSSA	tree-structured survival analysis
TTI	theory of triadic influence
TVSFP	Television, School and Family Project
USDHHS	U.S. Department of Health and Human Services
wk	week
Va	additive variance
VA	Veterans Affairs
VAMC	Veterans Affairs Medical Center
yr	year

I.

Psychosocial and Biological Mechanisms of Alcohol-Tobacco Use

Chapter 1

Integrating Basic, Clinical, and Public Health Research for Alcohol-Tobacco Interactions

David B. Abrams, Ph.D.

Research on alcohol-tobacco interactions can advance knowledge and inform treatment, prevention, and policy at many levels. To this end, it is valuable to encourage interdisciplinary integration of basic, clinical, and public health sciences.

In this chapter I wish to highlight some possible organizing themes and present a broad conceptual framework that will facilitate interdisciplinary collaboration, not only among alcohol and tobacco researchers, but also from the molecular to the molar levels of analysis. Bridging levels provides the obvious immediate benefits of cross-fertilization between basic and clinical research. Bridging also stretches our vision to include the public health domain. It is my hope that such a broad, general framework will help to serve as an overview to identify strategic long-range research priorities and gaps, to place specific research areas in their context, and to expand our awareness of creative possibilities.

Although this monograph is primarily focused on alcohol and tobacco, broader questions are raised about how best to study multiple risk factors and other addictive and lifestyle behaviors, including their commonalities and their differences, and how to delineate the important boundary conditions. Historically, it is common wisdom that alcohol and tobacco go together (Walton 1972; Ayers et al. 1976; Bobo and Gilchrist 1983; Miller et al. 1983; Kozlowski et al. 1986). Sobell and colleagues (1990) recommend that research on the role of tobacco dependence be

D.B. Abrams, Ph.D., is a professor and director of the Division of Behavioral and Preventive Medicine, Brown University School of Medicine, RISE Building, The Miriam Hospital, 164 Summit Avenue, Providence, RI 02906.

included in alcohol research at all levels. Similarly, the role of other related biobehavioral mechanisms, risk factors, and comorbidity (e.g., depression, diet, exercise, gambling) should be included in alcohol and tobacco research. In order to sharpen boundary conditions, we may need to examine how other addictions, eating disorders, other compulsive disorders, problems with impulse control, attention, and characterological factors such as sociopathy interact with alcohol and tobacco.

GENERALIZATION, SAMPLING, AND MODES OF DELIVERY

One advantage of an integrative perspective is that it sharpens our focus on the central question of generalization of research results across several domains, including individuals; biobehavioral mechanisms, lifestyle behaviors, situations, and time; aggregate units, such as groups, organizations, and communities; modes or channels of delivery (e.g., schools, work sites, physicians' offices, mass media); the developmental phases over the lifespan; and gender, education, ethnicity, and other sociodemographic variables. Related issues concerning generalization include the strengths and weaknesses of different research methods, ranging from animal and human laboratory analogs to clinical samples to large-scale applications in communities to epidemiological, policy, and public health research strategies.

In both tobacco and alcohol studies with humans, research volunteers, clinical samples, and reactive recruitment of volunteers produce biases. These relatively homogeneous groups have truncated ranges of individual difference measures that limit conclusions from laboratory and clinical research studies. By contrast, applied community research involves proactive enrollment and outreach to large and heterogeneous populations. This strategy produces its own set of biases and challenges in evaluating the impact of broad dissemination in public health populations. It is crucial that we develop standard definitions, measures, and ways of comparing studies and their samples.

Although many of the preceding points are basic to all research, it is worth noting that as tobacco research has moved from the individual to the public health arena over the last decade, many of these points either have not been addressed or have been taken for granted, resulting in gaps in knowledge and less scientific progress than was possible under ideal circumstances (Abrams et al. 1991). Research on alcohol-tobacco interactions will further complicate this picture. The lessons learned from tobacco research could also help us to address more explicitly the levels of sampling bias and generalization as we move from more basic to applied research.

We live in an era where there is also a strong need to more rapidly transfer technology from the laboratory in order to benefit society at large. Research can make a unique contribution to our understanding of service delivery mechanisms, including barriers to access, methods and channels of delivery, and the social marketing challenges to reach those clients who have special needs and to provide services to underserved populations. We need more focused research on the specific mechanisms that accelerate or attenuate dissemination from small-scale clinical trials to large defined population interventions.

The challenge of technology transfer raises other thematic issues around identification of the key variables to be measured, the context within which alcohol-tobacco issues are embedded, and the need to focus research on the process of technology transfer and dissemination. Closer research attention could be paid to the following issues:

- Constructing different profiles of client characteristics in terms of genetic and biobehavioral vulnerability, social networks, and social context.
- Identifying the best modes and methods of intervention delivery.
- Describing the nuances of different channels of access to clients such as schools, primary care physicians, work sites, tertiary care settings, and rehabilitative care settings.
- Describing the types of communications modalities, such as mass media, face-to-face counseling, self-help, interactive computers, and home-based interactive television.

We need to develop and evaluate health care services research questions, model standards of care, de-

velop clinical guidelines, and evaluate the training of larger numbers of less expensive generalist counselors versus more expensive highly trained professionals. For example, can alcohol counselors in alcohol treatment programs be effectively trained to deliver tobacco dependence treatment, and under what conditions should a specialist in nicotine dependence be consulted? Will different approaches produce different outcomes and, if so, in which types of clients?

MEASUREMENT

As we move from the basic sciences to clinical interventions to the public health arena, our measures, units of analysis, and timeframes also shift. We begin to cross over into different worlds and languages, from intraindividual neurochemical and cognitive self-regulatory mechanisms over relatively short timeframes of nanoseconds to hours; to overt individual behavior changes over days to months; to changes among social networks groups and larger units over months to years; to changes in policies and social norms over years to decades. We are all interested in similar research questions, albeit at different levels, such as the following:

- What mediating mechanisms and moderator variables facilitate or inhibit change?
- What are the causal processes and mechanisms that accelerate change within individuals, groups, and populations?

- How do processes relate to intermediate and final outcomes?

The measures of associations, causes, and effects also change from the neurochemical and cognitive-behavioral level to the level of treatment and prevention. Outcomes stretch beyond the neurochemical markers of alcohol or tobacco abuse—measures of motivation, use, exposure, and consumption—to societal considerations, including risk taking and alcohol-related problems such as incidence of violence, unsafe sex, quality of life, morbidity, mortality, and health care utilization and demand for services.

As we move to the public health arena, the bottom line outcome measures shift from individual clinical efficacy to cost-effectiveness and cost per unit of change per degree of penetration into the population (i.e., reach). Issues need to be considered, such as the sensitivity and specificity of outcome measures; choosing the appropriate metrics and units of measurement; and planning to include program, process, intermediate, and final outcomes into study designs.

With increasing awareness of the limitations of our resources come new questions involving health care utilization and financing. What is the relative value of the alcohol-tobacco research contribution to improving the overall quality of life, using standardized metrics such as quality-adjusted life years saved per unit of intervention of known cost and of known penetration or impact? What are the short- and long-term benefits and return on investment to managed care and health insurers? How do alcohol and tobacco compare with each other in terms of health risk reduction, morbidity, and mortality, and how do alcohol and tobacco programs compare with those for other chronic illnesses or wellness/lifestyle programs? Can research help us to develop more rational-empirical decisionmaking rules and algorithms?

THE IMPORTANCE OF THEORY AND RESEARCH DESIGN

Can we develop more focused and refined research questions when we think about how basic sciences can inform clinical and public health applications? Conversely, can population sciences, including epidemiology, health care services research, and health education and policy, help generate questions and hypotheses to advance basic and clinical arenas? This brings up another domain of concern involving research design, methodology, and the need for a common language. Such goals are facilitated by creating a sufficient critical mass of researchers working collaboratively from the outset as an interdisciplinary team. The result is the development of a common language, clearer definitions of terms, and a whole that is greater than the sum of the parts. This interdisciplinary approach is to be contrasted with the intermittent involvement of outside experts, which provides multidisciplinary input but stops short of true interdisciplinary collaboration. Innovations in theory and advances in knowledge may best be facilitated by the development of interdisciplinary centers of excellence.

Advances in statistical design and methodology also allow us to broaden our traditional research "gold standard" of the randomized group design so that we can apply the appropriate design, methods, and measurement to the question, sample, and context under investigation. Structural equation models and general estimating equations permit complex multivariate systems to be modeled as they dynamically change over time. How do changes in drinking patterns covary with changes in smoking, and how does depression relate to the separate and interactive patterns of use? Is it possible that research to date has inaccurately estimated the relationship between alcohol abuse and depression because it has failed to take into account the role of tobacco use as a form of self-medication against depression in alcohol abusers?

Interdisciplinary integration helps us to rethink our biases toward preferring traditional theory-driven randomized group designs. Observational studies, surveys, naturalistic studies, single-subject designs, case studies, and developmental and longitudinal cohort research not only can advance knowledge in their own right but also can help enhance hypothesis generation for the basic and clinical sciences.

This reciprocal interdisciplinary interaction between basic, clinical, and public health sciences can accelerate the development of more integrative theoretical models. This interaction will also encourage the development of consistent and clear definitions of terms, mechanisms, and measures. How do neuroregulatory pathways relate to behavioral self-regulation, and how do both of these factors in turn relate to community or societal patterns of acquisition, use, and abuse? What are the policy implications?

The clinical and public health sciences can inform basic sciences about what kinds of animal simulation studies to conduct and vice versa. The genetic epidemiology of alcohol, tobacco, and psychiatric comorbidity has influenced and is reciprocally influenced by neurobiological and animal research. Basic science can help confirm mechanisms and produce multivariate measures and markers with sufficient sensitivity and specificity to be incorporated into clinical treatment and prevention research. Assessment and screening tools with sufficient sensitivity and specificity can be developed to identify levels of vulnerability—those at risk. Presumably such identification will better inform intervention and policy research about how to allocate and tailor resources to individual and subgroup needs.

INTEGRATING THEMES FROM CLINICAL TO PUBLIC HEALTH INTERVENTIONS

Basic, clinical, and public health research all make valuable independent contributions to improving clinical and prevention applications. However, when we ask more challenging questions, such as how to allocate limited resources to optimize a continuum of care for the entire population across the lifespan, it is difficult to combine knowledge and data from all the necessary disciplines and levels for rational decisionmaking. By integrating alcohol and tobacco research on the one hand, and by stretching from the molecular to the molar level on the other hand, research can be challenged to explore new syntheses and models.

Figure 1 illustrates an integrated care model for a community population. We can begin to better define individual differences and important subgroups within an entire population and to examine a variety of essential program elements, such as clinical treatment and prevention, ranging from least to most intensive, costly, and interactive. At the same time we need to focus on the processes of change and sensitive intermediate and final outcomes, including measures of awareness, motivation, experimentation, normal use, intermittent abuse, and chronic dependence.

The related systems questions, such as the demand for services and the implications for costs, also need to be included in this integrated model. What are the separate and interactive contributions of alcohol and tobacco abuse to the often-cited health care statistic that 15 percent of the work-site population uses 85 percent of the health care dollar? Concepts such as stepped care and some form of treatment

matching will need to be more rigorously researched.

Generally, clinical treatments are quite intensive, expensive, and highly interactive, consisting of a professional specialist and either individuals or small groups participating in inpatient or outpatient care. There are also relatively few specialists in both alcohol and tobacco treatment, which limits access to larger populations. Such clinical treatment can be quite efficacious, but it is directed at a very self-selected and limited clinical population, such as those individuals with higher socioeconomic status, advanced dependence, or signs of medical illness. Comorbidity of medical and psychiatric illness, including depression, is likely to be more common in this clinical population.

The vast majority of alcoholics and smokers, including many less dependent individuals, do not seek formal treatment. Differences in social supports, marital status, education, and income also usually exist between clinical and general population samples. The truncated samples in clinical treatment research may be one reason why traditional patient-treatment matching research has not fulfilled its promise.

If we expand our intervention options from acute tertiary and rehabilitation settings to self-care and self-change programs and brief interventions in the work site, school, or primary care physician's office, we also can expand the range of people who can be reached for acute tertiary treatment, early intervention, or pri-

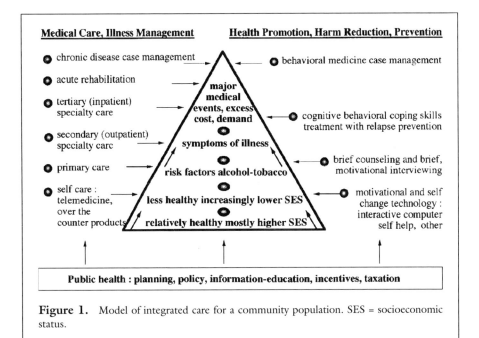

Figure 1. Model of integrated care for a community population. SES = socioeconomic status.

mary prevention. With this expansion in our conceptual framework, we would reach more people and also those at earlier stages of their tobacco and alcohol dependence. Subgroupings of individuals (at a more macro or population level) are likely to benefit from being matched to qualitatively different intervention programs that vary in their ease of dissemination, convenience, cost, and intensity. More research needs to be done on this kind of stepped-care or "macro-level" matching of population subtypes to extremely different types of intervention programs. Expanding the range of intervention options and penetrating a greater proportion of the whole population eventually produces a treatment continuum for the entire range of individuals in the general population. It conceptually combines a stepped-care approach with a treatment-matching strategy and a harm reduction philosophy.

A stepped-care conceptual approach suggests new research directions to inform the decisionmaking algorithms required for such a comprehensive approach. A new measurement metric is needed based on the overall population *impact* of the intervention. *Impact* provides a common language and a standardized measure to permit cross-fertilization between clinical and public health sciences. It also permits direct comparison across lifestyle risk factors such as alcohol, tobacco, and others. To illustrate from our work in tobacco research, table 1 shows the projected impact of different types of interven-

Table 1. Common Language Metrics for Individual-Population Research: Example From Tobacco Dependence Research.

Intervention Type	Efficacy (% Quit)	Reach (% Population)	Impact[1]
Clinical treatment: behavioral + pharmacotherapeutic	30–40	3–5	0.09–0.20
Clinical treatment: behavioral group	20–30	5–10	0.10–0.30
Brief primary care: behavioral + pharmacotherapeutic	10–20	10–20	0.10–0.40
Reactive: self-help programs	5–10	50?	0.25–0.50
Proactive: interactive computer interventions	15–25	50–70	0.75–1.75

[1]Impact = treatment efficacy x population reach (penetration).

tions that vary in their intensity, efficacy, and ability to penetrate a greater proportion of the whole population (Abrams 1993). Since interventions of different intensity and complexity will vary dramatically in cost, it follows that cost-effectiveness and overall impact become the most relevant measures of final outcome rather than the simple efficacy of traditional clinical outcomes trials, such as continuous abstinence for 1 year.

How can basic neurosciences, genetic epidemiology, and biobehavioral mechanisms researchers help to refine this kind of stepped-care model? A central question is, What clusters of individuals or subgroups of a defined population might be screened and triaged into what level or step

of intervention programming (minimal self-change, moderate brief interventions, and maximal acute care and rehabilitation)? For stepped care to work, an infrastructure is needed to guide assessment and decision rules and to triage the participants into appropriate levels of care and then to coordinate the delivery of services over time.

Research is needed to help design the parameters within a stepped-care model. Is a screening measure based on today's conceptualization of nicotine or alcohol dependence sufficiently sensitive and specific for large-scale public health planning? Some kind of screening with cut-points and benchmarks is needed for the identification of subgroups to be triaged into different types or levels of intervention. Some of the latest and best measures developed in the basic science laboratory would not be practical for use in the large-scale public health domain, but translational research could be directed at developing practical measures. Such research would lead to new decision rules or algorithms. Prospective demonstration research studies over reasonably long periods of time would also be needed to determine (1) which of several stepped-care approaches are most efficacious, practical, and cost-effective and (2) whether the best stepped-care model can indeed outperform secular trends or other models of service delivery.

Another related research opportunity comes from the realization that sensitive outcome measures at the biobehavioral mechanisms level can be very important process measures or intermediate outcome measures at the public health level. There is a need to conduct more process-to-outcome research in larger scale population-based interventions. Changes in biochemical markers, in cognitive motivational readiness, in self-efficacy, in acquisition of coping skills, in social supports, and in social norms can all be useful intermediate outcome measures along the way to evaluating overall population change. Essentially, the process and intermediate measures in population-based research could be the same measures considered to be the final outcome measures in biobehavioral mechanisms or clinical trials research. A related issue is to focus more explicitly on the ex-

pected timeframes for meaningful short-term change, for final outcomes, and for cost-effectiveness. Naturally, the timeframe and units of analysis would depend on the level of research and the questions being asked.

As we look more closely at health services delivery and utilization, related questions about morbidity and mortality are raised. Beyond the separate health-damaging effects of alcohol and tobacco, it is well known that there are synergistic effects for specific medical disorders such as laryngeal and esophageal cancers. The relative risk of smoking alone is 2.1 and that of alcohol alone is 2.2, but the combined risk is more than 4 times the relative risk of either one separately (Brownson and Chang 1987). The interaction of other lifestyle factors, such as the potential beneficial effects of increasing physical activity and changing dietary intake, also needs to be considered. Indeed, by focusing on alcohol and tobacco interactions, we may develop prototypes for the study of multiple risk factor behaviors related to chronic disease management more generally. These risk factors can then be linked to measures of overall health and well-being or to morbidity and mortality.

Dr. John Hughes (see chapter 10) and others have pointed out that heavy smoking can be a useful marker for alcohol-related problems in family practice or primary care settings. Furthermore, smokers tend to have poorer diets and are more sedentary than nonsmokers (Emmons et al. 1994). Given that over 85 percent of alcoholics are smokers, it is likely that many alcoholics will have three or more lifestyle risk factors co-occurring. In terms of outpatient medical services, one could envisage a clinic or rehabilitation program that would not only combine treatments for all addictive behaviors but would also include treatment of other health and lifestyle risk factors and psychiatric comorbidity issues in a more comprehensive approach to wellness. At the work site, we are already beginning to see that the traditional separation between programs such as health promotion, employee assistance, and occupational health and safety is beginning to dissolve as they are integrated into a continuum of interventions.

This kind of thinking flows logically from the integrative conceptual model presented earlier. It raises a host of potentially exciting research questions, including whether there are common skills that can be taught for one behavior that could generalize to others and whether there are commonalities or differences in trying to increase a low-frequency behavior such as exercise or fiber in the diet versus trying to decrease or eliminate a negative behavior such as drinking or tobacco abuse. Should behaviors be treated sequentially beginning with the most severely debilitating, such as alcohol first and tobacco second, or should behaviors be worked on concurrently? What are the similarities and differences in social network and social support variables across these lifestyle behaviors?

Computer-based technologies are beginning to open up very exciting possibilities. It is possible to develop computer-based interactive systems that can include screening algorithms and a variety of treatment elements that can be tailored to the individual response of the client (Skinner 1993; Velicer et al. 1993). This type of system allows for the possibility of a much higher level of tailoring within the privacy of a self-help or self-change approach. Interventions could be developed for use in the home, with interactive cable TV technology; in the workplace, where they could be combined with other screening and annual physical information; in schools; and in primary care offices and other health care facilities.

Brief training of subdoctoral health counselors could be combined with computer systems to deliver powerful interventions such as those based on Miller and Rollnick's (1991) motivational interviewing techniques. Physician or other professional time could then be used sparingly, as long as these limited services were backed up by brief counseling and telephone followup combined with home-based interactive learning modules. Research is needed to evaluate the reach, effectiveness, and cost (i.e., the impact) of various combinations of these intervention packages.

To develop the best decision algorithms for these interactive computer systems requires an enormous degree of interdisciplinary cooperation between basic and applied scientists as well as individuals in the communications arts and computer technologies.

Computer-based systems also have the capability of automatically collecting important individual and group information about program use, processes, and outcome that can be used to advance research hypotheses.

DEVELOPING THE COMPONENTS OF A COMPREHENSIVE APPROACH TO SERVICE DELIVERY

To demonstrate how these diverse ideas can come together, I would like to conclude with the presentation of a hypothetical stepped-care, population-based approach for comprehensive tobacco treatment (Abrams 1993). As illustrated in figure 2, if we look at the entire population of current smokers, they are distributed along a continuum of characteristics including severity of nicotine dependence; degree of comorbidity of alcohol, psychiatric, or medical conditions; and other factors affecting motivation, vulnerabilities, and risks. As their risk or vulnerability to relapse increases, there is a need for increased treatment complexity or excessive health care utilization. In treating the whole population, the essential elements include motivational factors along the continuum of being ready to change and degree of vulnerability in terms of dependence severity and comorbidity complications.

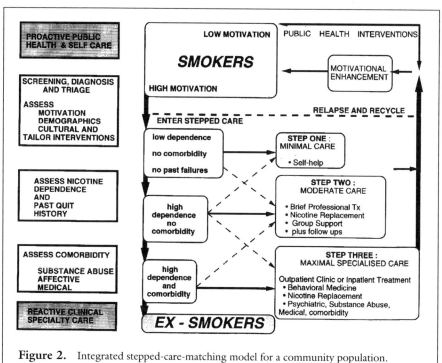

Figure 2.   Integrated stepped-care-matching model for a community population.

The first decision point in this stepped-care model is to assess the level of motivation so as not to use expensive skills training and behavior change interventions for those who are not interested or ready to change. By contrast, the whole range of health education and public health interventions, as well as motivational interviewing and other strategies, can be used to move individuals from lower to higher levels of motivation. This cycle is repeated until the individual is ready to change.

Once individuals are ready to change, that is, as they move from lower levels of motivational readiness to higher levels, then the next step of intervention can be considered. These intervention possibilities can be divided into one of several choice points, such as minimal self-change or self-help, moderate brief interventions, and maximal highly specialized acute care treatments. Individuals at any level who fail at a lower level of stepped care can either be recycled at the same level or stepped up to a more intensive and more specialized treatment specifically tailored to their needs. An infrastructure is needed to provide continuity of care and to track the current status and the past history of responses to treatments of all individuals in the program. Such a stepped-care delivery system needs to be sustained over many years so that the system never gives up on an individual, but also never coerces. The system should be patient centered and sensitive.

This approach combines the best of our limited knowledge of stepped-care treatments and individual differences that could be important for patient-treatment matching. This matching is actually on a large-scale population level (macromatching), in contrast to the traditional—and not very satisfactory—matching at the clinical treatment level (micromatching). In this example, one can see how many branches and disciplines need to be involved to provide rational decisionmaking information at every step of the model. While traditional matching algorithms have not fared well in psychotherapy or in alcohol treatment, the integration of population-level concepts and samples may warrant reconsideration.

The stepped-care model illustrates in concrete terms the issues touched on in this chapter, including generalization; the importance of the difference between clinical and general population samples; proactive reaching out versus reactive recruitment of clinical and research samples; the importance of common languages, definitions, and measures; understanding the processes of change over time, including motivational factors, and linking these processes to sensitive intermediate outcomes; intervention content, intensity, and mode of delivery; allowing for different timeframes for change to occur—from several weeks and months for those ready for action to many years for those who are very low in motivation; and incorporating sensitive measures of impact, including penetration, cost, efficacy, and reduced demand for acute tertiary and rehabilitative services.

To summarize, my main recommendations are as follows:

- Establish a standardized set of core measures and a common language to be used in an interdisciplinary approach to alcohol-tobacco interactions, from basic science to public health.
- Focus research on questions of technology transfer.
- Include short-term and more sensitive intermediate markers of the process of change as measures of intermediate outcomes.
- Include factors such as cost, penetration, and efficacy as outcome measures in an overall metric of impact.
- Conduct a search for common underlying mechanisms, differences, and boundary conditions within and across lifestyle behaviors and at different points in the lifespan from infancy to old age.
- Develop true interdisciplinary research and accept naturalistic, observational, and other research designs as a complement to theory-driven randomized trials.
- Begin to develop interdisciplinary centers of excellence that can combine research questions at a more integrative level.
- Develop measures and algorithms (decision rules) that can be used to screen and triage clients into different subgroups, which can be treated with different interventions, and that will prospectively predict differential outcomes.
- Develop and evaluate models along the lines of stepped-care and patient-treatment matching. Such research should, however, include true population-based samples and a wider range of qualitatively different intervention types (i.e., macromatching) than those matching variables that have traditionally been tested within the narrow samples of clinical trials research to date.
- Conduct more research on innovative technology such as computer-based interactive self-help programs.
- Focus research on selected delivery channels to reach defined populations such as work sites, schools, physicians' offices, hospitals, and mass media.
- Concentrate efforts on special populations, including the underserved, minorities, women, and those exposed to occupational risks that interact with tobacco and alcohol.
- Focus more research on health care utilization and cost-effectiveness issues.
- Address the question of return on investment for managed care organizations.

We are on the verge of an exciting opportunity as we move toward the year 2000, provided we can succeed in developing a critical mass of interdisciplinary research. This effort will involve new conceptual models and a common language based on the interests of the various disciplines involved. In this way we can move beyond multidisciplinary research, in which a number of experts are consulted but a new conceptual model and common language is rarely developed, to true interdisciplinary research. Multivariate structural models and other statistical approaches can now be used to integrate various levels of measurement, process, and intermediate outcomes over time. As more variance is accounted for by integrating alcohol and tobacco research from basic to public health sciences, our interventions will hopefully improve and reach more members of society with proper care.

ACKNOWLEDGMENTS

This work was supported in part by National Institute on Alcohol Abuse and Alcoholism grants 2R01 AA08734 and 1R01 AA07850, by National Heart, Lung, and Blood Institute grant HL32318, and by National Cancer Institute grants CA38309 and P01CA 50087. Grateful appreciation is expressed to the Brown University interdisciplinary team: Drs. Peter Monti, Raymond Niaura, Damaris Rohsenow, Richard Brown, Michael Goldstein, Karen Emmons, Bess Marcus, David Lewis, Richard Longabaugh, Suzanne Colby, Robert Swift, and many others. I especially appreciate the ideas of all our students and postdoctoral fellows over the last 15 years.

REFERENCES

Abrams, D.B. Treatment issues: Towards a stepped-care model. *Tobacco Control* 2 (suppl):S17–S37, 1993.

Abrams, D.B.; Emmons, K.M.; Niaura, R.; Goldstein, M.G.; and Sherman, C.B. Tobacco dependence: An integration of individual and public health perspectives. In: Nathan, P.E.; Langenbucher, J.W.; McCrady, B.S.; and Frankenstein, W., eds. *Annual Review of Addictions Research and Treatment.* New York: Pergamon Press, 1991. pp. 391–436.

Ayers, J.; Ruff, C.F.; and Templer, D.I. Alcoholism, cigarette smoking, coffee drinking and extraversion. *J Stud Alcohol* 37:983–985, 1976.

Bobo, J.K, and Gilchrist, L.D. Urging the alcoholic client to quit smoking cigarettes. *Addict Behav* 8:297–305, 1983.

Brownson, R.C., and Chang, J.C. Exposure to alcohol and tobacco and the risk of laryngeal cancer. *Arch Environ Health* 42:192–196, 1987.

Emmons, K.M.; Hammond, S.K.; and Abrams, D.B. Smoking at home: The impact of smoking cessation on nonsmokers' exposure to environmental tobacco smoke. *Health Psychol* 13:1–5, 1994.

Kozlowski, L.T.; Jelinek, L.C.; and Pope, M.A. Cigarette smoking among alcohol abusers: Continuing and neglected problem. *Can J Public Health* 77:205–207, 1986.

Miller, W.R.; Hedrick, K.E.; and Taylor, C.A. Addictive behaviors and life problems before and after treatment of problem drinkers. *Addict Behav* 8:403–412, 1983.

Miller, W.R., and Rollnick, S. *Motivational Interviewing: Preparing People To Change Addictive Behavior.* New York: Guilford Press, 1991.

Skinner, H.A. Early identification of addictive behaviors using a computerized lifestyle assessment. In: Baer, J.S.; Marlatt, G.A.; and McMahon, R.J., eds. *Addictive Behaviors Across the Lifespan: Prevention, Treatment and Policy Issues.* Newbury Park, CA: Sage, 1993. pp. 88–110.

Sobell, L.C.; Sobell, M.B.; Kozlowski, L.T.; and Toneatto, T. Alcohol or tobacco research versus alcohol and tobacco research. *Br J Addict* 85:263–269, 1990.

Velicer, W.F.; Prochaska, J.O.; Bellis, J.M.; DiClemente, C.C.; Rossi, J.S.; Fava, J.L.; and Steiger, J.H. An expert system intervention for smoking cessation. *Addict Behav* 18:269–290, 1993.

Walton, R.G. Smoking and alcoholism: A brief report. *Am J Psychiatry* 128:1455–1456, 1972.

Chapter 2

Associations Between Alcohol and Tobacco

Saul Shiffman, Ph.D., and Mark Balabanis, B.A.

Alcohol and tobacco seem to go together. Consumers of one drug are likely to consume the other. Moreover, alcohol and tobacco often are used at the same time. This chapter briefly reviews the epidemiology of the relationships between drinking and smoking and examines some of the mechanisms proposed to explain the linkage. An exhaustive review of the relevant literature is beyond this chapter's scope; instead, particular studies are cited as examples. The reader is referred to recent reviews for more comprehensive compendia (e.g., Istvan and Matarazzo 1984; Zacny 1990); we owe these reviewers a significant debt for making our task easier.

As suggested above, alcohol and tobacco use may be related in two ways. First, people who drink also may smoke (and vice versa); throughout this chapter, this is referred to as the person-level linkage. Second, there can also be a situational linkage: People who use both drugs may use them together in the same situations. The two relationships are conceptually and empirically independent: Each is logically possible without the other, each requires different empirical evidence, and each may be explained by different hypothetical mechanisms. Accordingly, this chapter discusses the two types of linkage separately.

Because the relationship between alcohol and tobacco may differ at different stages of a user's career, this chapter organizes the review according to three stages of drug use: initiation (i.e., the initial exposure to each

S. Shiffman, Ph.D., and M. Balabanis, B.A., are affiliated with the Department of Psychology, University of Pittsburgh, Bellefield Professional Building, 130 N. Bellefield Street, Suite 510, Pittsburgh, PA 15260.

drug and adoption of regular use), maintenance (i.e., ongoing use), and cessation/relapse (i.e., termination and reinitiation of use). Finally, we also consider the direction of the relationship tested in each study.

The relationship between alcohol and tobacco need not be bidirectional: Drinking may increase smoking, smoking may increase drinking, or both. The directionality of the relationship is defined most easily in experimental studies of the situational linkage between alcohol and tobacco, where one is manipulated and the other is observed. Cross-sectional correlational studies—the primary empirical basis for establishing an alcohol-tobacco link—cannot distinguish the direction of influence. Accordingly, most data on the person-level covariation in alcohol and tobacco use during the maintenance phase are nondirectional and are reviewed as such.

After reviewing the empirical evidence at each stage of drug use, we discuss additional issues relevant to the link between drinking and smoking and then examine potential mechanisms to explain the relationship. The chapter closes with conclusions and recommendations for future research.

INITIATION

The initiation phase of drug use involves initial exposure to, experimentation with, and adoption of a drug.

PERSON LINKAGE

Alcohol and tobacco are generally the first psychoactive drugs that young people experiment with, typically during the early teen years (Bachman et al. 1981; Kandel and Yamaguchi 1985). They initially try both drugs at around the same age (12 years for tobacco and 12.6 for alcohol) (Single et al. 1974). However, data about which drug is tried first are inconsistent (Kandel et al. 1992; U.S. Department of Health and Human Services [USDHHS] 1994). Both tobacco and alcohol share a role as "gateway drugs" that presage use of other psychoactive drugs; in other words, alcohol and/or tobacco use precedes most subsequent use of marijuana and cocaine (Kandel et al. 1992).

Do young people who drink also smoke and vice versa? According to study findings, the answer is "yes": A substantial body of evidence links alcohol and tobacco use during the initiation phase. Forty percent of teens who drink alcohol also smoke cigarettes (versus 10 percent of nondrinkers); conversely, 88 percent of those who smoke cigarettes also drink alcohol (versus 55 percent of nonsmokers) (USDHHS 1994). A slightly weaker relationship exists between alcohol and smokeless tobacco use (USDHHS 1994; O'Malley unpublished data 1995). Although causal direction cannot be discerned from survey data, the association appears to be asymmetric: The effect of drinking on smoking and smokeless tobacco use is more than twice as great as the converse (O'Malley unpublished data 1995). Studies of progression after initial use find that youths who drink alcohol are not more likely to accelerate their smoking (Ary and Biglan 1988); however, smokeless tobacco users are more likely to increase drinking (Ary et al. 1987; USDHHS 1994).

Similar psychosocial variables predict both tobacco and alcohol use (e.g., Bachman et al. 1981; Wills et al. 1994), which suggests that these relationships may account for the link between use of each drug. However, researchers have not tested such a hypothesis (i.e., whether the alcohol-tobacco link persists when these other variables are partialed out). In any case, the person-level linkage between drinking and smoking is evident from the very earliest stages of these behaviors.

SITUATIONAL LINKAGE

Are alcohol and tobacco used jointly early in users' careers? Perhaps more important, does use of one drug facilitate exposure to or experimentation with the other?

Alcohol to Tobacco

A link between drinking and smoking initiation is particularly plausible, because the disinhibiting effects of alcohol might help break down resistance to smoking. The only study that has examined this link (Friedman et al. 1985) found no evidence that teens were particularly likely to be drinking when they smoked their first few cigarettes. However, the likelihood that smoking was accompanied by drinking increased over the first three

smoking experiences. Friedman and colleagues (1985) speculated that situational associations may develop between behaviors that are clandestine. It is also possible that young users learn quickly about favorable pharmacologic interactions between the two drugs. In any case, two-thirds of teenagers reported that by the time they had been smoking for 2 years, they often smoked while drinking (McKennell and Thomas 1967).

Tobacco to Alcohol

We are not aware of any study that has examined the role of smoking in initiation to alcohol use. The idea that both behaviors are socially influenced, and that teens who smoke tend to drink, may cause some association to arise: The same friends who prompt drinking may prompt smoking. Otherwise, it is not clear by what mechanism smoking acutely might facilitate initiation of alcohol consumption.

MAINTENANCE

The initiation and cessation phases mark dramatic changes in drug-use patterns; however, users' careers are dominated by the relatively stable ongoing use that marks the maintenance phase.

PERSON LINKAGE

Do people who use alcohol also use tobacco? Is the converse true? The evidence for an association is striking: Smokers tend to drink and drinkers tend to smoke. Most smokers (86 percent) (Friedman et al. 1974) drink alcohol; smokers are 1.32 times more likely to drink than are nonsmokers. This relationship holds for both men and women (and thus is not an artifact of gender differences in prevalence of smoking and drinking) but is slightly stronger among women (Friedman et al. 1974; also see Carmody et al. 1985). Conversely, smoking prevalence is 75 percent higher among drinkers than among nondrinkers (Abelson et al. 1973).[1] Although the association between smoking and drinking is robust and consistent across studies, its magnitude is modest, with correlations typically hovering around 0.18 (Istvan and Matarazzo 1984). Epidemiological associations cannot distinguish the direction of influence. However, the link between smoking and drinking is asymmetrical: Drinking predicts smoking much better than smoking predicts drinking (based on analysis of data in Friedman et al. 1974).

The link between drinking and smoking shows a dose-response relationship. Heavier drinkers tend to be heavier smokers (Friedman et al. 1991; Abrams et al. 1992). Keenan et al. (1990) demonstrated that heavier drinkers also smoke each cigarette more intensely. Again, the association between smoking rate and drinking rate is reliable but modest, with correlations ranging from 0.15 to 0.20 (Craig and Van Natta 1977; Friedman et al. 1991). There is some suggestion that the dose-response relationship between smoking and drinking is nonlinear. In one study, occasional drinkers were slightly *more* likely to smoke heavily (≥ 20 cigarettes per day) than were nondrinkers (Cummins et al. 1981). Studies of very light smokers suggest that they are not necessarily light drinkers (Paty unpublished data 1991; Shiffman et al. 1994*b*).

Thus, the dose-response relationship does not hold up consistently at the low end of the dose distribution. Conversely, there is some evidence that the relationship between drinking and smoking is particularly strong at the high end of the dose distribution. In one study, the smoking rate did not rise with increased drinking until drinking exceeded three to four drinks per day (Cummins et al. 1981). In aggregate, these findings suggest that the overall correlation between drinking and smoking may be driven by persons who are both heavy smokers and heavy drinkers.

This is consistent with findings on smoking and alcoholism. Among alcoholics, prevalence rates over 90 percent are common (Maletzky and Klotter 1974; Bobo 1992). In a case-control study, smoking prevalence was much higher among alcoholics than nonalcoholics (Cyr and Wartman 1988; DiFranza and Guerrera 1990). Alcoholics also smoke more heavily than nonalcoholic smokers. In one study, the average smoking rate for alcoholics was

---

[1]Cigar and pipe smoking (in men only) is associated with only modest increases in drinking rates (Cummins et al. 1981); these behaviors produce highly variable nicotine levels and may have different dynamics (Craig and Van Natta 1977).

48.7 cigarettes per day (Maletzky and Klotter 1974), more than double the national average (USDHHS 1988). Also, drinking and smoking rates correlated very highly among alcoholics but not among nonalcoholic controls (Maletzky and Klotter 1974) (also see Abrams et al. 1992, who also showed that tobacco and alcohol dependence correlated as well).

Conversely, alcoholism is much more prevalent among smokers than nonsmokers, particularly among women (DiFranza and Guerrera 1990; Covey et al. 1994). In a recent study, 35 percent of heavy smokers had a lifetime history of alcoholism, versus 10 percent of never-smokers (the current prevalence was 13 percent versus 6 percent) (Hughes et al. in press), leading to the suggestion that heavy smoking should be used as a screening tool to identify potential alcoholics. Although both alcoholism and smoking are associated with other psychiatric disorders, the link between smoking and alcohol problems is not accounted for by common comorbidity; it persists when comorbidity is controlled (Covey et al. 1994).

Thus, drinking and smoking (both prevalence and rate) are consistently correlated in the general population, but the relationship appears to be particularly strong at high levels of use: Heavy drinkers are likely to be heavy smokers and vice versa.

SITUATIONAL LINKAGE

As previously discussed, many alcohol or tobacco users also use the other drug. Do they use the two drugs together? Specifically, does drinking potentiate smoking? Does smoking potentiate drinking?

Alcohol to Tobacco

Both observational and laboratory data demonstrate that alcohol consumption potentiates smoking. Laboratory studies that have manipulated alcohol consumption have demonstrated increased smoking. Classic studies by Griffiths and colleagues (1976) used small samples of alcoholic subjects (n = 2 - 3) who were required to consume 12 drinks of either alcohol or an inert vehicle each study day. Smoking rose by about 0.75 cigarettes per hour (an increase of 35 percent) on drinking days. Subsequent studies (see Mello and Mendelson 1986) have replicated and extended these findings.

Most of the early studies administered repeated doses of alcohol over 1 or more days and then observed smoking rates; this did not allow for evaluating the immediate effect of drinking on smoking. Subsequent studies have demonstrated that single doses of alcohol also increase smoking (Nil et al. 1984; Mintz et al. 1985). Two studies demonstrated that subjects who were administered alcohol increased their smoking by taking larger puffs even when the number of cigarettes was held constant experimentally (Nil et al. 1984; Mintz et al. 1985). The literature also suggests a dose-response effect: In one study, blood alcohol levels of 0.05 percent produced an alcohol effect on smoking, whereas levels of 0.025 percent did not (Nil et al. 1984).

One prominent limitation of the experimental literature is the unrepresentativeness of subjects. Subjects in most studies have been alcoholics or drug addicts. Very few of the experimental studies have examined social drinkers (e.g., Nil et al. 1984), and these studies generally have produced weaker findings (e.g., Henningfield et al. 1984), suggesting that the influence of drinking on smoking may be limited to heavy drinkers or alcoholics. It is possible that, like the person-level relationship between drinking and smoking, the situational association is driven primarily by the heaviest users.

The controlled laboratory studies have the advantage of internal validity; however, they lack ecological validity. The relationships established in such artificial environments may not generalize to the real world. Smokers' global self-reports suggest that drinking prompts smoking in the natural environment. In one study, 67 percent of the smokers stated that they smoked when they drank (McKennell and Thomas 1967). However, considerable evidence suggests that such self-reports are not valid measures of smoking patterns (Shiffman 1993; Shiffman et al. 1994a).

Our research group conducted a field study of the association of drinking and smoking using naturalistic monitoring in which subjects used small palm-top computers to record the circumstances of smoking (Shiffman et al. 1994a). The computers also "beeped" subjects at random to assess nonsmoking moments. Smoking was reliably associated with drinking: Subjects were almost twice as likely to report recent drinking when they had been smoking. However, the overall correlation of drinking and smoking was a modest 0.12. Nevertheless, alcohol consumption was the single strongest environmental correlate of smoking. The link between drinking and smoking could not be attributed to joint associations with other variables, such as mood or the presence of smoking models: Statistically controlling all likely environmental correlates did not weaken the relationship.

The study's findings also were inconsistent with the hypothesis that drinking increases smoking by disinhibiting smoking restraint.[2] The drinking-smoking association was somewhat stronger among the heavy drinkers but did not vary between the light and heavy smokers (i.e., all smoked $\geq$ 10 cigarettes per day). In another study, very light smokers (i.e., "chippers," who smoked $\leq$ 5 cigarettes per day) demonstrated a much stronger link between drinking and smoking than did heavy smokers (i.e., subjects who smoked 20-40 cigarettes per day) (Shiffman et al. unpublished data 1995). In any case, both laboratory and field data con-

---

[2]However, disinhibition effects may not be evident at low doses of alcohol; this study did not assess dose.

firm that alcohol consumption increases smoking. As with the person-level link, this relationship may be strongest for heavy drinkers, but may not vary linearly with dose.

Tobacco to Alcohol

Surprisingly, no human studies have been conducted, either in the laboratory or the field, to assess whether smoking primes drinking. In addition, we are aware of only one animal study relating to this issue. Potthoff and colleagues (1983) showed that rats implanted with nicotine-releasing pellets doubled their alcohol intake. This is the only study demonstrating that nicotine intake affects alcohol-seeking, thereby suggesting the importance of studying this direction of influence.

CESSATION/RELAPSE

Whatever the relationship between alcohol and tobacco during ongoing use, clinical concern centers around their interactions during cessation. In fact, much current interest in the relationship between drinking and smoking is motivated by concern and controversy regarding smoking cessation during alcoholism treatment—specifically, the possibility that stopping smoking might endanger one's effort to stop drinking. Although all data thus far suggest a positive association between drinking and smoking, this concern is predicated on an expected negative relationship: Reducing smoking is feared to lead to *increased* drinking. This

worry grows out of two related concerns: (1) that being deprived of one reinforcer (i.e., tobacco) may increase consumption of another (i.e., alcohol), as implied by the principles of behavioral economics (Carroll and Meisch 1984; Vuchinich and Tucker 1988) and (2) that expending energy toward a second challenge (i.e., quitting smoking) may undermine the success of efforts directed to a primary challenge (i.e., quitting drinking). (For example, there is some evidence that attempts to control weight gain can decrease success rates in smoking cessation [see Perkins 1994]).

PERSON LINKAGE

Are people who drink more or less successful at quitting smoking or are they more vulnerable to relapse? Are smokers more or less successful at stopping drinking?

Alcohol to Tobacco

There is mixed evidence that alcoholics and heavy drinkers are less likely to succeed in smoking cessation. According to Carmelli and colleagues (1993), smokers who were lighter drinkers were subsequently more likely to report having quit smoking over a 16-year followup period. DiFranza and Guerrera (1990) reported that although alcoholics were as likely as nonalcoholic controls to attempt quitting smoking, they were much less likely to succeed. Hughes (1993) found that smokers with past alcohol or drug problems (about one-half were current users) were less likely to quit smoking successfully. In a sample of alcoholics, Bobo and colleagues (1987) reported that severity of alcoholism was associated with failure to quit smoking. However, Hughes and Oliveto (1993) found that drinking rate had no influence on smoking relapse rates. Covey and colleagues (1993, 1994) similarly concluded that a history of alcoholism, per se, had no effect on smoking cessation; however, a subgroup of alcoholic men with histories of depression had significantly lower success rates. Thus, current or past alcoholism may impede smoking cessation efforts only in a subgroup of smokers.

Tobacco to Alcohol

The questions here are as follows: Are people who smoke more or less likely to succeed in quitting drinking than those who have quit smoking? And, particularly, does smoking cessation interfere with attempts to quit drinking? Several studies suggest that quitting smoking (or attempting to quit) has no effect on alcohol and other drug (AOD) treatment outcome (e.g., Abrams et al. 1992; Joseph et al. 1993; Seidner et al. 1993). Two studies that did find differences report that stopping smoking is associated with better outcomes in alcoholism treatment (Miller et al. 1983; Bobo et al. 1987; Bobo 1992). It should be noted that the existing studies are methodologically weak observational studies on select samples. Also, the ability to stop smoking may be correlated with success in alcoholism treatment for incidental reasons—for example, it may demonstrate the acquisition of skills for self-change or

the possession of personal characteristics associated with perseverance and success (see Joseph et al. 1993).

To date, no study has ever shown that quitting smoking increases the risk of alcoholism treatment failure. The studies that demonstrate any effect at all demonstrate a positive effect, consistent with all other findings on the tobacco-alcohol association. Thus, the literature currently provides little support for the concern that quitting smoking will undermine alcoholism treatment. However, the data to date derive from uncontrolled naturalistic observations of spontaneous cessation. The impact of systematic smoking treatment or smoking bans has not been evaluated adequately in controlled studies.

SITUATIONAL LINKAGE

The preceding section dealt with relapse as an outcome attained by a person who failed to permanently change drinking or smoking behavior. However, individual relapse episodes (or, more precisely, lapses) (Marlatt and Gordon 1985) also can be analyzed as particular situations in which abstinence is violated. This section considers the role that acute alcohol intake may have on promoting lapses to smoking and vice versa.

Alcohol to Tobacco

Data consistently demonstrate that alcohol consumption is linked acutely to smoking relapse. This has been demonstrated in several studies in which alcohol consumption was found to increase the risk of smoking relapse, compared with situations in which the smoker was tempted but did not relapse (Shiffman 1982) (see also Colletti et al. 1981; Cummings et al. 1985; Baer and Lichtenstein 1988). In a recent study using real-time data from subjects in which their relapse experiences were monitored via palm-top computers, alcohol consumption was almost five times more likely in first-lapse episodes than in temptation episodes (Shiffman et al. in press). Drinking also was more common in lapse situations than at randomly sampled times. There is some evidence that the role of alcohol in promoting relapse increases later in abstinence (Cummings et al. 1985).

There has been some speculation that alcohol may enhance relapse risk by engendering disinhibition and thus undermining coping (e.g., Shiffman 1982). However, the evidence for this is inconsistent (Curry and Marlatt 1985; Shiffman et al. in press), and other mechanisms are also plausible. For example, priming with one drug may reinstate use of other drugs (de Wit and Stewart 1983; Stewart and Wise 1992); conditioned associations between drinking and smoking also may be responsible for the association of drinking with smoking relapse (see Abrams et al. 1992 on elicitation of smoking urges via drinking cues; also see Niaura et al. 1988). In any case, drinking clearly increases the probability of lapses to smoking.

Tobacco to Alcohol

Establishing this linkage would require evidence that smoking helps cue alcohol relapse or is associated with it. Such cuing is plausible, given the fact that the typical heavy drinker-heavy smoker has a long history of using the two drugs simultaneously, thereby establishing a conditioned association between them. However, no data appear to be available bearing on this relationship.

OTHER ISSUES RELATED TO DRINKING AND SMOKING

THE MAGNITUDE OF THE LINKAGE AND ITS LIMITS

While our review confirms that highly reliable associations exist between drinking and smoking, the associations are modest in magnitude. Person-level correlations between alcohol use and tobacco use generally run between 0.12 and 0.13 (Istvan and Matarazzo 1984); for smoking rate and drinking rate, the correlations run from 0.15 to 0.22 (Craig and Van Natta 1977; Kaprio et al. 1982). The situational effects of drinking on smoking are also modest, accounting for only a small proportion of cigarettes smoked. The limits of alcohol's influence on smoking can easily be appreciated when one considers that an average smoker smokes about 20 cigarettes per day (USDHHS 1988), spaced approximately evenly throughout the day, whereas an average drinker drinks less than 2 drinks per day (Friedman et al. 1974; Klatsky et al. 1977), usually concentrated in the evening hours and limited to particular occasions or contexts. This is illustrated graphically in figure 1, which shows the distribution of smoking and drinking by time of day (Shiffman et al. 1994*a*). Because most drinking occurs in the evening and most smoking does not, alcohol can only prompt a minority of smoking occasions. In fact, the alcohol-smoking correlation only rises above 0.10 during periods when drinking incidence rises—at midday and after 6 p.m. Thus, drinking has limited influence over smoking, and the potential influence of smoking over drinking is likely to be similarly limited.

DRINKING AMONG EXSMOKERS AND SMOKING AMONG EXDRINKERS

The data reviewed above demonstrate the association between alcohol and tobacco at both the person and situation levels: People who use one drug tend to use the other and tend to do so at the same time. Furthermore, the person-level linkage is characterized by a dose-response relationship. It is conceivable that this dose-response relationship is due to the situational covariation between drinking and smoking. That is, a person who drinks might be a heavier smoker precisely because of the extra cigarettes that he or she smokes while drinking. Accordingly, the more one drinks, the more one smokes. This explanation can be tested with data from people who have stopped one of the two behaviors (e.g., if drinkers smoke more than nondrinkers because of the number of cigarettes smoked while drinking, then drinkers' smoking rates should drop back down to nondrinkers' levels once they stop drinking).

Studies that have examined smoking in people who have quit drinking show that their smoking does not return to nondrinkers' levels. Keenan and colleagues (1990) found that smoking rates and smoking topography profiles were similar in alcohol abusers who were abstinent and in those who currently drank an average of 34 drinks per week. Maletzky and Klotter (1974) similarly found no change in smoking when alcoholics quit drinking. Dyer and colleagues (1977) reported that exdrinkers smoked at rates equal to those who currently drank 3–4 drinks per day. Relatedly, Hughes (1993) reported reduced success in smoking cessation for those with past AOD problems, although none of the subjects were diagnosed as having current AOD abuse problems, and most past abusers (58 percent) were abstinent.

Similarly, studies of drinking in exsmokers consistently show that drinking does not revert to nonsmokers' levels. In one study (Perkins et al. 1993), long-time exsmokers (i.e., exsmokers with an average of 10 years of not smoking) reported drinking rates comparable to those of current smokers and higher than those of never-smokers. However, a small group of 24 subjects who quit during the 3-year study demonstrated a trend toward reduced drinking. Other studies (Cummins et al. 1981; Carmody et al. 1985) are generally

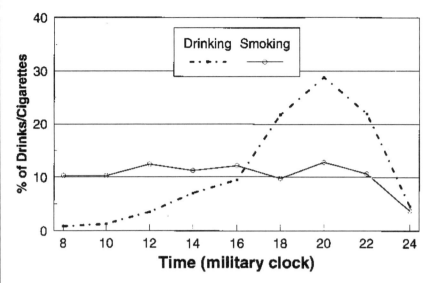

Figure 1. Distribution curves for percent drinking (squares and dashed line) and percent smoking (circles and solid line) by time of day.

consistent with this result. Hughes and colleagues (in press) also report that exsmokers show rates of alcoholism higher than those of never-smokers but lower than those of current smokers.[3] Hughes and Oliveto (1993) observed no change in drinking with smoking cessation.

One large longitudinal study that followed a cohort for 16 years produced complex results (Carmelli et al. 1993). Men who quit smoking increased their drinking over a 16-year period. However, the increase could not be attributed to their quitting, per se: Continuing smokers showed three times the increase in drinking over the same period. Thus, one could say that quitting smoking resulted in a relative decrease in drinking but was actually followed by an absolute increase. In general, the literature suggests that heavy drinking persists in exsmokers after they quit smoking.

Thus, the person-level effects generally persist even after joint use of the two drugs has ceased. This suggests that the person-level relationship is not due solely to the situational link; that is, drinkers do not smoke more simply because they smoke while drinking. The residual linkage may be attributed to persistent individual characteristics (e.g.,

---

[3]In this and similar studies, one needs to consider the antecedent rates of use. For example, the exsmokers may have been lighter smokers before quitting, and this might account for their lower alcoholism rates.

personality, genetics) or to the fact that the behaviors, once established, may be resistant to change. One practical implication relevant to the current controversy about joint treatment is that one should not expect quitting drinking, by itself, to have any effect on smoking.

MECHANISMS

While many empirical questions remain open, a review of the literature clearly demonstrates that drinking and smoking are associated. This chapter does not attempt to enumerate or evaluate the many mechanisms that have been proposed to account for the link between alcohol and tobacco (see Istvan and Matarrazo 1984; Zacny 1990). Instead, the discussion focuses on the conceptual and empirical tests that face any hypothesized mechanism.

It is important to reiterate that several potentially distinct phenomena need to be explained by candidate theories. Both the between-person and the situational covariation between alcohol and tobacco require explanation. While it is not necessary for a particular theory to explain all the relevant phenomena, doing so would make a theory more powerful.

Theories differ in their ability to explain both levels of linkage. For example, a stress-coping theory proposes that people resort to drug use when experienced stress exceeds coping capacity. This would explain why some people use both drugs: Some people may be chronically more stressed or less coping-competent. This theory also explains situational variability and covariance in drug use, because both drugs would be used in times of stress. In contrast, explanations relying on common genetic propensities to use alcohol and tobacco are best suited to explaining between-person covariance of alcohol and tobacco but are not well suited to explaining situational covariance.[4] Other researchers have proposed that people use tobacco when they drink in order to counteract alcohol's depressant effects with nicotine's stimulant effects, thereby reversing any alcohol-related performance decrement (Lyon et al. 1975; Michel and Battig 1989; Kerr et al. 1991). This would explain the situational covariation of the two drugs but not the individual covariation in use. Thus, some theories account for one level of the alcohol-tobacco link but not the other, whereas some theories may gain explanatory power from their ability to account for both levels of the relationship.

Theories also may differ in their ability to explain the alcohol-tobacco link at various stages in drinking and smoking careers. For example, it has been proposed that alcohol potentiates smoking by releasing inhibitions that restrain smoking (Shiffman

---

[4]A genetic factor may have modified the immediate interaction between the two drugs, thus explaining their situational covariance. However, such a genetic account would be far more complex (and accordingly less appealing) than any that have been offered to date.

1982; Shiffman et al. 1994*a*). This explanation only applies to situations in which smoking is being restrained and is perhaps most applicable to explaining how alcohol may potentiate smoking relapse in smokers trying to abstain. It seems considerably less apt for smokers in the maintenance stage who are not attempting to limit their smoking (see Shiffman et al. 1994*a*).

Theories also may differ in their ability to explain mutual influences between alcohol and tobacco. For example, the hypothesis that people smoke when they drink in order to reverse performance deficits caused by alcohol intoxication (Istvan and Matarazzo 1984; Zacny 1990) may help explain why drinking cues smoking, but it would not explain why nicotine might cue drinking, were such a relationship established (see Potthoff et al. 1983).

Conversely, some theories may do equally well at explaining each direction of influence. For example, pharmacokinetic and pharmacodynamic explanations, which suggest that each drug induces metabolic or functional cross-tolerance for the other (Burch et al. 1988), can explain a link in either direction. In fact, if cross-tolerance is symmetric, this theory would have difficulty explaining an asymmetric relationship. Thus, some theories may require a symmetric alcohol-tobacco relationship, whereas others are strictly one-directional. Accordingly, establishing the direction of influence between tobacco and alcohol can help discriminate among competing theories.

Theories also need to account for the dose-response effect that characterizes the alcohol-tobacco relationship. The extent to which there is an additional linkage between alcohol dependence and tobacco dependence (over and above dose, per se) is not fully clear. Ideally, a strong theoretical account should clarify whether the linkage is best conceptualized as relating to alcohol and/or tobacco use, rate of use, abuse, or dependence. Theories also need to account for nonlinear aspects of the dose-response function, if these are confirmed.

Explanations of the link between alcohol and tobacco are most powerful if they also explain the link between these drugs and the use of other psychoactive drugs. While this chapter focuses on the link between alcohol and tobacco, this association is, in fact, part of a larger nexus of drug use. At all stages of drug use, alcohol and tobacco use are correlated with the use of other psychoactive drugs (Goode 1972; Kozlowski et al. 1993; Martin et al. 1993; Schorling et al. 1994). Thus, at least some of the mechanisms linking these two drugs are likely to be general ones that encompass drug use in general (e.g., broad genetic influences, such as variations in dopamine systems, or broad psychosocial factors, such as extraversion, heightened life stress, or poor coping).

Several theoretical accounts explain the association between drinking and smoking by referring to the common causes of both forms of drug use. A key example is the stress-coping model, which suggests that both alcohol and tobacco are used to cope with stress (e.g., Wills and Shiffman 1985). Although there is good evidence that both forms of drug use are correlated with stress, it is not enough to establish this explanation of their association. To argue that a common cause is responsible for the covariation, one would need to demonstrate that when the common cause (e.g., stress, coping competence) is held constant statistically, the association between drinking and smoking disappears. This rarely has been done; when it has (e.g., Covey et al. 1994; Shiffman et al. 1994*a*), the common antecedents have in fact not been able to account for the alcohol-tobacco association. Thus, establishing common correlates is not sufficient to explain the link between alcohol and tobacco.

Finally, it should be noted that differing theories of the alcohol-tobacco link need not be mutually exclusive. First, two different theories can sometimes be manifestations of the same phenomenon at different levels of analysis. For example, some of the overlap between drinkers and smokers can be attributed to common genetic factors in alcohol and tobacco use. However, these genetic contributions may be expressed as differences in basic dimensions of personality, which appear to be heritable (Eysenck 1980; Rowe and Plomin 1981; Loehlin 1989; Clapper 1992). Thus, genetic and personality explanations of the drinking-smoking link may not only be compatible—they may be two ver-

sions of the same theory. Second, it is also possible that two genuinely different mechanisms work simultaneously and synergistically. For example, if nicotine has both stimulant and anxiolytic properties (Carmody 1989; Corrigall 1991; Jarvik 1991), then people who are stressed may use it together with alcohol, both to enhance the latter's tranquilizing properties and to antagonize its detrimental effects on performance.

It is a truism that nothing helps research better than a good theory. Research on alcohol and tobacco does not lack for speculation, but it is in need of more systematic theory development and testing.

SUMMARY AND CONCLUSIONS

Empirical evidence demonstrates a robust association between alcohol and tobacco use. The link is evident both among persons—users of one drug are likely to use the other—and across occasions—the two drugs tend to be used together. The association is of moderate magnitude: In the population as a whole, alcohol use is not the major determinant of tobacco use, and tobacco use is not the major determinant of alcohol use. However, the two behaviors seem to become more associated as smoking and drinking rates increase. It is likely that the association involves nicotine, per se, rather than cigarette smoking in particular, because the association is also evident for smokeless tobacco use; of course, the role of other tobacco constituents cannot be ruled out. The increased drinking and smoking seen in people who engage in both appear to persist even when one behavior is terminated.

The degree to which the influence between alcohol and tobacco is mutual cannot be determined confidently at this time. The epidemiologic data suggest that drinking influences smoking more than smoking influences drinking. Situationally, it is clear that alcohol administration can cue smoking, but there is a glaring absence of information regarding the influence of tobacco use on alcohol consumption. In general, more data exist on the comorbidity of alcohol and tobacco use among persons; the situational linkages between smoking and drinking are less thoroughly explored. Finally, there is no evidence that smoking cessation endangers alcoholism treatment. However, the controversy over this issue cannot be resolved firmly yet by empirical data.

RECOMMENDATIONS

Although much is known about the alcohol-tobacco link, much remains to be discovered. Several suggestions for future research (not in priority order) are as follows:

- Research should focus on developing and testing theoretical models of the alcohol-tobacco link. Although researchers have speculated about mechanisms linking drinking and smoking, almost no studies have truly tested any theory.

- Conclusions regarding the population correlation between drinking and smoking should not rely on convenience samples of persons presenting for treatment; population studies are needed.

- Research, perhaps in the form of secondary data analysis, should establish whether the observed relationship between alcohol and tobacco use is driven primarily by heavy users or is linear across the range of use.

- Research should assess the situational, as well as the individual, covariation of alcohol and tobacco. This requires both laboratory and field studies to ensure both internal validity and ecological credibility.

- Research is needed to assess the influence of tobacco on alcohol. While the influence of alcohol on tobacco use is well documented, the converse direction of influence is almost entirely unexplored. This issue seems particularly urgent, given the current concern about smoking cessation and alcoholism treatment.

- The effect of smoking cessation on alcoholism treatment is uncertain and is unlikely to be clarified by further retrospective studies of quitting; prospective longitudinal and experimental designs are needed. This line of research also needs to be guided by theory; behavioral economics offers a promising theoretical framework.

- In addition to controlled outcome research on smoking cessation in alcoholism treatment, process research is needed to assess, for example, how smoking urges (and efforts to resist them), feelings of deprivation relating to cigarettes, and symptoms of nicotine withdrawal may impact on alcohol abstinence.

ACKNOWLEDGMENTS

Preparation of this chapter was supported in part by National Institute on Drug Abuse grant DA06084 and by National Institute on Alcohol Abuse and Alcoholism grant AA07595–06. Patrick O'Malley and the staff of the Monitoring the Future project graciously conducted and provided data analyses from that study. We are grateful to Stephanie Paton and Yolanda DiBucci for assistance in preparing the manuscript and to Michael Sayette and Maryann Gnys for their comments on an earlier draft.

REFERENCES

Abelson, H.; Cohen, R.; Schrayer, D.; and Rappeport, M. Drug experience, attitudes and related behavior among adolescents and adults. In: *Drug Use in America: Problem in Perspective: Vol. 1. The Technical Papers of the Second Report of the National Commission on Marihuana and Drug Abuse, 1973.* Washington, DC: Supt. of Docs., U.S. Govt. Print. Off., 1973. pp. 488–871.

Abrams, D.B.; Rohsenow, D.J.; Niaura, R.S.; Pedraza, M.; Longabaugh, R.; Binkoff, J.A.; Beattie, M.C.; Noel, N.E.; and Monti, P.M. Smoking and treatment outcome for alcoholics: Effects on coping skills, urge to drink, and drinking rates. *Behav Ther* 23:283–297, 1992.

Ary, D.V., and Biglan, A. Longitudinal changes in adolescent cigarette smoking behavior: Onset and cessation. *J Behav Med* 11:361–382, 1988.

Ary, D.V.; Lichtenstein, E.; and Severson, H.H. Smokeless tobacco use among male adolescents: Patterns, correlates, predictors and the use of other drugs. *Prev Med* 16:385–401, 1987.

Bachman, J.G.; Johnston, L.D.; and O'Malley, P.M. Smoking, drinking, and drug use among American high school students: Correlates and trends, 1975–1979. *Am J Public Health* 71:59–68, 1981.

Baer, J., and Lichtenstein, E. Classification and prediction of smoking relapse episodes: An exploration of individual differences. *J Consult Clin Psychol* 56:104–110, 1988.

Bobo, J.K. Nicotine dependence and alcoholism epidemiology and treatment. *J Psychoactive Drugs* 24:123–129, 1992.

Bobo, J.K.; Gilchrist, L.D.; Schilling, R.F.; Noach, B.; and Schinke, S.P. Cigarette smoking cessation attempts by recovering alcoholics. *Addict Behav* 8:403–412, 1987.

Burch, J.B.; de Fiebre, C.M.; Marks, M.J.; and Collins, A.C. Chronic ethanol or nicotine treatment results in partial cross-tolerance between these agents. *Psychopharmacology* 95:452–458, 1988.

Carmelli, D.; Swan, G.E.; and Robinette, D. The relationship between quitting smoking and changes in drinking in World War II: Veteran twins. *J Subst Abuse* 5:103–116, 1993.

Carmody, T.P. Affect regulation, nicotine addiction, and smoking cessation. *J Psychoactive Drugs* 21:331–342, 1989.

Carmody, T.P.; Brischetto, C.S.; Matarazzo, J.D.; O'Donnell, R.P.; and Connor, W.E. Co-occurrent use of cigarettes, alcohol, and coffee in healthy, community-living men and women. *Health Psychol* 4:323–335, 1985.

Carroll, M.E., and Meisch, R.A. Increased drug reinforced behavior due to food deprivation. In: Thompson, T.; Dews, P.B.; and Barrett, J.E., eds. *Advances in Behavioral Pharmacology.* New York: Academic Press, 1984. pp. 47–88.

Clapper, R.L. The reducer-augmenter scale, the revised reducer-augmenter scale, and predicting late adolescent substance use. *Person Individ Diff* 13:813–820, 1992.

Colletti, G.; Supnick, J.A.; and Rizzo, A.A. "An Analysis of Relapse Determinants." Paper presented at the annual meeting of the American Psychological Association, Los Angeles, August 1981.

Corrigall, W.A. Understanding brain mechanisms in nicotine reinforcement. *Br J Addict* 86:507–510, 1991.

Covey, L.S.; Glassman, A.H.; Stetner, F.; and Becker, J. Effect of history of alcoholism or major depression on smoking cessation. *Am J Psychiatry* 150:1546–1547, 1993.

Covey, L.S.; Hughes, D.C.; Glassman, A.H.; Blazer, D.G.; and George, L.K. Ever-smoking, quitting, and psychiatric disorders: Evidence from the Durham, North Carolina, Epidemiologic Catchment Area. *Tobacco Control* 3:222–227, 1994.

Craig, T.J., and Van Natta, P.A. The association of smoking and drinking habits in a community sample. *J Stud Alcohol* 38:1434–1439, 1977.

Cummings, K.M.; Giovino, G.; Jaen, C.R.; and Emrich, L.J. Reports of smoking withdrawal symptoms over a 21 day period of abstinence. *Addict Behav* 10:373–381, 1985.

Cummins, R.O.; Shaper, A.G.; Walker, M.; and Wale, C.J. Smoking and drinking by middle-aged British men: Effects of social class and town of residence. *BMJ* 283:1497–1502, 1981.

Curry, S., and Marlatt, G.A. Strategies for coping with temptations to smoke. In: Shiffman, S., and Wills, T.A., eds. *Coping and Substance Abuse.* New York: Academic Press, 1985. pp. 243–265.

Cyr, M.G., and Wartman, S.A. The effectiveness of routine screening questions in the detection of alcoholism. *JAMA* 259:51–54, 1988.

de Wit, H., and Stewart, J. Drug reinstatement of heroin-reinforced responding in the rat. *Psychopharmacology* 79:29–31, 1983.

DiFranza, J.R., and Guerrera, M.P. Alcoholism and smoking. *J Stud Alcohol* 51:130–135, 1990.

Dyer, A.R.; Stamler, J.; Paul, O.; Berkson, D.M.; Lepper, M.H.; McKean, H.; Shekelle, R.B.; Lindberg, H.A.; and Garside, D. Alcohol consumption, cardiovascular risk factors, and mortality in two Chicago epidemiologic studies. *Alcohol, Risk Factors, and Mortality* 56:1067–1074, 1977.

Eysenck, H.J. *The Causes and Effects of Smoking.* Beverly Hills, CA: Sage, 1980.

Friedman, G.D.; Siegelaub, A.B.; and Seltzer, C.C. Cigarettes, alcohol, coffee and peptic ulcer. *N Engl J Med* 290:469–473, 1974.

Friedman, G.D.; Tekawa, I.; Klatsky, A.L.; Sidney, S.; and Armstrong, M.A. Alcohol drinking and cigarette smoking: An exploration of the association in middle-aged men and women. *Drug Alcohol Depend* 27:283–290, 1991.

Friedman, L.S.; Lichtenstein, E.; and Biglan, A. Smoking onset among teens: An empirical analysis of initial situations. *Addict Behav* 10:1–13, 1985.

Goode, E. Cigarette smoking and drug use on a college campus. *Int J Addict* 7:133–140, 1972.

Griffiths, R.R.; Bigelow, G.E.; and Liebson, I. Facilitation of human tobacco self-administration by ethanol: A behavioral analysis. *J Exp Anal Behav* 25:279–292, 1976.

Henningfield, J.E.; Chait, L.D.; and Griffiths, R.R. Effects of ethanol on cigarette smoking by volunteers without histories of alcoholism. *Psychopharmacology* 82:1–5, 1984.

Hughes, J.R. Treatment of smoking cessation in smokers with past alcohol/drug problems. *J Subst Abuse Treat* 10:181–187, 1993.

Hughes, J.R., and Oliveto, A.H. Coffee and alcohol intake as predictors of smoking cessation and tobacco withdrawal. *J Subst Abuse* 5:305–310, 1993.

Hughes, J.R.; Franco, K.S.N.; and Inatsuka, L.T. Using smoking as a screening tool to detect alcoholism. *J Addict Dis*, in press.

Istvan, J., and Matarazzo, J.D. Tobacco, alcohol and caffeine use: A review of their interrelationships. *Psychol Bull* 95:301–326, 1984.

Jarvik, M.E. Beneficial effects of nicotine. *Br J Addict* 86:571–575, 1991.

Joseph, A.M.; Nichol, K.L.; and Anderson, H. Effect of treatment for nicotine dependence on alcohol and drug treatment outcomes. *Addict Behav* 18:635–644, 1993.

Kandel, D.B., and Yamaguchi, K. Developmental patterns of the use of legal, illegal, and medically prescribed psychotropic drugs from adolescence to young adulthood. *Etiology of Drug Abuse: Implications for Prevention*. National Institute on Drug Abuse Research Monograph No. 56. Washington, DC: U.S. Govt. Print. Off., 1985. pp. 193–235.

Kandel, D.B.; Yamaguchi, K.; and Chen, K. Stages of progression in drug involvement from adolescence to adulthood: Further evidence for the gateway theory. *J Stud Alcohol* 53:447–457, 1992.

Kaprio, J.; Hammar, N.; Koskenvuo, M.; Floderus-Myrhed, B.; Langinvainio, H.; and Sarna, S. Cigarette smoking and alcohol use in Finland and Sweden: A cross-national twin study. *Int J Epidemiol* 11:378–386, 1982.

Keenan, R.M.; Hatsukami, D.K.; Pickens, R.W.; Gust, S.W.; and Strelow, L.J. The relationship between chronic ethanol exposure and cigarette smoking in the laboratory and the natural environment. *Psychopharmacology* 100:77–83, 1990.

Kerr, J.S.; Sherwood, N.; and Hindmarch, I. Separate and combined effects of the social drugs on psychomotor performance. *Psychopharmacology* 104:113–119, 1991.

Klatsky, A.L.; Friedman, G.D.; Siegelaub, A.B.; and Gerard, M.J. Alcohol consumption among white, black, or oriental men and women: Kaiser-Permanente health examination data. *Am J Epidemiol* 105: 311–323, 1977.

Kozlowski, L.T.; Henningfield, J.E.; Keenan, R.M.; Leigh, G.; Jelinek, L.C.; Pope, M.A.; and Haertzen, C.A. Patterns of alcohol, cigarette, and caffeine and other drug use in two drug abusing populations. *J Subst Abuse Treat* 10:171–179, 1993.

Loehlin, J.C. Partitioning environmental and genetic contributions to behavioral development. *Am Psychol* 44:1285–1292, 1989.

Lyon, R.J.; Tong, J.E.; Leigh, G.; and Clare, G. The influence of alcohol and tobacco on the components of choice reaction time. *J Stud Alcohol* 36:587–596, 1975.

Maletzky, B.M., and Klotter, J. Smoking and alcoholism. *Am J Psychiatry* 131: 445–447, 1974.

Marlatt, G.A., and Gordon, J.R. *Relapse Prevention.* New York: Guilford Press, 1985.

Martin, C.S.; Arria, A.M.; Mezzich, A.C.; and Bukstein, O.G. Patterns of polydrug use in adolescent alcohol abusers' addictive behavior. *Am J Drug Alcohol Abuse* 19:511–521, 1993.

McKennell, A.C., and Thomas, R.K. *Adults' and Adolescents' Smoking Habits and Attitudes.* London: British Ministry of Health, 1967.

Mello, N.K., and Mendelson, J.H. *Cigarette Smoking: Interactions With Alcohol, Opiates, and Marijuana.* National Institute on Drug Abuse Research Monograph No. 68. Washington, DC: Supt. of Docs., U.S. Govt. Print. Off., 1986. pp. 154–180.

Michel, C., and Battig, K. Separate and combined psychophysiological effects of cigarette smoking and alcohol consumption. *Psychopharmacology* 97:65–73, 1989.

Miller, W.R.; Hedrick, K.E.; and Taylor, C.A. Addictive behaviors and life problems before and after behavioral treatment of problem drinkers. *Addict Behav* 8:403–412, 1983.

Mintz, J.; Boyd, G.; Rose, J.E.; Charuvastra, V.C.; and Jarvik, M. Alcohol increases cigarette smoking: A laboratory demonstration. *Addict Behav* 10:203–207, 1985.

Niaura, R.S.; Rohsenow, D.J.; Binkoff, J.A.; Monti, P.M.; Pedraza, M.; and Abrams, D.B. Relevance of cue reactivity to understanding alcohol and smoking relapse. *J Abnorm Psychol* 97:133–152, 1988.

Nil, R.; Buzzi, R.; and Battig, K. Effects of single doses of alcohol and caffeine on cigarette smoke puffing behavior. *Pharmacol Biochem Behav* 20:583–590, 1984.

Perkins, K.A. Issues in the prevention of weight gain after smoking cessation. *Ann Behav Med* 16:46–52, 1994.

Perkins, K.A.; Meilahn, E.N.; Wing, R.R.; Matthews, K.A.; and Kuller, L.H. Diet, alcohol, and physical activity as a function of smoking status in middle-aged women. *Health Psychol* 12:410–415, 1993.

Potthoff, A.D.; Ellison, G.; and Nelson, L. Ethanol intake increases during continuous administration of amphetamine and nicotine, but not several other drugs. *Pharmacol Biochem Behav* 18:489–493, 1983.

Rowe, D.C., and Plomin, R. The importance of nonshared environmental influences in behavioral development.

Developmental Psychology 17:517–531, 1981.

Schorling, J.B.; Gutgesell, M.; Klas, P.; Smith, D.; and Keller, A. Tobacco, alcohol, and other drug use among college students. *J Subst Abuse* 6:105–115, 1994.

Seidner, A.L.; Burling, T.A.; Gaither, D.E.; and Salvio, M. "Work in Progress Update: Stop-Smoking Treatment for Drug/Alcohol Abuse Inpatients." Paper presented at the annual meeting of the Association for the Advancement of Behavior Therapy, Atlanta, GA, November 1993.

Shiffman, S. Relapse following smoking cessation: A situational analysis. *J Consult Clin Psychol* 50:71–86, 1982.

Shiffman, S. Assessing smoking patterns and motives. *J Consult Clin Psychol* 61:732–742, 1993.

Shiffman, S.; Fischer, L.A.; Paty, J.A.; Gnys, M.; Kassel, J.D.; Hickcox, M.; and Perz, W. Drinking and smoking: A field study of their association. *Ann Behav Med* 16:203–209, 1994*a*.

Shiffman, S.; Paty, J.A.; Kassel, J.D.; Gnys, M.; and Zettler-Segal, M. Smoking behavior and smoking history of tobacco chippers. *Exp Clin Psychopharmacol* 2:126–142, 1994*b*.

Shiffman, S.; Paty, J.A.; Gnys, M.; Kassel, J.A.; and Hickcox, M. First lapses to smoking: Within subjects analysis of real time reports. *J Consult Clin Psychol*, in press.

Single, E.; Kandel, D.; and Faust, R. Patterns of multiple drug use in high school. *J Health Soc Behav* 15:344–357, 1974.

Stewart, J., and Wise, R.A. Reinstatement of heroin self-administration habits: Morphine prompts and naltrexone discourages renewed responding after extinction. *Psychopharmacology* 108:79–84, 1992.

U.S. Department of Health and Human Services. *The Health Consequences of Smoking: Nicotine Addiction, A Report of the Surgeon General.* Washington, DC: the Department, 1988.

U.S. Department of Health and Human Services. *Preventing Tobacco Use Among Young People. A Report of the Surgeon General.* Atlanta, GA: the Department, 1994.

Vuchinich, R.E., and Tucker, J.A. Contributions from behavioral theories of choice to an analysis of alcohol abuse. *J Abnorm Psychol* 97:181–195, 1988.

Wills, T.A., and Shiffman, S. Coping behavior and its relation to substance use: A conceptual framework. In: Shiffman, S., and Wills, T.A., eds. *Coping and Substance Use.* New York: Academic Press, 1985. pp. 3–24.

Wills, T.A.; Cleary, S.D.; Mariani, J.; and Filer, M. "Stress-Coping Model for Alcohol/Tobacco Interactions in Adolescents." Paper presented at National Institute on Alcohol Abuse and Alcoholism Conference on Alcohol and Tobacco, San Diego, CA, November 1994.

Zacny, J.P. Behavioral aspects of alcohol-tobacco interactions. In: Galanter, M., ed. *Recent Developments in Alcoholism*: Vol. 8. *Combined Alcohol and Other Drug Dependence.* Plenum Press, 1990. pp. 205–219.

Chapter 3

The Theory of Triadic Influence: Preliminary Evidence Related to Alcohol and Tobacco Use

Brian R. Flay, D.Phil., John Petraitis, Ph.D., and Frank B. Hu, M.P.H.

There has been relatively little research on how biological influences contribute to tobacco and alcohol use. Our recent reviews of the theories of tobacco use (Flay and Petraitis 1994) and illicit drug use (Petraitis et al. 1995) concluded that biological influences are scarcely mentioned in the theories that dominate the field (e.g., the problem behavior theory). This is unfortunate because no understanding of tobacco and alcohol use is complete unless biological influences are addressed and the mechanisms by which biological factors contribute to the use of tobacco and alcohol are carefully described.

In this chapter we want to show how the biological views presented in other chapters in this monograph represent one piece of a larger puzzle that includes both biological and nonbiological influences. The nonbiological influences include (a) the influence of modeling, when parents show children how much pleasure they derive from alcohol and tobacco; (b) developmental influences, in which lifelong patterns of alcohol and tobacco use might begin in an adolescent's otherwise healthy desire for independence from parents; and (c) cultural influences, like advertising, in which tobacco and alcohol use

B.R. Flay, D.Phil., is a professor and the director of the Prevention Research Center, School of Public Health, University of Illinois at Chicago, 850 West Jackson Blvd., Suite 400, Chicago, IL 60607. J. Petraitis, Ph.D., is an assistant professor in the Department of Psychology, University of Alaska at Anchorage, 3211 Providence Drive, Anchorage, AK 99508. F.B. Hu, M.P.H., is a research associate with the Prevention Research Center, School of Public Health, University of Illinois at Chicago.

become linked as rewarding activities that people do to relax, to be sociable, and to treat themselves. We also want to focus on factors that cause adolescents to start smoking and start using alcohol. Toward these ends, we will describe (1) a theoretical framework that captures most (if not all) influences on experimental tobacco use (ETU) and experimental alcohol use (EAU) among adolescents; (2) some evidence for the causal processes that are articulated in our theoretical model, including research evidence on the onset of use of alcohol, tobacco, and other drugs (ATOD); and (3) implications of our model for understanding the causes of ETU and EAU, and for preventing ETU and EAU.

A THEORETICAL FRAMEWORK OF INFLUENCES ON ETU AND EAU

The dominant theories of EAU and ETU among adolescents include a long and diverse list of causal influences, ranging from factors that are intrinsically tied to ATOD use (e.g., beliefs about the consequences of smoking) to factors that on the surface have little to do with these problem behaviors (e.g., parenting styles and school characteristics) (Flay and Petraitis 1994; Petraitis et al. 1995). The diversity of theories and causal influences is not surprising given that ATOD use, like most behaviors, has a complex etiology. In fact, numerous scholars (e.g., Magnusson 1981;

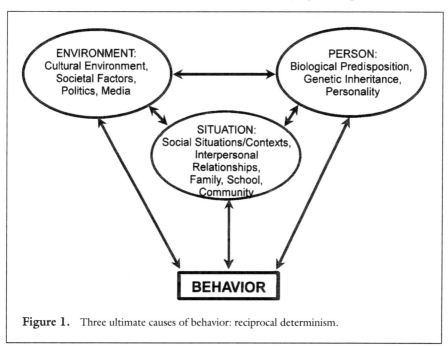

Figure 1. Three ultimate causes of behavior: reciprocal determinism.

Bandura 1986; Sadava 1987; Frankenhaeuser 1991; Jessor et al. 1991; DeKay and Buss 1992) have argued persuasively that a thorough understanding of any behavior must look at "the big picture." That picture must be based on a comprehensive and integrative analysis of (a) the broad social environment or cultural milieu surrounding the behavior, (b) the more immediate social situation or context in which the behavior occurs, (c) the characteristics or dispositions of the person performing the behavior, (d) the behavior itself and closely related behaviors, and (e) the interaction among all of these.

Figure 1, in a very general sense, represents "the big picture." It reminds researchers and theorists that ETU and EAU have roots in broad environmental or cultural factors (e.g., media depictions of smoking and alcohol use), situational factors (e.g., poor relationships with parents), and personal factors (e.g., individual sensitivities to nicotine) and that all of these factors affect each other and are also influenced by the behavior itself (i.e., reciprocal determinism). It also reminds us that any one factor is just one small part of a larger picture and is only likely to explain small portions of variance in either ETU or EAU.

The model depicted in figure 1 is not a testable theory; it is far too general and lacks important information about variables and relationships among variables. It is, however, the foundation of a theory that we call the theory of triadic influence (TTI).

According to TTI, the general cultural environment in which adolescents mature, the more immediate social situation in which adolescents find themselves from day to day, and intrapersonal differences among adolescents are the starting points for three "streams" of influence—streams that flow through different mediating variables and flow to different terminating variables.

THE THREE STREAMS: DEFINITIONS AND TERMINATING VARIABLES

Figure 2 begins to reveal these three streams in more detail. According to TTI, the first stream represents characteristics of the broad cultural environment and general social values that contribute to or terminate at adolescents' personal attitudes concerning ETU and EAU. Such *cultural/ attitudinal influences* include local crime and employment rates, media depictions and government policies concerning tobacco and alcohol use, lack of commitment to conventional values, and social alienation. The second stream represents characteristics of adolescents' more immediate social situations and more intimate social support systems that contribute to or terminate at the social pressure adolescents feel to experiment with tobacco or alcohol. Such interpersonal or *social/normative influences* include parenting styles, the strength of bonds between parents and adolescents, the strength of bonds between peers and adolescents, and tobacco and alcohol use by parents and peers.

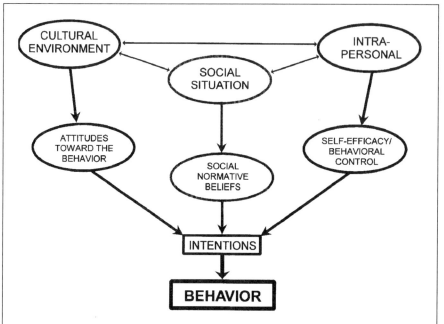

Figure 2. Basis of the theory of triadic influence: ultimate causes and proximal predictors.

The third stream represents characteristics of individual adolescents' biological makeup and basic personality that undermine their ability to resist pressures to smoke cigarettes and drink alcohol. Such *intrapersonal influences* include (among others) biological sensitivities to nicotine and alcohol, fundamental and stable personality characteristics (e.g., neuroticism, extraversion, openness, agreeableness, intellect), more transient affective states (e.g., depressed affect, low self-esteem), social skills, and, ultimately, resistance or refusal skills.

TIERS OF INFLUENCE

So far, our description of TTI has focused explicitly on its three streams of influence. Figure 3, however, reveals that there is more to TTI than just streams of influence; there are also several tiers or levels of influence. The lowest three tiers of figure 3 represent the most *proximal* level of influence. Proximal influences are fairly narrowly defined (e.g., intentions to smoke a cigarette within the next 30 days), are inherently tied to ETU and EAU (e.g., smoking-related attitudes), are probably the most immediate causes of ETU and EAU, and are the strongest predictors of ETU (Flay and Petraitis 1994) and EAU (Petraitis et al. 1994a).

The third and fourth tiers (from the bottom) of figure 3 are factors from more intermediate or *distal* lev-

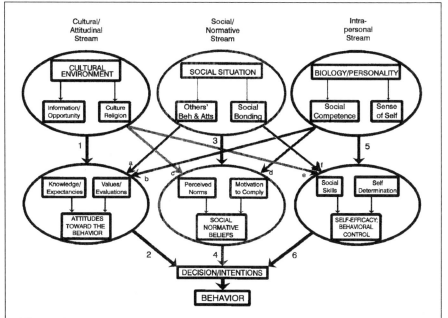

Figure 3. The theory of triadic influence. The causal streams are indicated by numbers 1–6, and the interstream influences are indicated by letters a–f (see text for an explanation of these pathways and influences).

els of influence. Distal influences are factors that probably contribute indirectly to ETU and EAU by contributing directly to tobacco- and alcohol-specific attitudes, normative beliefs, and self-efficacy.

Finally, the highest tier of figure 3 represents the *ultimate* influences. Unlike proximal and distal influences, ultimate influences (a) are beyond the easy control of adolescents, (b) are not inherently tied to alcohol or tobacco use, (c) are broader in scope and not as narrowly defined, and (d) are more deeply rooted in an adolescent's environment, personality, or biological makeup. As such, ultimate influences are likely to affect ETU and EAU in a variety of ways.

EMPIRICAL EVIDENCE FOR TTI

In the previous section we argued that TTI's three streams of influence have different tiers or levels of influence. According to TTI, however, each stream also has a unique set of mediating variables and causal pathways through which causal influences primarily flow. Furthermore, causal processes are not thought to exist exclusively within one stream or the other. Rather, factors in one stream may cross streams and influence factors in another stream. In this section, we briefly describe these pathways and some of their empirical support. We provide a detailed review of studies of causal process in another paper (Flay et al. unpublished manuscript 1995).

PATHS AND MEDIATING VARIABLES IN THE CULTURAL/ ATTITUDINAL STREAM

According to TTI, the cultural/ attitudinal stream begins in the general cultural environment in which adolescents mature, the information they derive from their culture about tobacco and alcohol, and the general social values they adopt from their culture. In turn, these factors combine to affect (a) adolescents' subjective expectations about the personal consequences of ETU or EAU, (b) their personal evaluations concerning the goodness-badness of those consequences, and (c) their overall attitudes toward their own ETU or EAU. This causal process is represented by path 1 in figure 3 and is supported by numerous empirical studies. For instance, after comparing the causal processes that lead to alcohol use in the United States and Greece, Marcos and Johnson (1988) concluded that teen alcohol use in the United States, unlike that in Greece, is a sign of social alienation and deviant attitudes. Grube and Wallack (1994) found that cultural images of beer in the United States (as provided by television advertisements) might affect attitudes toward drinking by leading many children to link "drinking with positively valued activities and consequences such as romance, sociability, and relaxation" (pp. 257–258).

TTI then argues that tobacco- or alcohol-related expectations, evaluations, and attitudes play a major role in shaping adolescents' decisions or intentions to use (or avoid) tobacco and alcohol in the future (see path 2 of figure 3). In line with this, several studies have demonstrated that attitudes influence drug use through the mediating effects of intentions (e.g., Bentler and Speckart 1979; Schlegel et al. 1992; Flay et al. 1994; Flay et al. unpublished manuscript 1994; Petraitis et al. 1994b).

PATHS AND MEDIATING VARIABLES IN THE SOCIAL/ NORMATIVE STREAM

Social/normative influences have their roots in the characteristics of adolescents' parents, peers, and immediate surroundings, especially the tobacco- and alcohol-related attitudes and behaviors of family members and those peers to whom adolescents most closely bond. As depicted by path 3, TTI asserts that these characteristics affect (a) adolescents' subjective perceptions about the normativeness of ETU and EAU, (b) with whom adolescents are most motivated to comply (e.g., conventional parents or deviant peers), and (c) the social pressures adolescents feel to experiment with either tobacco or alcohol. Several studies support this assertion. For instance, we found that parental and peer smoking indirectly affected adolescents' smoking initiation and escalation by first affecting adolescents' outcome expectancies regarding smoking, perceived approval of smoking, and refusal skills self-efficacy (Flay et al. 1994).

Perceived norms, motivation to comply, and social normative beliefs are important because they are among the few factors that directly affect adolescents' decisions or intentions to use (or avoid) ETU or EAU in the future (see path 4 on figure 3). Several studies have demonstrated that attitudes influence drug use through the mediating effects of intentions (Ellickson and Hays 1991, 1992; Flay et al. 1994; Flay et al. unpublished manuscript 1994).

PATHS AND MEDIATING VARIABLES IN THE INTRAPERSONAL STREAM

Whereas the first two streams began with characteristics of the general culture in which adolescents mature and characteristics of their more immediate social situations, the intrapersonal stream begins with fundamental and stable characteristics of the individual adolescents (e.g., their personalities and biological makeups), their general levels of competence (e.g., social and academic skills), and their sense of self (e.g., the strength of their self-concepts). As depicted by path 5 on figure 3, these influences are thought to affect (a) adolescents' skills at dealing with situations where they are offered cigarettes or alcohol, (b) their determination to either use or avoid cigarettes and alcohol, and (c) their tobacco- and alcohol-related self-efficacy. In support of this causal process, Dielman and colleagues (1989) found that adolescents' locus

of control influenced alcohol use indirectly by first affecting adolescents' self-esteem, social competence, and social skills.

The second link in the causal process of intrapersonal influences runs to tobacco- or alcohol-related decisions or intentions from refusal skills, self-determination, and self-efficacy (see path 6 on figure 3). Supporting this link, Ellickson and Hays (1991) found that resistance self-efficacy regarding use of alcohol, cigarettes, and marijuana affected adolescents' use of these drugs both directly and indirectly through intentions.

INTERSTREAM PATHS: INTERACTIONS AND MODERATION

So far, this section has focused on within-stream, or *intrastream*, pathways. Paths 1–6 probably explain most of the variance in ETU and EAU. However, we do not believe that all causal processes lie neatly within one stream or the other. Rather, factors in one stream might exert some influence on factors in other streams. Moreover, such *interstream* influences are sometimes the effects of variables on a higher level within one stream being mediated by variables at a lower level in another stream. These interstream influences are depicted by paths a–f in figure 3.

Interstream influences may also take the form of statistical interactions such that the effect of a variable in one stream moderates the influence of a variable in another stream. For instance, intrapersonal influences (e.g., personality characteristics and biological makeups) might make some adolescents more susceptible to some social influences (e.g., peer pressures to smoke). In line with this, Bauman and colleagues (1992) showed that high testosterone levels (an intrapersonal characteristic of adolescents) exaggerate the effects of peer or parental smoking (which are social influences in TTI). The stress-coping model (see chapter 6 in this monograph; see also Wills and Shiffman 1985) is a special case of this type of interaction. This model postulates that experiences of stress (from higher in the intrapersonal stream) may be moderated by expectancies, reasons for use, or coping functions (from lower in the cultural/ attitudinal stream).

Interstream influences of ethnicity and gender are of particular interest. Although we assume that TTI describes the causal process of ETU and EAU for all ethnic groups, we also assume that the specific weights applied to particular paths probably vary by ethnicity. For example, we found that the effects of friends' smoking on adolescents' initiation of smoking were both direct and indirect—the latter mediated through refusal skills self-efficacy for whites and Hispanics, whereas the effects of friends' smoking for blacks were only direct (Flay et al. 1994). The TTI describes the causal process of ETU and EAU for both males and females, even though the specific weights applied to paths probably differ and males and females probably react differently to some

known predictors of ATOD use. As with ethnicity, we suspect that some of these differences are due to biological differences whereas others are due to cultural differences in how males and females are raised.

Several studies suggest that factors in one stream do, in fact, moderate factors in the other two streams. Risk factors from two (sub)streams may interact such that one increases the effects of the other. For example, high-risk-taking adolescents may be less susceptible to family influences than are low-risk-takers because the former are more likely to seek independence. Similarly, adolescents with low refusal skills are more prone to peer pressure than those with adequate refusal skills. We tested these hypotheses in the context of smoking onset from grade 7 to grade 8. Data for the analyses were collected as part of the Television, School and Family Project (TVSFP) smoking prevention program in Southern California (Flay et al. 1988, 1995). Baseline data were collected in 1986 from 6,695 seventh grade students from 47 schools in Los Angeles County and San Diego County.

Figure 4 shows the interactive effects of two distal risk factors: family conflict (a 3-item scale, Cronbach's alpha = 0.74, median split into low and high family conflicts) and risk-taking (a 3-item scale, Cronbach's alpha = 0.77, median split into low- and high-risk-takers). Smoking onset rates were 25.9 percent for low-risk-takers with low family conflict and 41.8 percent for low-risk-takers with high family conflicts, whereas the onset rates for high-risk-takers were 34.6 percent and 38.4 percent for low and high family conflict, respectively. The relative risk of smoking onset imposed by family conflict is higher for low-risk-takers than for high-risk-takers (odds ratios 2.06 versus 1.18). These findings suggest that low-risk-taking adolescents are more reactive to family environment than high-risk-taking adolescents.

Figure 4 also shows the interactive effects between two proximal risk factors: friends' smoking and refusal skills self-efficacy. The relative

risk of smoking onset imposed by friends' smoking shows a decreasing trend with increasing refusal skills (odds ratios are 2.97, 2.73, and 1.75, respectively, for low-, medium-, and high-refusal-skill adolescents). These results indicate that adolescents with inadequate refusal skills self-efficacy are more susceptible to peer pressure.

FEEDBACK AND LONGITUDINAL EFFECTS

Feedback or reciprocal effects postulated by TTI (Flay and Petraitis 1994) reflect the broad idea of reciprocal determinism (cf. Bandura

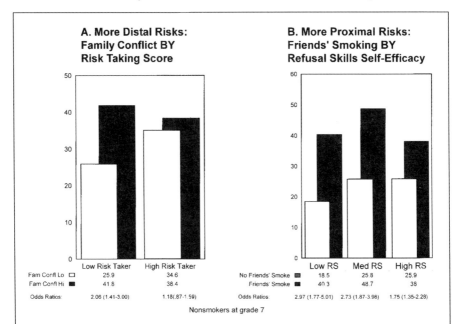

Figure 4. Risk of smoking onset by grade 8: Two interactions of grade 7 social and intrapersonal risks. (A) Interactive effects of family conflict and risk-taking. (B) Interactive effects of friends' smoking and refusal skills (RS) self-efficacy. Data are from the Television, School and Family Project smoking prevention program in Southern California.

1986). Feedback influences are concerned with the role of prior behavior. Though it has been well documented that prior drug use is the best predictor of later drug use, there is little research on how experiences derived from prior drug use influence later drug use. TTI proposes a feedback mechanism by which this might happen. Specifically, feedback loops connecting prior and later behaviors are formed in each stream of influence through a dynamic interplay between causal factors and behaviors (figure 5). Initially, drug use is affected by variables such as social bonding and attitudes. Once adolescents start to use drugs, the causal

ordering reverses and these variables are subsequently shaped by the drug use behavior. These modified factors, in turn, affect later drug use.

Several studies have provided support for the idea of a feedback mechanism. For example, Krohn and colleagues (1985) found that prior smoking affected smoking maintenance both directly and indirectly through positive and negative consequences of smoking. Similarly, Kaplan and colleagues (1988) found that earlier drug use influenced later drug use both directly and through its impact on association with drug-using peers and perceived negative social sanctions. In a well-

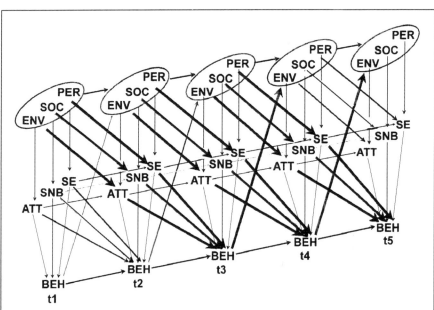

Figure 5. Longitudinal and developmental effects according to the theory of triadic influence. ATT = attitudes; BEH = behavior; ENV = cultural environment; PER = biology/personality; SE = self-efficacy; SNB = social normative beliefs; SOC = social situation; t1–t5 = times 1–5.

known study, Bentler and Speckart (1979) tested the effects of prior behavior within the framework of Fishbein and Ajzen's (1975) theory of reasoned action and found that some of the effects of prior drug use were mediated by intention and some of the effects were direct. In a replication and extension of this study, our group (Petraitis et al. 1994b) found that prior smoking had several indirect (mediated) effects: (1) it promoted more positive attitudes toward smoking, (2) it altered adolescents' beliefs in the normative nature of smoking, and (3) it undermined adolescents' resolve to resist smoking; it also had direct ef-

fects on intentions to smoke in the future and on future smoking.

Unfortunately, these studies only focused on two-wave data and ignored the dynamic nature of the effects. In figure 6, we model both feedback and longitudinal effects using three-wave data from the TVSFP. In this model, drug use is a latent variable with smoking and alcohol use as indicators. Risk-taking and friends' smoking are latent predictor constructs measured over time. Note how drug use at one wave "feeds back" to cause changes in the risk predictor variables. Note also that the size of these effects may change over time.

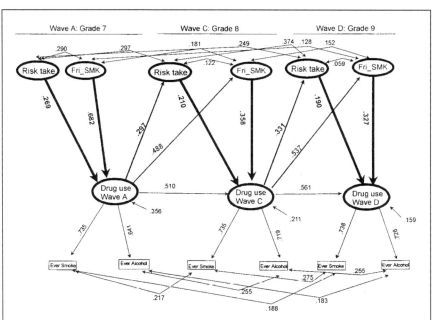

Figure 6. Three-wave latent variable model of two risk factors and drug use. χ^2 = 122.09 (df = 33). Adjusted goodness-of-fit index = 0.970. All coefficients are standardized and are significant at $p < 0.05$. Data are from the Television, School and Family Project smoking prevention program in Southern California.

ROLE OF RELATED BEHAVIORS

Influence of Related Behaviors

Related behaviors (e.g., tobacco, alcohol, and marijuana use) may influence each other. It has been frequently found that adolescents who use one drug are more likely to use another one, leading to the widely accepted conclusion that the use of one drug serves as a gateway for use of other drugs. This unidimensional conceptualization of drug use behaviors, however, may be too simplistic without considering other risk factors.

TTI postulates that the influence of related behaviors might be modified by psychosocial factors. Figure 7 shows the interactions of two variables, one cultural and one intrapersonal, with prior alcohol use on the onset of cigarette smoking. Among those who did not regularly attend religious worship, prior alcohol users were more likely to initiate cigarette smoking than those who had not used alcohol (odds ratio = 3.5). For those who regularly attended religious worship, the risk for the transition from alcohol use to cigarette smoking was much less (odds ratio = 1.9).

Figure 7 also shows that the risk for the transition from alcohol use to cigarette smoking was much higher for those who had low refusal skills self-efficacy than for those who had medium and high refusal skills self-efficacy (odds ratios were 3.76, 2.00, and 1.90, respectively). Alcohol use puts students at risk for future smoking, as the gateway hypothesis predicts, but much more so for those who do not attend church, and more so for those with low refusal skills self-efficacy.

The preceding example (figure 7) describes how other risk factors affect the influence of alcohol use on the use of cigarettes. This moderating process, however, does not stop there. The line in figure 8 shows the well-known phenomenon of prior alcohol and tobacco use increasing the risk for marijuana use, illustrating the gateway drug hypothesis.

The gateway metaphor, however, may be too simplistic when we consider the effects of risk factors in the process of drug escalation, because related behaviors may also interact with risk factors to influence subsequent behavior. Figure 8 shows that the basic gateway drug hypothesis is true only for students who are otherwise also at high risk (who score high on risk-taking and whose friends also smoke cigarettes); it is not true for those not otherwise at risk (who score low on risk-taking and whose friends do not smoke). Specifically, for those students who were low-risk-takers and had no smoking peers, marijuana use was independent of prior use of alcohol and cigarettes. For those who were high-risk-takers but had no smoking peers and for those who were low-risk-takers but had smoking peers, marijuana use was much higher for prior cigarette smokers compared with those who used alcohol. This kind of "stepping-stone" phenomenon of adolescent drug involvement was most pronounced for the stu-

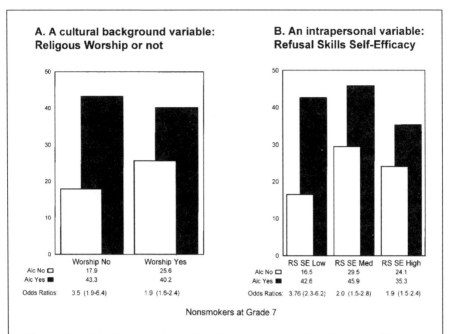

A. A cultural background variable: Religous Worship or not

	Worship No	Worship Yes
Alc No ☐	17.9	25.6
Alc Yes ■	43.3	40.2
Odds Ratios:	3.5 (1.9-6.4)	1.9 (1.6-2.4)

B. An intrapersonal variable: Refusal Skills Self-Efficacy

	RS SE Low	RS SE Med	RS SE High
Alc No ☐	16.5	29.5	24.1
Alc Yes ■	42.6	45.9	35.3
Odds Ratios:	3.76 (2.3-6.2)	2.0 (1.5-2.8)	1.9 (1.5-2.4)

Nonsmokers at Grade 7

Figure 7. Risk of smoking by grade 8: Two interactions with prior (grade 7) alcohol use. (A) Interaction of religious worship with prior alcohol use. (B) Interaction of refusal skills self-efficacy (RS SE) with prior alcohol use. Data are from the Television, School and Family Project smoking prevention program in Southern California.

dents at highest risk (they were both high-risk-takers and had smoking peers). These findings suggest that relying on a single risk factor orientation runs counter to the known heterogeneity of behavior. We need to consider multiple risk factors and their interactions to find out who is at risk and under what conditions.

Prediction of Closely Related Behaviors

Researchers are often asked whether or not the various drug use behaviors are part of the same latent construct. These behaviors have been conceptually characterized to form a unidi-

mensional structure, that is, problem behaviors (Jessor and Jessor 1977). TTI suggests that closely related behaviors may have the same, or very similar causes, and less related behaviors less so (Flay and Petraitis 1994). The more dissimilar the behavior, the less the overlap of the causal structure. The overlap varies most at the most proximal levels and least at the most distal levels (see figure 7 in Flay and Petraitis 1994). The ultimate or root causes of related behaviors are generally the same.

Related behaviors obviously do correlate with each other (that is, after all, part of what we mean by

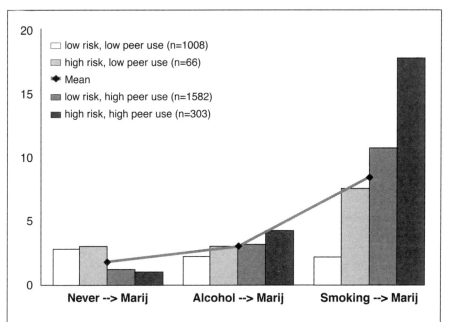

Figure 8. Risk of marijuana use by grade 8: Effects of prior behavior (grade 7), peer behavior, and risk-taking. Data are from the Television, School and Family Project smoking prevention program in Southern California.

"related"). They probably also have most of the same causes. We may ask whether these causes interrelate with each other and influence related behaviors in the same ways. If alcohol use and smoking had a similar causal structure and influenced related behaviors in the same ways, the model shown in figure 9 would describe the relations among their causes. In this model, smoking and alcohol behaviors are characterized as one latent phenomenon, which is influenced by risk-taking preferences and the number of smoking friends. Demographic variables like gender and race mainly affect the adolescents' risk-taking (personality) and the exposure to smoking friends. This model does, in-

deed, provide a good statistical fit to our data.

Despite the good fit of the "one-factor" model, we can fit an alternative "two-factor" model. In this model, smoking and alcohol use are treated as separate constructs, but they are assumed to have the same causes. However, the model allows for the causes to behave in different ways; that is, it allows for different causal processes. Even the same causes may act in slightly different ways with respect to different behaviors. The model shown in figure 10 (which does fit better than the model of figure 9 at a statistically significant level), suggests that gender, ethnicity, risk-taking and friends' smoking all act differently for

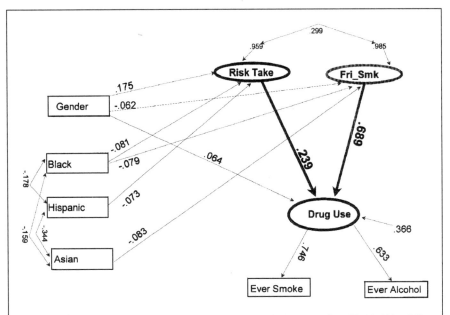

Figure 9. One-factor model of smoking and alcohol onset. χ^2 = 91.46 (df = 10). Adjusted goodness-of-fit index = 0.947. All coefficients are standardized. Data are from the Television, School and Family Project smoking prevention program in Southern California.

alcohol and tobacco use. In particular, gender and race still have differential direct effects on smoking and alcohol use, even after accounting for their indirect effects through the other risk factors. In broad terms, white adolescents drink more (and earlier) than adolescents of other races, and girls drink less than boys.

This finding suggests that we revisit our earlier model of the longitudinal effects of drug use, this time separating alcohol and tobacco use. In figure 11, we see that the risk variables not only predict the two behaviors at different levels, but that experience with the behavior also changes these relationships over time.

IMPLICATIONS AND CONCLUSIONS

The relations between alcohol use and cigarette smoking are complex. The traditional gateway or unidimensional explanations for experimentation may be too simplistic. So far, we have demonstrated four main points. First, alcohol use and cigarette smoking do share several causes and pathways, which are described by the generic theoretical framework provided by TTI. Second, the relation between alcohol use and cigarette smoking can be modified by other risk factors. For example, the transition from alcohol use to cigarette smoking is more likely to occur among adolescents who have other risk factors, such as low refusal skills and exposure to smoking peers. Third, alcohol use and cigarette smoking can be conceptualized either as one latent phenomenon or as different behaviors. Generally speaking, the two behaviors (perhaps along with other deviant behaviors) have more similarities than differences in terms of causes. However, differences in causal processes may have important implications for understanding and prevention. Fourth, the relation between alcohol use and cigarette smoking is dynamic, as are the relations between other risk factors and drug use. In order to understand the developmental process of drug use, we need to take several effects into consideration, including growth effects (longitudinal or time effects), reciprocal effects, mediating effects, and moderating effects. These effects are all incorporated into TTI.

All of the points made above have implications not only for understanding why adolescents start to experiment with alcohol or tobacco, but also for behavior change in general and prevention in particular. The mul-

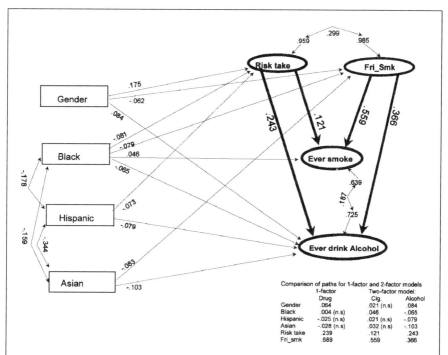

Comparison of paths for 1-factor and 2-factor models

| | 1-factor | Two-factor model: | |
	Drug	Cig.	Alcohol
Gender	.064	.021 (n.s)	.084
Black	.004 (n.s)	.046	-.065
Hispanic	-.025 (n.s)	.021 (n.s)	-.079
Asian	-.028 (n.s)	.032 (n.s)	-.103
Risk take	.239	.121	.243
Fri_smk	.689	.559	.366

Figure 10. Two-factor model of smoking and alcohol onset. $\chi^2 = 2.38$ (df = 5). Adjusted goodness-of-fit index = 0.997. All coefficients are standardized. Data are from the Television, School and Family Project smoking prevention program in Southern California.

tilevel and multidimensional nature of TTI suggests that intervention and prevention programs for adolescent alcohol and tobacco use should also be multilevel and multidimensional (figure 12). At more distal levels, TTI suggests that legislative, media, and community interventions are needed to change the informational, cultural/values, normative, and social support aspects of the broader cultural or social environment. At more proximal levels, adolescents (and parents) need to be taught appropriate attitudes (and supportive knowledge and values), normative beliefs (with appropriate models and social approval/

disapproval), and social skills (with appropriate opportunities for practice and reinforcement).

RECOMMENDATIONS FOR FUTURE RESEARCH

Research is needed to establish more clearly the links and causal relationships between intrapersonal, interpersonal, and environmental risks and protective factors, and the relationships of all of these with behavior. We make the following recommendations for future research:

- *Studies of causal process.* In general, we encourage more studies of the

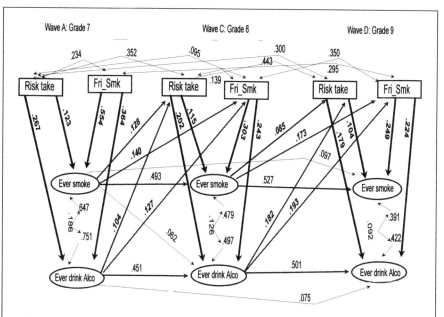

Figure 11. Three-wave latent variable model of two risk factors and two drug use behaviors, showing changes over time in influence of risk factors on behavior and of behavior on risk factors. $\chi^2 = 168.40$ (df = 27). Adjusted goodness-of-fit index = 0.950. All coefficients are standardized and are significant at $p < 0.05$. Data are from the Television, School and Family Project smoking prevention program in Southern California.

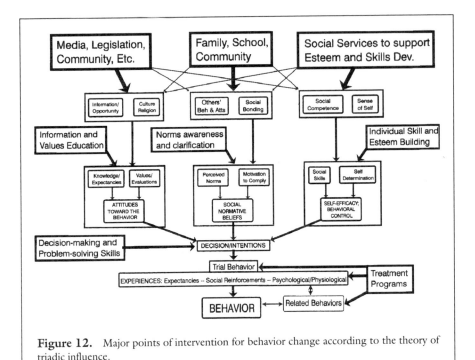

Figure 12. Major points of intervention for behavior change according to the theory of triadic influence.

causal processes by which risk factors contribute to adolescents' experimental use of tobacco and alcohol. As TTI postulates, the etiology of ETU and EAU use is complex and involves both direct and indirect paths, moderating effects, and feedback or reciprocal effects. Unfortunately, past research has too rarely reflected this complexity. Although there are signs of change among more recent studies, too often past studies have stopped at describing univariate or multivariate predictors of alcohol and tobacco use and have not described the complex causal process by which variables contribute to drinking and smoking. Therefore, we

encourage researchers to move from finding predictors to describing causal processes.

- *Studies of causal processes involving sociocultural environmental factors.* Although future studies should focus on causal processes in general, there is a particular need for studies that focus on the causal processes by which sociocultural factors contribute to tobacco and alcohol use. More research is needed to examine the influences of macrolevel sociocultural factors, such as public policies, neighborhood, poverty, and media. Grube and Wallack (1994) provided one of the few examples of such a study by examining how exposure to alcohol advertisements influences adolescents' drinking intentions.

- *Studies of causal processes involving intrapersonal characteristics.* We also recommend that more studies focus on the causal pathways by which ETU and EAU are rooted in intrapersonal characteristics, especially biological factors and fundamental personality traits. In fact, our recent review of theories of experimental drug use (Petraitis et al. 1995) suggested no clear causal pathways that link biological or personality variables to drug use. More research is also needed on the interactive effects of biological and psychosocial factors on tobacco and alcohol use.

- *Studies of causal processes leading to dependence and addiction.* Although there are numerous studies on the etiology of ETU (Flay and Petraitis 1994) and experimental drug use (Petraitis et al. 1994*a*; Flay et al. unpublished manuscript 1995), few studies describe the predictors of tobacco or alcohol dependence and addiction, and even fewer studies describe the causal processes of becoming dependent or addicted. Therefore, more research is needed to examine the natural history of tobacco and alcohol use and the potentially different etiologic factors and pathways associated with experimental use and abuse.

- *Studies of developmental changes.* In addition, we recommend more studies of developmental changes in the influence on tobacco and al-

cohol use. Influences on tobacco and alcohol use may vary with different stages of adolescence. A time-varying design (e.g., multiple waves of observations over critical periods of adolescence) and a time-varying statistical analysis (e.g., random effects or multilevel models) are crucial in investigating the developmental paths leading to tobacco and alcohol use.

- *Multiwave and intervention studies of tobacco and alcohol use.* The preceding recommendations are based on our belief that too few studies have attempted to untangle the complex etiology that leads to the use of tobacco, alcohol, or both. Our final recommendation is that researchers design more studies that can untangle the causal factors, moderating effects, feedback effects, and other direct and indirect effects and can test complex causal processes. In particular, we recommend that researchers design future studies of etiology with enough waves of data (probably six or more) to allow them (a) to carry out sensitive tests of complex and interwoven causal processes, (b) to test feedback mechanisms and reciprocal effects, and (c) to test for developmental changes over time. In addition, the suggested causal relationships should be subjected to the ultimate test—by designing interventions to change the presumed causes and then determining if such change leads to changes in behavior (less or no alcohol or tobacco use). It is only with such linked tests of theory and preventive interventions that a true science of prevention can develop fully (Kellam 1994).

ACKNOWLEDGMENTS

This chapter was prepared with support from National Institute on Drug Abuse grant DA06307. Ohid Siddiqui, M.S., helped with data analysis.

REFERENCES

Bandura, A. *Social Foundations of Thought and Action: A Social Cognitive Theory.* New York: Prentice-Hall, 1986.

Bauman, K.E.; Foshee, V.A.; and Haley, N.J. The interaction of sociological and biological factors in adolescent cigarette smoking. *Addict Behav* 17:459–467, 1992.

Bentler, P.M., and Speckart, G. Models of attitude-behavior relations. *Psychol Rev* 86:452–464, 1979.

DeKay, W.T., and Buss, D.M. Human nature, individual differences, and the importance of context: Perspectives from evolutionary psychology. *Curr Direct Psychol Sci* 1(6):184–189, 1992.

Dielman, T.E.; Shope, J.T.; Butchart, A.T.; Campaneilli, P.C.; and Caspar, R.A. A covariance structure model test of antecedents of adolescent alcohol misuse and a prevention effort. *J Drug Educ* 19(4):337–361, 1989.

Ellickson, P.L., and Hays, D. Beliefs about resistance self-efficacy and drug prevalence: Do they really affect drug use? *Int J Addict* 25(11A):1353–1378, 1991.

Ellickson, P.L., and Hays, D. On becoming involved with drugs: Modeling adolescent drug use over time. *Health Psychol* 11:377–385, 1992.

Fishbein, M., and Ajzen, I. *Belief, Attitude, Intention and Behavior: An Introduction to Theory and Research.* Reading, MA: Addison-Wesley, 1975.

Flay, B.R., and Petraitis, J. The theory of triadic influence: A new theory of health behavior with implications for preventive interventions. In Albrecht, G.L., ed. *Advances in Medical Sociology: Volume IV. A Reconsideration of Models of Health Behavior Change.* Greenwich, CT: JAI Press, 1994. pp. 19–44.

Flay, B.R.; Brannon, B.R.; Johnson, C.A.; Hansen, W.B.; Ulene, A.; Whitney-Saltiel, D.A.; Gleason, L.R.; Gavin, D.M.; Glowacz, K.M.; Sobol, D.F.; Spiegel, D.C.; and Sussman, S. The television, school and family smoking prevention/cessation project: I. Theoretical basis and television program development. *Prev Med* 17(5):585–607, 1988.

Flay, B.R.; Hu, F.B.; Siddiqui, O.; Day, E.L.; Hedeker, D.; Petraitis, J.; Richardson, J.; and Sussman, S. Differential influences of parental and friends' smoking on adolescent initiation and escalation of smoking. *J Health Soc Behav* 35(3):248–265, 1994.

Flay, B.R.; Miller, T.Q.; Hedeker, D.; Siddiqui, O.; Brannon, B.R.; Johnson, C.A.; Hansen, W.B.; Sussman, S.; and Dent C. The television, school and family smoking prevention and cessation project: VIII. Student outcomes and mediating variables. *Prev Med* 24(1):29–40, 1995.

Frankenhaeuser, M. The psychophysiology of workload, stress, and health: comparison between sexes. *Ann Behav Med* 13:197–204, 1991.

Grube, J.W., and Wallack, L. Television beer advertising and drinking knowledge, beliefs, and intentions among schoolchildren. *Am J Public Health* 84:254–259, 1994.

Jessor, R., and Jessor, S.L. *Problem Behavior and Psychosocial Development*. New York: Academic Press, 1977.

Jessor, R.; Donovan, J.E.; and Costa, F.M. *Beyond Adolescence: Problem Behavior and Young Adult Development*. New York: Cambridge University Press, 1991.

Kaplan, H.B.; Johnson, R.J.; and Bailey, C.A. Explaining adolescent drug use: An elaboration strategy for structural equations modeling. *Psychiatry* 51:142–163, 1988.

Kellam, S.G. Testing theory through developmental epidemiologically based prevention research. In: Cazares, A., and Beatty, L.A., eds. *Scientific Methods for Prevention Intervention Research*. NIDA Research Monograph No. 139. Rockville, MD: National Institute on Drug Abuse, 1994. pp. 37–58.

Krohn, M.D.; Skinner, W.F.; Massey, J.L.; and Akers, R.L. Social learning theory and adolescent cigarette smoking: A longitudinal study. *Soc Probl* 32:455–471, 1985.

Magnusson, D. Wanted: A psychology of situations. In: *Toward a Psychology of Situations: An Interactional Perspective*. Hillsdale, NJ: Erlbaum, 1981. pp. 9–23.

Marcos, A.C., and Johnson, R.E. Cultural patterns and causal processes in adolescent drug use: The case of Greeks versus Americans. *Int J Addict* 23(6):545–572, 1988.

Petraitis, J.; Flay, B.R.; Miller, T.Q.; Torpy, E.J.; and Greiner, B. "A Review of Prospective Studies of Illicit Substance Use." Poster session presented at the annual meeting of the Western Psychological Association, Kono, HI, May 1994*a*.

Petraitis, J.; Flay, B.R.; Siddiqui, O.; and Day, E. "A longitudinal comparison of three models of adolescent smoking." Poster session presented at the annual meeting of the Western Psychological Association, Kona, HI, May 1994*b*.

Petraitis, J.; Flay, B.R.; and Miller, T.Q. Reviewing theories of adolescent substance use: Organizing pieces in the puzzle. *Psychol Bull* 117(1):67–86, 1995.

Sadava, S.W. Psychosocial interactionism and substance use. *Drugs Soc* 2:1–30, 1987.

Schlegel, R.P.; d'Avernas, J.R.; Zanna, M.P.; DeCourville, N.H.; and Manske, S.R. Problem drinking: A problem for the theory of reasoned action? *J Appl Soc Psychol* 22:358–385, 1992.

Wills, T.A., and Shiffman, S. Coping and substance use: A conceptual framework. In: Shiffman, S., and Wills, T.A., eds. *Coping and Substance Use*. Orlando, FL: Academic Press, 1985.

Chapter 4

Genetic and Environmental Influences on Alcohol and Tobacco Dependence Among Women

Carol A. Prescott, Ph.D., and Kenneth S. Kendler, M.D.

This chapter examines the evidence for genetic influences on alcohol and tobacco dependence in a large sample of female twins. These preliminary results suggest that genetic factors and environmental influences shared by siblings are important in the development of alcohol and tobacco dependence and their overlap. The analyses also illustrate a number of methodological challenges facing researchers investigating genetic contributions to alcohol, tobacco, and other drug (ATOD) dependence.

GENETIC INFLUENCES ON ALCOHOL DEPENDENCE

Historically, researchers have gathered evidence for genetic influences on alcohol dependence using three genetic epidemiologic methods: family, adoption, and twin studies. More recently, genetic marker and association studies have provided evidence for genetic influences on negative consequences of alcohol consumption. In addition, findings from animal studies have suggested a genetic basis for components of addiction such as tolerance, withdrawal, and physical dependence.

The empirical literature on genetic epidemiology of alcohol dependence has been the subject of several recent reviews. The evidence is summarized briefly here; for more comprehensive reviews, see works by Merikangas (1990), Sher (1991), and McGue (1994, in press).

Researchers have studied hundreds of families through family histories and

C.A. Prescott, Ph.D., and K.S. Kendler, MD, are affiliated with the Psychiatric Genetics Research Program, Medical College of Virginia, Virginia Commonwealth University, P.O. Box 980710, Richmond, VA 23298–0710.

personal interviews in attempts to understand the familiality of alcoholism. With few exceptions, results from family studies have shown alcoholism to be highly familial (Cotton 1979; Merikangas 1990). Having a first-degree relative with alcohol dependence is associated with a fourfold to fivefold increase in risk of alcoholism.

Although based on small samples, the available adoption studies of alcoholism strongly suggest the importance of genetic effects in the development of alcoholism among males. As shown in figure 1A, aside from a small study by Roe (1945), males adopted away from their alcoholic fathers were significantly more likely to develop alcoholism than adoptees whose biological parents were not alcoholic.

Researchers have conducted four adoption studies of women, but these comprised small samples, with only one sample including more than 50 women born to alcoholic parents (figure 1B). In two of the four studies, women with alcoholic biological parents were significantly more likely to develop alcoholism than adoptees whose biological parents were not alcoholic. In the other two studies, no differences were found between the two groups of adoptees. Thus, the data from studies of female adoptees are mixed in implicating genetic influences in the development of alcoholism.

Adoption studies have two substantial limitations. First, researchers may not be justified in assuming that biological and adoptive environments

are uncorrelated. Adoption agencies often practice *selective placement* in which prospective adoptees are matched to parents based on appearance, ethnicity, or religion. Second, the generalizability from adoption studies alone is limited: Families adopt children for nonrandom reasons, and adoptees and their biological parents generally have higher rates of psychopathology and adopting parents have lower rates of psychopathology than the population average. Because of these limitations, it

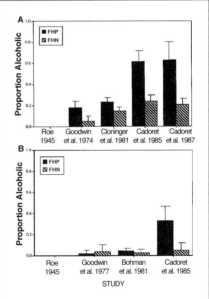

Figure 1. Risk of alcoholism among adoptees with a positive (FHP) or negative (FHN) family history of alcoholism: (A) male adoptees; (B) female adoptees. Bar indicates one standard error. Roe (1945) found no familial resemblance for alcoholism among either type of adoptee. Adapted from McGue 1994.

is important to consider the adoption evidence in conjunction with family and twin study results.

TWIN STUDIES

During the past 5 years, the number of published twin studies on alcoholism has increased rapidly. The majority of studies on male twins have found evidence of significant genetic influences on liability for alcoholism, with less evidence of the importance of shared environmental influences (figure 2A). However, the results

from studies of female twins are less consistent, with some studies finding no evidence of genetic effects and other studies yielding heritability estimates as high as 0.60 (figure 2B). Partly because of the small sample sizes, the estimates have depended on the definitions used. For example, in the study conducted by Pickens and colleagues (1991), the estimate of genetic effects was 0.42 for alcohol dependence and 0.26 for abuse and dependence, whereas in an overlapping sample, McGue and colleagues (1992) found an estimate of 0.0 for abuse and dependence.

Most available twin data are based on cases ascertained through clinic or archival records. In contrast, the female twin subjects used in the Medical College of Virginia (MCV) Stress and Coping Twin Study were ascertained through the population-based Virginia Twin Registry (Kendler et al. 1992*b*). The best fitting models for alcohol dependence in this sample produced estimates of genetic contributions ranging from 50 to 61 percent, with little evidence of shared environmental effects.

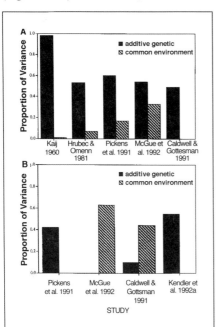

Figure 2. Estimates of additive genetic and common environmental contributions from twin studies of alcohol dependence: (A) male twins; (B) female twins. The Pickens et al. and McGue et al. studies contain overlapping samples. Adapted from McGue 1994.

GENETIC INFLUENCES ON TOBACCO DEPENDENCE

A large number of studies have investigated the familiality of tobacco use, but few have studied tobacco dependence. Family data suggest that children of smokers have a twofold to fourfold greater risk of becoming smokers than children of nonsmokers (Hughes 1986). A single adoption study (Eysenck and Eaves 1980) found modest evidence that the smoking habits of adoptees were more similar to the smoking habits of their biological relatives than of their adopting families.

Twin studies of tobacco use have consistently found smoking to be moderately familial. However, the results are inconsistent in assigning this resemblance to shared genes or shared environments. Several studies have attributed the resemblance only to genetic effects (Pedersen 1981; Carmelli et al. 1990, 1992; Swan et al. 1990), other studies support both genetic and shared environmental influences (Todd and Mason 1959; Conterio and Chiarelli 1962; Kaprio et al. 1982), and one study suggests only shared environmental influences (Kaprio et al. 1984). Evidence for gender differences in tobacco use is also mixed, with most studies suggesting no difference, but two studies finding genetic influences among women but not men (Raaschou-Nielsen 1960; Crumpacker et al. 1979).

Part of this discrepancy may be attributed to the samples' wide variations in prevalence of smoking, age cohort, and ethnic background. In addition, some studies have analyzed smoking versus nonsmoking, whereas others have studied quantity of smoking. Studies of smoking quantity have varied in the handling of nonsmoking twins. As will be addressed later, exclusion of nonsmokers may alter estimates of genetic and environmental effects.

METHOD

SUBJECTS AND DESIGN

The MCV Stress and Coping Twin Study was begun in 1987. Subjects are Caucasian female twins born in Virginia who were between the ages of 17 and 55 when originally studied. Twins were ascertained through a population-based twin registry originally formed by a sequential search of State birth records and then matching to State records for current addresses. (See Kendler et al. 1992b for more details on subject ascertainment and assessment.)

Table 1 shows some characteristics of the sample. The original study included 2,163 women who were administered individual structured psychiatric interviews. The assessment included personality characteristics and alcohol use as well as various psychiatric disorders, including alcohol dependence as defined by the *Diagnostic and Statistical Manual of Mental Disorders, Third Edition, Revised* (DSM–III–R) (American Psychiatric Association 1987). The complete sample includes 590 monozygotic (MZ) and 440 dizygotic (DZ) twin pairs as well as 3 pairs of uncertain zygosity and 97 women whose co-twins did not participate. Zygosity was determined from a combination of questionnaire responses and examination of photographs. For uncertain cases, blood typing was conducted. At the time of the first interview, the sample had a mean age of 30 and was generally middle class, with educational and income levels similar

Table 1. Sample Characteristics of 2,163 Female Subjects in the Medical College of Virginia Stress and Coping Twin Study.

Sample Characteristics	Mean	(SD)	Range	Median
Age (years)	30.1	(7.6)	17–55	29
Education (years)	13.5	(2.0)	3–17+	13
Family income (thousands)	37.8	(20.0)	2–75+	33
Alcohol Use				
Consumption during year of heaviest use ($n = 1,667$)				
Quantity (drinks per day)	2.5	(1.7)	1–16	2
Frequency (days per month)	5.0	(6.3)	0–30	2
Typical past-year consumption among current drinkers ($n = 1,534$)				
Quantity (drinks per day)	2.1	(1.3)	1–11	2
Frequency (days per month)	5.0	(6.4)	0–30	3
Tobacco Use				
Use among women who had ever smoked regularly ($n = 636$)				
Onset regular use (years)	18.1	(3.9)	9–47	18
Heaviest use (cigs per day)	22.4	(14.2)	1–80	20
Fagerstrom score	4.9	(2.3)	0–11	5
Past-year quantity[1]	17.4	(10.4)	1–60	20
Time since quit[2] (years)	8.4	(7.5)	0–37	7

Subjects were first interviewed between 1987 and 1988. The past-year tobacco use and Fagerstrom score were obtained during followup assessment (in progress) for 1,677 women. The average interval between assessments was 60.7 months (range 44–79). Postbaccalaureate education was categorized as 17. Highest income category was $75,000 or more. Consumption data exclude abstainers.
[1]Among current smokers ($n = 335$).
[2]Among former smokers ($n = 301$).

to U.S. census data for Caucasian women in this age range.

About 90 percent of these women were reinterviewed in 1990–1991. A third wave, begun in early 1993, had obtained 1,677 completed interviews as of this report. The interview included questions on current and lifetime smoking patterns and the eight-item version of the Fagerstrom Tolerance Questionnaire (FTQ) (Fagerstrom 1978). In addition, approximately 2 years before the first interview, the subjects completed a mailed questionnaire that included items on tobacco and alcohol use. This assessment also asked each subject about her co-twin's use of alcohol and tobacco.

For women who had not yet been interviewed in wave three, questionnaire data or a co-twin report was used

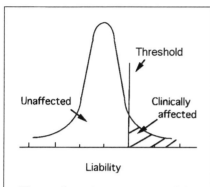

Figure 3. Schematic model of the distribution of liability in a population. Liability is assumed to be the sum of genetic and environmental risk. A clinical disorder is expressed if liability exceeds a theoretical threshold.

to establish lifetime tobacco use or abstinence. A co-twin report was not employed for quantity of substance use, because this was believed to be less valid than knowledge of whether or not a co-twin had ever smoked.

MEASURES

The current research utilizes seven measures of alcohol and tobacco use and dependence:

1. *Alcohol abstinence:* Use denied on all three occasions (i.e., waves 1 and 3 and on initial questionnaire).
2. *Alcohol dependence:* As defined by DSM–III–R. To increase the information value, the current analyses employ the number of symptoms (out of nine) rather than a dichotomous rating of present or absent.
3. *Alcohol intake quantity:* Typical number of drinks consumed per day when drinking. The highest value across the three occasions of measurement was employed.

4. *Alcohol intake frequency:* The typical number of days per month that alcohol was consumed. The highest value across the three occasions of measurement was employed.
5. *Tobacco use:* Acknowledged ever smoked cigarettes regularly.
6. *Heaviest smoking:* Number of cigarettes smoked during period of heaviest use.
7. *Tobacco dependence:* Score on eight-item FTQ.

RESEARCH QUESTIONS

The seven variables listed above will be used to address five questions. Because ATOD dependence is contingent upon ATOD use, the first two questions involved influences on the onset of ATOD use:

1. How important are genetic influences on the initiation of alcohol and tobacco use among women?
2. Are genetic influences on alcohol and tobacco use the same, partially overlapping, or completely independent?

The remaining three questions concern the overlap between alcohol and tobacco dependence and the processes that may produce this overlap:

3. Are demographic and personality characteristics significant predictors of the covariance between alcohol and tobacco dependence?
4. To what extent are alcohol and tobacco dependence expressions of a unitary addiction factor versus drug-specific factors?
5. How important are genetic influences on the risk for alcohol and tobacco dependence among women?

MODELS AND ANALYSES

When studying the genetic epidemiology of complex disorders, researchers usually assume that a continuum of liability exists that is continuously distributed in the population (figure 3). This liability arises from a multifactorial process comprising both genetic and environmental risk factors that together produce total liability. People who exceed a certain threshold of liability are assumed to express the clinical disorder, or *phenotype*. A person may have high liability because of genetic predisposition, environmental factors, or both. As shown in figure 4, people who have low genetic risk would need a severe environmental stimulus to develop the disorder, whereas those at high genetic risk might require only average stress levels to become alcoholic.

Figure 5 shows the basic model used in genetic epidemiology. The box indicates the observed characteristic—for example, the presence or absence of the clinical diagnosis of alcoholism. However, when genetic and environmental effects on a dichotomous variable are studied, it is actually their contribution to the liability for alcoholism that is estimated. This is an unobserved, or *latent*, variable, inferred from the distributional characteristics of diagnosis in the sample, and is represented in figure 5 as an oval. In the results presented in this chapter, both dichotomous and continuous measures are employed. In subsequent diagrams, only the observed phenotype is shown, but the latent liability is an

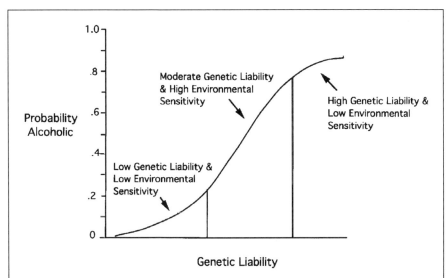

Figure 4. Genetic and environmental effects combine additively to increase or decrease the probability of alcoholism. Adapted from McGue 1994.

implicit component of all analyses of categorical variables.

In the most common etiological model, liability for ATOD is attributed to three latent sources. The first source is termed additive genetic effects (abbreviated as "A") and represents large numbers of alleles that combine additively. It is also possible for researchers to investigate the presence of nonadditive genetic mechanisms, such as genetic dominance, but in previous empirical studies of alcohol and tobacco abuse and dependence, the evidence for these has been negligible. In this chapter, discussion of genetic effects is limited to additive genetic mechanisms.

A second source of liability is common environmental effects shared by siblings (abbreviated as "C"). By defi-

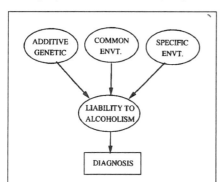

Figure 5. Theoretical model for variance components contributing to liability for development of alcoholism. Components include additive genetic effects, common environmental sources shared by siblings, and environmental sources specific to individuals. Liability is unobserved and its distribution inferred from clinical presentation.

nition, these are assumed to be perfectly correlated for twins or siblings reared together. This is a broader category than what is usually termed "environmental" and includes all nongenetic sources of similarity. With respect to ATOD use and misuse, common environmental effects might include the following: parental drinking habits and teachings about alcohol, shared peer groups, and sociocultural influences. For twins, these components also would include intrauterine effects.

The third source of liability includes all environmental influences and experiences not shared by relatives (abbreviated as "E"). These might include job loss, marital separation, or unshared peer groups. In practice, this component usually includes any random measurement error, such as from misclassification, although multivariate models can be used to separate the effects of error and unique environment.

In most models it is assumed that the three components are independent (i.e., uncorrelated), linear, and additive in effect. Under these simplifications, the expectation for liability for an individual i is as follows:

$$L_i = a(A_i) + c(C_i) + e(E_i)$$

and the total liability variance for the population is thus

$$V_i = a^2 + c^2 + e^2$$

where the lower case letters a, c, and e are used to designate the amount of each component contributed to the outcome. In the case of a threshold

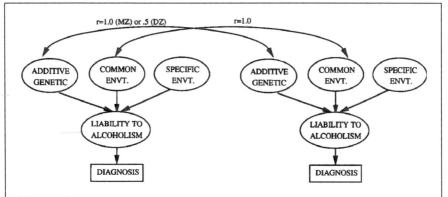

Figure 6. Schematic path model for same-sex twin studies of alcoholism. Monozygotic (MZ) twins are correlated 1.0 and dizygotic (DZ) twins are correlated 0.5 for additive genetic effects.

characteristic (such as using alcohol or not), the liability can be turned into an estimate of the probability using a probit function:

Probability (Alcoholism) =

$$e^{Li} / (1 + e)^{Li}$$

The *heritability* of a characteristic is the proportion of genetic variance relative to total variance in the population. In other words:

Heritability = $a^2 / (a^2 + c^2 + e^2)$

This is an important concept because it means that two groups may differ in heritability for several reasons. For example, if the observed heritability of alcoholism is lower among women, this could mean that the *absolute* influence of genetic effects is less in women than men (i.e., lower a^2), or it might mean that genetic influences are operating to the same degree in both sexes but that the *relative* importance of environmental influences is greater among women (i.e., equal a^2 but greater $c^2 + e^2$).

THE TWIN MODEL

Figure 6 shows how the three components are estimated as part of the twin design. At conception, MZ twins are genetic replicates. Although genetic mutations arise and adult MZ twins may differ in which genes are currently active, the impact of these differences on the development of ATOD is believed to be small. The genes of MZ twins are thus assumed to be perfectly correlated (i.e., indicated by a correlation of 1 for their A components). Under random mating, first-degree relatives, including DZ twins, on average have one-half their genes in common, indicated by a 0.5 correlation for genotypes for DZ twins. Thus, the expected correlation between MZ twins is

$$R_{mz} = a^2 + c^2$$

whereas the expected correlation for DZ twins is

$$R_{dz} = 0.5a^2 + c^2$$

Estimates for the various components can then be obtained using the algebra of simultaneous equations. For example, if the observed correlation for MZ pairs is 0.7 and for DZ pairs 0.4, the estimated components would be 60 percent for additive genetic, 10 percent for common environment, and 30 percent for unique environment plus measurement error. To the extent that MZ twins are more highly correlated for a characteristic than DZ twins, genetic influences are implicated as an explanation for familial resemblance. If MZ and DZ twin pairs are equally similar, then any similarity is attributed to shared environmental factors.

While empirical evidence supports some assumptions required to estimate genetic and environmental parameters from twin data (such as independence and additivity of the latent variables), the validity of other assumptions is less clear. One important example is *assortative mating* (i.e., the tendency for people to choose mates nonrandomly with respect to physical or behavioral characteristics). The standard twin design assumes the absence of assortative mating. However, when there is positive assortative mating for alcohol and tobacco use (as is typical) (e.g., Price et al. 1981; Hall et al. 1983; Jacob and Bremer 1986), the genetic correlation between DZ twins exceeds 0.50, leading to an underestimation of the magnitude of genetic influence.

Another assumption crucial for both twin and adoption studies is the *equal environment assumption* (EEA). The EEA requires that MZ and DZ twin pairs are equally similar in their shared, or common, environments (i.e., the C component). To the extent that the EEA is violated, the importance of shared environment will be underestimated and the importance of genetic influence will be overestimated.

Attempts to address the EEA with respect to alcohol intake have yielded mixed results (Lykken et al. 1990; Rose et al. 1990; Prescott et al. 1994). In the current sample, the EEA was addressed with respect to several forms of psychopathology. MZ and DZ twin pairs were asked a variety of questions about similarity of treatment and rearing environment. Although there were clear differences, with MZ pairs reporting more similar environments than DZ pairs, these differences did not significantly predict similarity for alcoholism or other psychiatric disturbances. That is, within zygosity groups, twins with very similar rearing environments were only slightly more likely to be similar in their risk for alcoholism than twins with dissimilar environments (Kendler et al. 1992*a*).

Researchers have not studied the EEA adequately in regard to initiation of alcohol and tobacco use. Because the onset of alcohol and tobacco use typically occurs in adolescence, it may well be true that MZ twins are more similar for environmental variables relevant to ATOD use, such as shared peer groups than DZ twins. If this is true, current modeling techniques will overestimate the importance of genetic effects on the initiation of ATOD use.

ASSUMPTIONS ABOUT ABSTAINERS

An important consideration for twin studies of ATOD dependence is how to treat twin pairs in which one or both members have abstained from ATOD use. One approach is to consider abstaining subjects as unaffected and thus at the low end of the continuum of liability for developing dependence. However, some alcoholics' offspring (who are presumably at *increased* genetic risk for alcoholism) will abstain from drinking to avoid developing alcohol problems. An alternative approach is to exclude those who abstain (and their co-twins) from the analyses, because their risk is unexpressed and unknown. This approach, however, is defensible only in the unlikely situation in which abstinence is uncorrelated with liability.

Twin pairs that are discordant in terms of their ATOD use provide some information regarding this issue. Researchers have applied multidimensional scaling techniques (Heath et al. 1991*a*; Meyer et al. 1992) and nested probability models (Hannah et al. 1985) to twin data on smoking and drinking. Heath and colleagues (1991*a*) found that nonsmokers could be considered at the low end of a single dimension of smoking quantity but that nondrinkers could not be assumed to be on the same dimension as drinkers. This means that studying only ATOD users may restrict the range of liability and attenuate the correlations observed in the data.

The issue of handling ATOD abstainers in twin studies applies to pairs of variables as well as to pairs of relatives. If the reason alcohol and tobacco dependence tend to co-occur is because users of one drug tend to use the other, then excluding nonusers could result in a zero correlation between dependence on the two drugs. Thus, it is important to account for the mechanism of subject selection in any analysis of ATOD dependence.

RESULTS

ALCOHOL AND TOBACCO USE

Table 1 displays sample characteristics for lifetime and past year alcohol and tobacco use. Approximately three-fourths of the sample had used alcohol sometime during the past 8 years. Among the women who drank, their reported intake during the year of heaviest use was approximately two drinks five times per month. However, substantial variation existed among the subjects, with some women drinking daily and consuming as many as 16 drinks per day. Nearly all the women who had consumed alcohol sometime in the past 8 years also had consumed alcohol in the past year, with a typical intake of two drinks a few days per month.

Only 39 percent of the sample had ever smoked regularly, and 53 percent of these subjects were still smoking when last interviewed. Among the smokers, regular use typically began in late adolescence and consisted of a one-pack-per-day habit. Most former smokers had been nonsmokers for several years.

TWIN RESEMBLANCE AND MODELING RESULTS FOR USE VERSUS ABSTINENCE

Table 2 displays twin pair resemblance and resulting parameter estimates for lifetime use of alcohol and tobacco. As with most previously conducted twin studies, extensive similarity existed within twin pairs for ever engaging in ATOD use. For both alcohol and tobacco, the MZ twins' tetrachoric correlation was high and nearly twice as large as that for DZ twins.

The pair resemblance for both alcohol and tobacco use is estimated to be attributed primarily to shared genotypes rather than shared environments. The additive genetic contribu-

Table 2. Twin Pair Resemblance and Parameter Estimates for Lifetime Alcohol and Tobacco Use Versus Abstinence.

Alcohol	MZ Twins	DZ Twins
No. of pairs	590	440
Pair status		
Both use	68.6%	63.8%
Both abstain	13.4%	9.6%
Discordant	18.0%	26.6%
Tetrachoric correlation (r)	0.72	0.42
	Proportion of variance (std error)	
Parameter estimates		
Additive genetic	61% (4)	
Common environment	11% (4)	
Specific environment	28% (1)	

Tobacco	MZ Twins	DZ Twins
No. of pairs	520	376
Pair status		
Both use	27.7%	29.3%
Both abstain	54.8%	35.4%
Discordant	17.5%	35.4%
Tetrachoric correlation (r)	0.85	0.47
	Proportion of variance (std error)	
Parameter estimates		
Additive genetic	77% (4)	
Common environment	8% (3)	
Specific environment	15% (1)	

Lifetime alcohol use is defined as any reported alcohol consumption at any of three waves of assessment across 8+ years based on a self-report or a co-twin report. Lifetime tobacco use is defined as regular use any time during one's lifetime based on a self-report or a co-twin report. MZ = monozygotic; DZ = dizygotic.

tion to using alcohol was estimated as 61 percent, with common environment as 11 percent and specific environment and measurement error as 28 percent. The genetic influence on developing a regular smoking habit was estimated as 77 percent among these women, with only 8 percent of the variance attributed to common environment and 15 percent attributed to specific environment and measurement error.

In this sample, about one-half of the women who had used alcohol had smoked regularly and nearly 90 percent of the smokers had used alcohol. To what extent do these behaviors have similar sources? This question was addressed by comparing the cross-twin, cross-variable correlations of MZ and DZ twin pairs. In this sample, the within-person tetrachoric correlation between alcohol and tobacco use was $r = 0.38$. Among the MZ twin pairs, the correlation between one twin's smoking and the other twin's alcohol use was equally high at $r = 0.39$. This means that knowing that a woman smokes tells as much about the probability that her identical twin uses alcohol as it does about her own drinking. The correlation between one twin's smoking and the other twin's alcohol use among DZ pairs also was positive but lower (i.e., $r = 0.29$), suggesting a role for both genetic and shared environmental influences on the covariance of drinking and smoking.

Figure 7 shows the parameter estimates for these data. The shared variance was moderate, accounting for approximately 32 percent of the variance in alcohol use and 24 percent of

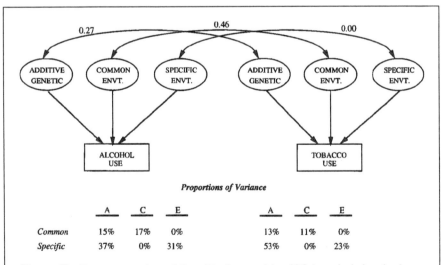

Figure 7. Parameters estimated from bivariate models of lifetime alcohol and tobacco use versus abstinence ($n = 504$ monozygotic and 363 dizygotic female twin pairs). All nonzero parameters are significantly different from zero (T > 1.96).

the variance in tobacco use. This shared variance was divided about equally between additive genetic and common environmental factors. The figure also illustrates that the additive genetic influences on alcohol use were correlated at $r = 0.27$ with the genetic influences on tobacco use. The correlation between shared environmental factors was quite strong at $r = 0.46$. Perhaps most remarkable is that these data suggested no overlap of specific, or unique, environmental factors. This means that all the environmental influences that jointly affected alcohol and tobacco use were those shared by siblings, such as parental teachings, peer groups, and religious beliefs.

INCLUSION OF ABSTAINING SUBJECTS

The methodological problems concerning the exclusion of abstainers were particularly salient in this sample, because fewer than 40 percent of the women had ever smoked. Restricting analyses to pairs in which both women had smoked resulted in 273 pairs, only 31 percent of the complete pairs studied in wave 3. Bivariate analyses of alcohol and tobacco dependence would have included only the 26 percent of these pairs with both twins current or former users of both alcohol and tobacco.

The effects of this selection were examined in two ways. First, the correlation between alcohol dependence (i.e., the number of DSM–III–R symptoms) and tobacco dependence (i.e., the FTQ score) was calculated under a variety of exclusion condi-

tions. Abstinent subjects were assigned a score of zero on the relevant measure. Table 3 shows the effects of this selection. As one moves to the right across the table, there is greater selection based on alcohol intake. The first column does not select on alcohol use, the second column includes only drinkers, and the third column includes only those subjects who had acknowledged a period of excessive drinking. The first row does not select on tobacco use, the second row includes only regular smokers, and the final row is restricted to those subjects who smoked at least one pack of cigarettes per day. The upper value in each cell is the observed correlation; the lower value is the proportion of the sample included in the estimate.

For 100 percent of the sample, the correlation between severity of alcohol and tobacco dependence was $r = 0.29$. However, among the 37 percent of the sample that had used both tobacco and alcohol, the correlation was $r = 0.16$, and among the 6 percent of women who smoked moderately or heavily and who had problem alcohol use, the correlation was $r = 0.14$. Not surprisingly, dropping nonsmokers from the sample had the greatest impact on the correlation because this excluded more than 60 percent of the sample.

A second approach to evaluating the effects of selection was to examine the resulting changes in the twin correlations. MZ twin correlations for the FTQ were 0.57 for the entire sample, 0.28 among pairs in which both twins were regular smokers, and 0.01 among pairs in which both twins smoked at least one pack of cigarettes per day. The corresponding DZ correlations were 0.36, 0.44, and 0.33, respectively.

These preliminary approaches indicate that exclusion of abstainers could have a major and unpredictable impact on the results of twin analyses. However, it is difficult to say which approach is more "correct." Therefore, twin analyses were conducted with and without abstainers.

TWIN RESEMBLANCE FOR USE QUANTITY AND DEPENDENCE

Table 4 shows the MZ and DZ pair correlations for the indices of problem

Table 3. The Effects of Changing Threshold on the Covariance of Alcohol and Tobacco Dependence.

		ALCOHOL			
		All Subjects	*Drinkers*	*Problem Drinkers*	**n**
TOBACCO	*All Subjects*	r = 0.29 (100%)	r = 0.27 (77.6%)	r = 0.18 (16.6%)	1,899
	Smokers	r = 0.15 (42.1%)	r = 0.16 (37.4%)	r = 0.11 (11.8%)	799
	≥ 1 Pack Smokers	r = 0.13 (21.5%)	r = 0.13 (19.5%)	r = 0.14 (6.4%)	409
	n	1,899	1,473	315	

r = Pearson correlations calculated under differing conditions of selection. Each percentage shown is the proportion of the sample contributing to the estimate. The upper left cell includes all subjects (*n* = 1,899). Table columns and rows are nested and are not independent. Moving right in the table represents raising the alcohol threshold. Moving down in the table represents raising the tobacco threshold.

Table 4. Twin Pair Resemblance for Problem Alcohol and Tobacco Use.

	MZ Pairs	**DZ Pairs**
Among Drinkers	*n* = 399	*n* = 275
Alcohol dependence symptoms	r = 0.35	r = 0.20
Intake quantity	r = 0.48	r = 0.15
Intake frequency	r = 0.53	r = 0.29
Among Regular Smokers	*n* = 97	*n* = 68
Fagerstrom score	r = 0.25	r = 0.43
Heaviest use	r = 0.50	r = 0.35

n = number of pairs; *r* = Pearson correlation; MZ = monozygotic; DZ = dizygotic. Correlations are based on pairs in which both twins have used the drug.

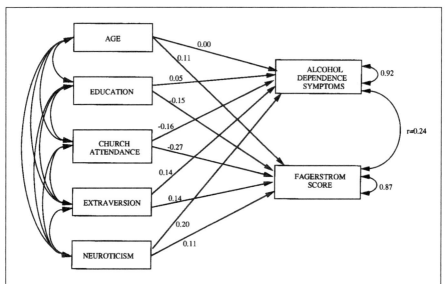

Figure 8. Prediction of alcohol and tobacco dependence from demographic and personality characteristics (*n* = 1,635 women). Nonusers were assigned scores of zero for substance-related measures. Values shown are standardized weights and residuals.

alcohol and tobacco use among pairs in which both twins use the drug. All measures were positively skewed and, therefore, were transformed for further analyses by taking the square root. For each of the alcohol measures, the MZ correlation is substantially higher than the DZ correlation, implicating the importance of genetic influences on consumption and dependence. The picture is more mixed for smoking-related variables. Genetic factors appear to have some influence on quantity of cigarettes smoked. However, among twin pairs concordant for smoking, the DZ twins are actually more similar than the MZ twins on the Fagerstrom scale, suggesting an absence of genetic effects. Rather than estimating genetic effects separately for these indicators, they were combined in factor analyses, as described below.

COVARIATES OF ALCOHOL AND TOBACCO DEPENDENCE

The next series of analyses addressed sources of covariation between alcohol and tobacco dependence. One important question is whether this covariation can be accounted for by variation in personality and demographic characteristics. To address this, five predictors were used to predict severity of dependence symptoms. These included age, years of education, frequency of church attendance, and neuroticism and extraversion as assessed by the short form of the Eysenck Personality Questionnaire (Eysenck et al. 1985). At a univariate level, these variables accounted for 8 percent of the variance in the number of alcohol-dependence symptoms and 13 percent of the variance in FTQ scores.

Not surprisingly, these variables also accounted for little of the covariance between the two dependence measures. Figure 8 shows the standardized parameter estimates for the regression weights and residual correlation based on data from all available subjects. Compared to the original correlation of 0.29, the residual correlation of 0.24 indicates that these variables account for a relatively small portion of the common influence on alcohol and tobacco dependence. Similar results were obtained when the sample was restricted to the 541 women who had used both alcohol and tobacco, with the original correlation of 0.16 decreasing to 0.14.

STRUCTURE OF ALCOHOL AND TOBACCO DEPENDENCE

The next issue to be addressed concerns the underlying structure among the measures of dependence and problem use. Do these measures assess a unitary construct of ATOD dependence or are these separate components that are drug specific? Several confirmatory factor models were used to test a priori hypotheses about the relationships among the observed variables. The first model used was a single-factor model, which represented the hypothesis of a unitary addiction factor (figure 9A). An alternative was a two-factor model of ATOD dependence and ATOD use (figure 9B), which hypothesized that

heavy tobacco use would be correlated with heavy alcohol use but that these would be less correlated with dependence symptoms. The third model posited distinct alcohol and tobacco-specific factors (figure 9C).

Table 5 displays information on the statistical fit of these alternative models for both the entire sample and the subgroup of alcohol and tobacco users. Fit is indicated by a chi-square statistic indexing the similarity between the model expectations and the observed statistics. Better models have smaller chi-square values. (See Neale and Cardon 1992 for a discussion of evaluating model fit in genetic modeling.) The first line shows the fit of a null model, representing no correlation among any of the variables. This fit poorly; the model based on the entire sample obtained a chi-square of 6,016 for 10 degrees of freedom (df) and a goodness-of-fit index (GFI) of 0.55 on a scale of 0 to 1. The single-factor model greatly improved the fit relative to the null model. The two-factor model— with separate dependence and use factors—offered little improvement in fit relative to the single-factor model. In contrast, the drug-specific two-factor model offered a very good fit, with a GFI of 0.99 for both the entire sample and subset of alcohol and tobacco users.

Figure 10 shows the parameter estimates from the final two-factor model based on data from the entire sample. Of primary interest is the correlation between the two factors. The factor for alcohol addiction was correlated

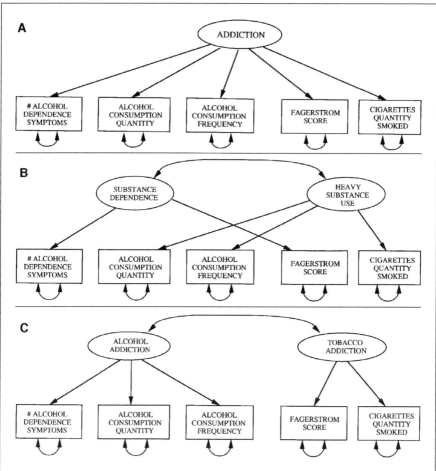

Figure 9. Alternative factor models for measures of alcohol and tobacco dependence: (A) single-factor model of a unitary addiction factor; (B) two-factor model of heavy use and dependence symptoms; (C) two-factor model of substance-specific factors.

0.37 with that for tobacco addiction, indicating substantial overlap in liability to develop problem use for the two drugs. Also of note is that the alcohol factor was marked primarily by consumption characteristics and less by dependence symptoms. The tobacco factor was somewhat underidentified and was marked equally by consump-

tion and Fagerstrom scores, which were highly correlated.

When the analysis was repeated for the subsample of subjects who had used both tobacco and alcohol, the correlation between the alcohol and tobacco factors was $r = 0.08$, providing little evidence of covariance of dependence on the two drugs. This

Table 5. Model Fitting Results for Addiction Factors.

Hypothesis	All Subjects		
	χ^2	df	GFI
No covariance among measures	6,016.0	10	0.55
Single factor	1,124.1	5	0.82
Two factors: dependence and use	1,121.8	4	0.82
Two factors: alcohol and tobacco	69.5	4	0.99
Hypothesis	Nonabstainers Only		
	χ^2	df	GFI
No covariance among measures	536.7	10	0.76
Single factor	400.7	5	0.82
Two factors: dependence and use	395.4	4	0.83
Two factors: alcohol and tobacco	20.1	4	0.99

The top portion of the table shows the results for models based on all available subjects ($n = 1,734$). The lower portion is based only on subjects who have used both alcohol and tobacco ($n = 566$). χ^2 is chi-square associated with model fit; df = degrees of freedom; GFI = goodness-of-fit index.

suggests that the observed covariance may be attributed to the large group of nondrinkers who were also non-smokers and thus had low scores on both factors. However, the factor loadings among the subgroup were very similar to those found among the entire sample. This suggests that the factor structure observed previously was not solely attributable to the group of nonusers who had zero scores on the consumption and symptom measures. Heavier use correlated significantly with greater dependence among the group of users as well.

TWIN RESEMBLANCE FOR DEPENDENCE FACTORS

The final series of analyses examined the sources for the resemblance between the alcohol and tobacco factors identified previously (e.g., figure 10).

Because the covariance between the factors was so small for the subsample of users, these analyses were conducted only for the whole sample. Figure 11 displays the correlations among the alcohol and tobacco factor scores for MZ and DZ twin pairs. For these data, the cross-twin, cross-variable correlation for MZ twin pairs ($r = 0.36$) was very similar to that for DZ pairs ($r = 0.31$), suggesting that most of the covariance is attributable to shared environmental factors.

Table 6 presents fit results for a series of nested models. Relative to the null model of no twin resemblance ($\chi^2 = 5,688$; df = 105; GFI = 0.43), the model allowing twin resemblance for the alcohol and tobacco factors produced a large fit increase ($\chi^2 = 475$; df = 96; GFI = 0.87). The next four models test the importance of various components in accounting for the covariance between the alcohol and tobacco factors. The best fit was achieved by including both genetic and shared environmental factors. As with the earlier results for covariance of alcohol and tobacco use, there was no evidence that specific environmental influences produce similarity for alcohol and tobacco dependence. The

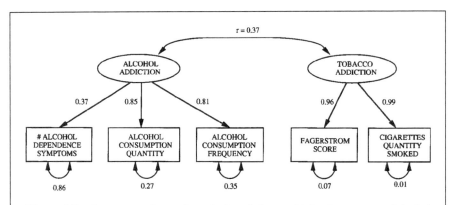

Figure 10. Parameter estimates from the best fitting model for the structure of alcohol and tobacco dependence measures (n = 1,734 women). Nonusers were included and assigned scores of zero. χ^2 = 69; degrees of freedom = 4; goodness-of-fit index = 0.99.

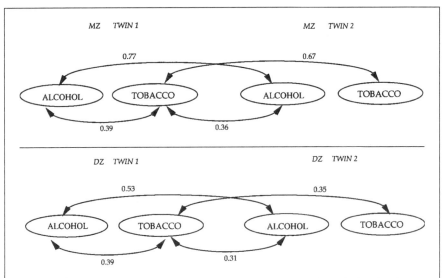

Figure 11. Within-person and cross-twin correlations of alcohol and tobacco dependence factors (n = 428 monozygotic and 275 dizygotic female twin pairs). Nonusers were included and assigned scores of zero.

final model tested whether the dependence factors accounted for all the twin resemblance or whether some genetic and environmental effects were unique to the individual measures. The large improvement in the fit of this model indicates that in addition to the common factors, important specific influences exist.

Table 7 shows the resulting parameter estimates from the final model in table 6. The genetic influences on the two disorders were correlated at $r = 0.40$, but this is a relatively small effect, because shared genetic variance accounted for only about 4 percent of the variance in the alcohol factor and

8 percent of the variance in the tobacco factor. The common environmental sources of variance were correlated at $r = 0.55$, and this is relatively more important, accounting for 36 percent of the variance in the alcohol factor and 13 percent of the variance in the tobacco factor. Because there was no evidence for specific environmental influences on the covariance, the correlation between the two specific components was nonexistent. Estimates for the remaining variance (that was not shared between the two drugs) are shown in the lower portion of table 7.

Table 6. Genetic Model Fitting Results for Addiction Factors.

Hypothesis	χ^2	df	GFI
No twin resemblance	5,688.4	105	0.43
Twin resemblance for alcohol and tobacco; no alcohol-tobacco covariance	475.3	96	0.87
Covariance of alcohol and tobacco factors due to:			
Specific environment only	450.0	95	0.88
Additive genetic and specific environment	343.9	94	0.91
Common environment and specific environment	341.1	94	0.91
Additive genetic, common environment, and specific environment	334.9	93	0.91
Additive genetic, common environment, and specific environment factors + variable-specific covariance	187.5	83	0.93

Models based on 428 monozygotic and 275 dizygotic twin pairs with complete alcohol and tobacco data (including nonusers). χ^2 is chi-square associated with model fit; df = degrees of freedom; GFI = goodness-of-fit index.

Table 7. Genetic and Environmental Contributions to Dependence Factors.

Drug	Sources of Variance Contributing to Both Drugs		
	Additive Genetic	Common Environment	Specific Environment
Alcohol	4%[1]	36%	0%
Tobacco	8%[1]	13%	0%
Correlation of factors	0.40	0.55	0.00

Drug	Sources of Variance Unique to Each Drug		
	Additive Genetic	Common Environment	Specific Environment
Alcohol	28%	0%	32%
Tobacco	45%	0%	34%

Parameter estimates based on 428 monozygotic and 275 dizygotic twin pairs with complete alcohol and tobacco data (including nonusers).
[1]Parameter was not significantly different from zero (T < 1.96).

CONCLUSIONS

Use of tobacco and alcohol appears to be strongly influenced by genetically mediated characteristics. Environmental influences shared by twins apparently play only a minor role in affecting use versus abstinence.

The covariance between alcohol and tobacco use is modest and about equally attributable to genetic and shared environmental factors. Specific environmental influences appear to have little impact.

These data suggest that the overlapping liability for alcohol and tobacco use and for alcohol and tobacco dependence is modest, approximately 20–30 percent of the variance in these characteristics. This shared variation appears to be attributable primarily to a large group of subjects who abstained from use of one or both drugs. Among users of both alcohol and tobacco, there was little covariance for level of use or intensity of dependence symptoms across the two drugs.

Demographic and personality characteristics accounted for approximately 10–15 percent of the variance in measures of alcohol and tobacco dependence. However, these variables explained only a small portion of the covariance between the two and cannot be the source of the shared environmental variance.

There appear to be specific factors for alcohol and tobacco dependence. The hypothesis of a unitary addiction liability factor was not supported. The covariance between the alcohol- and tobacco-dependence factors was mediated primarily by environmental influences shared by the twins and, to a lesser extent, by genetic sources.

LIMITATIONS

Because the study was conducted on young adult to middle-age Caucasian females born in Virginia, the results may not be representative of other demographic groups.

The data presented limited opportunity to address whether abstainers had randomly distributed risk versus low risk for developing alcohol or tobacco dependence. Because the exclusion of abstainers altered the patterns in the data, it is likely that the distribution was not random. However, it is not justified to assume that all abstainers had low risk. At the time this information was compiled, data were available only on regular smokers. In future research with this sample, lifetime smoking history will be assessed in more detail. This will enable distinctions between those subjects who tried a few cigarettes or drinks and did not become regular users (i.e., presumably low risk) from those who completely abstained (i.e., unknown risk).

The analyses presented here did not address potential violations of the equal environment assumption or include estimates of assortative mating. To the extent that the environments of MZ twin pairs relevant to ATOD use and dependence are more similar than the environments of DZ pairs, the genetic influences may have been overestimated. To the extent that the mothers and fathers of these twins had correlated liability for alcohol or tobacco dependence, the current results may have underestimated the role of genetic influences. Data are available for this sample on measures of pair contact and similarity of rearing environment, twin report of parental smoking, and assessment of alcohol dependence from interviews with the parents of this sample (Kendler et al. 1994). Future analyses will address the existence of violations of these assumptions and their potential impact on estimates of genetic influences.

IMPLICATIONS

Although this chapter focuses on genetic influences on alcohol and tobacco use and dependence, initiation of drug use is also clearly environmentally influenced. The current study is somewhat unusual in finding no evidence for shared environmental influences and only modest specific environmental influences on initiation of use. Other twin studies have found that 30–80 percent of the variation in alcohol use and 30–70 percent of the variation in tobacco use are attributable to environmental sources (Kaprio et al. 1984; Swan et al. 1990; Heath et al. 1991a; Boomsma et al. 1994; Prescott et al. 1994; Heath 1995). Although a "just say no" approach to prevention is overly simplistic, both self-regulation and external regulation of ATOD use and availability can limit the potential for expression of genetic vulnerability.

These findings suggest that the sources of liability for alcohol and tobacco dependence among women are not shared between the two drugs. This implies that environmental interventions could be targeted separately for alcohol and tobacco dependence.

DIRECTIONS FOR FUTURE RESEARCH

These results suggest several strategies for future research on potential genetic influences on liability for alcohol and tobacco dependence. The strong twin pair resemblance for alcohol and tobacco use underscores the importance of studying the mechanisms of initiation of use as a means of understanding risk for ATOD dependence. By explicitly studying twin resemblance for environmentally mediated variables, such as attitudes about ATOD use and similarity of peer experiences—and genetically influenced characteristics, such as individual differences in pharmacology and reinforcing characteristics of drugs—researchers may be better able to characterize the basis of twins' similarity and identify avenues for potential interventions.

A second strategy is to specifically study the influence of sibling ATOD use on the behavior of other siblings. The fact that most twins are living together when they begin using alcohol and tobacco suggests that co-twin behavior may play a crucial role in influencing initiation of use. To the extent that one's co-twin serves as an environmental influence, MZ twins may experience more similar environments than DZ twins. If twin behavior is a substantial factor in influencing use, the apparent genetic influences on initiation of use may actually be attributed to environmental sources. Under certain assumptions, twin data can be used to model the effects of

sibling interaction (Eaves 1976; Carey 1986). Another strategy would be to compare pair resemblance for ATOD dependence among subjects who began using the drug before rather than after twin separation.

A major unresolved question is whether women and men differ in genetic influences on the development of alcohol and tobacco dependence. Figure 12 illustrates how studying male and female same-sex pairs allows researchers to calculate separate estimates of genetic and environmental effects for each sex (e.g., a_m and a_f). However, one cannot assume that the genes and environments that influence the development of alcoholism are the same in both sexes. For example, Heath and colleagues (1991a,b) found evidence for different genetic sources of alcohol and tobacco use among men and women. Different environmental factors may be more salient for one sex. For example, family environment might be more important for adolescent girls but peer relations more influential for boys.

Using opposite sex pairs, researchers can test such differences explicitly. For example, if the opposite sex environmental correlation r_c (figure 12) is estimated below 1.0, this provides evidence that different environmental mechanisms influence women and men. If the correlation between the genotypes of male and female twins is less than 0.5, one can infer that the genes relevant for alcoholism do not overlap completely in women and men.

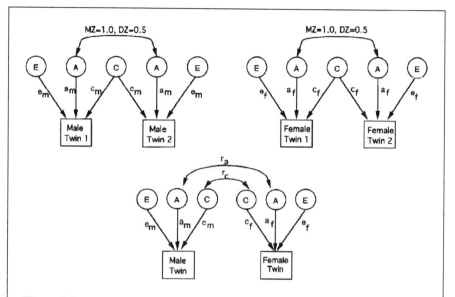

Figure 12. Schematic path model for opposite-sex twin studies of alcoholism. Additive genetic (a) common environmental (c), and specific environmental (e) parameters are estimated separately in the two sexes, permitting estimation of the opposite-sex correlation of additive genetic (r_a) or common environment (r_c) effects.

Another important avenue for future research is studying parent-offspring transmission of liability to develop ATOD dependence. By studying those at high risk, such as children of alcoholics, researchers will be able to identify genotype by environment interactions to determine which particular environments are especially risky for genetically vulnerable persons. Some evidence to support this line of research comes from adoption studies in which biological children of alcoholics placed with adoptive parents with alcohol problems were at even greater risk for alcoholism than adoptees placed in nonalcoholic homes (Cloninger et al. 1981).

Researchers can use the parent-twin design to address a variety of environmental questions, such as the following: Once genetic influences are included, do parents contribute anything further? If so, what is the mechanism of this transmission? Do mothers and fathers differ in either the magnitude or mechanism of transmitted genetic or environmental liability? Does the strength of transmission differ for sons and daughters?

These questions are similar to those that can be addressed using opposite-sex twin pairs. However, parent-twin models incorporate assortative mating, permitting more valid estimates of genetic effects than those available from twin data alone. In addition, parent-offspring patterns may differ from twin results if there are important cohort or age effects on the expression of a characteristic. The increasing prevalence of alcohol dependence among younger women (Helzer et al. 1991) or secular changes in smoking would result in less similarity between relatives of different generations (e.g., mothers and daughters) than between relatives in the same generation (i.e., sisters).

In conclusion, genetically informative designs offer a variety of possibilities for addressing the etiology of alcohol dependence, tobacco dependence, and their interaction.

ACKNOWLEDGMENTS

This chapter was prepared with support from National Institute on Mental Health grants MH–40828 and MH–49492 and National Institute on Alcohol Abuse and Alcoholism grant AA–09095. The Virginia Twin Registry is maintained by Linda Corey, Ph.D., and Walter Nance, M.D, Ph.D., and supported by National Institutes of Health grants HD–26746 and NS–25630.

REFERENCES

American Psychiatric Association. *Diagnostic and Statistical Manual of Mental Disorders, Third Edition, Revised.* Washington, DC: The Association, 1987.

Bohman, M.; Sigvardsson, S.; and Cloninger, C.R. Maternal inheritance of alcohol abuse: Cross-fostering analysis of adopted women. *Arch Gen Psychiatry* 38: 965–969, 1981.

Boomsma, D.I.; Koopmans, J.R.; Van Doornen, L.J.P.; and Orlebeke, J.F. Genetic and social influences on starting to smoke: A study of Dutch adolescent twins and their parents. *Addiction* 89: 219–226, 1994.

Cadoret, R.J.; O'Gorman, T.W.; Troughton, W.; and Heywood, E. Alcoholism and antisocial personality: Interrelationships, genetic and environmental factors. *Arch Gen Psychiatry* 42:161–167, 1985.

Cadoret, R.J.; Troughton, E.; and O'Gorman, T.W. Genetic and environmental factors in alcohol abuse and antisocial personality. *J Stud Alcohol* 48:1–8, 1987.

Caldwell, C.B., and Gottesman, I.I. Sex differences in risk for alcoholism: A twin study. *Behav Genet* 21:563(abstract), 1991.

Carey, G. Sibling imitation and contrast effects. *Behav Genet* 16:319–341, 1986.

Carmelli, D.; Swan, G.E.; Robinette, D.; and Fabsitz, R. Heritability of substance use in the NAS-NRC twin registry. *Acta Genet Med Gemellol* 39:91–98, 1990.

Carmelli, D.; Swan, G.E.; Robinette, D.; and Fabsitz, R. Genetic influence on smoking: A study of male twins. *N Engl J Med* 327:829–833, 1992.

Cloninger, C.R; Bohman, M.; and Sigvardsson, S. Inheritance of alcohol abuse: Cross-fostering analysis of adopted men. *Arch Gen Psychiatry* 38:861–868, 1981.

Conterio, F., and Chiarelli, B. Study of the inheritance of some daily life habits. *Heredity* 17:347–359, 1962.

Cotton, N.S. The familial incidence of alcoholism: A review. *J Stud Alcohol* 40: 89–116, 1979.

Crumpacker, D.W.; Cederlof, R.; Friberg, L.; Kimberling, W.J.; Sorensen, S.; Vandenberg, S.G.; Williams, J.S.; McClearn, G.E.; Grever, B.; Iyer, H.; Krier, M.J.; Pedersen, N.L.; Price, R.A.; and Roulette, I. A twin methodology for the study of genetic and environmental control of variation in human smoking behavior. *Acta Genet Med Gemellol* 28: 173–195, 1979.

Eaves, L.J. A model for sibling effects in man. *Heredity* 36:205–214, 1976.

Eysenck, H.J., and Eaves, L.J. *The Causes and Effects of Smoking*. London: Maurice Temple Smith, 1980.

Eysenck, S.B.G.; Eysenck, H.; and Barrett, P. A revised version of the psychoticism scale. *Person Individ Diff* 6: 21–29, 1985.

Fagerstrom, K.-O. Measuring degree of physical dependence to tobacco smoking with reference to individualization of treatment. *Addict Behav* 3:235–241, 1978.

Goodwin, D.W.; Schulsinger, F.; Moller, N.; Hermansen, L.; Winokur, G.; and Guze, S.B. Drinking problems in adopted and nonadopted sons of alcoholics. *Arch Gen Psychiatry* 31:164–169, 1974.

Goodwin, D.W.; Schulsinger, F.; Knop, J.; Mednick, S.; and Guze, S.B. Psychopathology in adopted and nonadopted daughters of alcoholics. *Arch Gen Psychiatry* 34:1005–1009, 1977.

Hall, R.L.; Hesselbrock, V.M.; and Stabenau, J.R. Familial distribution of alcohol use. II. Assortative mating of alcoholic probands. *Behav Genet* 13:373–382, 1983.

Hannah, M.C.; Hopper, J.L., and Mathews, J.D. Twin concordance for a binary trait. II. Nested analysis of ever-smoking and ex-smoking traits and unnested analysis of a "committed smoking" trait. *Am J Hum Genet* 37:153–165, 1985.

Heath, A.C. Genetic influences on drinking behavior in humans. In: Begleiter, H.J., and Kissin, B. *The Genetics of Alcoholism*. New York: Oxford University Press, 1995. pp. 82–121.

Heath, A.C.; Meyer, J.; Eaves, L.J.; and Martin, N.G. The inheritance of alcohol consumption patterns in a general population twin sample: I. Multidimensional scaling of quantity/frequency data. *J Stud Alcohol* 52:345–352, 1991*a*.

Heath, A.C.; Meyer, J.; Jardine, R.; and Martin, N.G. The inheritance of alcohol consumption patterns in a general population twin sample: II. Determinants of consumption frequency and quantity consumed. *J Stud Alcohol* 52:425–433, 1991*b*.

Helzer, J.; Burnam, A.; and McEvoy, L.T. Epidemiology of alcohol addiction: United States. In: Robins, L.N., and Regier, D.A., eds. *Psychiatric Disorders in America*. New York: Free Press, 1991. pp. 81–115.

Hrubec, Z., and Omenn, G.S. Evidence of genetic predisposition to alcoholic cirrhosis and psychosis: Twin concordances for alcoholism and its biological end points by zygosity among male veterans. *Alcohol Clin Exp Res* 5:207–215, 1981.

Hughes, J.R. Genetics of smoking: A brief review. *Behav Ther* 17:335–345, 1986.

Jacob, T., and Bremer, D.A. Assortative mating among men and women alcoholics. *J Stud Alcohol* 47:219–222, 1986.

85

Kaij, L. *Alcoholism in Twins.* Stockholm: Almqvist and Wiksell, 1960.

Kaprio, J.; Hammar, N.; Koskenvuo, M.; Floderus-Myrhed, B.; Langinvainio, H.; and Sarna, S. Cigarette smoking and alcohol use in Finland and Sweden: A cross-national twin study. *Int J Epidemiol* 11:378–386, 1982.

Kaprio, J.; Koskenvuo, M; and Langin-vainio, H. Finnish twins reared apart: IV. Smoking and drinking habits. *Acta Genet Med Gemell* 33:425–433, 1984.

Kendler, K.S.; Heath, A.C.; Neale, M.C.; Kessler, R.C.; and Eaves, L.J. A popula-tion-based twin study of alcoholism in women. *JAMA* 268:1877–1882, 1992*a*.

Kendler, K.S.; Neale, M.C.; Kessler, R.C.; Heatch, A.C; and Eaves, L.J. A popula-tion-based twin study of major depression in women. The impact of varying defini-tions of illness. *Arch Gen Psychiatry* 49: 257–266, 1992*b*.

Kendler, K.S.; Neale, M.C.; Heath, A.C.; Kessler, R.C.; and Eaves, L.J. A twin-family study of alcoholism in women. *Am J Psychiatry* 151:707–715, 1994.

Lykken, D.T.; McGue, M.; Bouchard, T.J.; and Tellegen, A. Does contact lead to similarity or similarity to contact? *Be-hav Genet* 20:547–561, 1990.

McGue, M. Genes, environment and the etiology of alcoholism. In: Zucker, R.; Boyd, G.; and Howard, J., eds. *The De-velopment of Alcohol Problems: Exploring the Biopsychosocial Matrix of Risk.* Nation-al Institute on Alcohol Abuse and Alco-holism Research Monograph No. 26. DHHS Pub. No. (ADM)94–3495. Wash-ington, DC: Supt. of Docs., U.S. Govt. Print. Off., 1994. pp. 1–40.

McGue, M. Moderators and mediators of alcoholism inheritance. In: Turner, R.;

Cardon, L.; and Hewitt, J.K. *Behavior Genetic Approaches in Behavioral Medi-cine.* New York: Plenum Press, in press.

McGue, M.; Pickins, R.W.; and Svikis, D.S. Sex and age effects on the inheri-tance of alcohol problems: A twin study. *J Abnorm Psychol* 101:3–17, 1992.

Merikangas, K.R. The genetic epidemiol-ogy of alcoholism. *Psychol Med* 20:11–2, 1990.

Meyer, J.M.; Heath, A.C.; and Eaves, L.J. Using multidimensional scaling on data from pairs of relatives to explore the di-mensionality of categorical multifactorial traits. *Genet Epidemiol* 9:87–107, 1992.

Neale, M.C., and Cardon, L.R. *Method-ology for Genetic Studies of Twins and Families.* Dodrecht, The Netherlands: Kluwer Academic Publishers, 1992.

Pedersen, N. Twin similarity for usage of common drugs. In: Gedda, L; Parisis, P.; and Nance, W., eds. *Twin Research 3: Epidemiological and Clinical Studies.* New York: Alan R. Liss, 1981. pp. 53–59.

Pickens, R.W.; Svikis, D.S.; McGue, M.; Lykken, D.T.; Heston, L.L.; and Clayton, P.J. Heterogeneity in the inheritance of alcoholism: A study of male and female twins. *Arch Gen Psychiatry* 48:19–28, 1991.

Prescott, C.A.; Hewitt, J.K.; Heath, A.C.; Truett, K.R.; Neale, M.C.; and Eaves, L.J. Environmental and genetic influences on alcohol use in a volunteer sample of older twins. *J Stud Alcohol* 55:18–33, 1994.

Price, R.A.; Chen, K-h.; Cavalli-Sforza, L.L.; and Feldman, M.W. Models of spouse influence and their application to smoking behavior. *Soc Biol* 28:14–29, 1981.

Raaschou-Nielsen, E. Smoking habits in twins. *Dan Med Bull* 7:82–88, 1960.

Roe, A. The adult adjustment of children of alcoholic parents raised in foster homes. *Q J Stud Alcohol* 5:378–393, 1945.

Rose, R.J.; Kaprio, J.; Williams, C.J.; Viken, R.; and Obemski, K. Social contact and sibling similarity: Facts, issues and red herrings. *Behav Genet* 20:763–778, 1990.

Sher, K.J. *Children of Alcoholics: A Critical Appraisal of Theory and Research.* Chicago: University of Chicago Press, 1991.

Swan, G.E.; Carmelli, D.; Rosenman, R.H.; Fabsitz, R.R.; and Christian, J.C. Smoking and alcohol consumption in adult male twins: Genetic heritability and shared environmental influences. *J Subst Abuse* 2:39–50, 1990.

Todd, G.F., and Mason, J.I. Concordance of smoking habits in monozygotic and dizygotic twins. *Heredity* 13:417–444, 1959.

Chapter 5

Genetic and Environmental Influences on Tobacco and Alcohol Consumption in World War II Male Veteran Twins

Dorit Carmelli, Ph.D., and Gary E. Swan, Ph.D.

It has long been recognized that smoking and drinking tend to cluster in families. The growing interest in this familial clustering relates primarily to the question of whether research findings support the contribution of genetic factors to this clustering, in addition to the contribution of environmental factors, which are communicated rather than inherited. A second issue of importance is whether genetic and environmental influences contribute equally to various aspects of alcohol and tobacco consumption (e.g., initiation, persistence, intensity). A third, related topic is the question of commonality and specificity of the genetic and environmental influences underlying joint use of tobacco with other drugs.

In this review, we summarize results from a series of studies that ad- dressed these issues using epidemiological data collected on a large sample of adult U.S. male twins. After a brief outline of the principles of quantitative genetics and a description of the data collection methods, we present findings that suggest a significant role of genetics (1) in various aspects of smoking behaviors; (2) in joint use of tobacco, alcohol, and coffee; and (3) in changes in alcohol and coffee consumption after cessation of tobacco smoking.

GENETIC APPROACHES TO ANALYSES OF TWIN DATA

Evidence for the influence of genetic factors on smoking and drinking comes mainly from twin and adoption studies. Traditionally, heritability estimates (h^2) based on twin data are

D. Carmelli, Ph.D., and G.E. Swan, Ph.D., are with the Health Sciences Program, Stanford Research Institute, 333 Ravenswood Ave., Menlo Park, CA 94025.

calculated by doubling the difference between identical (monozygotic [MZ]) and fraternal (dizygotic [DZ]) twin correlations: $h^2 = 2(r_{MZ} - r_{DZ})$, where h^2 represents the part of the total, or phenotypic, variance that is accounted for by genetic factors and r_{MZ} and r_{DZ}, respectively, are the intraclass correlations in MZ and DZ twins (Falconer 1989). When $r_{MZ} < 2r_{DZ}$, the additional familial resemblance indicates the importance of the common environment shared by twin siblings. This common environment may be created by influences from family members or common peers. The contribution from common or shared environment (c^2) to the phenotypic variance can be estimated by the formula $c^2 = 2r_{DZ} - r_{MZ}$ (Eaves et al. 1989).

For dichotomous traits (e.g., ever or never smoked, light or heavy smoker), a comparison of the probandwise concordance rates of MZ twins with those of DZ twins serves a similar purpose. The assumption is made that when one member of a pair is a smoker, the probability of smoking in the co-twin is increased, beyond that expected from the prevalence of smoking in the sample (Falconer 1965). A ratio, therefore, of observed to expected concordances that is significantly greater than 1 will imply the presence of familial influences, and a ratio in MZ twins that is significantly greater than that in DZ twins will suggest genetic influences. This simple method of comparison serves as an important first step, but it is not a formal test of a genetic/environmental model. Furthermore, it works only with twins and does not generalize to more complex data sets (Fulker 1982).

In nuclear family designs, correlations between siblings and/or correlations between parents and offspring can also provide estimates of the nature and degree of familial clustering. These correlations, however, do not permit making the distinction between shared genes and shared family environments (Rao 1991). For this and many other reasons, heritability estimates obtained from twin data are often higher than estimates obtained from other family study designs (Hunt et al. 1989). The higher heritability observed in twin studies often has been interpreted to reflect a greater environmental correlation for twins than nontwins, an age dependency in the expression of genetic effects, or a cross-generation correlation of genetic effects among family relatives that is less than unity.

Twin and family studies are also characterized by the fact that subjects are often measured on more than one variable or on more than one occasion. For twin data, the univariate model can be extended easily to the multivariate situation, where one can investigate the degree to which genetic and environmental factors explain persistence or change in single variables measured at different times or the covariances between two or more variables assessed simultaneously. The standard analytic procedure for estimating the contribution of genetic and environmental influences to trait variation and covariation is path analysis (Neale and Cardon 1992). These methods are essentially factor analysis methods in which the unobserved sources of covariation are characterized as genetic and environmental in origin. The unobserved latent factors can be characterized as such since we work with genetically related individuals where a priori knowledge about the relationships among factors is given (e.g., a correlation of 1 in MZ twins and a correlation of 0.5 in DZ twins).

Figure 1 represents the standard path diagram used in twin analysis of a single trait. We see influences from three sources: common family background (C), individual environmental factors (E), and additive genetic influences (A). These influences will differ in MZ and DZ twins, since the correlation between genotypes is 1 in MZ twins and 0.5 in DZ twins. The model presented in figure 1 can be extended easily to the multivariate case, although more than one formulation of a multivariate genetic model exists, depending on assumptions about the relationship of latent variables to the observed phenotypic correlations within individuals and across traits.

The general multivariate model from which we begin the multivariate analyses presented in this review is the *independent pathway model* (Neale and Cardon 1992). In this model, a set of common genetic and environmental factors (A, C, and E) independently influence each observed measure and account for the associations of the measures within and among twin

pairs. Alternatives to the independent pathway model include the common factor model, the simplex model, and a hierarchical formulation of dependence. These models are discussed in more detail later in this chapter.

THE NAS-NRC WORLD WAR II TWIN REGISTRY

SUBJECTS AND DATA COLLECTION

The National Academy of Sciences-National Research Council (NAS-NRC) Twin Registry consists of white male twins born between 1917 and 1927 who both served in the military, primarily in World War II (Hrubec and Neel 1978). Beginning in 1967 and continuing into 1970, an

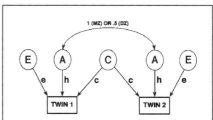

Figure 1. Path diagram for twins showing environmental factors that are not shared between twins (E), shared environmental influences (C), and additive genetic influences (A); e, c, and h represent the path coefficients of these respective factors. The proportion of variance due to genetic and environmental influences equals the squared path coefficients. The correlation between genetic factors is 1 for monozygotic (MZ) twins and 0.5 for dizygotic (DZ) twins. The correlation between shared environmental factors is c^2.

91

extensive epidemiological questionnaire was mailed to these individuals in a collaborative study with investigators of the Twin Registry of the Karolinska Institute in Stockholm. Among the objectives of this questionnaire, which was the English translation of one used in Sweden (Cederlof and Lorich 1978), were to obtain a history of tobacco and alcohol consumption and to collect information on health and social factors related primarily to coronary and respiratory diseases. Respondents to the first epidemiological questionnaire were sent an identical followup questionnaire during 1983–85 to assess changes in smoking, drinking, and health status. Response rates to the 1967–70 and 1983–85 epidemiological surveys were 78 percent and 66 percent, respectively. Twin zygosity was determined by self-report questionnaire and confirmed by fingerprints and anthropometric similarity scores. Assessments of the accuracy of the twins' opinions of their zygosity suggest that 95 percent of the self-report classifications were correct.

MEASURES

Data on smoking and on alcohol and coffee consumption were available for 2,317 MZ and 2,482 DZ complete pairs of twins out of a total of 13,000 individual respondents to the first epidemiological survey (Carmelli et al. 1990, 1992). Among those who responded to the 1967–70 survey, 80 percent reported ever-smoking and 52 percent were current cigarette smokers; 26 percent of smokers were heavy smokers (> 30 cigarettes/d). The prevalence of smoking in the registry is about 10 percent higher than that reported in the Health Interview Survey for noninstitutionalized white males in the United States (U.S. Department of Health and Human Services 1989).

Smokers in 1967–70 smoked an average of 18.6 cigarettes per day (SD = 16.1) and drank an average of 3.7 cups of coffee per day (SD = 2.4). Approximately 16 percent of the sample reported abstaining from alcohol consumption in the year prior to the time that the first epidemiological survey was conducted. Monthly use of alcohol was reported by 38 percent of all drinkers; 33 percent were drinking once or twice weekly; and the remaining 29 percent reported daily use of alcohol. The average number of alcoholic drinks consumed by drinkers weekly was 9.5 (SD = 13.3). Pairwise correlations for joint consumption of tobacco, alcohol, and coffee in 1967–70 were $r = 0.22$ ($p < 0.001$) between tobacco and alcohol, $r = 0.28$ ($p < 0.001$) between tobacco and coffee, and $r = 0.14$ ($p < 0.001$) between alcohol and coffee.

The 1983–85 followup survey obtained responses from a total of 8,956 individuals of this cohort, including 1,039 MZ pairs, 865 DZ pairs, and 5,148 individuals. There was no difference in mean age between respondents to both surveys and nonrespondents to the followup survey (Carmelli et al. 1993). The groups differed significantly on socioeconomic status and on smoking and drinking habits in 1967–

70; the prevalence of both smoking and alcohol consumption was lower among respondents than among non-respondents. Test-retest correlations for alcohol use at baseline and followup were significant and indicated moderate stability: 0.58 for frequency and 0.42 for quantity consumed per drinking occasion. The prevalence of cigarette smoking was lower at followup: 26 percent among MZ twins and 27 percent among DZ twins. These figures represent a quit rate of 45 percent among the MZ twins and 42 percent among the DZ twins. However, the proportion of heavy smokers among the continuing smokers in 1983–85 was higher than that in 1967–70 (37 percent versus 27 percent).

GENETIC AND ENVIRONMENTAL DETERMINANTS OF SMOKING BEHAVIOR

Using available data from 4,755 twin-pair respondents (2,305 MZ pairs and 2,450 DZ pairs) to the 1967–70 epidemiological survey, we estimated concordance rates for current cigarette smoking of 78 percent in MZ twins and 67 percent in DZ twins, compared with a prevalence of 53 percent in the total sample of 13,000 respondents. Corresponding rates for never-smoking were 38 percent in MZ twins and 29 percent in DZ twins, compared with a prevalence in the sample of 18 percent. These figures yield ratios of observed to expected concordance rates that are significantly greater than 1 and significantly greater in MZ twins than in DZ twins.

When changes in smoking behaviors were examined, the calculated ratios suggested genetic influences on the ability to quit smoking: MZ cotwins were more likely than DZ cotwins to quit smoking before the time the first epidemiological survey was conducted and in the time between the two surveys (relative risk ratios of 1.59 and 1.24, respectively). Evidence was also obtained for genetic influences on the intensity of smoking. We found significantly higher concordance ratios in MZ twins than in DZ twins for light (1–10 cigarettes/d) and heavy (> 30 cigarettes/d) smoking but not for moderate smoking (11–30 cigarettes/d).

One can proceed further with analysis of these data by attempting to quantify the contribution to smoking behaviors as influenced by (1) genetic effects, (2) shared environmental effects, and (3) unique environmental effects. These effects can be estimated for categorical variables by fitting a threshold model (Eaves et al. 1978). In this model, it is assumed that the underlying distribution of the behavior studied (e.g., smoking) is continuous and normal because of multiple influences of genetic and environmental factors. A threshold divides the distribution into two or more categories; for example, "never-smoker" versus "ever-smoker" or "current smoker" versus "former smoker." The correlation between the observed categories (e.g., current smoking in twin 1 with current smoking in twin 2) is known as the tetrachoric correlation. Since sample sizes are relatively large in the present study, a good approximation can be obtained for an estimate of additive genetic variance by doubling the difference between MZ and DZ tetrachoric correlations. Subtracting the MZ correlation from twice the DZ correlation provides an estimate of the shared environmental variance, and subtracting the MZ correlation from unity is an upper-bound estimate of the nonshared environmental variance (Eaves 1982).

Applying these methods to the NAS-NRC smoking data yields a heritability estimate of 65 percent for current smoking, with no significant shared environmental influences. The corresponding heritability estimate for the risk of becoming a smoker is 59 percent, with shared environmental effects accounting for an additional 21 percent of the variance. The estimated heritability for heavy consumption of tobacco (> 30 cigarettes/d) is 49 percent, with shared environmental influences nonsignificant.

Heath and Madden (in press) have reviewed results from several smoking studies of adult twins ranging in date of birth from 1870 to 1967. They report consistent evidence for highly significant genetic influences on the risk of becoming a smoker and the likelihood of smoking persistence. Shared environmental influences, in most studies, were significant for initiation of smoking but not for amount smoked and smoking persistence. The authors of this review argue that non-genetic influences unique to the twinning condition tend to play a larger role in smoking initiation than in other aspects of this behavior. Analyses of data from two Australian and U.S. twin samples (Heath and Martin 1993) have shown a significant and consistent twin reciprocal environmental influence on smoking initiation. This environmental influence, however, had no effect on the genetic contribution to the probability of becoming a smoker, which remained substantial (46 percent to 77 percent). Only the magnitude of the shared environmental estimate of total variance decreased because of the significance of this reciprocal influence.

In summary, the NAS-NRC data and data from other studies confirm the important contribution of genetic influences to all aspects of smoking behavior, especially the risk of becoming a smoker, the amount smoked, and the likelihood of becoming a long-term smoker. Shared environmental influences seem to have a role only for smoking initiation. For smoking persistence or number of cigarettes smoked daily, there is no strong evidence for shared environmental influences. These findings suggest that once regular smoking is initiated, other mechanisms determine the regulation of tobacco use. These mechanisms may include individual sensitivities to the pharmacological and toxicological effects of nicotine, the ability to develop tolerance to the effects of nicotine, and the severity of withdrawal symptoms (Pomerleau et al. 1993).

Strong evidence for the role of genetics in tobacco smoking also comes from animal studies. Collins and Marks (1989) found evidence that sensitivity to the effects of nicotine may be under genetic control partly because of differences among inbred strains of mice in the number of receptors that bind nicotine. Strain differences were also evident for the development of tolerance. Strains of inbred mice that were most sensitive to an acute dose of nicotine also developed tolerance more readily. Translating these results to humans suggests that individual differences in genetic makeups, such as differences in number of nicotinic receptors, could eventually determine susceptibility to long-term use of this drug.

TOBACCO, ALCOHOL, AND COFFEE: SAME OR DIFFERENT GENETIC INFLUENCES?

The pattern of observed associations in the joint use of tobacco, alcohol, and coffee suggests at least one and possibly two common genetic or environmental etiologies. The phenotypic correlations between smoking and alcohol consumption and between smoking and coffee consumption are significant and on the order of 0.25–0.35. The correlation between alcohol and coffee consumption is weaker—on the order of 0.12 (Istvan and Matarazzo 1984). A genetic etiology for the tobacco-alcohol association is supported by animal studies indicating that alcohol and

nicotine share common neural pathways and receptors (Collins 1990) and by human studies that show significant associations of the D_2 dopamine receptor with both tobacco and alcohol consumption (Noble 1993). These findings, coupled with the consistent pattern of correlations seen in many epidemiological studies, have led some to suggest that the determinants of the alcohol-tobacco relationship are different from those of the tobacco-coffee relationship (Carmody et al. 1985). Others, however, believe in a common pathophysiological pathway underlying the use of all three substances (Istvan and Matarazzo 1984; Kaprio and Koskenvuo 1988). Empirical testing of these two competing hypotheses requires a model that incorporates the two hypotheses, of independent versus shared etiologies, as submodels.

To address this question, we have developed a path model (Cardon et al. in press) and applied this model to the NAS-NRC twin data obtained in 1967–70. The model postulates two correlated sets of genetic and environmental factors, one contributing to the covariation of tobacco with alcohol, the other to the covariation of tobacco with coffee. As part of this formulation, the correlations between these two pleiotropic factors can be tested to determine the degree of genetic/environmental overlap. The following measures of tobacco smoking and of alcohol and coffee consumption were used in these analyses: average number of cigarettes smoked daily; total number of alcoholic beverages (beer, wine, and spirits) consumed in a typical week; and average number of cups of coffee consumed daily. To reduce the skewness in the distribution of these measures, the data were log-transformed.

Table 1 summarizes the following twin correlations by zygosity:

- Within-person cross-trait correlations (e.g., alcohol with tobacco, alcohol with coffee, or tobacco with coffee); these are all significant and show no variation as a function of zygosity.

- Intra-twin-pair correlations; these suggest genetic influences on alcohol, tobacco, and coffee consumption, since MZ intraclass correlations (0.48, 0.36, and 0.38, respectively) are greater than the corresponding DZ correlations (0.31, 0.10, and 0.19).

- Cross-trait within-pair correlations (e.g., twin 1 alcohol with twin 2 tobacco); these are informative in suggesting the presence of genetic

influences on joint consumption of substances. For example, these correlations are consistently higher in MZ twins than in DZ twins.

DESCRIPTION OF BIOMETRIC MULTIVARIATE MODELS

There are a number of biometric models that one can fit to such data; the most commonly used include the common factor model (Carmelli et al. 1994a), the Cholesky factorization, the simplex model, and a hierarchical formulation of dependence (see Neale and Cardon 1992 for their application to twin data). The common factor model requires one source of commonality for all three phenotypes, which is one of the hypotheses we aimed to test. The Cholesky factorization allows multiple groupings but imposes a factor structure that does not correspond to the pattern of phenotypic correlations observed in this sample. A simplex model of dependence (Boomsma and Molenaar 1987)

Table 1. Twin Correlations for Alcohol (ALC), Tobacco (TOB), and Coffee (COF) Consumption.

	Twin 1			Twin 2		
	ALC	TOB	COF	ALC	TOB	COF
Twin 1						
ALC		0.20	0.12	0.31	0.08	0.05
TOB	0.28		0.30	0.06	0.10	0.07
COF	0.10	0.25		0.03	0.05	0.19
Twin 2						
ALC	0.48	0.12	0.08		0.19	0.15
TOB	0.17	0.36	0.07	0.26		0.32
COF	0.08	0.11	0.38	0.12	0.27	

Note: Monozygotic correlations are shown below the diagonal, and dizygotic correlations are shown above the diagonal.

can be fitted to these data but requires that the phenotypes be ordered as in table 1 (i.e., tobacco use intermediate to alcohol and coffee use). This assumption imposes a priori the causal relationship between tobacco, alcohol, and coffee use.

The most accurate description of the observed pattern of correlations suggests a hierarchical model, with alcohol-tobacco and tobacco-coffee as primary subgroup factors and a second-order factor relating all three traits. Since the appropriate specification of this model requires the smok-ing variable to load on each of the subgroup factors, we constructed a constrained model that combined the order dependence of the simplex model with the factor structure of a hierarchical model. This model does not impose the strong structural assumptions of causality inherent in the more general simplex model and maintains the second-order or partial correlation between alcohol and coffee after removal of the effects of tobacco smoking.

Figure 2 presents the path diagram used for model fitting of the

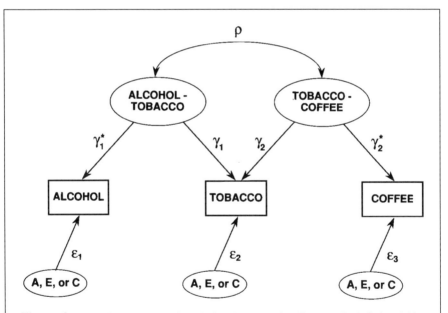

Figure 2. Two-factor model of alcohol, tobacco, and coffee use. Encircled variables "ALCOHOL-TOBACCO" and "TOBACCO-COFFEE" represent the unmeasured (latent) associations between tobacco smoking and alcohol consumption and between tobacco smoking and coffee drinking. The latent variables A, C, and E represent substance-specific factors contributing to variation in alcohol, tobacco, and coffee consumption. Trait-specific effects, accounting for genetic and environmental effects specific to each behavior, are indicated by ε_1, ε_2, and ε_3. The genetic factor correlation is indicated by ρ. Model parameters γ^*_1 and γ^*_2 are constrained for model identification.

correlation matrices described in table 1. The model allows for additive genetic effects (A), shared environmental effects (C), and nonshared individual environmental effects (E). It assumes two groupings of latent factors, reflecting the stronger correlation between alcohol and tobacco or coffee and tobacco, and imposes a second- order weaker association among all three variables. The extent to which all three substances share a common source of covariance is reflected in the factor correlation ρ. A shared genetic etiology for tobacco, alcohol, and coffee consumption will result in a significant estimate of the genetic factor correlation, ρ, whereas independence between the two subclusters will result in ρ being zero. Trait-specific effects, accounting for genetic and environmental effects specific to each behavior, are also assumed to contribute to the phenotypic variance of each variable. These effects are shown in figure 2 as ε_1, ε_2, and ε_3. Note that in the actual application of this model to twin data, all the parameters in figure 2 are specified for each of the three components of variance—A, C, and E.

The model described in figure 2 was fitted to the observed variance-covariance matrices of table 1 with the Mx computer program (Neale 1991). To identify the most parsimonious model and test the statistical significance of the various parameters of this model, the full model was compared, by using the likelihood ratio chi-square test, with submodels in which selected parameters were set to zero

(Neale and Cardon 1992). Parameters evaluated for significance in the sequence of models tested included the higher order factor correlation (ρ), shared influences for each cluster (γ_1 for alcohol-tobacco correlations and γ_2 for tobacco-coffee correlations), and trait-specific effects (ε_1, ε_2, ε_3) for each covariance component: additive genetic, shared environmental, and nonshared environmental.

Alternative models were compared by using the difference in the chi-square statistic relative to the difference in degrees of freedom. We considered a model to provide a significantly better fit than an alternative model if the chi-square difference was significant at the 0.05 level. It is important to emphasize that the acceptability of a model depends not only on how well the model fits the data but also on the extent to which the model is consistent with observations, the model is simple, and the parameters of the model are significant.

RESULTS OF MODEL FITTING

When the two-factor model described in figure 2 was fitted to the twin correlation matrices of table 1, it provided a good fit to the data (goodness of fit $\chi^2_{24} = 23.66$, $p = 0.48$). The shared environmental latent factor for both subgroups could be omitted without loss of fit (the difference in likelihood yielded a $\chi^2_3 = 2.61$, $p > 0.30$). Similarly, trait-specific shared environmental influences for tobacco smoking and coffee drinking could be omitted from the model without loss of fit. However, the shared environmental influences specific to alcohol consumption were found to be significant (χ^2_1 = 17.5, $p < 0.001$). The genetic correlation between the smoking-alcohol latent factor and the smoking-coffee latent factor could not be omitted from the model without a significant decrease in model fit (χ^2_1 = 104.46, $p < 0.0001$). The estimated genetic correlation (ρ = 0.73) was significantly different from 0 but also significantly different from 1, suggesting a significant but not total overlap of genetic influences.

The most parsimonious model fitting these data is shown in figure 3. The goodness-of-fit statistic for this model was χ^2_{30} = 26.5, $p = 0.61$. Summary statistics derived from the final model are shown in figure 4. We also notice from figure 3 that the correlation between the alcohol-tobacco and tobacco-coffee latent factors is unity, suggesting a strong overlap of environmental influences underlying the use of all three substances. As further seen in figure 4, tobacco smoking shows higher heritability (h^2 = 0.57) than alcohol and coffee drinking. The heritability of alcohol use is h^2 = 0.37, with most of the heritable variation being trait specific (63 percent). In contrast, genetic

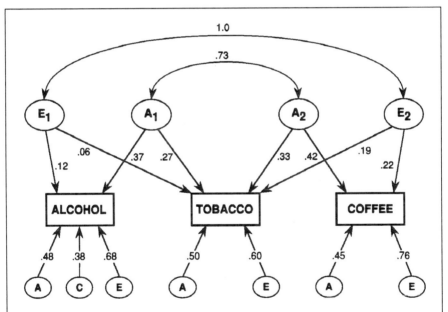

Figure 3. Parameter estimates from best fitting, most parsimonious model of regular use of alcohol, tobacco, and coffee, χ^2_{30} = 26.5, $p = 0.61$. Parameter estimates that were not significantly different from 0 were omitted from the diagram. A represents additive genetic influences; C represents shared environmental influences; E represents nonshared environmental factors. Subscripts 1 and 2 indicate overlapping influences between alcohol and tobacco and between tobacco and coffee, respectively.

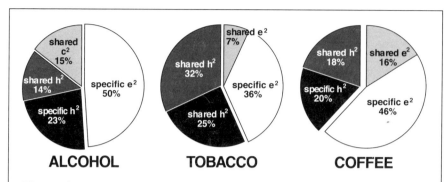

Figure 4. Shared and specific genetic (h^2) and environmental (e^2) components of variance contributing to the overall variability in alcohol, tobacco, and coffee consumption in the NAS-NRC twin cohort. The proportion of shared environmental factors in alcohol consumption is c^2.

influences on tobacco smoking and coffee drinking are divided equally between shared and specific genetic effects.

Genetic and environmental correlations can be derived by tracing the routes or path coefficients shown in figure 3. The estimated genetic correlation between tobacco smoking and alcohol consumption is 0.41, that between tobacco smoking and coffee drinking is 0.48, and that between alcohol and coffee consumption is 0.30. Environmental correlations are much smaller: 0.07 between alcohol and tobacco, 0.11 between tobacco and coffee, and 0.05 between alcohol and coffee.

To summarize, these results suggest stronger genetic than environmental influences underlying the joint use of alcohol, tobacco, and coffee in this cohort of World War II veteran twins. Furthermore, as seen from figure 4, the estimated overlap of genetic influences—14 percent, 18 percent, and 32 percent, respectively, of the total variance in alcohol, coffee, and tobacco consumption—is not uniform across substances. Finally, all environmental influences, with the exception of those for heavy alcohol use, accounting for 15 percent of the total variance, are nonshared environmental influences (i.e., environmental influences that make co-twins dissimilar rather than similar).

CHANGES IN ALCOHOL AND COFFEE CONSUMPTION FOLLOWING CESSATION OF TOBACCO SMOKING

Another important feature of twin research is the matched co-twin design, which simultaneously controls for shared genetic and early environmental influences (Carmelli et al. 1994*b*). Such control is impossible to achieve in any study of individual subjects, because only members of MZ pairs are identical genetically. In addition, being of the same age, co-twins share many other familial, societal, and cultural influences. In previous sections of this chapter, we have demonstrated the use of quantitative genetic analysis to estimate the contributions of genetic and environmental influences to the phenotypic variance of smoking and drinking behaviors. In this section, we demonstrate the use of the co-twin matched design for a study of the effect of smoking cessation on changes in alcohol and coffee consumption.

Twin pairs who differ on smoking behaviors can be selected, and intrapair relationships with respect to consumption of other substances can be compared with a priori expectations. In a matched twin analysis we attempt to describe how heredity and the environment (e.g., pressure to quit smoking) interact rather than estimating their relative importance. For example, if we postulate that genetic susceptibility to become a long-term tobacco smoker increases the susceptibility to alcohol consumption, we would expect a different pattern of change in alcohol consumption in quitter twins whose brothers continued to smoke than in quitters whose brothers were nonsmokers.

The NAS-NRC longitudinal data offer a unique opportunity to examine the interaction between heredity and the environment in long-term changes of tobacco, alcohol, and coffee consumption. Using the combined data from twin respondents to the first and second epidemiological surveys, we identified in this cohort 155 MZ pairs in which both twins quit smoking between the 1967–70 and 1983–85 surveys, 117 pairs in which both twins continued to smoke, and 290 pairs in which both twins were nonsmokers. Table 2 describes consumption of tobacco, alcohol, and coffee at baseline and at followup in these pairs.

Continuing smokers consumed significantly higher amounts of alcohol and coffee at baseline and at followup than continuing nonsmokers. Concordant quitters consumed intermediate amounts of all three substances. In addition, there was a significant increase ($p < 0.01$) in alcohol consumption in continuing smokers (mean change 8.8 drinks/mo), a moderate ($p < 0.05$) increase in quitters (mean change 4.7 drinks/mo), and no change in continuing nonsmokers (mean change 2.4 drinks/mo). For coffee consumption, however, the relationships with smoking were different. No significant change was observed in continuing nonsmokers and smokers (mean changes -0.3 and -0.2 cups/d, respectively), and a significant decrease ($p < 0.01$) in coffee consumption was found in concordant quitters (mean change -0.7 cups/d).

Even more informative are the same comparisons within MZ twins discordant for smoking cessation (i.e., pairs in which one twin quit smoking and the co-twin persisted in smoking). Table 3 shows baseline and followup consumption of alcohol and coffee. Quitters had a significant increase in alcohol consumption after

Table 2. Tobacco, Alcohol, and Coffee Consumption by Demographic Characteristics and Smoking Concordance Status in Monozygotic Twins.

Variable	Concordant Nonsmokers (n = 290)	Concordant Quitters (n = 155)	Concordant Smokers (n = 117)
Age in 1967–70 (yr)	46.4	46.3	46.0
Socioeconomic (index)	70.2	70.2	67.4
Age started smoking (yr)	—	18.3	17.5
No. cigarettes/d	—	23.6	26.0
Percent heavy smokers	—	20.0	35.0
1967–70 characteristics			
BMI (kg/m²)	171.2	170.6	172.0
Alcohol (drinks/mo)	20.2	39.5	48.9
Coffee (cups/d)	2.6	3.9	4.6
1983–85 characteristics			
BMI (kg/m²)	175.1	179.2	175.8
Alcohol (drinks/mo)	22.6	44.2	57.7
Coffee (cups/d)	2.3	3.2	4.4
Change variables			
BMI (kg/m²)	2.8	8.6	3.8
Alcohol (drinks/mo)	2.4	4.7	8.8
Coffee (cups/d)	-0.3	-0.7	-0.2

Note: BMI = body mass index.

cessation of smoking (mean change 10.4 drinks/mo). This increase was significantly larger than that of co-twins who continued to smoke (mean change 3.7 drinks/mo). In 1967–70, the twin who smoked and subsequently quit consumed less alcohol than his brother who continued to smoke (38.0 versus 48.5 drinks/mo). At followup, however, the two brothers, although now discordant for smoking, did not differ in alcohol consumption (48.4 versus 52.2 drinks/mo). With respect to coffee consumption, there was no difference in consumption at baseline, when co-twins were concordant for smoking, and there was a significant difference at followup as they became discordant for smoking.

How can we interpret these results? The data clearly suggest a different pattern of cross-use of tobacco with alcohol than of tobacco with coffee. Pomerleau and colleagues (1993) argued that initial low sensitivity to nicotine eventually leads— via high exposure to nicotine—to

Table 3. Tobacco, Alcohol, and Coffee Consumption Within Monozygotic Twins Discordant for Smoking Cessation.

Variable	Quitter Twin (n = 190)	Continuing Smoker Twin (n = 190)
Age started smoking (yr)	18.9	18.0
No. cigarettes/d	24.0	25.6
Percent heavy smokers	25.0	40.0
1967–70 characteristics		
BMI (kg/m²)	173.0	172.8
Alcohol (drinks/mo)	38.0	48.5
Coffee (cups/d)	3.9	3.9
1983–85 characteristics		
BMI (kg/m²)	182.7	174.7
Alcohol (drinks/mo)	48.4	52.2
Coffee (cups/d)	2.9	3.6
Change variables		
BMI (kg/m²)	9.7	1.9
Alcohol (drinks/mo)	10.4	3.7
Coffee (cups/d)	-1.0	-0.3

Note: BMI = body mass index.

nicotine dependence and the development of extensive tolerance. Following this argument of genetic differences in sensitivity and the development of tolerance, one will note that the pattern of change in alcohol consumption in MZ twin quitters whose brothers were continuing smokers differs from that of quitters whose brothers were nonsmokers. A genetic theory of cross-drug tolerance would predict a significant increase in alcohol consumption in quitters whose genetically identical brothers continued to smoke (i.e., genetically susceptible users) but no increase in alcohol consumption in quitters whose brothers were nonsmokers (i.e., genetically nonsusceptible users), which is exactly the situation observed in the present study.

In contrast, changes in coffee consumption fit the expectations of a theory of behavioral cross-drug tolerance. Smoking-discordant quitters did not differ in coffee consumption at baseline when both co-twins were smokers, but they differed significantly at followup when the co-twins were discordant for smoking. The continuing smoker, as one would expect, consumed more coffee than his brother who quit smoking. These changes are also consistent with a behavioral reciprocal activation theory, whereby a decrease in coffee consumption is expected when the eliciting environmental conditions (i.e., nonsmoking) are less frequent.

To summarize, we have demonstrated in this simple analysis how longitudinal data coupled with the twinning condition can shed further light on the relationship of tobacco smoking to consumption of other substances. A more thorough examination of other relevant variables, including behavioral, physiological, and biochemical observations that can be subjected to the types of analyses presented in this review, may ultimately make possible the creation of a theory of drug dependence that is both rational and predictive.

LIMITATIONS AND RECOMMENDATIONS FOR FUTURE RESEARCH

The results from this study apply to male subjects only. The interaction between genetic and environmental influences that determine the consumption of tobacco or other substances may be different in females. Analyses similar to those described in this chapter with cohorts that include female and opposite-sex twins are critical for understanding the extent to which gender mediates the genetic and environmental determinants of substance use.

Another limitation of this study is that the subjects do not represent a random sample of the U.S. twin population in this age range. The present sample, screened for health at induction into the military and selected for

longitudinal study participation, limits inference to a "high-functioning" sample whose members are less likely to have been diagnosed for abuse of alcohol and alcoholism during their lifetime. However, we have identified in this sample a sizable subgroup of alcohol abusers and have conducted separate analyses to examine the relative contributions of genetic and environmental influences on joint heavy use of alcohol and tobacco.

Results from the present study are also limited by the validity and reliability of self-report data, an issue of particular concern in investigating continued use of tobacco and alcohol. The validity of the self-report data in the NAS-NRC registry is supported by the significant agreement between the responses to the two survey questionnaires and the same data obtained by a physician interview from a subset of twins in the National Heart, Lung, and Blood Institute Twin Study (Feinleib et al. 1977; Swan et al. 1990). We also have good evidence of the reliability of our measures based on the high stability in this sample for repeated measures of quantity and frequency of alcohol consumption (Carmelli et al. 1993).

We have demonstrated in this review how structural equation models, coupled with the twin design, can be used to formulate and test hypotheses of the relative contribution of genetic and environmental effects to the observed phenotypic correlation between tobacco smoking and alcohol consumption. The results, however, should not be viewed as precise estimates and should be used only in relative terms.

In recent years, human genetics and molecular biology have sparked a revolution in medical science on the basis of the improbable notion that one can locate the genes underlying "complex traits" without any prior knowledge as to how they function (Lander and Schork 1994). Molecular biologists have developed the technology, and genetic epidemiologists have improved on their statistical methods to use this new information for gene mapping. The time is therefore ripe for these two groups to work together rather than in isolation.

ACKNOWLEDGMENTS

This research was supported by National Institute on Alcohol Abuse and Alcoholism grant AA08925.

REFERENCES

Boomsma, D.J., and Molenaar, P.C.M. The genetic analysis of repeated measures. *Behav Genet* 17:111–123, 1987.

Cardon, L.R.; Swan, G.E.; and Carmelli, D. A model of genetic and environmental effects for the joint use of alcohol, smoking, and caffeine. *Behav Genet*, in press.

Carmelli, D.; Swan, G.E.; Robinette, D.; and Fabsitz, R.R. Heritability of substance use in the NAS-NRC Twin Registry. *Acta Genet Med Gemellol (Roma)* 39:91–98, 1990.

Carmelli, D.; Swan, G.E.; Robinette, D.; and Fabsitz, R.R. Genetic influence on smoking—a study of male twins. *N Engl J Med* 327:829–833, 1992.

Carmelli, D.; Heath, C.H.; and Robinette, D. Genetic analysis of drinking behavior in World War II veteran twins. *Genet Epidemiol* 10:201–213, 1993.

Carmelli, D.; Cardon, L.R.; and Fabsitz, R.R. Clustering of hypertension, diabetes, and obesity in adult male twins: Same genes or same environments? *Am J Hum Genet* 22:566–573, 1994a.

Carmelli, D.; Robinette, D.; and Fabsitz, R.R. Concordance, discordance, and prevalence of hypertension in World War II male veteran twins. *J Hypertens* 12:323–332, 1994b.

Carmody, T.P.; Brischetto, C.S.; Matarazzo, J.D.; O'Donnel, R.P.; and Conner, W.E. Co-occurrent use of cigarettes, alcohol, and coffee in healthy community living men and women. *Health Psychol* 4:323–335, 1985.

Cederlof, R., and Lorich, U. The Swedish twin registry. In: Nance, W.E., ed. *Twin Research, Part B: Biology and Epidemiology.* New York: Alan R. Liss, 1978. pp. 189–198.

Collins, A.C. Interactions of ethanol and nicotine at the receptor level. In: Galanter, M., ed. *Recent Developments in Alcoholism: Volume 8. Combined Alcohol and Other Drug Dependence.* New York: Plenum Press, 1990. pp. 221–231.

Collins, A.C., and Marks, M.J. Chronic nicotine exposure and brain nicotinic receptors—influence of genetic factors. *Prog Brain Res* 79:137–146, 1989.

Eaves, L.J. The utility of twins. In: Anderson, V.E.; Hauser, W.A.; Penry, J.K.; and Sing, C.F., eds. *Genetic Basis of the Epilepsies.* New York: Raven Press, 1982. pp. 249–276.

Eaves, L.J.; Last, K.; Young, P.A.; and Martin, N.G. Model fitting approaches to the analysis of human behavior. *Heredity* 41:249–320, 1978.

Eaves, L.J.; Eysenck, H.J.; and Martin, N.G. *Genes, Culture and Personality. An Empirical Approach.* London: Academic Press, 1989.

Falconer, D.S. The inheritance of liability to certain diseases estimated from the incidence among relatives. *Ann Hum Genet* 29:51–76, 1965.

Falconer, D.S. *Introduction to Quantitative Genetics.* 3d ed. London: Longman, 1989.

Feinleib, M.; Garrison, R.J.; Fabsitz, R.R.; Christian, J.C.; Hrubec, Z.; Borhani, N.O.; Kannel, W.B.; Rosenman, R.H.; Schwartz, J.T.; and Wagner, J.O. The NHLBI Twin Study: Methodology and summary of results. *Am J Epidemiol* 106:284–295, 1977.

Fulker, D.W. Extensions of the classical twin method. In: Bonne-Tamir, B., ed. *Human Genetics. Part A: The Unfolding Genome.* New York: Alan R. Liss, 1982. pp. 395–406.

Heath, A.C., and Madden, P.A.F. Genetic influences on smoking behavior. In: Turner, J.R.; Cardon, L.R.; and Hewitt, J.K., eds. *Behavior Genetic Approaches in Behavioral Medicine.* New York: Plenum Press, in press.

Heath, A.C., and Martin, N.G. Genetic models for the natural history of smoking: Evidence for a genetic influence on smoking persistence. *Addict Behav* 18:19–34, 1993.

Hrubec, Z., and Neel, J.V. The National Academy of Sciences-National Research Council Twin Registry: Ten years of operation. In: Nance, W.E., ed. *Twin Research, Part B: Biology and Epidemiology.* New York: Alan R. Liss, 1978. pp. 153–172.

Hunt, S.C.; Hasstedt, S.J.; Kuida, H.; Stults, B.M.; Hopkins, P.N.; and Williams, R.R. Genetic heritability and common pedigrees and twins. *Am J Epidemiol* 129:625–638, 1989.

Istvan, J., and Matarazzo, J.D. Tobacco, alcohol, and caffeine use: A review of their interrelationships. *Psychol Bull* 95:301–326, 1984.

Kaprio, J., and Koskenvuo, M. A prospective study of psychological and socioeconomic characteristics, health behavior and morbidity in cigarette smokers prior to quitting compared to persistent smokers and non-smokers. *J Clin Epidemiol* 41:139–150, 1988.

Lander, E.S., and Schork, N.J. Genetic dissection of complex traits. *Science* 265:2037–2048, 1994.

Neale, M.C. *Mx: Statistical Modeling.* Richmond, VA: Medical College of Virginia, Department of Human Genetics, 1991.

Neale, M.C., and Cardon, L.R. *Methodology for Genetic Studies of Twins and Families.* Boston: Kluwer, 1992.

Noble, E.P. The D_2 dopamine receptor gene: A review of association studies in alcoholism. *Behav Genet* 23:119–129, 1993.

Pomerleau, O.F.; Collins, A.C.; Shiffman, S.; and Pomerleau, C.S. Why some people smoke and others do not: New perspectives. *J Consult Clin Psychol* 61:723–731, 1993.

Rao, D.C. Statistical considerations in applications of path analysis in genetic epidemiology. In: Rao, C.R., and Chakraborty, R., eds. *Handbook of Statistics.* Vol. 8. Amsterdam: Elsevier Science Publishers, 1991. pp. 63–80.

Swan, G.E.; Carmelli, D.; Rosenman, R.H.; Fabsitz, R.R.; and Christian, J.C. Smoking and alcohol consumption in adult male twins: Genetic heritability and shared environmental influences. *J Subst Abuse* 2:39–50, 1990.

U.S. Department of Health and Human Services. *Reducing the Health Consequences of Smoking: Twenty-five Years of Progress. A Report of the Surgeon General.* DHHS Pub. No. (CDC)89–8411. Washington, DC: Supt. of Docs., U.S. Govt. Print. Off., 1989.

Chapter 6

Stress-Coping Model for Alcohol-Tobacco Interactions in Adolescence

Thomas Ashby Wills, Ph.D., and Sean D. Cleary, M.P.H.

It has been known for some time that alcohol and tobacco use tend to be intercorrelated, both in adolescent and adult populations (Istvan and Matarazzo 1984). The epidemiology of adolescent alcohol, tobacco, and other drug (ATOD) use shows that between the ages of 12 and 18, adolescents' rates of regular alcohol and tobacco use increase from low single-digit figures to substantial prevalence rates (Johnston et al. 1991). Because the typical progression for adolescent ATOD use is an increase in both frequency and intensity of use (Kandel 1975; Donovan and Jessor 1983), researchers typically find tobacco, alcohol, and marijuana use intercorrelated in adolescent sam-

ples (Jessor and Jessor 1977; Hays et al. 1984; Wills 1986). Although some research has been conducted relevant to this subject (e.g., Donovan and Jessor 1985; Hays et al. 1987), researchers have paid less attention to the theoretical basis of such a relationship. Although the basis of a relationship for early ATOD use is not necessarily the same as the processes that operate later, a better understanding of the tobacco-alcohol relationship in adolescence may help to clarify and advance theory in this area.

This chapter presents the tenets of a stress-coping model, which provides a behavioral perspective for the basis of alcohol-tobacco interactions. The model proceeds from the postulate

T.A. Wills, Ph.D., is an associate professor of psychology, epidemiology, and social medicine, Ferkauf Graduate School of Psychology, Albert Einstein College of Medicine, 1300 Morris Park Avenue, Bronx, NY 10461. S.D. Cleary, M.P.H., is an instructor in epidemiology, Department of Epidemiology and Social Medicine, Albert Einstein College of Medicine, 1300 Morris Park Avenue, Bronx, NY 10461.

that drugs such as tobacco or alcohol have coping functions that assist a person in regulating emotion or experience. Although nicotine and alcohol have somewhat different physiological effects, studies on the perceived coping functions of smoking and drinking show notable similarities. Acknowledging that ATOD use in early adolescence may be influenced by several different types of factors, including parental ATOD use and peer networks, the stress-coping model focuses on the role of life stress and coping variables as factors that make a subgroup of adolescents vulnerable to multiple ATOD use (Wills and Shiffman 1985; Wills and Filer in press).

COPING FUNCTIONS OF TOBACCO AND ALCOHOL USE IN ADULTS

Before reviewing data on adolescents, it should first be established that coping motives are relevant for tobacco and alcohol use in adults. This chapter does not review the whole body of literature on this topic but instead presents some typical studies. Table 1 summarizes studies on perceived functions for cigarette smoking in adults. In these studies, the researchers administered a number of items about reasons for smoking to a large sample of adult smokers, factor-analyzed the items, and then correlated the motive scores with level of use. Typically, the researchers grouped the empirical factors under two broad domains: *negative affect functions* and *positive affect functions*.

In table 1, negative affect functions indicate that smoking helps a person cope with anxiety, frustration, and anger (e.g., "When I'm feeling upset, few things help more than cigarettes"). Positive affect functions indicate that cigarettes help provide pleasurable and relaxing sensations (e.g., "Smoking cigarettes is pleasant and relaxing"). Within the studies, scores on negative affect reduction tend to correlate with measures of addictive smoking and with indices of high-frequency use. Measures of social smoking, which are not strongly correlated with the other dimensions, are related to low levels of use. Study findings also indicate that smoking helps one to cope with boredom or inactivity, thereby representing a function for coping with a different type of unpleasant condition (i.e., inactivity rather than overload).

This chapter does not consider all the evidence on how cigarette smoking provides these functions; this has been reviewed in detail in various publications, such as the 1988 Surgeon General's Report (U.S. Department of Health and Human Services 1988). It should be noted that the evidence on how smoking provides these functions is respectable although by no means complete.

Table 2 summarizes some typical studies on the coping functions of alcohol. In these studies, the researchers used methods that were more diverse and included both clinical samples and college drinkers;

however, the dimensional structure of the studies is similar to the structure used in the studies on smoking motives. In this table, negative affect functions indicate that drinking helps a person reduce tension, relieve depression, forget worries, and cope with anger. The positive affect functions tend to be more socially based, reflecting the typical use of alcohol during social occasions. The category "other" is more difficult to interpret in these studies: It indicates that alcohol may increase self-confidence or relieve boredom, again suggesting coping functions, not just social use.

In two other studies, the researchers used a composite score for coping-related alcohol use. Cooper and colleagues (1988) used a composite

Table 1. Studies of Perceived Functions for Smoking in Adults.

Reference	N	Item Type	Functions
Ikard et al. 1969	2,094	Likert	NA: Negative affect reduction, addictive smoking PA: Pleasurable relaxation OTHER: Stimulation, habit
McKennell 1970	1,140[1]	Situation	NA: Nervous irritation, smoking alone, food substitution PA: Relaxation, social confidence OTHER: Activity accompaniment, social smoking
Coan 1973	595	Motive	NA: Negative affect reduction, distraction, addiction, agitated state PA: Pleasurable relaxation, sensorimotor pleasure, mental state OTHER: Stimulation, concentration, habit
Leventhal and Avis 1976	186	Motive	NA: Anxiety reduction, addiction PA: Pleasure, taste OTHER: Stimulation, habit, social reward, "fiddling"
Best and Hakstian 1978	331	Situation	NA: Nervous tension, frustration, discomfort, anger/impatience, restlessness PA: Relaxation OTHER: Automatic, sensory stimulation, concentration, social smoking, inactivity/boredom

Note: NA = Negative affect functions; PA = Positive affect functions; OTHER = functions not clearly classifiable as either negative-affect reduction or positive-affect enhancement.
[1]The McKennell (1970) study included some older adolescents.

Table 2. Studies of Perceived Functions of Alcohol Use in Adults.

Reference	N	Item Type	Functions
Cahalan et al. 1969	2,746	Motive	NA: Relieve tension/nervousness, help forget worries, cheer up from bad mood PA: Relaxation OTHER: Social drinking, special occasions, taste enhancement, improves appetite
Deardorff et al. 1975	385 (C + GP)	Situation	NA: Tension reduction, physical discomfort OTHER: Social liveliness, sense of power
Wanberg and Horn 1983	5,000 (C)	Mixed	NA: Manage mood (i.e., feel less depressed, relieve tension, forget worries) OTHER: Improve mental functioning (i.e., think better, have better thoughts), improve sociability (i.e., make friends, relate better, feel less inferior)
Segal et al. 1980	854	Situation	NA: Feeling lonely, sad, under pressure; having problems; feeling mad PA: Feel happier, get-togethers more fun OTHER: More self-confidence, feel less shy, get along better with others, nothing else to do
Brown et al. 1980	440[1]	Expectancy	NA: Tension reduction (i.e., decrease muscular tension, worry less) PA: Enhancement (i.e., future seems brighter, feel less restricted) OTHER: Social drinking (i.e., special occasions), sexual responsiveness, increased power, increased self-confidence
McCarty and Kaye 1984	465	Motive	NA: Negative affect reduction (i.e., reduce tension, forget worries, cheer up when sad) PA: Enjoyment, positive affect OTHER: Social drinking, increase sensations (i.e., get high, nothing better to do), taste

Note: NA = Negative affect functions; PA = Positive affect functions; OTHER = functions not clearly classifiable as either negative affect reduction or positive affect enhancement. Subjects are from general population samples unless noted otherwise; C = clinical sample; GP = general population sample.
[1]This study was conducted with adolescents.

measure of drinking-to-cope (e.g., to forget worries, cheer one's self up when in a bad mood, help when feeling depressed or nervous, feel more self-confident, and relieve boredom) and found this to be a strong predictor of alcohol abuse. McKirnan and Peterson (1988) used a combined measure of tension reduction/mood enhancement and found the relationship between stress and alcohol and other drug (AOD) use to be particularly strong for persons who scored high on coping expectancies. The suggested mechanisms for how alcohol provides coping functions have been considered in detail elsewhere (see, for example, Hull and Bond 1986; Cappell and Greeley 1987; Steele and Josephs 1990). Again, one could say that the evidence is generally supportive of the reported functions, although the literature does include some null results.

SIMILARITY OF COPING FUNCTIONS FOR ALCOHOL AND TOBACCO USE

Overall, the similarity between the coping functions reported for alcohol and tobacco use is striking. In both cases consistent evidence indicates that these drugs are perceived as helping people cope with anxiety, frustration, or depression, as well as providing self-related coping functions such as increased self-confidence. As in Diener's (1984) model of subjective well-being (which posits independent domains of negative affective experience and positive affective experience),

the functional reports suggest that ATOD use is perceived as having the ability both to reduce negative affect and to enhance positive affect, representing a kind of "double whammy" for coping with various conditions. Consequently, the reported coping functions of alcohol and tobacco use map well onto what is known about the structure of affective experience. This evidence, generated by a stress-coping model of ATOD use, suggests one explanation for the co-occurrence of alcohol and tobacco use: They both provide functions that are useful for helping persons to cope, at least in the short term.

The reported functions for smoking tend to emphasize increased attention and concentration (see Wesnes and Warburton 1983; Revell et al. 1985), whereas the functions for alcohol emphasize distraction and forgetting (see Steele and Josephs 1990). However, this is not damaging for a coping model, but rather it suggests that tobacco and alcohol may have complementary coping functions, such that tobacco use increases when one wants to concentrate on something and alcohol consumption increases when one wishes to forget about something. Thus, selective use can help to achieve different coping goals. In addition, researchers have suggested that biphasic or dose-dependent effects are involved in coping functions, such that drugs may be used in some instances to decrease arousal (e.g., when one is tense or overloaded) and at other times to increase arousal (e.g., when one is inactive or bored). Researchers do not know how these various coping functions relate to characteristics of different ecological settings or to situational variations in people's daily lives, but the evidence suggests that such differences do exist.

One point that tends to be underemphasized in research is the role of alcohol and tobacco in coping with frustration and anger. The tendency to become easily and intensely upset is one of the strongest predictors of ATOD use in early adolescence (e.g., Kellam et al. 1982; Wills 1986), but the relation of anger to alcohol and tobacco use has received little theoretical attention. Khantzian (1990) discusses this topic in an intriguing paper on adult ATOD abusers, considering, from a clinical standpoint, how patients use ATOD's to help cope with anger.

STRESS-COPING MODEL FOR ADOLESCENTS

How is the stress-coping model applied for adolescents? In brief, the stress component of this model proposes that adolescents may be under stress because their parents are experiencing difficulties, such as financial strain or illness, or because the adolescents themselves are experiencing difficulties meeting developmental demands in domains such as academic performance, acceptance in peer social systems, or relationships with adults. An adolescent's subjective perception of stress derives from an accumulation of demands from these various domains and is based on feelings that things are not controllable and that one is unable to meet or resolve all the demands. Researchers postulate that a person's response to a high level of unresolved demands manifests as feelings of emotional distress, lack of control, and anger. Believing that one is unable to cope with situations and feelings leads to a search for alternative ways to self-regulate emotion and experience.

Table 3 includes a summary of the empirical evidence for the stress component of the model. Several studies conducted in various parts of the United States and Canada and across the age range of 12–16 years have found a relationship between stress and adolescent ATOD use. The typical stress measure used was a checklist of the major negative life events that occurred during the previous year, but these studies also included measures of weekly "hassles" or subjective stress. Several studies were prospective, indicating that stress is a predictor, not a consequence, of ATOD use. Wills and colleagues (in press b) showed in a grouping analysis that life stress was a predictor of escalated ATOD use among adolescents between 7th and 9th grades. Thus, much evidence indicates that life stress is a predisposing factor for alcohol and tobacco use in adolescence. Similar findings occur in studies of adult ATOD use and relapse (see Wills 1990; Wills and Hirky in press).

The coping component of the stress-coping model for early adoles-

Table 3. Studies of Stress and Drug Use in Adolescents.

Reference	Site	Age (years)	Stress Measure	DV
Castro et al. 1987	Los Angeles, CA	15–17	Negative life events	Tobacco
Chassin et al. 1988	Columbia, MO	13	Negative life events	Alcohol
Labouvie 1986	New Jersey (regional sample)	12–16	Subjective	Alcohol, marijuana
Mitic et al. 1985	Halifax, NS	12–18	Subjective	Tobacco
Newcomb and Harlow 1986	Los Angeles, CA; New Jersey (regional sample)	12–16 (P)	Negative life events	Alcohol, marijuana, other illicit drugs
Wills 1986	Manhattan, NY	12–13 (P)	Negative life events, hassles, subjective	Tobacco, alcohol
Wills et al. 1992	Bronx, NY	12–13	Negative life events, negative affect[1]	Tobacco, alcohol, marijuana
Wills et al. in press *b*	NYC area	12–14 (P)	Negative life events	Escalation in combined use

Note: DV = dependent variable; P indicates prospective analysis; otherwise, design is cross-sectional.
[1]This study also found a negative affect x positive affect interaction.

cence posits that patterns of coping with problems relate to the probability of early ATOD use. An active, problem-solving approach is likely to reduce one's feelings of distress and increase self-confidence; therefore, active coping may be inversely related to early ATOD use. Conversely, three types of coping methods are likely to make things worse: (1) anger (i.e., getting mad at people), (2) avoidance (i.e., doing things to avoid the problem), and (3) helplessness (i.e., giving up on trying to cope). These types of coping methods may be related to a greater likelihood of ATOD use in early adolescence.

Some relevant studies of coping and adolescent ATOD use are summarized in table 4. In these studies active types of coping are inversely related to early ATOD use, whereas anger and helplessness are positively related to ATOD use and show reverse interactions (i.e., worsen the impact of life stress on ATOD use). Thus, evidence indicates that the way adolescents cope with problems affects the likelihood of their becoming involved in early ATOD use.

COROLLARIES AND DERIVATIONS

There are three corollaries from the basic postulates of the stress-coping model. First is the prediction that the perception of coping functions in adolescence increases as a person gets older. If a person smokes only once a month, as is typical in early adolescence, it is difficult for that person to be very aware of nicotine's effects. However, as one's frequency of smoking increases over time, one's awareness of tobacco's effects should become more salient. This also would hold true regarding alcohol. This corollary provides a theoretical account for the observed increase in frequency of use during adolescence, because using a drug more frequently makes people more cognizant of its coping functions.

The second corollary suggests that to the extent that active coping abilities are well developed, the coping functions of ATOD use should be less compelling, because alternatives are available. Conversely, a deficiency in active types of coping should increase the attractiveness of the perceived coping functions of ATOD use. This suggests a dynamic system along the lines of Boyle's Law and generates the prediction of a constructive cycle and

Table 4. Studies of Coping and Drug Use in Adolescents.

Reference	Age (years)	Measure	Findings on Coping
Wills 1986	12–13 (P)	Factorial	Behavioral ==> less drug use Anger ==> more drug use
Kaplan et al. 1986	12–20 (L)	Scale	Avoidance ==> escalated marijuana use
Hirschman et al. 1984	8–16	Item	Helplessness ==> transition to 2d and 3d cigarettes
Stacy, Newcomb, and Bentler 1991	16–24 (P)	Composite (cognitive motivations)	Composite score ==> increase in drug use
Labouvie et al. 1990	14–16	Factorial	Anger ==> high-intensity drug use
Sussman et al. 1993	12	Factorial	Anger, partying ==> more drug use Coping effort ==> stress-buffer
Wills in press	12–14 (P)	Intention	Behavioral ==> less drug use (+ buffer) Anger, helplessness, hanging out ==> less drug use; general avoidance ns[1] Reverse interactions: anger, hangout Buffer interaction: Σ(active) x Σ(avoidant)

Note: P = prospective analysis; L = longitudinal analysis.
[1]Nonsignificant.

a "vicious cycle," respectively (see Wills in press).

The constructive cycle starts with a moderate level of active coping, which contributes both to further development of active coping (as a person receives feedback on the effectiveness of his or her coping efforts) and to a decline in the perceived coping functions of any drugs ever used. The vicious cycle starts with early perception of ATOD use as a coping mechanism, which reduces the development of active types of coping, thereby enhancing the perceived coping function of ATOD's, thus producing even further decrements in active coping, and so on. In this way, the stress-coping model provides a theoretical account for the progressive increase in the extent of ATOD use observed among adolescents.

The third corollary suggests that coping processes may be involved in mediating the impact of sociocultural factors on tobacco or alcohol use. For example, adolescent epidemiology has shown consistently that African-American teenagers have relatively low rates of tobacco and alcohol use compared with Caucasian teenagers (see Bachman et al. 1991), but this differential has not been totally explained. It is possible that differences in the perceived coping functions of ATOD use can help to account for this differential.

For another example, during recent years a female differential has been shown for adolescent cigarette smoking, which has been the subject of considerable discussion (see Ensminger et al. 1982; Gritz 1986; Biener 1987). The possibility that males and females have differential weights for coping functions of tobacco is a possible theoretical mechanism to account for ways in which the effect of gender on ATOD use is mediated, but there is relatively little evidence on this aspect of sociocultural influences. Analogously, although females' rates of alcohol and marijuana use are low relative to those for males, several studies have suggested that emotion-management functions may be a factor in women's risk for ATOD abuse (Wilsnack et al. 1991; Kaplan and Johnson 1992). As a case in point, Wilsnack and colleagues (1991) summarized their results by suggesting that "onset of problem drinking may be facilitated by a woman's long-term tendency to use various psychoactive drugs to feel better, to have a good time, or to cope with problems" (p. 316).

Thus, the stress-coping model suggests a basis for how the impact of sociocultural factors is mediated.

SUMMARY

To summarize, the stress-coping model provides a theoretical account for the co-occurrence of alcohol and tobacco use in adolescence. The model suggests that a high level of stress during early adolescence primes one for ATOD experimentation, and deficits in active coping ability contribute to an increase in the frequency of ATOD use. As the level of ATOD use increases, the coping functions of tobacco and alcohol (as noted in adult studies) become more salient. If subjective distress continues during adolescence, there is a likelihood that ATOD use will continue to escalate to high-intensity use. Hence, the stress-coping model suggests both a mechanism for the increase in ATOD use during adolescence and the co-occurrence of tobacco and alcohol use.

The stress-coping model is not the only theory that bears on this phenomenon; problem behavior theory (Jessor and Jessor 1977) also has postulates addressing the co-occurrence of alcohol use, marijuana use, and other types of problem behavior among adolescents. In fact, the ability of problem behavior theory to account for the covariation of problem behaviors is one of its strengths (see Jessor et al. 1980; Donovan and Jessor 1985). However, we shall discuss subsequently why problem behavior theory does not provide the whole story.

In emphasizing individual differences in perceived coping functions among adolescents, the stress-coping model does not try to minimize the significance of parental ATOD use as an influencing factor (Sher et al. 1991; Merikangas et al. 1992; Chassin et al. 1993; Fitzgerald et al. 1993; Wills et al. 1994a). However, research findings also indicate that 75 percent of adult alcoholics have no family history of alcohol abuse (Russell 1990). This implies that processes occur in the general population that influence how adolescents perceive tobacco and alcohol use. Therefore, it is important for researchers to study representative samples of adolescents as well as high-risk samples, because each provides insights into how risk or protection processes occur.

FINDINGS ON ADOLESCENT ALCOHOL AND TOBACCO USE

Recent data from a research program on adolescent ATOD use have a bearing on several questions about alcohol-tobacco interactions. We collected the data through school-based research in which self-report questionnaires were administered in classrooms to students between the 7th and 10th grades. The sample totaled approximately 1,700 cases. The samples were multiethnic, and the demographics for the families were representative of the New York State population.

The items on ATOD use indexed the typical frequency of use for cigarettes, alcohol, or marijuana on a 1–6 scale, with scale points ranging from "Never Used" to "Use Every Day." Regarding alcohol use, an additional item on heavy drinking, with a 1–3 scale, specifically asked whether there was a time in the past month when the respondent consumed three or more drinks on one occasion. This item had scale points ranging from "None" to "Twice or More" ("Three Times or More" for older subjects, on a 1–4 scale). These same items were used across all surveys of adolescents. Older subjects also were asked about cocaine use.

INTERCORRELATION OF ALCOHOL AND TOBACCO USE

A first question is the degree of intercorrelation of alcohol and tobacco use. The cohort from which the data were obtained was surveyed yearly, between 7th grade and 10th grade. The Pearson correlations among the ATOD use indices are reported in table 5. This table includes, for each drug, the mean for the continuous score and the percentage of students who had engaged in ATOD use at least monthly. These data show the typical increase in ATOD use during adolescence; for example, the percentage of smokers increased from 5 to 22 percent, and the prevalence of heavy drinking (twice a month or more) increased from approximately 3 percent in 7th grade to about 15 percent in 10th grade. Rates of marijuana use were generally low, but they increased to nontrivial levels by the 9th and 10th grades.

Regarding intercorrelations for the three primary drugs (i.e., alcohol, tobacco, and marijuana), the mean correlations were 0.28, 0.37, 0.50, and 0.54 across the four grades. Thus, the degree of intercorrelation increased, partly for statistical reasons (i.e., one cannot have high correlations when variance is low), but also because the students were using more drugs. It should be noted that the intercorrelation of tobacco and alcohol use was already present at around age 12, reflecting the typical pattern that teens who begin to smoke cigarettes also begin to use alcohol. The correlation between tobacco and alcohol use was $r = 0.35$ in 7th grade and increased to $r = 0.54$ in 10th grade; therefore, the degree of relationship between alcohol and tobacco use was substantial in absolute terms in this adolescent population. Thus, there was substantial co-occurrence of tobacco and alcohol use in this sample. The use of illicit drugs (e.g., marijuana and cocaine) also was related to the use of tobacco and alcohol; although the correlations for cocaine were lower (the rates of use were fairly skewed), the correlations for marijuana were substantial.

PREDICTIVE TEST OF MOTIVES FOR TOBACCO AND ALCOHOL USE

In one study, we administered an inventory of motives for cigarette smoking and alcohol use to a sample of 1,698 students in 10th grade. The items were based on the studies of adult motives previously cited and included items to tap a range of different motives. Identical items were used in nine-item measures of motives for smoking and alcohol use. They were administered with a 5-point Likert scale ("Not at All True" to "Very True") in which the subjects indicated the extent to which each item was a reason for their smoking or alcohol use. The subjects were instructed to answer only if they had used the drug (i.e., these were motive reports and not expectancies). A factor analysis identified one clear factor for coping motives and one

Table 5. Intercorrelations of Tobacco, Alcohol, and Other Drug Use Among Adolescents in 7th–10th Grades.

Correlations for 7th Grade (below diagonal) and 8th Grade (above diagonal)

	Cig	Alc	Hvy	Marj	Range	M(8th)	% ≥ Monthly
Cig smoking	—	0.41	0.32	0.34	1–6	1.86	10%
Alcohol use	0.35	—	0.51	0.30	1–6	1.90	7%
Heavy drinking	0.36	0.37	—	0.31	1–3	1.22	5%
Marijuana use	0.17	0.23	0.17	—	1–6	1.09	1%
Range	1–6	1–6	1–3	1–6			
M(7th)	1.54	1.62	1.16	1.04			
% ≥ monthly	5%	3%	3%	< 1%			

Correlations for 9th Grade (below diagonal) and 10th Grade (above diagonal)

	Cig	Alc	Hvy	Marj	Coc	Range	M(10th)	% ≥ Monthly
Cig smoking	—	0.54	0.43	0.56	0.15	1–6	2.47	22%
Alcohol use	0.54	—	0.66	0.55	0.27	1–6	2.40	20%
Heavy drinking	0.42	0.59	—	0.50	0.26	1–4	1.53	15%
Marijuana use	0.48	0.50	0.48	—	0.37	1–6	1.64	10%
Cocaine use	0.16	0.29	0.30	0.44	—	1–6	1.07	1%
Range	1–6	1–6	1–4	1–6	1–6			
M(9th)	2.23	2.14	1.37	1.37	1.05			
% ≥ monthly	19%	13%	10%	6%	< 1%			

Note: Cig = cigarette smoking; Alc = alcohol use; Hvy = heavy drinking; Marj = marijuana use; Coc = cocaine use. *N* for analyses = 1,690–1,890 cases.
M(x) = mean substance use score for 7th, 8th, 9th, and 10th grades, respectively..

factor for social pressure. The items concerning boredom relief and self-confidence enhancement loaded about equally on both of the extracted factors. The fact that boredom and self-confidence items load about equally on the coping factor and the social pressure factor has, we think, a substantive meaning: that worry about either social acceptance or lack of activity is a problem that must be coped with in some way. To retain information about these different aspects of motives for ATOD use, the inventory was scored for a four-item factor for coping motives and a two-item factor for social pressure, and the other three items were analyzed singly.

What motive dimensions are most related to ATOD use in adolescence? To test this question, we entered the five motive variables simultaneously in multiple regression, with the appropriate ATOD use index as criterion. For smoking motive reports, the cigarette smoking index (1–6 scale) was used as the criterion variable; for drinking motive reports, the heavy drinking index (1–4 scale) was used as the criterion variable. Similar results were found using the index of overall alcohol use.

The scores for coping motives for smoking and drinking were strongly related to level of use, with beta's of 0.56 and 0.45, respectively. Boredom also had a significant, unique contribution, with beta's of 0.08 and 0.12, respectively. Although these latter figures are not huge, they represent an independent contribution for an item that was substantially correlated with the coping motive dimension. The motive of curiosity was inversely related to level of use. The factor score for social pressure was nonsignificant in the simultaneous analysis. This was an interesting finding, because peer pressure is commonly suggested as a major cause of adolescent ATOD use, although the evidence for overt pressure is fairly weak. In this case, the effect for social pressure was nonsignificant when compared with the effects for other motives. When these analyses were replicated with demographic controls (i.e., gender, ethnicity, family structure, and socioeconomic status), the results were not substantially altered. Thus, these findings indicate that coping motives contribute strongly to level of ATOD use in middle adolescence: The subjects who perceived that coping motives were important showed a high level of ATOD use. Of course these data are cross-sectional, and the direction of effect cannot be conclusively demonstrated. It is possible that persons who engage in heavy ATOD use become more aware of coping functions. Most likely some reciprocity occurs in the relationship, as was previously hypothesized.

DIFFERENCES IN COPING MOTIVES BY GENDER AND ETHNICITY

Do coping motives differ by gender or ethnicity? To test this question, we performed 2 (gender: female versus male) x 3 (ethnicity: African-American versus Hispanic versus Caucasian) analyses of variance. For smoking, significant effects for gender indicated that females were marginally higher on coping motives ($p = 0.08$) and curiosity ($p = 0.04$), whereas males scored higher on motives for social pressure ($p = 0.05$), boredom relief ($p = 0.01$), and self-confidence enhancement ($p = 0.03$). Significant effects for ethnicity indicated that Caucasians scored significantly higher on coping motives and African-Americans scored significantly lower ($p < 0.0001$), with the same pattern observed for boredom relief ($p < 0.01$). These effects are consistent with previously observed demographic differences in cigarette smoking. The results of analyses for gender and smoking motives are presented graphically in figure 1.

For alcohol, there was no significant gender difference in coping motives. Males scored significantly higher than females on social pressure ($p < 0.001$), boredom relief ($p < 0.001$), and self-confidence enhancement ($p < 0.01$). Significant effects for ethnicity indicated that Caucasians scored significantly higher on coping motives ($p < 0.0001$) and boredom motives ($p < 0.01$), whereas African-Americans scored significantly lower on these dimensions.

These results are generally consistent with previous epidemiologic data. The females scored somewhat higher on coping motives for cigarette smoking, where there was a female differential; however, the effect was not a large one, and other variables may have been operative for producing the differential. The females equaled the males on coping motives for alcohol use, where rates in recent years tend to be comparable for males and females. With regard to ethnicity, African-Americans scored lower on coping, self-confidence, and boredom motives for both tobacco and alcohol, consistent with the lower rates of ATOD use previously observed for African-American adolescents. We observed a lower prevalence rate of ATOD use among African-American adolescents in these data sets and verified this finding for cigarette smoking with carbon monoxide measurements (Wills and Cleary unpublished data 1995).

COPING MOTIVES AND TYPES OF USERS

It is possible that there are different types of ATOD users (e.g., primarily smokers versus primarily drinkers) within the adolescent ATOD user population. If so, the previous data on co-occurrence of alcohol and tobacco use, and the overall correlations of motives with level of use, could be missing relationships that occur in specific subgroups of users. To address this issue, we applied disjoint clustering analysis to the four ATOD use items (i.e., smoking, alcohol, marijuana, and heavy drinking) from the 10th-grade data. The analysis indicated that there were discriminable subgroups within the population of ATOD users, and the analysis was scored for five clusters. The largest group was termed "nonusers"; this

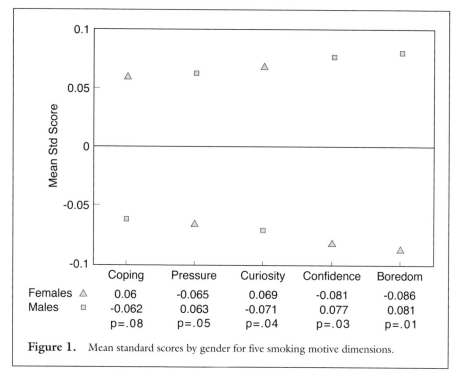

Figure 1. Mean standard scores by gender for five smoking motive dimensions.

group of adolescents had, at most, tried cigarettes or alcohol once during their lives. The four other clusters were termed "experimenters," "marijuana users," "smokers," and "heavy users." The "experimenters" had some acquaintance with alcohol (typically they had tried alcohol more than four times), but their means for other types of ATOD use were low. The "marijuana users" had elevated rates of exposure to marijuana, with means closer to monthly use, but they had low rates for smoking and alcohol use relative to other types of users. The "smokers" had relatively high rates for cigarette smoking, representing daily smoking, but they had low rates for alcohol and marijuana use. Finally, the

"heavy users" had high rates for tobacco, alcohol, and marijuana use. It is evident that the co-occurrence of alcohol and tobacco use mostly occurred among the heavy user subgroup, although the three other user subgroups also contributed to the overall correlation. The subgroup of heavy users represented 9.5 percent of the overall sample; thus, while this group was a relatively small part of the adolescent population, its size was by no means trivial.

Is pattern of ATOD use related to motives for use? To address this question, we tested for variation in motives across the four user subgroups. (The nonusers did not have motive scores.) For both tobacco and alcohol, the heavy users subgroup scored particularly high on coping motives as well as on boredom relief and self-confidence enhancement, thereby supporting the hypothesis that perception of ATOD use as a coping mechanism contributes to high-intensity use. However, the smokers subgroup was particularly elevated on coping motives for cigarette smoking and was lowest on coping motives for alcohol use. This supports a differential effect of coping motives, such that for persons who are primarily cigarette smokers, coping motives for tobacco are more salient. Also noteworthy was the patterning for the marijuana users subgroup. This subgroup scored relatively low on coping motives and self-confidence enhancement but scored relatively high on the motive for relieving boredom. This suggests that marijuana use among this group was more a reaction to lack of environmental stimulation. However, it should be noted that when marijuana smoking occurs together with high levels of tobacco and alcohol use, it is related to personal coping motives.

DISCUSSION

This chapter outlines the propositions of a stress-coping model of ATOD use and argues that coping functions of tobacco and alcohol provide a theoretical explanation for their co-occurrence. The examples provided show that this is true both in adult populations and in samples of adolescents. The data reported here demonstrate that coping motives of tobacco and alcohol use are salient for adolescents and that coping motives are a strong predictor of level of use. The data on motives for ATOD use show some gender and ethnicity differences, and the patterning of these effects is consistent with previously observed demographic differences in adolescent ATOD use. Findings also indicate that there are different subgroups of adolescent ATOD users and that there is some evidence for differential motive effects. The group of heavy ATOD users scored highest on all motive indices, but the coping functions associated with tobacco were more salient for a subgroup who were primarily cigarette smokers.

The theoretical arguments and empirical data presented in this chapter support a stress-coping model for the co-occurrence of alcohol and tobacco use in adolescence. However, there is an alternative model: the problem behavior theory of Jessor and Jessor (1977). From this perspective, alcohol, marijuana use, and other problem behaviors are all manifestations of deviance-prone attitudes. Furthermore, in this alternative, sociocognitive model, the underlying factor is a rejection of conventional values, and adolescents who are not bonded to conventional institutions, such as school and family, will exhibit various forms of behavior that are construed as deviant by conventional socializing agents (e.g., parents and teachers). The intercorrelation of adolescent problem behaviors was, in fact, a starting point for problem behavior theory, and the theory has had notable success in showing that various problem behaviors are intercorrelated, have similar predictors, and fit a common-factor model (e.g., Jessor et al. 1980; Donovan and Jessor 1985).

It is not the intention here to review criticisms of problem behavior theory, for its strengths are notable ones. Our view is that this theory is tenable but that it does not cover the range of variables that are involved in adolescent problem behavior. First, it does not address affective or stress-related factors in adolescent ATOD use, nor does it consider how alienation from conventional institutions can be generated by patterns of maladaptive coping. In addition, researchers have conducted several studies to provide differential tests of constructs from problem behavior theory (e.g., tolerance for deviance, independence-achievement value discrepancy) compared with variables from stress-coping theory. The results show that constructs from problem behavior theory are related to adolescent ATOD use, but this occurs together with independent contributions from stress-coping variables (Wills et al. in press *b*). In addition, clustering analyses show that problem youth exhibit elevations on constructs from both theories (Wills et al. 1994*b*). Thus, constructs from problem behavior theory may be useful for predicting adolescent tobacco and alcohol use, but the evidence suggests that coping functions also contribute to producing high-intensity ATOD use.

A second theoretical issue concerns the convergence of stress-coping theory with behavior genetic research. A classical problem in social epidemiology has been the question of how abstract demographic factors are related to actual physical health (see Wills et al. 1995*b*), or as Mary Haan phrased the question with regard to socioeconomic status, "How does it [socioeconomic status] get *inside* the body?" In recent years there has been much activity in behavior genetic research on ATOD abuse, and it seems clear that this research shows that risk for ATOD abuse is influenced to some extent by heritable factors (see Merikangas et al. 1992; McGue 1993; Tarter et al. 1985). However, a comparable theoretical question can be asked about the findings on risk from behavior genetic research: "How does it [genetic risk] get *outside* the body?"

The stress-coping model suggests that some persons may be at increased risk for ATOD use because they are more reactive to stress, have greater susceptibility to mood-regulating effects of drugs, or have different approaches to coping with problems, which are based to some extent on temperamental factors (Wills et al. 1995*a*). While behavior genetic research has made major advances in predicting risk for ATOD use, the theoretical questions about how these effects are mediated at the behavioral level largely remain to be addressed. In this context, the stress-coping model appears to have implications for understanding how contributions to risk actually occur in the daily lives of adolescents.

RECOMMENDATIONS FOR RESEARCH

Recommendations for further research are as follows:

- Research should be conducted to obtain detailed assessment of the perceived functions of ATOD use in adolescent samples. This could include descriptive research to explore the way ATOD use is perceived by adolescents and psychometric research to provide reliable measures of perceived functions.
- Research should be conducted to examine the convergence of constructs from stress-coping theory with research generated by models of alcohol expectancies (e.g., Christiansen et al. 1989). The question may be posed: To what extent are these bodies of research examining similar or different constructs?
- Research should be conducted to investigate the ecological contexts in which tobacco and alcohol are used. It can be hypothesized that the co-occurring use of alcohol and tobacco occurs because of situational factors, but little evidence exists that would help to resolve this issue.
- The relation of perceived coping functions of ATOD use to temperament factors, such as activity level, emotionality, or sociability, needs to be investigated. Previous research suggests patterns of onset and progression may be shaped by

factors that operate prior to adolescence; however, studies conducted after time of onset have provided little evidence in this regard.
- Research should be conducted on the relation of ATOD use to the daily lives of adolescents, with particular attention to the social contexts of use. It is not known whether the co-occurrence of alcohol and tobacco is temporally related to periods of distress or whether ATOD use is substantially influenced by particular membership or reference groups. The role of coping motives in relation to ATOD use and high-risk behavior is a topic of particular importance (see McKirnan and Peterson 1988, 1989; Kelly et al. 1991; Folkman et al. 1992; Leigh and Stall 1993).
- Research should be conducted to investigate factors that characterize adolescents who are at high risk but do not use drugs intensively or at all. A focus on risk factors should not deflect attention from investigating the operation of protective or resiliency factors (Wills et al. in press *a*).

ACKNOWLEDGMENTS

This research was supported by grants 1–R01–DA05950 and 1–R01–DA08880 from the National Institute on Drug Abuse. A version of this chapter was presented at the Third Annual Meeting of the Society for Prevention Research, West Palm Beach, Florida, in June 1994. The authors would like to thank the participating schools for their cooperation and Marnie Filer, John Mariani, Grace McNamara, Donato Vaccaro, and Caroline Zeoli for their assistance with the research.

REFERENCES

Bachman, J.G.; Wallace, J.M.; O'Malley, P.M.; Johnston, L.D.; Kurth, C.L.; and Neighbors, H.W. Racial/ethnic differences in smoking, drinking, and illicit drug use among American high school seniors, 1976-89. *Am J Public Health* 81: 372–377, 1991.

Best, J.A., and Hakstian, A.R. A situation-specific model for smoking behavior. *Addict Behav* 3:79–92, 1978.

Biener, L. Gender differences in the use of substances for coping. In: Barnett, R.C., Biener, L., and Baruch G.K., eds. *Gender and Stress*. New York: Free Press, 1987. pp. 330–349.

Brown, S.A.; Goldman, M.S.; Inn, A.; and Anderson, L.R. Expectations of reinforcement from alcohol: Their domain and relation to drinking patterns. *J Consult Clin Psychol* 48:419–426, 1980.

Cahalan, D.; Cisin, I.H.; and Crossley, H.M. *American Drinking Practices: A National Study of Drinking Behavior and Attitudes*. New Brunswick, NJ: Rutgers University, 1969. 260 pp.

Cappell, H., and Greeley, J. Alcohol and tension reduction. In: Blane, H.T., and Leonard, K.E., eds. *Psychological Theories of Drinking and Alcoholism*. New York: Guilford Press, 1987. pp. 15–54.

Castro, F.G.; Maddahian, E.; Newcomb, M.D.; and Bentler, P.M. A multivariate model of the determinants of cigarette smoking among adolescents. *J Health Soc Behav* 28:273–289, 1987.

Chassin, L.A.; Mann, L.M.; and Sher, K.J. Self-awareness theory, family history, and adolescent alcohol involvement. *J Abnorm Psychol* 97:206–217, 1988.

Chassin, L.A.; Pillow, D.R.; Curran, P.J.; Molina, B.; and Barrera, M. Relation of parental alcoholism to early adolescent substance use: A test of three mediating mechanisms. *J Abnorm Psychol* 102:3–19, 1993.

Christiansen, B.A.; Smith, G.T.; Roehling, P.V.; and Goldman, M.S. Using alcohol expectancies to predict adolescent drinking behavior after one year. *J Consult Clin Psychol* 57:93–99, 1989.

Coan, R.W. Personality variables associated with cigarette smoking. *J Pers Soc Psychol* 26:86–104, 1973.

Cooper, M.L.; Russell, M.; and George, W.H. Coping, expectancies, and alcohol abuse. *J Abnorm Psychol* 97:218–230, 1988.

Deardorff, C.M.; Melges, F.T.; Hout, C.N.; and Savage, D.J. Situations related to drinking alcohol: A factor analysis of questionnaire responses. *J Stud Alcohol* 36:1184–1195, 1975.

Diener, E. Subjective well-being. *Psychol Bull* 95:542–575, 1984.

Donovan, J.E., and Jessor, R. A Guttman scalogram analysis of adolescent drug use. *Am J Public Health* 73:543–552, 1983.

Donovan, J., and Jessor, R. Structure of problem behavior in adolescence and young adulthood. *J Consult Clin Psychol* 53:890–904, 1985.

Ensminger, M.E.; Brown, C.H.; and Kellam, S.G. Sex differences in antecedents of substance use among adolescents. *J Soc Issues* 38(2):25–42, 1982.

Fitzgerald, H.E.; Sullivan, L.A.; Ham, H.P.; Zucker, R.A.; Bruckel, S.;

Schneider, A.M.; and Noll, R.B. Predictors of behavior problems in three-year-old sons of alcoholics: Early evidence for the onset of risk. *Child Dev* 64:110–123, 1993.

Folkman, S.; Chesney, M.A.; Pollack, L.; and Phillips, C. Stress, coping and high-risk sexual behavior. *Health Psychol* 11: 218–222, 1992.

Gritz, E. Gender and the teenage smoker. In: Ray, B.A., and Braude, M.C., eds. *Women and Drugs.* DHHS Publication No. (ADM) 86–1447. Rockville, MD: National Institute on Drug Abuse, 1986. pp. 70–79.

Hays, R.; Stacy, A.W.; and DiMatteo, M.R. Covariation among health-related behaviors. *Addict Behav* 9:315–318, 1984.

Hays, R.D.; Widaman, K.F.; DiMatteo, M.R.; and Stacy, A.W. Structural equation models of current drug use. *J Pers Soc Psychol* 52:134–144, 1987.

Hirschman, R.S.; Leventhal, H.; and Glynn, K. The development of smoking behavior: Cross-sectional survey data. *J Appl Soc Psychol* 14:184–206, 1984.

Hull, J.G., and Bond, C.F., Jr. Social and behavioral consequences of alcohol consumption and expectancy. *Psychol Bull* 99:347–360, 1986.

Ikard, F.F.; Green, D.E.; and Horn, D. A scale to differentiate between types of smoking as related to the management of affect. *Int J Addict* 4:649–659, 1969.

Istvan, J., and Matarazzo, J.D. Tobacco, alcohol, and caffeine use: A review of their interrelationships. *Psychol Bull* 95:301–326, 1984.

Jessor, R.; Chase, J.A.; and Donovan, J.E. Psychosocial correlates of marijuana use and problem drinking in a national sample of adolescents. *Am J Public Health* 70: 604–613, 1980.

Jessor, R., and Jessor, S. *Problem Behavior and Psychosocial Development.* New York: Academic Press, 1977. 281pp.

Johnston, L.D.; O'Malley, P.M.; and Bachman, J.G. *Drug Use Among American High School Seniors, College Students, and Young Adults, 1975–1990.* DHHS Publication No. (ADM) 91–1813. Rockville, MD: National Institute on Drug Abuse, 1991. 199 pp.

Kandel, D.B. Stages in adolescent involvement in drug use. *Science* 190:912–914, 1975.

Kaplan, H.B., and Johnson, R.J. Circumstances surrounding initial illicit drug use and escalation of use: Moderating effects of gender and early adolescent experiences. In: Glantz, M., and Pickens, R., eds. *Vulnerability to Drug Abuse.* Washington, DC: American Psychological Association, 1992. pp. 299–358.

Kaplan, H.B.; Martin, S.S.; Johnson, R.J.; and Robbins, C.A. Escalation of marijuana use. *J Health Soc Behav* 27:44–61, 1986.

Kellam, S.G.; Brown, C.H.; and Fleming, J.P. Adaptation to first grade and teenage drug, alcohol and cigarette use. *J Sch Health* 52:301–306, 1982.

Kelly, J.; St. Lawrence, J.; and Brasfield, T. Predictors of vulnerability to AIDS risk behavior relapse. *J Consult Clin Psychol* 59:163–166, 1991.

Khantzian, E.J. Self-regulation and self-medication factors in alcoholism and the addictions. In Galanter, M., ed. *Recent Developments in Alcoholism.* Vol. 8. New York: Plenum Press, 1990. pp. 255–271.

Labouvie, E.W. Alcohol and marijuana use in relation to adolescent stress. *Int J Addict* 21:333–345, 1986.

Labouvie, E.W.; Pandina, R.J.; White, H.R.; and Johnson, V. Risk factors of adolescent drug use: An affect-based interpretation. *J Subst Abuse* 2:265–285, 1990.

Leigh, B.C., and Stall, R. Substance use and risky sexual behavior for exposure to HIV. *Am Psychol* 48:1035–1045, 1993.

Leventhal, H., and Avis, N. Pleasure, addiction, and habit: Factors in verbal report or factors in smoking behavior? *J Abnorm Psychol* 85:478–488, 1976.

McCarty, D., and Kaye, M. Reasons for drinking: Motivational patterns and alcohol use among college students. *Addict Behav* 9:185–188, 1984.

McGue, M. The behavioral genetics of alcoholism. In: Plomin, R.C., and McClearn, G.E., eds. *Nature, Nurture, and Psychology.* Washington, DC: American Psychological Association, 1993. pp. 245–268.

McKennell, A.C. Smoking motivation factors. *Br J Soc Clin Psychol* 9:8–22, 1970.

McKirnan, D.J., and Peterson, P.L. Stress, expectancies, and vulnerability to substance abuse. *J Abnorm Psychol* 97:461–466, 1988.

McKirnan, D.J., and Peterson, P.L. AIDS risk behavior: The role of attitudes and substance abuse. *Psychol Health* 3:161–171, 1989.

Merikangas, K.R.; Rounsaville, B.J.; and Prusoff, B.A. Familial factors in vulnerability to substance abuse. In: Glantz, M., and Pickens, R., eds. Vulnerability to Drug Abuse. Washington, DC: American *Psychological Association*, 1992. pp. 75–98.

Mitic, W.R.; McGuire, D.P.; and Neumann, B. Perceived stress and adolescents' cigarette use. *Psychol Rep* 57:1043–1048, 1985.

Newcomb, M.D., and Harlow, L.L. Life events and substance use among adolescents. *J Pers Soc Psychol* 51:564–577, 1986.

Revell, A.D.; Warburton, D.M.; and Wesnes, K. Smoking as a coping strategy. *Addict Behav* 10:209–224, 1985.

Russell, M. Prevalence of alcoholism among children of alcoholics. In: Windle, M., and Searles, J.S., eds. *Children of Alcoholics: Critical Perspectives.* New York: Guilford Press, 1990. pp. 9–38.

Segal, B.; Huba, G.J.; and Singer, J.L. Reasons for drug and alcohol use by college students. *Int J Addict* 15:489–498, 1980.

Sher, K.J.; Walitzer, K.S.; Wood, P.K.; and Brent, E.E. Characteristics of children of alcoholics: Putative risk factors, substance use and abuse, and psychopathology. *J Abnorm Psychol* 100:427–448, 1991.

Stacy, A.W.; Newcomb, M.D.; and Bentler, P.M. Cognitive motivation and drug use: A 9-year longitudinal study. *J Abnorm Psychol* 100:502–515, 1991.

Steele, C.M., and Josephs, R.A. Alcohol myopia: Its prized and dangerous effects. *Am Psychol* 45:921–933, 1990.

Sussman, S.; Brannon, B.R.; Dent, C.W.; Hansen, W.B.; Johnson, C.A.; and Flay, B.R. Relations of coping strategies, perceived stress, and cigarette smoking among adolescents. *Int J Addict* 28:599–612, 1993.

Tarter, R.E.; Alterman, A.I.; and Edwards, K. Vulnerability to alcoholism in men: A behavior-genetic perspective. *J Stud Alcohol* 46:329–356, 1985.

U.S. Department of Health and Human Services. *The Health Consequences of Smoking: Nicotine Addiction.* DHHS Publication No. (CDC) 88–8406. Washington, DC: Supt. of Docs., U.S. Govt. Print. Off., 1988. 639 pp.

Wanberg, K.W., and Horn, J.L. Assessment of alcohol use with multidimensional concepts and measures. *Am Psychol* 38:1055–1069, 1983.

Wesnes, K., and Warburton, D.M. Smoking, nicotine, and human performance. *Pharmacol Ther* 21:189–208, 1983.

Wills, T.A. Stress and coping in early adolescence: Relationships to smoking and alcohol use in urban school samples. *Health Psychol* 5:503–529, 1986.

Wills, T.A. Stress and coping factors in the epidemiology of substance use. In: Kozlowski, L.T.; Annis, H.M.; Cappell, H.D.; Glaser, F.B.; Goodstadt, M.S.; Israel, Y.; Kalant, H.; Sellers, E.M.; and Vingilis, E.R., eds. *Research Advances in Alcohol and Drug Problems.* Vol. 10. New York: Plenum Press, 1990. pp. 215–250.

Wills, T.A. Coping relates to important external criteria. In Pickering, T., ed. *Concepts and Controversies in Behavioral Medicine.* Hillsdale, NJ: Erlbaum, in press.

Wills, T.A., and Shiffman, S. Coping and substance use: A conceptual framework. In: Shiffman, S., and Wills, T.A., eds. *Coping and Substance Use.* Orlando, FL: Academic Press, 1985. pp. 3–24.

Wills, T.A., and Filer, M. Stress-coping model of adolescent behavior problems. In: Ollendick, T.H., and Prinz, R.J., eds. *Advances in Clinical Child Psychology.* Vol. 18. New York: Plenum Press, in press.

Wills, T.A., and Hirky, A.E. Coping and substance abuse. In: Zeidner, M., and Endler, N.S., eds. *Handbook of Coping:*

Theory, Research, and Applications. New York: Wiley, in press.

Wills, T.A.; Vaccaro, D.; and McNamara, G. The role of life events, family support, and competence in adolescent substance use: Test of vulnerability and protective factors. *Am J Community Psychol* 20:349–374, 1992.

Wills, T.A.; Schreibman, D.; Benson, G.; and Vaccaro, D. The impact of parental substance use on adolescents: A test of a mediational model. *J Pediatr Psychol* 19:537–555, 1994a.

Wills, T.A.; Vaccaro, D.; and McNamara, G. Novelty seeking, risk taking, and related constructs as predictors of adolescent substance use: An application of Cloninger's theory. *J Subst Abuse* 6:1–20, 1994b.

Wills, T.A.; DuHamel, K.; and Vaccaro, D. Activity and mood temperament as predictors of adolescent substance use: Test of a self-regulation model. *J Pers Soc Psychol* 68:901–916, 1995a.

Wills, T.A.; McNamara, G.; and Vaccaro, D. Parental education related to adolescent stress-coping and substance use. Health Psychol 14:464–478, 1995b.

Wills, T.A.; Blechman, E.A.; and McNamara, G. Family support, coping and competence. In: Hetherington, E.M., ed. *Stress, Coping, and Resiliency in Children and the Family.* Hillsdale, NJ: Erlbaum, in press a.

Wills, T.A.; McNamara, G.; Vaccaro, D.; and Hirky, A.E. Escalated substance use: A longitudinal grouping analysis in early adolescence. *J Abnorm Psychol*, in press b.

Wilsnack, S.C.; Klassen, A.D.; Schur, B.E.; and Wilsnack, R.W. Predicting onset and chronicity of women's problem drinking: Five-year longitudinal analysis. *Am J Public Health* 81:305–318, 1991.

Chapter 7

Animal Models of Alcohol-Nicotine Interactions

Allan C. Collins, M.S., Ph.D., and
Michael J. Marks, M.S., Ph.D.

Over 35 years ago, Cartwright and colleagues (1959) noted that people who consume alcohol regularly are more likely to be cigarette smokers. By 1984, when Istvan and Matarazzo reviewed the literature, it was clear that smokers consume more alcohol than nonsmokers and, among smokers, heavy smokers consume more alcohol than light smokers. Laboratory studies indicate that alcohol use evokes increased tobacco use. This was seen in short-term studies of male alcoholics (Mello and Mendelson 1972; Griffiths et al. 1976; Henningfield et al. 1983, 1984) and in long-term studies of hospitalized nonalcoholic men and women (Mello et al. 1980, 1987).

Although the prevalence of smoking has decreased in the general popu-

lation since the early 1970's, smoking has not decreased markedly in alcoholics (Kozlowski et al. 1986; Bobo 1989; Hughes 1993, 1994). Hughes (1994) reported that about 70 percent of alcoholics are heavy smokers (i.e., smoke more than 29 cigarettes per day), compared with 10 percent of the general population. Furthermore, one of every seven heavy smokers meets the criteria for active alcoholism, whereas among never-smokers and exsmokers, only one of 20 meets these criteria.

The bases for these interactions are largely unknown; however, it is well established that genetic factors are important in the development of alcoholism (National Institute on Alcohol Abuse and Alcoholism 1993), and they also seem to influence smoking

A.C. Collins, M.S., Ph.D., is a professor and M.J. Marks, M.S., Ph.D., is a research associate at the Institute for Behavioral Genetics, Campus Box 447, University of Colorado, Boulder, CO 80309–0447.

(see Collins and Marks 1991 for a review of this literature). Genetic factors may be more important in regulating smoking than they are in determining alcoholism, because the heritability estimates for smoking persistence are higher than are the heritability estimates for alcoholism (McGue 1993; Heath and Madden 1994). It seems reasonable to suspect, given the high incidence of their simultaneous use, that some overlap may exist in those genes that regulate the use and abuse of alcohol and nicotine.

Among the biological factors that may relate to genetic influences on alcoholism is sensitivity to alcohol. Studies emanating from Schuckit's group (Schuckit et al. 1985) indicate that sons of alcoholics are less sensitive (i.e., more tolerant) to one or more of alcohol's effects than sons of nonalcoholics. These observations have led to the suggestion that people who are less sensitive to alcohol can ingest more alcohol, which facilitates the development of dependence on alcohol.

Similar arguments have been made concerning tobacco use. Almost all smokers report that their first experience with smoking was not pleasant (Bewley et al. 1974), and it may be that some people may not become dependent on nicotine because they have high innate sensitivity to the toxic actions of nicotine (Silverstein et al. 1982; U.S. Department of Health and Human Services 1988). People with less sensitivity to nicotine may experience fewer unpleasant effects and, consequently, may be more likely to continue using tobacco (Friedman

et al. 1985). In an alternative hypothesis, Pomerleau and colleagues (1993) argue that the development of tolerance to nicotine is more important than initial sensitivity. This supposition is based on recent human studies (Shiffman 1991) and animal studies (Marks et al. 1992) showing that humans or animals that are more sensitive to a first dose of nicotine develop more tolerance to nicotine with chronic exposure. This model assumes that the first experience with nicotine of those people with high innate sensitivity to the drug produces both aversive effects and reinforcing consequences and that as tolerance to the aversive effects develops, reinforcing effects emerge.

The sensitivity models are derived, at least in part, from animal studies. Studies in inbred strains and selectively bred lines of rodents have consistently shown that genetic factors influence a broad array of responses to acute doses of alcohol (see Phillips and Crabbe 1991 for a review of this literature). Similarly, strains and lines of rats and mice differ in sensitivity to many behavioral and physiological effects produced by nicotine (for examples, see Freund et al. 1988; Marks et al. 1989b; Miner and Collins 1989). These results stimulated a series of studies from our laboratory that were intended to assess whether common genes regulate sensitivity to alcohol and nicotine. The vast majority of our studies used the long-sleep (LS) and short-sleep (SS) mouse lines (McClearn and

Kakihana 1981), which were selectively bred for differences in duration of loss of the righting response (i.e., alcohol "sleep time"). Initial studies (de Fiebre et al. 1987) using the LS-SS mice yielded a provocative result: The alcohol-sensitive LS mice were more sensitive to nicotine, as measured by a battery of behavioral and physiological responses (to be enumerated later in this chapter), than were the alcohol-resistant SS mice. A parallel study (de Fiebre et al. 1991) using rat lines that had been selectively bred for differences in sleep time (Deitrich et al. 1988)— the high and low alcohol sensitivity (HAS-LAS) rat lines—yielded comparable results. These results indicate that one or more common genes may, indeed, regulate first-dose sensitivities to several responses elicited by alcohol and nicotine.

LS-SS and HAS-LAS differences could also arise because of chance inbreeding. One strategy that can be used to determine whether an apparent association between two traits is due to common genetic regulation or to fortuitous associations arising because of inbreeding is to determine whether the traits are transmitted together in segregating populations. We tried such a study by assessing the segregation of the sleep-time response to alcohol and seven responses to nicotine in F1 and F2 generations and backcross generations (F1 x LS and F1 x SS) derived from the LS-SS mice using generation means for the analyses (de Fiebre and Collins 1992). The segregation patterns for

alcohol-induced sleep time did not differ from any of the segregation patterns for nicotine, which supported the common gene argument.

A more powerful method that can be used to test for associations is to use recombinant inbred (RI) strains. The RI method also allows a convenient access to quantitative trait loci (QTL) mapping methods, which may be extraordinarily helpful in identifying the genes of interest. RI strains have been derived from the LS and SS mouse lines by crossing the two progenitor lines to generate first the F1 and then the F2 generations (DeFries et al. 1989). Chance association (i.e., linkage) among genetic loci should be broken down in the segregating F2 generation. The genes are fixed in new constellations by inbreeding starting from the F2 generation. Inbreeding of the LS-SS–derived RI strains was started using 40 sibling pairs derived from 12 F2 families; ultimately, 27 RI strains were developed.

METHODS

We used 26 of the LS-SS–derived RI strains to test the hypothesis that common genes regulate sensitivities to acute doses of alcohol and nicotine. The studies used young adult (i.e., ages 60–90 days) female mice. The sensitivities of the LS-SS–derived RI strains to seven effects of nicotine were measured following acute injections of the drug. Potential correlations between sensitivities to nicotine and alcohol were sought using alcohol-related data that had been reported previously by other researchers (DeFries et al. 1989; Erwin et al. 1990, 1993; Erwin and Jones 1993).

A neutralized stock of nicotine was prepared by dissolving nicotine base (Sigma) in physiological saline containing 0.1 N HCl. The relative sensitivities of the strains to the effects of nicotine were determined by constructing dose-response curves. Three doses of nicotine (i.e., 0.5, 1.0, and 1.5 mg/kg), plus the saline control, were used in all the strains. Additional doses were added, depending on the sensitivity of each strain, so that accurate estimates of parameters, such as the ED_{50}, could be calculated from linear portions of the dose-response curves. Each animal was tested only once, and a minimum of six animals were tested at each of the challenge doses.

The animals were tested following injection with either saline (control) or low doses of nicotine using a test battery described below. The times used for testing each measure represent the times of maximal drug effect for the measure and were selected from previous studies (Marks et al. 1985; de Fiebre et al. 1987). Sensitivity to nicotine-induced seizures was measured in separate animals.

Respiratory rate was measured 1 minute after injection for a period of 1 minute. The nicotine dose that increased respiratory rate by 50 breaths per minute (ED_{+50}) was calculated for each strain. Acoustic startle was measured using a Columbus Instruments Responder Startle Reflex Monitor 3 minutes after injection. The slopes of the dose-response curves were determined and used to compare the strains. Activity in an automated Y-maze was measured for a 3-minute period starting 5 minutes after injection. The nicotine doses that decreased crossing and rearing activities by 50 percent (ED_{50}) were calculated for each strain. Heart rate was measured 9 minutes after injection using an E&M Physiograph. The nicotine dose that decreased heart rate by 100 beats per minute (ED_{-100}) was calculated for each strain. Body temperature was measured 15 minutes after injection. The nicotine dose that decreased body temperature by 2°C ($ED_{-2°}$) was calculated for each strain.

Nicotine-induced seizures were measured in separate animals than were used for the other tests. Animals were injected with nicotine, placed in a glass jar, and observed for a 5-minute period. The presence, or absence, of overt clonic-tonic seizures was recorded. The nicotine dose that produced seizures in 50 percent of the animals (ED_{50}) was calculated for each strain.

The number of effective factors (i.e., genes) regulating each response was estimated using the following formula derived by Falconer (1981): Gene # = $R^2/8V_A$. R is the difference between mean values of the extreme responders, and V_A is the additive variance.

RESULTS

Nicotine injection produced both stimulant and depressant actions, which varied among the strains. This is illustrated in figures 1 and 2, in which dose-response curves are presented for the LS and SS mice and for four of the RI strains. Each response to nicotine seems to have been polygenically determined. The estimates of the number of effective factors, or number of genes, that influenced response to nicotine (obtained by using effective dose values calculated for all 26 of the RI strains that were tested) are as follows: 6.71 for respiration rate, 3.19 for acoustic startle, 5.33 for Y-maze crossing activity, 6.00 for Y-maze rearing activity, 6.40 for heart rate, 3.22 for body temperature, and 2.31 for nicotine-induced seizures.

As is evident from figure 1, nicotine injection elicited a dose-dependent increase in respiration rate in virtually all the mouse strains. Differences in control respiration rate were seen among the strains ($F_{25, 305} = 2.06$, $p < 0.01$) and differences in sensitivity to nicotine were seen as well, as indicated by a significant strain-by-dose interaction ($F_{75, 1230} = 1.33$, $p < 0.05$) obtained with the two-way analysis of variance (ANOVA) of the four common doses (i.e., 0, 0.5, 1.0, and 1.5 mg/kg) used in all the strains. The ED_{+50} value (i.e., the nicotine dose that increased respiration rate by 50 breaths per minute) for the LS was among the lowest of the strains, whereas the ED_{+50} value for the SS was in the midrange of strain sensitivities. The variation in sensitivity to nicotine's effects on respiration rate among the strains was large; the range in ED_{+50} values was as much as sevenfold.

Variation was seen among the strains in basal startle ($F_{25, 305} = 10.29$, $p < 0.001$), but the two-way ANOVA failed to detect apparent strain differences when the four common doses were compared ($F_{75, 1230} = 1.08$, $p = 0.31$). A comparison of the slopes of the dose-response curves, which were constructed using all the test doses, suggested that nicotine did not affect the strains similarly. The slopes of the dose-response curves were nearly zero in most of the strains but were positive in some of the strains (i.e., nicotine-enhanced startle), whereas others showed a depressed startle response yielding a negative slope for the dose-response curve; these slopes ranged between -2 and +2.

Nicotine depressed the two Y-maze measures. The strains showed differences in control Y-maze activities (crosses, $F_{25, 305} = 6.85$, $p < 0.001$; rears, $F_{25, 305} = 5.31$, $p < 0.001$), and nicotine injection resulted in decreases in both of these activities. The strains differed in sensitivity to nicotine as indicated by significant strain-by-dose interaction terms detected by the two-way ANOVA (crosses, $F_{75, 1230} = 2.04$, $p < 0.001$; rears, $F_{75, 1230} = 2.35$, $p < 0.001$). The parental LS mice were among the most sensitive, the SS mice were among the most resistant, and the RI strains showed wide variance in sensitivity to these depressant effects of nicotine. The ED_{50} values of the least sensitive strains were approximately 2.5 times those of the most sensitive strains.

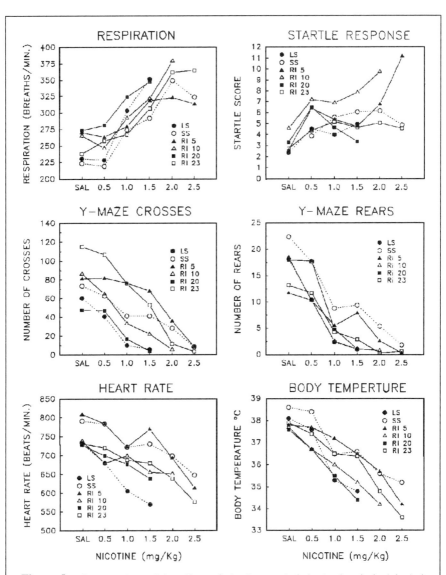

Figure 1. A comparison of the effects of nicotine on six behavioral and physiological measures. Dose-response curves for nicotine effects were constructed as described in the Methods section of this chapter. The data obtained from the progenitor long-sleep (LS) and short-sleep (SS) mice (n = 10–12 for each sex in both lines) as well as four representative recombinant inbred (RI) strains (n = 6–10 for each dose in both sexes for each strain) are presented.

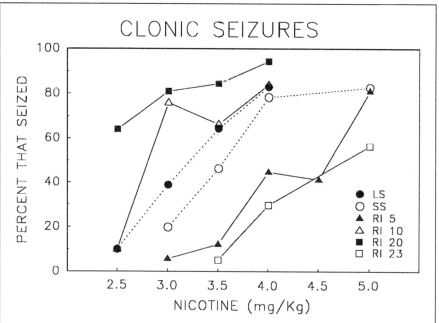

Figure 2. A recombinant inbred (RI) strain comparison of nicotine-induced seizures. Dose-response curves for nicotine-induced seizures were constructed as described in the Methods section of this chapter. Data presented were obtained from the progenitor long-sleep (LS) and short-sleep (SS) mice *(n = 10–12 for each sex in both lines)* as well as four representative RI strains *(n = 10–12 for each dose in both sexes for each strain)*. The nicotine dose that evoked seizures in 50 percent of the animals (ED_{50}) was calculated for each strain.

Heart rate following saline injection differed among the strains ($F_{25, 305} = 4.54$, $p < 0.001$), and nicotine injection elicited a dose-dependent decrease in heart rate. The strains differed in sensitivity as indicated by a significant dose-by-strain interaction term ($F_{75, 1230} = 2.07$, $p < 0.001$). The LS mice were among the most sensitive strains, and the SS mice were intermediate in sensitivity. The range between the least and the most sensitive RI strains, as measured by the ED_{100} value, was approximately eightfold.

Nicotine injection produced a dose-dependent decrease in body temperature in all the strains. Small differences in control body temperatures were seen among the strains ($F_{25, 305} = 1.97$, $p < 0.01$), and strain differences in nicotine's hypothermic actions were detected ($F_{75, 1230} = 1.69$, $p < 0.001$). A comparison of the strain sensitivities using the dose that decreased body temperature by 2°C ($ED_{-2°}$) revealed that the LS mice were among the more sensitive strains and that the SS mice were less sensitive than average but were not among the least sensitive strains. The least sensitive strains had $ED_{-2^{\circ}}$ values that were approximately 2.5-fold higher than those of the most sensitive strains.

The LS and SS mice were equisensitive to the seizure-inducing effects of nicotine (figure 2), but the RI strains showed a broad range of responsiveness. The ANOVA of the two doses that were used in all the strains (3.5 and 4.0 mg/kg) detected significant overall strain differences. This was confirmed by an analysis of the ED_{50} (i.e., the dose that evoked seizures in 50 percent of the animals), in which the ED_{50} value of the least sensitive strain was approximately 2.5 times that of the most sensitive strain.

The correlations between responses to nicotine, as measured by effective doses, and four responses of the RI strains to alcohol also were calculated and are presented in table 1. None of the correlations were significant.

DISCUSSION

The RI strain distribution patterns and estimates of effective factors suggest that the actions of nicotine that have been studied are polygenically determined. Similarly, estimates of the number of effective factors that regulate responses to alcohol—made using the LS-SS–derived RI strains—suggest that more than one gene regulates alcohol actions; effective factor estimates are 7.1 for the sleep-time response (DeFries et al. 1989), 4.1 for the hypothermic action, and 3.1 for effects on locomotor activity

(Erwin and Jones 1993). Thus, the results of the RI analysis is an analysis of the covariance of polygenically determined traits.

As noted previously, several earlier studies had demonstrated that the LS-SS mice differ in sensitivity to several effects of nicotine (de Fiebre et al. 1987, 1990; de Fiebre and Collins 1988, 1989). The apparent association between alcohol and nicotine sensitivity was not dissociated by a classical cross analysis (de Fiebre and Collins 1992), but the more powerful RI analysis reported here indicates that common genetic regulation of several acute responses to these two drugs may not exist.

The finding that the apparent association between sensitivity to alcohol and sensitivity to nicotine broke down when more powerful methods were used does not mean that common genes do not influence first-dose sensitivity to alcohol and nicotine in humans. The responses that we have measured to both drugs may not be the relevant ones to measure. Both alcohol and nicotine affect a broad array of behaviors and physiological responses, and it may well be that one or more of these "other" responses is the critical measure that should have been analyzed.

From a genetics perspective, it is becoming increasingly clear that genetic regulation of alcohol-related behaviors is quite complex. Given this genetic complexity, it may be that approaches other than comparing phenotypes (i.e., drug responses) should be used to identify (if they exist) common sites of action for nicotine.

Markel and colleagues (1995) have used the QTL method to search for loci that regulate alcohol-induced sleep time. This study utilized the LS-SS–derived RI strains in an initial screen and F2 mice as a confirmation. Both of these analyses detected a QTL on chromosome 2. The gene that encodes for the major brain nicotinic receptor subunit, α4, is found on chromosome 2 (Bessis et al. 1990) at almost precisely the site where Markel and colleagues (1995) found their major QTL. Thus, although our results suggest that there may be no overlap in the genes that regulate sensitivity to alcohol and nicotine, it may very well be that discarding the common gene hypothesis at this time would be premature. Further comparisons using other behavioral and physiological responses should, in all probability, be done.

While the results of this RI analysis do not confirm the conclusion that many of the same genes regulate acute responses to alcohol and nicotine, the data reported here confirm several previous studies of the genetics of nicotine action (Marks et al. 1989a, 1989b; Miner and Collins 1989). For example, a principal components analysis of the RI data indicated that the Y-maze crossing and rearing responses were highly correlated with nicotine-induced effects on body temperature and that nicotine-induced seizures were unrelated to any of the other responses. This identical finding was made using 19 inbred mouse strains (Marks et al. 1989a). Indeed, the similarity between the RI data reported here and our earlier study of nicotine actions using the same tests and 19 inbred mouse strains is remarkable.

Table 1. Correlation Between Responses to Nicotine and Alcohol.

Responses to Alcohol	Responses to Nicotine						
	RESP	START	CROSS	REAR	HRATE	BTEMP	SEIZ
SLEEP	-0.14	-0.03	-0.26	-0.11	-0.08	0.15	0.07
TEMP	0.06	0.01	-0.03	-0.01	-0.44	0.27	0.09
DISTANCE	0.05	0.04	0.18	-0.17	-0.18	-0.10	0.22
REAR	0.22	-0.24	0.08	0.01	0.12	-0.10	-0.36

Correlations between effective doses for nicotine responses (ED values) and several responses to alcohol (i.e., sleep-time, body temperature, total distance, and rearing activity) were calculated as described in the Methods section of this chapter. Alcohol values are those published previously (DeFries et al. 1989; Erwin et al. 1990; Erwin and Jones 1993; Erwin et al. 1993). SLEEP = sleep-time following an alcohol dose of 4.1 g/kg; TEMP = change in body temperature 30 min after injection with a 4.1 g/kg dose of alcohol; DISTANCE = total distance traveled in an Omnitech activity apparatus (5 min) following a 1.75 g/kg dose of alcohol; REAR = rearing activity during a 5-min test period following a 1.75 g/kg dose of alcohol; RESP = respiration rate; START = acoustic startle score; CROSS and REAR = Y-maze crossing and rearing activities; HRATE = heart rate; BTEMP = body temperature; SEIZ = seizures.

It may very well be that the most important thing to study at the behavioral level, given that alcohol administration increases smoking in humans, is the interaction between alcohol and nicotine when these two drugs are given together. As an example, de Fiebre and Collins (1989) measured the relative potency of alcohol as an anticonvulsant in cases in which seizures were induced by high doses of nicotine. This study demonstrated that alcohol pretreatment was more effective at blocking nicotine-induced seizures in the LS mice than in the SS mice. It may be somewhat simplistic, but an increased use of tobacco could result when alcohol is consumed if alcohol blocks one or more of nicotine's actions. Kozlowski (1980) has argued that smokers adjust their tobacco intake to maintain brain nicotine levels below a concentration that evokes toxic responses and above a level that is associated with increased craving and/or withdrawal symptoms.

de Fiebre and Collins (1989) also studied the effect of alcohol on a behavioral desensitization phenomenon. They noted that pretreatment with low doses of nicotine resulted in reduced sensitivity to seizures induced by higher doses of nicotine. This behavioral desensitization was enhanced by pretreatment with alcohol, was seen at lower alcohol doses, and was more pronounced in LS mice. Thus, alcohol seems to antagonize some actions of nicotine and augment others, but the magnitude of these effects seems to be influenced by genetic factors.

Another potential site of interaction is at the level of cross-tolerance. We have completed several such studies (Burch et al. 1988; Collins et al. 1988, 1993; de Fiebre and Collins 1993; Luo et al. 1994). In these studies, mice of four different strains (i.e., DBA/2, C57BL/6, LS, and SS) were chronically treated with alcohol or nicotine, and tolerance and cross-tolerance were measured using most of the tests used in the RI strain studies reported in detail earlier in this chapter. These studies demonstrated that tolerance to both drugs can be evoked by chronic treatment and that some cross-tolerance (e.g., reduced sensitivity to the other drug) also developed, particularly for the body temperature measure. LS-SS differences in tolerance and cross-tolerance were detected, with the LS mice developing more of each (Collins et al. 1993; de Fiebre and Collins 1993; Luo et al. 1994).

Minimal progress has been made in understanding how alcohol and nicotine might interact at the molecular level, but an elegant series of studies conducted by Miller and colleagues (for examples see Forman et al. 1989; Fraser et al. 1990; Wood et al. 1991; Wu et al. 1994) suggest that studies of the effects of alcohol on brain nicotinic receptor function might be useful. These studies have demonstrated that under certain circumstances alcohol may enhance nicotinic receptor function and under other circumstances it may inhibit function by enhancing the rate of receptor desensitization. All of these studies have utilized the nicotinic receptor found in the electric organ of *Torpedo californica*, which is similar, but not identical, to the brain nicotinic receptors. Given that there are several brain nicotinic receptor subtypes that differ in structure, function, pharmacology, and regulation (see Sargent 1993 for a recent review), it does not seem unreasonable to suggest that in-depth studies of the effects of alcohol on brain nicotinic receptor function could be valuable.

CONCLUSION AND RECOMMENDATIONS

Although some early studies suggested an overlap of the genes that influence acute actions of alcohol and nicotine, data presented here do not support this notion. Bearing in mind the caveats outlined above, the RI data do not support a common gene hypothesis for initial sensitivity. However, there are many other ways that these two drugs could interact, and available evidence suggests potential genetic influences on many of these interactions. Included among these are antagonism or enhancement of drug action (e.g., alcohol might decrease one or more of the toxic actions of nicotine), enhancement by one drug of the reinforcing actions of the other, and cross-tolerance (to toxic actions) or sensitization (to reinforcing effects) following chronic treatment. Any or all of these could occur and could result in increased use of tobacco when alcohol is consumed.

Although it has been known for over 35 years (and perhaps longer, when common knowledge is considered) that smoking and drinking go hand-in-hand, we still have almost no knowledge as to why this occurs. The field has not moved forward for a number of reasons, not the least of which is that very few scientists have attempted to resolve the difficult questions that arise when drug interactions are considered. If progress is to be made, additional human resources must be recruited to the research effort. Scientists should be encouraged to address new issues. More than enough studies have been done concerning whether alcohol consumption promotes tobacco use. Human studies should attempt to unravel questions such as whether common genetic factors regulate alcohol and tobacco use and alcoholism and should attempt to resolve mechanistic questions.

Additional studies using animals and model systems also should be encouraged. While our genetic studies of initial sensitivity may have been inconclusive, it is clear from other studies that have been done that alcohol and nicotine interact. Animal models that focus on acute and chronic cotreatment with alcohol and nicotine should be encouraged to define the behavioral and physiological interactions between these two drugs. In addition, attempts should be made to define sites and mechanisms of interaction at the molecular level. Tremendous progress has been made in the last 5 years in identifying and characterizing brain nicotinic receptors. Given the results obtained by Miller's group (Forman et al. 1989; Fraser et al. 1990; Wood et al. 1991; Wu et al. 1994) using the *Torpedo* nicotinic receptor, it seems possible that an in-depth analysis of alcohol's effects on brain nicotinic receptors could yield much-needed insight into the reasons underlying alcohol-nicotine co-abuse.

ACKNOWLEDGMENTS

These studies were supported by National Institute on Alcoholism and Alcohol Abuse grant AA–06391. A.C. Collins was supported, in part, by Research Scientist Award DA–00197 from the National Institute on Drug Abuse.

REFERENCES

Bessis, A.; Simon-Chazottes, D.; Devillers-Thiery, A.; Guenet, J.-L.; and Changeux, J.P. Chromosomal localization of the mouse genes encoding for α2, α3, α4 and β2 subunits of neuronal nicotinic acetylcholine receptor. *FEBS Lett* 264:48–52, 1990.

Bewley, B.R.; Bland, J.M.; and Harris, R. Factors associated with the starting of cigarette smoking by primary school children. *Br J Prev Soc Med* 28:37–44, 1974.

Bobo, J.K. Nicotine dependence and alcoholism epidemiology and treatment. *J Psychoactive Drugs* 21:323–329, 1989.

Burch, J.B.; de Fiebre, C.M.; Marks, M.J.; and Collins, A.C. Chronic ethanol or nicotine treatment results in partial cross-tolerance between these agents. *Psychopharmacology* 95:452–458, 1988.

Cartwright, A.; Martin, F.M.; and Thomson, J.G. Distribution and development of smoking habits. *Lancet* 2:725–727, 1959.

Collins, A.C., and Marks, M.J. Genetic studies of nicotinic and muscarinic agents. In: Harris, R.A., and Crabbe, J.C., eds. *The Genetic Basis of Alcohol and Drug Actions.* New York: Plenum Publishing Co., 1991. pp. 323–352.

Collins, A.C.; Burch, J.B.; de Fiebre, C.M.; Marks, M.J. Tolerance to and cross tolerance between ethanol and nicotine. *Pharmacol Biochem Behav* 29:365–373, 1988.

Collins, A.C.; Romm, E.; Selvaag, S.; Marks, M.J. A comparison of the effects of chronic nicotine infusion on tolerance to nicotine and cross-tolerance to ethanol in Long-Sleep and Short-Sleep mice. *J Pharmacol Exp Ther* 266:1390–1397, 1993.

de Fiebre, C.M., and Collins, A.C. Decreased sensitivity to nicotine-induced seizures as a consequence of nicotine pretreatment in long-sleep and short-sleep mice. *Alcohol* 5:55–61, 1988.

de Fiebre, C.M., and Collins, A.C. Behavioral desensitization to nicotine is enhanced differentially by ethanol in long-sleep and short-sleep mice. *Alcohol* 6:45–51, 1989.

de Fiebre, C.M., and Collins, A.C. Classic genetic analyses of responses to nicotine and ethanol in crosses derived from long-sleep and short-sleep mice. *J Pharmacol Exp Ther* 261:173–180, 1992.

de Fiebre, C.M., and Collins, A.C. A comparison of the development of tolerance to ethanol and cross-tolerance to nicotine following chronic ethanol treatment in Long-Sleep and Short-Sleep mice. *J Pharmacol Exp Ther* 266:1398–1406, 1993.

de Fiebre, C.M.; Medhurst, L.J.; and Collins, A.C. Nicotine response and nicotinic receptors in long-sleep and short-sleep mice. *Alcohol* 4:493–501, 1987.

de Fiebre, C.M.; Marks, M.J.; and Collins, A.C. Ethanol-nicotine interactions in long-sleep and short-sleep mice. *Alcohol* 7:249–257, 1990.

de Fiebre, C.M.; Romm, E.; Collins, J.; Draski, L.J.; Deitrich, R.A.; and Collins, A.C. Responses to cholinergic agonists of rats selectively bred for differential sensitivity to ethanol. *Alcohol Clin Exp Res* 15:270–276, 1991.

DeFries, J.C.; Wilson, J.R.; Erwin, V.G.; and Petersen, D.R. LS x SS recombinant inbred strains of mice: Initial characterization. *Alcohol Clin Exp Res* 13:196–200, 1989.

Deitrich, R.A.; Spuhler, K.P.; Baker, R.C.; and Erwin, V.G. Development and characteristics of rats selectively bred for sensitivity to ethanol. In: Kuriyama, K.; Takada, A.; and Ishii, H., eds. *Biomedical and Social Aspects of Alcohol and Alcoholism*. New York: Elsevier, 1988. pp. 419–422.

Erwin, V.G., and Jones, B.C. Genetic correlations among ethanol-related behaviors and neurotensin receptors in Long Sleep (LS) x Short Sleep (SS) recombinant inbred strains of mice. *Behav Gen* 23:191–196, 1993.

Erwin, V.G.; Jones, B.C.; and Radcliffe, R. Further characterization of LSxSS recombinant inbred strains of mice: Activating and hypothermic effects of ethanol. *Alcohol Clin Exp Res* 14:200–204, 1990.

Erwin, V.G.; Radcliffe, R.; Hinkle, B.; and Jones, B.C. Genetic-based differences in neurotensin levels and receptors in brains of LS x SS mice. *Peptides* 14:821–828, 1993.

Falconer, D.S. *Introduction to Quantitative Genetics*. 2d ed. London: Longman, 1981.

Forman, S.A.; Righi, D.L.; and Miller, K.W. Ethanol increases agonist affinity for nicotinic receptors from *Torpedo*. *Biochem Biophys Acta* 987:95–103, 1989.

Fraser, D.M.; Louro, S.R.; Horváth, L.I.; Miller, K.W.; and Watts, A. A study of the effect of general anesthetics on lipid-protein interactions in acetylcholine receptor enriched membranes from *Torpedo nobiliana* using nitroxide spin-labels. *Biochemistry* 29:2664–2669, 1990.

Friedman, L.S.; Lichtenstein, E.; and Biglan, A. Smoking onset among teens: An empirical analysis of initial situations. *Addict Behav* 10:1–13, 1985.

Freund, R.K.; Martin, B.J.; Jungschaffer, D.A.; Ullman, E.A.; and Collins, A.C. Genetic differences in plasma corticosterone levels in response to nicotine injection. *Pharmacol Biochem Behav* 30:1059–1064, 1988.

Griffiths, R.R.; Bigelow, G.E.; and Liebson, I. Facilitation of human tobacco self-administration by ethanol: A behavioral analysis. *J Exp Anal Behav* 25:279–292, 1976.

Heath, A.C., and Madden, P.A.F. Genetic influences on smoking behavior. In: Turner, J.R.; Cardon, L.R.; and Hewitt, J.K., eds. *Behavior Genetic Applications in Behavioral Medicine Research*. New York: Plenum Publishing, 1994.

Henningfield, J.E.; Chait, L.D.; and Griffiths, R.R. Cigarette smoking and subjective response in alcoholics: Effects of pentobarbital. *Clin Pharmacol Ther* 33:806–812, 1983.

Henningfield, J.E.; Chait, L.D.; and Griffiths, R.R. Effects of ethanol on cigarette smoking by volunteers without histories of alcoholism. *Psychopharmacology* 82:1–5, 1984.

Hughes, J.R. Treatment of smoking cessation in smokers with past alcohol/drug problems. *J Subst Abuse Treat* 10: 181–187, 1993.

Hughes, J.R. Smoking and alcoholism. In: Cos, J.L., and Hatsukami, D.K., eds. *Behavioral Approaches to Addiction.* Belle Mead, NJ: Cahners Healthcare Communications, 1994. pp. 1–3.

Istvan, J., and Matarazzo, J.D. Tobacco, alcohol and caffeine use: A review of their interrelationships. *Psychol Bull* 95:301, 1984.

Kozlowski, L.T. The role of nicotine in the maintained use of cigarettes. *Drug Merchandizing (Can)* 36–43, 1980.

Kozlowski, L.T.; Jelinek, L.C.; and Pope, M.A. Cigarette smoking among alcohol abusers: A continuing and neglected problem. *Can J Public Health* 77:205–207, 1986.

Luo, Y.; Marks, M.J.; and Collins, A.C. Genotype regulates the development of tolerance to ethanol and cross-tolerance to nicotine. *Alcohol* 11:167–176, 1994.

Markel, P.D.; Fulker, D.W.; Bennett, B.; Corley, R.P.; DeFries, J.; Erwin, V.G.; and Johnson, T.E. Detection of quantitative trait loci for ethanol sensitivity in the LSxSS recombinant inbred strains: An interval-mapping approach. *Behav Gen,* in press.

Marks, M.J.; Romm, E.; Bealer, S.; and Collins, A.C. A test battery for measuring nicotine effects in mice. *Pharmacol Biochem Behav* 23:325–330, 1985.

Marks, M.J.; Romm, E.; Campbell, S.M.; and Collins, A.C. Variation of nicotinic binding sites among inbred strains. *Pharmacol Biochem Behav* 33:679–689, 1989*a*.

Marks, M.J.; Stitzel, J.A.; and Collins, A.C. Genetic influences on nicotine responses. *Pharmacol Biochem Behav* 33: 667–678, 1989*b*.

Marks, M.J.; Pauly, J.R.; Gross, S.D.; Deneris, E.S.; Hermans-Borgmeyer, I.; Heinemann, S.F.; and Collins, A.C. Nicotine binding and nicotinic receptor subunit RNA after chronic nicotine treatment. *J Neurosci* 12:2765–2784, 1992.

McClearn, G.E., and Kakihana R: Selective breeding for ethanol sensitivity: Short-sleep and long-sleep mice. In: McClearn, G.E.; Deitrich, R.A.; and Erwin, V.G., eds. *Development of Animal Models as Pharmacogenetic Tools.* DHHS Publication No. (ADM)81–1133. Washington, DC: Supt. of Docs., U.S. Govt. Print. Off., 1981. pp. 147–159.

McGue, M. Genes, environment, and the etiology of alcoholism. In: Zucker, R.; Boyd, G.; and Howard, J., eds. *The Development of Alcohol Problems: Exploring the Biopsychosocial Matrix of Risk.* National Institute on Alcohol Abuse and Alcoholism Research Monograph 26. NIH Pub No. 94–3495. Rockville, MD: National Institutes of Health, 1993.

Mello, N.K., and Mendelson, J.H. Drinking patterns during work-contingent and noncontingent alcohol acquisition. *Psychosom Med* 34:139–164, 1972.

Mello, N.K.; Mendelson, J.H.; Sellers, M.L.; and Kuehnle, J.C. Effect of alcohol and marihuana on tobacco smoking. *Clin Pharmacol Ther* 27:202–209, 1980.

Mello, N.K.; Mendelson, J.H.; and Palmieri, S.L. Cigarette smoking by women: Interactions with alcohol use. *Psychopharmacology* 93:8–15, 1987.

Miner, L.L., and Collins, A.C. Strain comparison of nicotine-induced seizure sensitivity and nicotinic receptors. *Pharmacol Biochem Behav* 33:469–475, 1989.

National Institute on Alcohol Abuse and Alcoholism. *Eighth Special Report to the U.S. Congress on Alcohol and Health.* NIH Pub. No. 94–3699. Bethesda, MD: National Institutes of Health, 1993.

Phillips, T.J., and Crabbe, J.C., Jr. Behavioral studies of genetic differences in alcohol action. In: Crabbe, J.C., Jr., and Harris, R.A., eds. *The Genetic Basis of Alcohol and Drug Actions.* New York: Plenum Press, 1991. pp. 25–104.

Pomerleau, O.F.; Collins, A.C.; Shiffman, S.; and Pomerleau, C.S. Why some people smoke and others do not: New perspectives. *J Consult Clin Psychol* 61:723–731, 1993.

Sargent, P.B. The diversity of neuronal nicotinic acetylcholine receptors. *Annu Rev Neurosci* 16:403–443, 1993.

Schuckit, M.A.; Li, T.-K.; Cloninger, C.R.; and Deitrich, R.A. Genetics of alcoholism. *Alcohol Clin Exp Res* 9:475–492, 1985.

Shiffman, S. Refining models of dependence: Variations across persons and situations. *Br J Addict* 86:611–615, 1991.

Silverstein, B.; Kelly, E.; Swan, J.; and Kozlowski, L.T. Physiological predisposition toward becoming a cigarette smoker: Evidence for a sex difference. *Addict Behav* 7:83–86, 1982.

U.S. Department of Health and Human Services. *The Health Consequences of Smoking: Nicotine Addiction (1988 Report of the Surgeon General).* Rockville, MD: Public Health Service, Office on Smoking and Health, 1988.

Wood, S.C.; Forman, S.A.; and Miller, K.W. Short chain and long chain alkanols have different sites of action on nicotinic acetylcholine receptor channels from *Torpedo. Mol Pharmacol* 39:332–338, 1991.

Wu, G.; Tonner, P.H.; and Miller, K.W. Ethanol stabilizes the open channel state of the *Torpedo* nicotinic acetylcholine receptor. *Mol Pharmacol* 45:102–108, 1994.

Chapter 8

Neurobiological Interactions of Alcohol and Nicotine

Ovide F. Pomerleau, Ph.D.

There is a natural synergy between nicotine and alcohol use. Smokers are more likely to drink alcohol than nonsmokers; people who drink alcohol are more likely to smoke than nondrinkers. Moreover, heavy smokers drink more than light smokers, and heavy drinkers smoke more than light drinkers (Zacny 1990).

In 1965 over 50 percent of adult males in the United States smoked, but by 1985 the rate had dropped to 33.5 percent. In contrast, smoking rates for outpatient alcoholics (male) exceeded 90 percent in the 1960's and remained nearly the same in the 1980's (Bien and Burge 1990). Recent data from the University of Michigan Alcohol Research Center, which studies geriatric populations, indicate that the discrepancy between alcoholics and normal controls persists over the life span. In a comparison of age-matched cohorts (mean age 60), only 10 percent of the nonalcoholic men were still smoking, but over 60 percent of the alcoholic men continued to smoke (Marks et al. 1994).

The relationship between smoking and drinking is evident, but the neurobiological mechanisms that underlie this phenomenon are not well understood. Among the major possibilities are that one drug increases tolerance to the toxic/aversive effects of the other drug (herein referred to as "cross-tolerance"). Alternatively, one drug may enhance or prolong the reinforcing effects of the other (herein referred to as "cross-reinforcement"). This chapter focuses on what is known about some of these mechanisms

O.F. Pomerleau, Ph.D., is Director of Behavioral Medicine and Professor of Psychology in Psychiatry at the University of Michigan School of Medicine, 475 Market Pl. (Suite L), Ann Arbor, MI 48108.

in order to identify possible explanations for further study in drug interaction paradigms.

CROSS-TOLERANCE

Tolerance can be defined as decreased sensitivity to a given dose of a drug as a result of repeated administration over time or the need for a larger dose to maintain the effect originally obtained (Pomerleau et al. 1993). Tolerance can be divided into two major subtypes: *metabolic tolerance* and *functional tolerance*. Metabolic (pharmacokinetic) tolerance involves accelerated drug elimination (i.e., increased distribution and clearance) as the explanation for diminished effects observed after repeated dosing; functional (pharmacodynamic) tolerance involves loss of sensitivity that occurs even when the contribution of metabolic tolerance can be ruled out. In the case of alcohol and nicotine, the assumption is that the concentration of one drug at the receptor site (estimated in humans by plasma concentration) causes the other drug to have smaller effects as a result of induced changes in the receptor (e.g., decreased sensitivity due to down-regulation).

METABOLIC CROSS-TOLERANCE

One of the reasons for the association of smoking with drinking is that nicotine might increase alcohol metabolism and vice versa. Adir and colleagues (1980) reported that when rats were pretreated with alcohol, plasma nicotine/cotinine levels from nicotine administration were decreased due to increased volume of distribution and clearance. Benowitz and colleagues (1986), however, were unable to demonstrate metabolic cross-tolerance in humans to an extent sufficient to account for increased cigarette smoking during alcohol consumption. In mice, Collins (1990) found that although chronic alcohol and nicotine treatment produced cross-tolerance in a number of response systems, the rate of metabolism was not much altered for either drug. He therefore concluded that individual variability in cross-tolerance was probably mediated by functional (pharmacodynamic) differences involving central nervous system (CNS) sensitivity to alcohol and nicotine.

FUNCTIONAL CROSS-TOLERANCE

The possibility that chronic use of nicotine might decrease some of the effects of alcohol or vice versa, producing compensatory changes in use or dosage, has been examined. Studies by Burch and colleagues (1988) on the effects of chronic nicotine and alcohol exposure in mice are illustrative: predosing with one drug does, in fact, diminish responsivity to the other drug, at least in some response systems. The implications of these observations were examined in a series of studies on receptor function by Collins (1990) and his colleagues. Their research indicates that by disrupting the regulation of brain lipid membranes, alcohol seems to modify nicotine receptor structure and function. Collins also suggested that there may be concordance between some of the gene products that regulate sensitivity to nicotine and those that regulate sensitivity to alcohol; thus, a person who is sensitive to one drug may have heightened reactivity to the other (see chapter 7 of this monograph for a review of this topic).

ARGININE VASOPRESSIN MEDIATION OF ALCOHOL TOLERANCE IN ANIMALS

Hoffman (1982) hypothesized that alcohol tolerance might share certain underlying mechanisms with memory-related processes known to be mediated by neurohypophyseal hormones. Specifically, arginine vasopressin (AVP), the mammalian antidiuretic hormone secreted by the neurohypophysis (posterior pituitary), prolonged the duration of functional tolerance to alcohol well beyond the time when such tolerance dissipated in untreated animals. Tolerance also was maintained by several vasopressin analogs (AVP-related peptides), and Hoffman's findings suggested that maintenance of alcohol tolerance was mediated by direct peptidergic activation in the CNS. Of particular interest was the observation that the peptides implicated inhibited extinction of active and passive avoidance—effects suggesting neuromodulation of memory consolidation. Furthermore, some of the peptides attenuated amnesia caused by various agents, apparently by influencing retrieval or expression of stored information.

The basic procedure used in Hoffman's research involved giving mice a liquid diet laced with alcohol (7 percent v/v) for 7 days. On the morning of the eighth day, administration of a control diet that did not contain alcohol precipitated withdrawal symptoms. On the ninth day, a test dose of alcohol (3.1 g/kg) was administered to determine degree of tolerance to alcohol's hypnotic effects (duration of loss of righting reflex, or "sleep time"). Groups were then given different peptides on the third day of withdrawal. As can be seen in figure 1, subjects that had received AVP (and some closely related peptides) showed clear continuation of tolerance (i.e., continued exhibition of shorter sleep times despite no further exposure to alcohol), compared with saline control subjects, which lost their tolerance to alcohol over the 9 days of nonexposure.

In a review on subsequent research on AVP, Hoffman and colleagues (1990) came to the following conclusions:

1. The effects of AVP on tolerance require intact brain noradrenergic (norepinephrine) and serotonergic (5-hydroxytryptamine [5–HT]) projections.

2. AVP acts on V_1 receptors localized presynaptically on catecholaminergic neuronal terminals (in the mouse lateral septum), suggesting that vasopressin modulates catecholamine release.

3. AVP antagonists (V_1 selective) increase the rate of dissipation of alcohol tolerance.

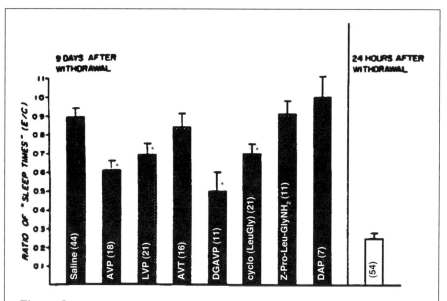

Figure 1. Effect of neurohypophysial hormones, analogs, and related peptides on maintenance of alcohol tolerance in C57BL mice. Values are shown as mean ± SEM of the ratios of sleep time in alcohol-treated mice (E) and their matched controls (C). When the ratio for alcohol-fed mice is less than 1.0, these animals are exhibiting tolerance to alcohol; the ratio approaches 1.0 as tolerance is lost. The number in parentheses is the number of alcohol-fed animals tested. *$p < 0.05$, peptide-treated compared with saline-treated groups (analysis of variance). AVP = [8-arginine]vasopressin; LVP = [8-lysine]vasopressin; AVT = [8-arginine]vasotocin, [Ile³,Arg⁸]vasopressin; DGAVP = [des-9-glycinamide, 8-arginine]vasopressin; Z = benzyloxycarbonyl protecting group; DAP = deamino pressinamide. Reprinted from *Pharmacology, Biochemistry and Behavior*, Volume 17, P.L. Hoffman, "Structural Requirements for Neurohypophyseal Peptide Maintenance of Ethanol Tolerance," pp. 685–690, Copyright 1982, with kind permission from Elsevier Science Ltd, The Boulevard, Langford Lane, Kidlington 0X5 1GB, UK.

4. Brattleboro rats (which lack AVP but are otherwise normal) lose alcohol tolerance much more rapidly than ordinary rats.

5. Hypothalamic vasopressin mRNA—and by implication AVP synthesis—is decreased by chronic alcohol exposure in mice and rats, though the effects on vasopressin levels released into plasma differ in the two species.

6. Plasma AVP levels are increased in alcoholics, though there was a suggestion that the higher AVP levels observed might be a response to the stress of alcohol withdrawal.

Overall, the research suggested that extrahypothalamic vasopressin activity in brain (in septum, hippocampus, etc.) mediates alcohol tolerance and that normal hypothalamic control of AVP release into systemic circulation by the neurohypophysis may be impaired by chronic alcohol exposure.

INDIVIDUAL DIFFERENCES IN ALCOHOL TOLERANCE AND AVP ACTIVITY

Stable strain differences in animals have been studied in an effort to explain behavioral differences in drug response in terms of variations in neuroregulatory activity. For example, Ebel and colleagues (1991) described the effects of chronic alcohol exposure in alcohol-adaptive and nonadaptive mouse lines. The term "alcohol-adaptive" was used to characterize strains that exhibited greater capacity to cope with alcohol intoxication and that showed greater capacity to develop tolerance (evinced by more rapid recovery of the righting reflex after successive exposures to alcohol).

An examination of the brains of alcohol-adaptive mice revealed enhanced hypothalamic synthesis of AVP compared with nonadaptive mice; there was a fivefold increase in AVP mRNA activity in the hypothalamus of the alcohol-adaptive mice even when there was no noticeable enhancement of AVP release into plasma. Compared with nonadaptive mice, the AVP levels of alcohol-adaptive mice were markedly elevated in the amygdala and septum, and Ebel and colleagues (1991) concluded that the ability to handle alcohol intoxication was most likely due to the enhancement of AVP activity in those limbic projection fields, along with greater activity in the serotonergic and noradrenergic systems that regulate AVP in the medial hypothalamus. This study and others like it strongly implicate AVP in alcohol tolerance.

EFFECTS OF NICOTINE ADMINISTRATION ON AVP IN ALCOHOLICS

About 10 years ago, my research group and I attempted to quantitate the effects of nicotine on hypophyseal hormone release (see review by Pomerleau and Rosecrans 1989). The procedure involved comparing the hormonal response to smoking two 0.48-mg nicotine research cigarettes versus two 2.87-mg cigarettes (order of conditions counterbalanced). As can be seen in figure 2, nicotine had a potent effect on hypophyseal hormones. Higher dose levels caused significant elevations in beta-endorphin, adrenocorticotropic hormone, cortisol, AVP, neurophysin (the carrier protein for AVP), growth hormone, and prolactin released into circulation (Seyler et al. 1986).

In nonalcoholic subjects, baseline plasma AVP was 2.7 pg/mL and did not change much after smoking two low-nicotine cigarettes, as can be seen in figure 3. In contrast, the peak AVP response to smoking two high-nicotine cigarettes in a usual manner was 12.1 pg/mL, and the response to smoking two high-nicotine cigarettes intensively was 75 pg/mL (Pomerleau et al. 1983; Seyler et al. 1986). The correlation between peak plasma nicotine and peak AVP levels was 0.985 and highly significant ($p < 0.001$), suggesting a linear dose-response relationship between nicotine and AVP release within the dose range studied.

The same procedure yielded very different results in alcoholic subjects tested after completing 2 weeks of

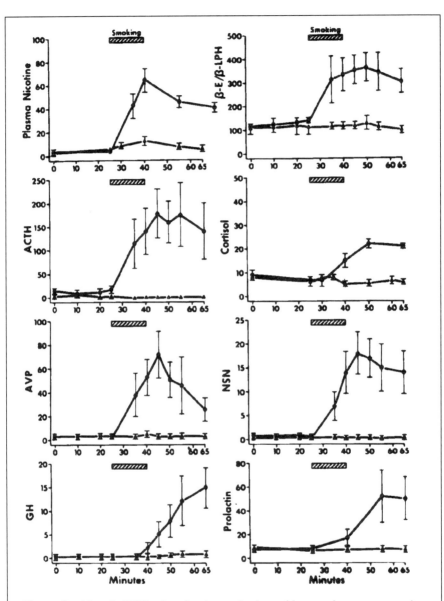

Figure 2. Mean (± SEM) values for plasma nicotine and hormonal responses over time for four subjects; circles indicate the high-nicotine condition and triangles the low-nicotine condition. Units: nicotine in ng/mL; adrenocorticotropic hormone (ACTH) in pg/mL; arginine vasopressin (AVP) in pg/mL; growth hormone (GH) in ng/mL; beta-endorphin/beta-lipotropin (β-E/β-LPH) in pg/Ml; cortisol in μg/dL; neurophysin (NSN) in ng/mL; prolactin in ng/mL. Reprinted from Seyler et al. Pituitary hormone response to cigarette smoking. *Pharmacol Biochem Behav* 24:159–162, 1986.

detoxification. Despite extensive hydration of all subjects to bring AVP to very low baseline levels (all subjects drank 1 L of water just before the session, resulting in urine specific gravity of 1.01), the baseline plasma AVP of alcoholic subjects was twice that of nonalcoholic subjects (approximately 6 pg/mL versus 3 pg/mL). Moreover, compared with nonalcoholic subjects, alcoholic subjects were insensitive to stimulation of AVP by nicotine, achieving only modest boosts in AVP (1–2 pg/mL) and showing no significant relationship between plasma nicotine and AVP. At the time, we considered these findings aberrant and pursued the question no further; now it seems that our observations provide additional support for the hypothesis that chronic, heavy drinking disrupts normal hypothalamic control of AVP, and that the effects persist well beyond alcohol detoxification. Subsequent investigators (e.g., Eisenhofer et al. 1985) also found that AVP baselines are elevated during alcohol withdrawal.

These findings suggest a new explanation for increased smoking during heavy drinking. If heavy drinking blunts the AVP response to normal physiological stimulation, heavy drinkers may use smoking to compensate for disruption of homeostasis by alcohol; thus, nicotine stimulation of AVP is used to lessen the physiological

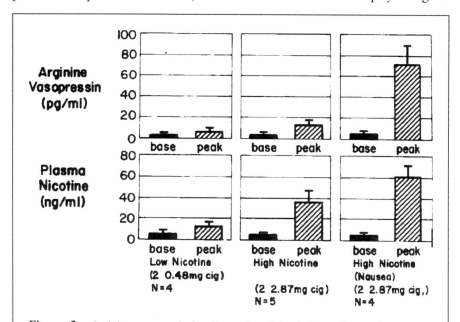

Figure 3. Arginine vasopressin baseline and peak levels in smokers. Adapted from Pomerleau et al. Neuroendocrine reactivity to nicotine in smokers. *Psychopharmacology* 81:61–67, 1983, and Seyler et al. Pituitary hormone response to cigarette smoking. *Pharmacol Biochem Behav* 24:159–162, 1986.

impact of alcohol (e.g., to dampen perturbations in fluid balance) and/or to reduce psychological impairment (e.g., to lessen memory disruption or loss of attentional focus) during heavy drinking. Thus, nicotine may serve to relieve the physiological and behavioral toxicity of alcohol consumption.

CROSS-REINFORCEMENT

ACETALDEHYDE MEDIATION OF REINFORCEMENT FOR ALCOHOL

Acetaldehyde is a major component of alcohol metabolism and a breakdown product of several metabolic pathways—alcohol dehydrogenase, the microsomal ethanol-oxidizing system (MEOS), and the peroxisome H_2O-catalase system (Lieber 1981). Accumulation of large amounts of acetaldehyde in the periphery is extremely toxix—sufficiently so as to constitute the basis for aversion therapy for alcoholism using disulfiram, an aldehyde dehydrogenase inhibitor. At lower concentrations, acetaldehyde may possess positive reinforcing properties; in fact, the reinforcing effects attributed to alcohol may actually be mediated by acetaldehyde modulation of catecholamine metabolism in midbrain structures controlling consummatory activity and reward (Amir et al. 1980).

The reinforcing properties of moderate concentrations of acetaldehyde are well documented. For example, as shown in figure 4, Amit and Smith (1985) found that non-alcohol-dependent animals self-administered acetaldehyde intracerebrally (animals could receive up to 0.5 mg over 5 minutes). Multiple infusions of acetaldehyde resulted in the establishment of a conditioned place preference;[1] furthermore, individual differences in the amount of acetaldehyde self-administered predicted subsequent self-administration of alcohol.

In related research, Takayama and Uyeno (1985) reported that acetaldehyde and alcohol via drinking solution or intravenous infusion maintained self-administration reliably, though acetaldehyde was preferred in a choice situation (figure 5). Acetaldehyde has been estimated to be 10 times as potent as alcohol in maintaining self-administration (Holtzman and Schneider 1974). Brown and colleagues (1983) even showed that inhibition of acetaldehyde metabolism by disulfiram could produce euphoria in humans if the dose of alcohol was kept sufficiently low.

ACETALDEHYDE MEDIATION OF REINFORCEMENT FOR NICOTINE

Acetaldehyde was featured prominently in the news in 1994 as a result of Congressional hearings on cigar-

---

[1] Some drugs, such as psychomotor stimulants or opiates, have potent effects on motor activity, confounding the use of response rate as an indicator of reinforcement value. The place-preference procedure was an attempt to get around this problem (Riecher and Holman 1977). In this procedure, the drug of interest is administered in the same distinctive location each time and, subsequently, when the rate-modulating effects of the drug have worn off, the amount of time the animal spends in that particular location can be calculated.

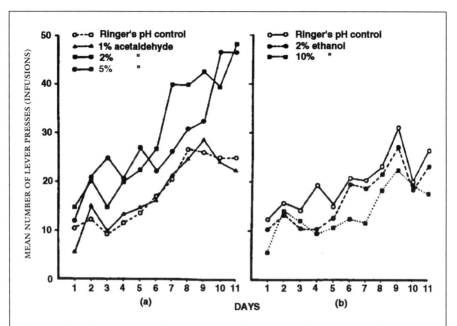

Figure 4. Mean number of lever presses (infusions) over 11 consecutive days for rats receiving (a) acetaldehyde solutions (1%, 2%, or 5% v/v) or the vehicle and (b) rats receiving alcohol (ethanol) solutions (2% or 10% v/v) or the vehicle. Reprinted from *Alcohol*, Volume 2, Z. Amit and B.R. Smith, "A Multi-Dimensional Examination of the Positive Reinforcing Properties of Acetaldehyde," pp. 367–370, Copyright 1985, with kind permission from Elsevier Science Ltd, The Boulevard, Langford Lane, Kidlington 0X5 1GB, UK.

ette manufacturing (e.g., *New York Times*, Friday, April 29, 1994). During testimony before Congress, Victor DeNoble, a former tobacco company scientist, described unpublished research that he had conducted more than 10 years earlier showing that acetaldehyde (8 µg/kg) potentiated self-administration of nicotine in rats by a factor of 3 (Raloff 1994). He stated that he had been interested in the biobehavioral effects of acetaldehyde (a pyrolysis product of tobacco), but that his research was abruptly terminated when his em-ployer concluded that there might be some potential for increased product liability. DeNoble's testimony and disclosure that up to 1.4 mg of acetaldehyde was available in inhaled smoke from a standard cigarette fueled considerable speculation that acetaldehyde might serve as a second psychoactive ingredient in cigarette smoking—that it might insidiously strengthen the habit by potentiating nicotine reinforcement.

As noted by Kitson (1978), however, inhaling 1.4 mg of acetaldehyde into the lungs does not guarantee

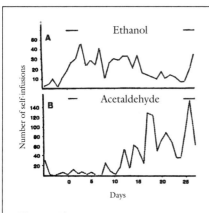

Figure 5. Typical daily patterns of intravenous self-infusion of (A) 18 μM/kg/infusion of alcohol (ethanol) or (B) 6 μM/kg/infusion of acetaldehyde. μM = micromolar. The number of self-infusions is presented as the daily number of lever pressings to activate the self-administration system during 24 hours. The rats were allowed to self-administer alcohol or acetaldehyde solution for 27 days following 5 successive days of saline self-infusion. Reprinted with permission from Takayama, S., and Uyeno, E.T. Intravenous self-administration of ethanol and acetaldehyde by rats. *Japanese Journal of Psychopharmacology* 5:331, 1985.

delivery into systemic circulation. He estimated that acetaldehyde accumulation from smoking was actually less than that produced continuously by microbial fermentation in the gastrointestinal tract. Recent empirical studies corroborate this, showing that smoking causes transient increases in breath acetaldehyde without detectable changes in blood acetaldehyde levels (McLaughlin et al. 1990); the findings suggest rapid excretion of acetaldehyde involving mechanisms such as breath exhalation and active pulmonary metabolism (von Wartburg 1980). The critical point is that, if levels of acetaldehyde from cigarette smoking are low in systemic circulation, brain concentrations will also be low. The amount of acetaldehyde generated by cigarette smoking in isolation seems too low to contribute much to the reinforcement of smoking; on the other hand, if DeNoble's observations are correct, acetaldehyde generated by drinking alcohol could contribute to smoking by potentiating reinforcement for nicotine self-administration.

INDIVIDUAL DIFFERENCES IN BRAIN-REWARD RESPONSES TO ALCOHOL AND NICOTINE

A final set of observations on reinforcement potentiation is worth noting. Fadda and colleagues (1991) compared the effects of alcohol in alcohol-preferring and nonpreferring lines of rats 60 minutes after dosing. They found significant increases in concentration of the dopamine metabolites (dihydroxyphenylacetic acid and homovanillic acid) in the caudate nucleus, olfactory tubercle, and medial prefrontal cortex in alcohol-preferring rats but not in nonpreferring rats. The finding of heritable differences in the sensitivity of the dopamine response to alcohol corresponding to alcohol preference is significant, for it involves the brain-reward pathways shown to mediate reinforcement for various drugs of abuse, including nicotine (Wise and Bozarth 1987). Similar observations have been made by McBride and colleagues (1990), who noted that acute

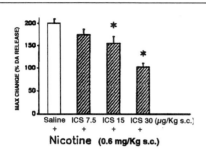

Figure 6. Effect of different doses of ICS 205–930 (7.5, 15, and 30 µg/kg subcutaneously [SC]) on the in vivo release of dopamine from the nucleus accumbens induced by nicotine (0.6 mg/kg SC). Each column represents the mean ± SEM peak response based on the results from four experiments. *$p < 0.05$, compared with saline + nicotine. Reprinted from *European Journal of Pharmacology*, Volume 164, E. Carboni, E. Acquas, R. Frau, and G. Di Chiara, "Differential Inhibitory Effects of a 5-HT$_3$ Antagonist on Drug-Induced Stimulation of Dopamine Release," pp. 515–519, Copyright 1989, with kind permission from Elsevier Science Ltd, The Boulevard, Langford Lane, Kidlington 0X5 1GB, UK.

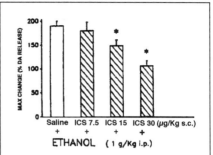

Figure 7. Effect of different doses of ICS 205–930 (7.5, 15, and 30 µg/kg subcutaneously) on the in vivo release of dopamine from the nucleus accumbens induced by alcohol (ethanol) (1 g/kg intraperitoneally). Each column represents the mean ± SEM peak response based on the results from four experiments. *$p < 0.05$, compared with saline + nicotine. Reprinted from *European Journal of Pharmacology*, Volume 164, E. Carboni, E. Acquas, R. Frau, and G. Di Chiara, "Differential Inhibitory Effects of a 5-HT$_3$ Antagonist on Drug-Induced Stimulation of Dopamine Release," pp. 515–519, Copyright 1989, with kind permission from Elsevier Science Ltd, The Boulevard, Langford Lane, Kidlington 0X5 1GB, UK.

administration of alcohol increased the activity in 5–HT and dopamine projections to the nucleus accumbens in alcohol-preferring rats; chronic administration produced tolerance in the 5–HT and dopamine response, providing a plausible explanation for the high alcohol consumption of alcohol-preferring rats.

Blockade of drug-stimulated dopamine activity in the nucleus accumbens of rats by a 5–HT$_3$ antagonist, ICS 205–930, has been used to demonstrate a remarkable symmetry between nicotine and alcohol (Carboni et al.

1989), as shown in figures 6 and 7. Prevention of drug-induced stimulation of dopamine activity caused a diminution of the manifestations of drug reinforcement, including loss of the place-preference response. The similarity of the dopamine response for nicotine and alcohol supports the possibility of common brain-reward pathways by which nicotine might enhance reinforcement for alcohol, and alcohol for nicotine. Potentiation of dopamine activity is common to a number of drugs with abuse potential, however, suggesting that this mechanism for mutual induction may not be specific to nicotine and alcohol.

SUMMARY AND CONCLUSIONS

This brief examination of neurobiological interactions of nicotine with alcohol has focused on cross-tolerance and cross-reinforcement as mechanisms to explain mutual induction. Thus, expression of gene products that regulate functional sensitivity by either drug may cause shifts in tolerance that cause compensatory increases in self-administration of the other. Heavy alcohol drinking may also engender smoking because nicotine, by stimulating central peptides such as AVP, dampens some of the physiological and behavioral toxicity of inebriation, providing temporary avoidance or escape. Acetaldehyde generated by alcohol consumption may potentiate nicotine self-administration by acting on the midbrain structures that mediate consummatory activity and reward. Finally, nicotine and alcohol may have additive effects on dopamine brain-reward pathways, allowing the administration of one drug to enhance the reinforcing value of the other.

Some caveats are in order. First, the critical experiments needed to show that a given mechanism is *necessary* for drug induction have not been carried out. Second, fundamental relationships are still sketchy; for example, there is no quantitative information available on how an increase in tolerance caused by one drug might translate into changes in reinforcement

value and self-administration of another drug. Third, the list of possible mechanisms presented in this chapter is by no means exhaustive and was extracted from a research literature that is haphazard. Fourth, the degree of symmetry that may exist among mediators of mutual induction is unknown, nor is it possible to determine the relative contribution of the different mechanisms identified to date. The latter is troublesome because the mechanisms are not mutually exclusive. Fifth, there have been no parametric explorations of the effects of different dose combinations of nicotine and alcohol on putative mechanisms, nor has previous history of exposure been adequately taken into account; in addition, there is little information on how individual differences in drug metabolism or in neuroregulatory activity might influence susceptibility to induction of self-administration of one drug by the other. Though the mechanisms proposed here do have some empirical support, they should be considered provisional as explanations until the findings are more definitive.

RECOMMENDATIONS

Drugs like nicotine and alcohol have profound effects on neuroregulatory activity, but as already indicated, not much is known about the interactions of different neurobiological systems. A major opportunity may come from the availability of new tools for studying individual differences in humans and animals; behavioral and molecular genetics may provide the methodology needed to link variations in behavior to demonstrable differences in neuroregulatory activity. The rationale for selecting individuals with differences in behavioral or physiological responsivity is simply that their CNS—the aggregate of receptors, pathways, and neuroregulatory products—may vary in ways that can now be determined.

Approaches that involve the induction of intake of one drug by another show promise as a tool for obtaining useful information. For example, paradigms for testing the effects of alcohol and nicotine, comparing responses to the two in combination with responses to each alone, may provide new opportunities for elucidating biobehavioral mechanisms. The similarities that emerge between the drugs should help identify common pathways that are critical and necessary for the development of dependence; differences between the drugs should lead to a better appreciation of the unique properties of each substance and of the specific neuroregulatory patterns needed to support drug self-administration.

Finally, the elucidation of critical factors that contribute to combined alcohol and nicotine use may make it possible to identify individuals who are particularly susceptible to both drugs. Building on findings that might devolve from the basic research described above, tailored interventions might result. The neurobiological patterns that put the individual at special risk could be taken into account and modified accordingly.

REFERENCES

Adir, J.; Wildfeuer, W.; and Miller, R.P. Effect of ethanol pretreatment on the pharmacokinetics of nicotine in rats. *J Pharmacol Exp Ther* 212:274–279, 1980.

Amir, S.; Brown, Z.; and Amit, Z. The role of acetaldehyde in the psychopharmacological effects of ethanol. In: Rigter, H., and Crabbe, J.C., eds. *Alcohol Tolerance and Dependence.* New York: Oxford, 1980. pp. 317–337.

Amit, Z., and Smith, B.R. A multidimensional examination of the positive reinforcing properties of acetaldehyde. *Alcohol* 2:367–370, 1985.

Benowitz, N.L.; Jones, R.T.; and Jacob, P. Additive cardiovascular effects of nicotine and ethanol. *Clin Pharmacol Ther* 40: 420–424, 1986.

Bien, T.H., and Burge, R. Smoking and drinking: A review of the literature. *Int J Addict* 25:1449–1454, 1990.

Brown, Z.W.; Amit, Z.; Smith, B.R.; Sutherland, E.A.; and Selvaggi, N. Alcohol-induced euphoria enhanced by disulfiram and calcium carbamide. *Alcohol Clin Exp Res* 7:276–278, 1983.

Burch, J.B.; de Fiebre, C.M.; Marks, M.J; and Collins, A.C. Chronic ethanol or nicotine treatment results in partial cross tolerance between these agents. *Psychopharmacology* 95:452–458, 1988.

Carboni, E.; Acquas, E.; Frau, R.; and Di Chiara, G. Differential inhibitory effects of a 5–HT_3 antagonist on drug-induced stimulation of dopamine release. *Eur J Pharmacol* 164:515–519, 1989.

Collins, A.C. Interactions of ethanol and nicotine at the receptor level. In: Galanter, M., ed. *Recent Developments in Alcoholism: Volume 8. Combined Alcohol and Other Drug Dependence.* New York: Plenum Press, 1990. pp. 221–231.

Ebel, A.; Strosser, M.T; Felix, M.; Kempf, J.; and Kempf, E. Are chronic alcohol-induced central vasopressin changes determinant in strain dependency of tolerance in mice? *Alcohol Alcohol Suppl* 1:207–210, 1991.

Eisenhofer, G.; Lambie, D.G.; Whiteside, E.A; and Johnson, R.H. Vasopressin concentrations during alcohol withdrawal. *Br J Addict* 80:195–199, 1985.

Fadda, F.; Colombo, G.; and Gessa, G.L. Genetic sensitivity to effect of ethanol on dopaminergic system in alcohol preferring rats. *Alcohol Alcohol Suppl* 1:439–442, 1991.

Hoffman, P.L. Structural requirements for neurohypophyseal peptide maintenance of ethanol tolerance. *Pharmacol Biochem Behav* 17:685–690, 1982.

Hoffman, P.L.; Ishizawa, H.; Giri, P.R.; Dave, J.R.; Grant, K.A.; Liu, L.-I.; and Tabakoff, B. The role of arginine vasopressin in alcohol tolerance. *Ann Med* 22:269–274, 1990.

Holtzman, S.G., and Schneider, F.H. Comparison of acetaldehyde and ethanol: Depression of motor activity in mice. *Life Sci* 14:1143–1250, 1974.

Kitson, T.M. Letter to the editor. *Alcohol Clin Exp Res* 2:396–398, 1978.

Lieber, C.S. Metabolic effects of ethanol on the liver and other digestive organs. In: Leevy, C.M., ed. *Clinics in Gastroenterology.* Vol. X. London: Saunders, 1981. p. 227.

Marks, J.L.; Hill, E.M.; Pomerleau, C.S.; Mudd, S.A.; and Blow, F.S. DSM–III–R tobacco dependence in male alcoholic and non-alcoholic ex-smokers. *Ann Behav Med* 16:S113 (abstract), 1994.

McBride, W.J.; Murphy, J.M.; Lumeng, L.; and Li, T.K. Serotonin, dopamine and GABA involvement in alcohol drinking of selectively bred rats. *Alcohol* 7:199–205, 1990.

McLaughlin, S.D.; Scott, B.K.; and Peterson, C.M. The effect of cigarette smoking on breath and whole blood-associated acetaldehyde. *Alcohol* 7:285–287, 1990.

Pomerleau, O.F., and Rosecrans, J. Neuroregulatory effects of nicotine. *Psychoneuroendocrinology* 14:407–423, 1989.

Pomerleau, O.F.; Fertig, J.B.; Seyler, L.E.; and Jaffe, J. Neuroendocrine reactivity to nicotine in smokers. *Psychopharmacology* 81:61–67, 1983.

Pomerleau, O.F.; Collins, A.C.; Shiffman, S.; and Pomerleau, C.S. Why some people smoke and others do not: New perspectives. *J Consult Clin Psychol* 61:723–731, 1993.

Raloff, J. Cigarettes: Are they doubly addictive? *Sci News* 145:294, 1994.

Riecher, M.A., and Holman, E.W. Location preference and flavor aversion reinforced by amphetamine in rats. *Anim Learn Behav* 5:343–346, 1977.

Seyler, L.E.; Pomerleau, O.F.; Fertig, J.B.; Hunt, D.; and Parker, K. Pituitary hormone response to cigarette smoking. *Pharmacol Biochem Behav* 24:159–162, 1986.

Takayama, S., and Uyeno, E.T. Intravenous self-administration of ethanol and acetaldehyde by rats. *Jpn J Psychopharmacol* 5:329–334, 1985.

von Wartburg, J.P. Acetaldehyde. In: Sandler, M., ed. *Psychopharmacology of Alcohol.* New York: Raven Press, 1980. pp. 137–147.

Wise, R., and Bozarth, M.A. A psychomotor stimulant theory of addiction. *Psychol Rev* 94:469–492, 1987.

Zacny, J.P. Behavioral aspects of alcohol-tobacco interactions. In: Galanter, M., ed. *Recent Developments in Alcoholism: Volume 8. Combined Alcohol and Other Drug Dependence.* New York: Plenum Press, 1990. pp. 205–219.

Chapter 9

Overview of Section I: Psychosocial and Biological Mechanisms

Raymond Niaura, Ph.D., and Saul Shiffman, Ph.D.

Smoking creates an unnatural thirst, and leads to the use of spiritous liquors. I will not vouch for the truth of the common observation, that great smokers are generally tipplers. They appear to be however different strands of the same rope.
—*Benjamin Waterhouse, M.D.*
Cambridge, MA, 1804

The links between use of alcohol and use of tobacco are multiple and complex. Epidemiological studies have established their association in terms of levels of use, abuse, and dependence. Heavy drinkers tend to be heavy smokers and vice versa. There are developmental links, with the two substances initiated in relative proximity, and often in a particular sequence. Clinical studies suggest that alcoholics are much more likely to smoke than their nonalcoholic counterparts. Experimental studies have established that consumption of alcohol provokes more vigorous smoking. Studies of twins suggest genetic involvement in the covariation between use of alcohol and use of tobacco. Animal studies point to activation of common neurobiological mechanisms that mediate reward. There are also numerous theoretical links between alcohol consumption and smoking.

Although the links between alcohol and tobacco use are many, satisfactory explanations for their association are few. This is due, in part, to the long neglect of the covariation between

R. Niaura, Ph.D., is associate professor of psychiatry at Brown University School of Medicine and in the Division of Behavioral Medicine, The Miriam Hospital, 164 Summit Avenue, Providence, RI 02906. S. Shiffman, Ph.D., is professor in the Department of Clini-cal Psychology, University of Pittsburgh, 604 Old Engineering Hall, 4015 O'Hara Street, Pittsburgh, PA 15213.

use of alcohol and tobacco and also, in part, to the complexity of the phenomenon. It is unlikely that a single explanation will be found; rather, multiple levels of explanation are likely to be required to reach a comprehensive understanding of the association between the two drugs.

GENETIC INFLUENCES

Studies of both male and female human twins (see chapters 4 and 5) underscore the substantial heritability for liability to use alcohol or tobacco. More specifically, genetically mediated characteristics significantly influence use of alcohol or tobacco. However, different findings are obtained when the covariation in the use of both drugs is considered. Among men, genetic mechanisms continue to explain a substantial degree of covariation, whereas among women the genetic contribution is more modest and is matched by the influence of shared environmental factors. Specific environmental factors also play a prominent role in affecting the joint use of alcohol and tobacco among men.

These findings emphasize the need to consider gender differences and similarities in explaining liability to use both alcohol and tobacco, but they also suggest that other differences, including ethnicity, should be considered. Sophisticated genetic statistical modeling techniques are available to test explicitly whether various study populations differ in how genetic and environmental factors influence covariation separately in alcohol and tobacco

use, but these techniques have not been applied to the study of covariation between alcohol and tobacco use. The fact that gender moderates genetic influences on alcohol and tobacco use suggests that other individual differences (e.g., personality or psychiatric comorbidity) may also act as moderators and thus muddy the observed relationships in studies that do not take moderators into account.

Interpretation of genetic studies may be helped or hindered depending on the degree to which outcome measures are clearly specified, relevant, and similar across studies. For example, alcohol, tobacco, and other drug (ATOD) use may be characterized by some sort of quantity/frequency index, but this may tell us little about dependence-related processes. Measures of dependence and diagnostic criteria also vary from study to study, and this may be responsible for different results. There needs to be an integration of data on psychiatric diagnosis, ATOD dependence, and patterns of ATOD use if we are to reach some understanding of the complexity of genetic and environmental influences on the developmental trajectory spanning initial use, regular use, persistence, escalation, development of dependence, cessation, and relapse. This is a significant challenge when studying just one drug, and the task is particularly daunting when two or more drugs are considered.

Another issue relates to the range of ATOD use/abuse that is studied. For example, inclusion or exclusion of nonusers may profoundly affect results of statistical analyses and corresponding interpretation of the results. The problem here is that one cannot be sure why someone is not using either alcohol or tobacco. For example, are nonusers those for whom the drug has little appeal, or are nonusers abstaining because they recognize their potential for developing dependence on alcohol or tobacco? Further, some individuals may have become nonusers because they sampled tobacco or alcohol, found it unappealing, and abandoned its use; others may be nonusers because they never tried tobacco or alcohol, perhaps due to limited access or social restrictions on experimentation. Some individuals in the latter group may be inclined to use, abuse, or dependence but have never had the opportunity to express this inclination.

Levels of inquiry must also be integrated in comprehensive studies. For example, developmental twin studies should include measures of sociocultural, psychological, physiological, and molecular genetic factors. Only in this way will it be possible to map specific pathways describing, for example, how gene and environment affect behavior separately and interactively. However, this sort of integration is complicated by its scope, cost, and myriad choice of variables upon which to focus. Less ambitious efforts to integrate levels of inquiry are underway, for example, by including measures of personality in developmental twin studies that focus upon ATOD use, but more can be done.

This is best accomplished by communication among investigators representing various disciplines.

Data on genetic influences also point up the need to understand effects of environmental influences; these environmental influences often account for as much covariation in alcohol and tobacco use as do genetic mechanisms. Shared and unique environmental events and forces are poorly understood in studies of genetic influences. It is here that sociocultural and psychological theories of drug use can inform genetic studies. More attention must be paid to family and peer influences and to the social-environmental matrix to which individuals are exposed, and through which they must attempt to find their way and cope effectively. Individuals react differently to the life stresses and strains they encounter; some are resilient, others quickly succumb, and others vary in how they meet life's demands. Our goal should be to understand how environment and genes express healthy as well as abnormal behaviors.

The implications of genetic research for developing interventions are also complex. It is possible to envision development of gene therapies, but complex drug use behaviors (not to mention their covariation) are probably under polygenic control and not subject to simple interventions. Moreover, the genetic studies themselves illustrate the importance of environmental determinants, suggesting further avenues for interventions. It is also important to distinguish between risk and realization of risk. For example, even if covariation in alcohol and tobacco use was 100 percent genetic, environmental interventions, such as limiting access to these drugs, could work. Thus, recognition of genetic influences on alcohol and tobacco use should not limit our attempts to implement behavioral and policy interventions.

We should recognize that to discover that a phenomenon has a genetic origin is not to have achieved an understanding of its causes and mechanisms. In the end, genetic studies of the alcohol-tobacco link may be most fruitful in helping us understand the physiological (and, perhaps, behavioral) mechanisms that underlie the association. Several speculative biological mechanisms have been proposed (see chapters 2, 7, and 8), but none of them are well supported by evidence. Research that addresses these mechanisms is of the greatest importance.

The potential association of smoking and drinking with other variables, such as psychiatric comorbidity, deserves mention. Here we must evaluate our theoretical models concerning the cause of the association between alcohol and tobacco use. For example, is there reciprocal causation, with one drug clearly provoking use of the other and vice versa? Is there a common cause, some third variable, which influences the covariation between smoking and drinking? As of yet, there are no good answers to these questions, although there is some evidence from experimental and genetic studies to support both inter-

pretations. Epidemiological studies have established strong links between smoking and major depression on the one hand, and between drinking and major depression on the other. Studies have also shown that the covariation between smoking or nicotine dependence and major depression results in large part from a genetic influence that predisposes toward both conditions. No studies have examined the relative contribution of genetic and environmental factors to the co-occurrence of depression and use of alcohol and tobacco.

To state the obvious, genetic studies aim to explain some of the differences among individuals. Thus, genetics may account for some of the between-person covariation in drinking and smoking. It cannot easily explain their situational covariation. Given the robust situational linkage between drinking and smoking, genetics will necessarily leave much to be explained.

NEUROBIOLOGICAL MECHANISMS

Neurobiological mechanisms that could account for the covariation in use of alcohol and tobacco are diverse. Most explanations, though, fall into two general categories: cross-tolerance and cross-reinforcement.

Cross-tolerance could develop for both the rewarding and aversive effects of alcohol and nicotine. Thus, perhaps the drinker learns that nicotine can be consumed at a faster rate when drinking because nicotine's ill effects are somewhat blunted. However, cross-tolerance to rewarding effects would reinforce consumption of each drug to reestablish the desired effects. Smoking-induced increases in brain peptides such as arginine vasopressin may potentiate alcohol tolerance, thus potentiating alcohol consumption. The heavy drinker may also smoke to increase arginine vasopressin, to compensate for undesirable behavioral and physiological effects of alcohol. There is also preliminary evidence suggesting that alcohol may desensitize some areas of the brain responsible for mediating the rewarding effects of nicotine. Thus, alcohol consumption could provoke more intense smoking to reestablish nicotine's reinforcing effects. Note that the relationships between these neurobiological mechanisms and drug seeking are not well established: both blockade and synergistic activation can be used to explain either increased or decreased drug seeking. It should be noted, too, that neuromolecular mechanisms that could account for cross-tolerance between alcohol and nicotine have not been firmly established.

Cross-reinforcement refers to the potential for one drug to enhance or prolong the effects of another. Although this is a well-documented phenomenon, research has not focused intensively on exploring specific pharmacological mechanisms whereby alcohol could increase the rewarding effects of nicotine and vice versa. Acetaldehyde mediation of reinforcement for both alcohol and

nicotine is an intriguing hypothesis that currently is supported by circumstantial evidence. It is unlikely, however, that acetaldehyde generated by cigarette smoking would reinforce or potentiate alcohol consumption, because the amounts absorbed seem so low as to be physiologically meaningless. However, drinking alcohol would raise acetaldehyde sufficiently so as to potentiate reinforcement for nicotine self-administration. This theory would also explain the seeming but as yet unproved (in humans) lack of symmetry in the effects of one drug on the level of consumption of the other; it appears that alcohol is a more powerful stimulus for smoking than vice versa.

Cross-reinforcement could occur because the drugs have additive or synergistic effects on areas of the brain that mediate reinforcement and reward. One drug may also increase sensitivity to the effects of the other. An enormous amount of animal experimentation has gone into characterizing similarities among all drugs of abuse in their actions on certain brain areas that are known to be vitally involved in pleasure, reward, and motivation to consume drugs. Most, if not all, drugs of abuse activate dopaminergic neurotransmission in the ventral tegmental area of the brain. It is therefore conceivable that the actions of one drug on this neural system somehow sensitizes it to reinforcement from the other. Moreover, the individual who is sensitive to one drug may have heightened reactivity to the other by virtue of activation of a common neural circuit. Animals differ in sensitivity of this brain system to effects of alcohol and nicotine, and these individual differences may explain, in part, abuse potential. For example, high initial sensitivity to the effects of alcohol and nicotine, coupled with development of tolerance to the aversive effects of each substance, could explain escalation and persistence of drug self-administration. A key research strategy will be to contrast individuals who are similar and different in sensitivity to alcohol and nicotine effects on behavioral, physiological, and neurophysiological responses, to better understand common mechanisms that may explain the covariation between consumption of alcohol and nicotine.

Evaluation of cross-tolerance and cross-reinforcement mechanisms must consider the longevity of these effects. Some mechanisms imply longstanding changes in individual pharmacodynamics or kinetics, which could help explain why a person who uses alcohol may be predisposed to smoke (though not necessarily while drinking). In contrast, other mechanisms imply acute synergistic effects (whether via acetaldehyde or other mediators), which can help explain why alcohol and tobacco are used at the same time. It is possible that different mechanisms will be needed to explain the enduring person-level association between drinking and smoking and the acute situational linkage between the two.

Many of these cross-tolerance and cross-reinforcement mechanisms (e.g., involving final common pathways in the brain) may also apply to other psychoactive drugs besides alcohol and tobacco. Thus, the relationship between alcohol and tobacco may be best explored in the context of a larger nexus of drug use and abuse.

Because of the ability to breed and isolate strains and lines of animals selectively to express different sensitivities to particular drug effects, animal research is much more advanced than human research with respect to exploring the neurobiological mechanisms involved in explaining sensitivity to drug effects and subsequent self-administration. This research, while supporting the notion of activation of common neural substrates by various drugs of abuse, also suggests caution in embracing this as a simple explanation for addiction and cross-addiction. The neural circuitry underlying drug effects is complex and involves simultaneous activation of several mechanisms. There are different sites of action for different drug effects, and drug sensitivity is not unidimensional as it is expressed in physiological and behavioral changes. Different neural circuits may underlie development of tolerance to drug effects, motivation to seek and use drugs, and rewarding or pleasurable effects of drugs. Drugs may activate these circuits to varying degrees. Thus, differences in drug effects should not be ignored in explaining covariation, or lack thereof, in their use. To complicate matters, the evidence is mixed concerning genetic regulation of initial sensitivity to alcohol and nicotine. More rigorous studies have failed to support the notion that there is overlap in genetic regulation of sensitivity to alcohol and nicotine, although it should be emphasized that only a small sample of behavioral and physiological measures of sensitivity have thus far been investigated.

The contribution of learning factors to the simultaneous use of alcohol and tobacco should not be ignored. If psychoactive drugs of abuse potential share the ability to enhance mesotelencephalic dopamine neurotransmission, then what are the psychological functions of this system? The mesotelencephalic dopamine system is thought to mediate reward. Another, perhaps more important, function of this system is to attribute incentive salience to stimuli associated with activation of this system, thus making these stimuli attractive and wanted. From the point of view of associative learning, as the pairing between drug use and stimulation of dopaminergic neurotransmission becomes stronger, the drug will increasingly become sought after. And as the individual tries other drugs and learns that they produce similar effects in terms of increasing dopaminergic neurotransmission, then these drugs become associatively connected with the other drugs the individual has come to use habitually. Thus, for example, as alcohol use and smoking become intertwined, one should provoke use of the other because incentive salience for the drugs, and all of the stimuli surrounding use of the drugs, is interchangeable.

However, there may be a problem with this interpretation. There is strong evidence that drinking alcohol provokes smoking, but there is little evidence to suggest that smoking provokes drinking. There is also some evidence to suggest that use of other psychoactive drugs such as opiates or stimulants provokes smoking, but it is unclear whether smoking provokes use of these other drugs. This may reflect the degree to which each drug increases dopaminergic activity. For example, alcohol might increase dopaminergic activity to a substantially greater degree than smoking a few cigarettes. Once the activity of the neural system is entrained by alcohol, cigarettes become increasingly wanted, especially if they are readily available. In contrast, smoking may not sufficiently activate the system to immediately increase the incentive salience of alcohol-related stimuli, which may also be less readily available. It may also be true that smoking may increase the incentive salience of other drugs, but the addict is able to restrain drug-seeking behavior until it is more appropriate, for example, by going to a bar after work or going home to smoke and drink.

There is accumulating evidence that, for some individuals, repeated use of drugs renders the system hypersensitive to drugs and drug-related stimuli. The basic idea is that use of the drug will stimulate increased desire for the drug, subject to certain physical and physiological constraints (e.g., running out of the drug, getting arrested, lapsing into stupor, or becoming ill).

But what is really sought after is increased priming of dopamine neurotransmission, which can also be accomplished by simultaneous use of another drug, such as nicotine. In fact, with nicotine, this effect can be more finely titrated than with alcohol, and it is probably more rapid. In addition, as noted earlier, alcohol and nicotine may have complementary effects.

Sensitization to drug effects may be permanent or at least very long-lived. This suggests the possibility that, even in the abstinent individual, risk for return to drug use and abuse is always present, and that use of one drug may incur relapse to use of the other. Researchers are only now beginning to investigate whether, for example, continued smoking among abstinent alcoholics contributes to risk of alcohol relapse. Several studies suggest that mesotelencephalic dopaminergic neurotransmission can also be primed by stress and negative affect, which then, by virtue of associative learning processes, come to elicit drug seeking. This may, in part, explain some of the interrelationships among alcohol, nicotine, and negative affect. One key issue will be the ability to identify individuals who are vulnerable to increasing sensitivity to dopaminergic drug effects. Is this predisposition inherited or acquired? Is this brain lesion or abnormality functionally relevant to species survival? What are other psychological and behavioral correlates of this abnormality?

It is also tempting to speculate about how some aspects of brain circuitry relevant to drug use map onto psychological constructs. Borrowing from the work of Jeffrey Gray, it appears there are two brain circuits responsible for mediating motivation and inhibition of behavior in general. These are the behavioral activation and behavioral inhibition systems, which are thought to be somewhat mutually inhibitory, but not entirely so. These systems can be characterized in terms of incentive salience, negative affectivity, and the personality dimensions of extroversion and neuroticism, and attention to some of these constructs may also help to explain the use of multiple drugs. For example, smokers tend to be extroverts and neurotics, but different drugs may have different reinforcing consequences depending on one's personality predisposition, which is again tied directly to an inherited set of neural circuitry. So there are probably distinct subgroups of alcohol drinkers and smokers, and, of those who smoke and drink, there may exist predisposing brain circuitry and personality factors that determine the effects of these drugs and their co-occurrence. There may be a cluster of smokers and drinkers for whom both alcohol and nicotine are having similar effects on behavioral activation circuitry. There may also be a cluster for whom both drugs have similar effects on the behavioral inhibition system.

Finally, it should be noted that the exploration of neurobiological mechanisms to explain the covariation in alcohol and tobacco use is still in its infancy. Although some promising leads have been developed, the complexity of studying drug-brain-behavior relationships is daunting. Continued progress will depend on supporting behavioral, physiological, and pharmacological studies in both humans and animals and will rely to a large degree on advances in molecular biological and genetic technology.

SOCIOCULTURAL AND PSYCHOLOGICAL INFLUENCES

Sociocultural and psychological theories point up the importance of the developmental perspective. Both alcohol and tobacco are first sampled early in life. Despite almost universal experimentation with tobacco and alcohol, only a subset of individuals go on to continued use or develop dependence. Of those who do, most use both alcohol and tobacco.

The risk factor approach to understanding use of alcohol and tobacco focuses on those biological, psychological, and social factors that increase vulnerability to drug abuse and dependence. However, risk factors are expressed in a dynamic and reciprocally interacting developmental matrix. For example, biological predispositions to react to and cope with social, environmental, and developmental demands in particular ways will determine, to some extent, how well these demands are met. Predispositions interacting with environmental forces will determine how both adaptive and problem behaviors are expressed. Individuals learn that drugs will help them to meet certain life demands, or at least to cope with them, reinforcing their continued use. However, family, peer, and other cultural factors will impinge on this process and will, to varying degrees, determine subsequent drug-taking behaviors.

The stress-coping model posits that alcohol and tobacco serve coping functions that assist in regulation of emotion and experience. Life stress and coping factors may be particularly important for a subgroup of adolescents who are highly vulnerable to use both alcohol and tobacco. Studies have noted striking similarities in motives to use alcohol and tobacco and in situations where both are used. In addition, there appear to be complementary motives for alcohol and tobacco use. Patterns of coping motives mirror actual patterns of alcohol and tobacco use in adolescents. Therefore, perceived stress and coping responses may help to explain epidemiological differences in patterns of drug use (e.g., gender and ethnic differences). However, that stress and coping variables help explain both alcohol and tobacco use does not necessarily imply that they explain the link between the two drugs. Studies of stress and coping should specifically address the joint use of tobacco and alcohol, rather than analyzing each in parallel.

Although perceived stress and coping functions may explain much about use of alcohol and tobacco, the contribution of other perspctives cannot be ignored. For example, alcohol and tobacco use may be part of a constellation of other problem behaviors that manifest themselves in adolescence. Studies of adolescents have found links between depression and smoking and alcohol use, mirroring findings in adult populations and suggesting that these links are established early in life. Stress and coping and related drug use fluctuate over time according to prevailing social and environmental influences. Some individuals come to depend on alcohol and tobacco to serve coping and other functions. Maladaptive coping, characterized by anger, avoidance, and helplessness, appears to contribute to escalation in the use of these drugs.

Many questions remain. Adolescents who face great developmental and environmental challenges and who are exposed to alcohol and tobacco use at an early age do not invariably go on to use these drugs regularly or to develop dependence. Stress and coping are only part of the equation. Other vulnerabilities may interact with environmental and social forces to influence the perception of stress and subsequent coping. For example, individuals differ in their emotional and physiological reactions to stress; in their temperament and personality, which influence their reactions to novel stimuli and prevailing affect; and in their susceptibility to the mood-regulating effects of alcohol and tobacco. Long-term longitudinal studies are needed to assess vulnerability factors early in life and to see how these factors interact with environmental influences over time to influence perceived stress coping and drug use well into adulthood. Only in this way can we begin to understand how destructive patterns of drug use behavior emerge, wax, and wane, and thereby identify those individuals who may be in greatest need for early interventions.

SUMMARY

The chapters in this section have mapped the association between alcohol and tobacco use and have suggested genetic, neurobiological, associative, and psychosocial mechanisms for their strong linkage. Given that research is just beginning to focus on this association, it is not surprising that very little is known beyond a descriptive or speculative level. Advancement of this field of study will require studies of alcohol and tobacco epidemiology, behavior genetics, neuropharmacology, associative learning, personality and social psychology, and clinical treatment. Research methods must encompass laboratory animal and in vitro studies, human pedigree studies, human laboratory studies, and naturalistic field studies. Research effort must particularly be directed toward studies that address the mechanisms that link alcohol and tobacco, studies that consider interactions among multiple factors, and studies that recognize the association of alcohol and tobacco at both the individual and situational levels.

ACKNOWLEDGMENTS

This chapter was prepared with support from National Institute on Drug Abuse grant DA 06084 and National Heart, Lung, and Blood Institute grant HL 32318.

II.

Alcohol-Tobacco Use and Dependence: Treatment, Early Intervention, and Policy

Chapter 10

Clinical Implications of the Association Between Smoking and Alcoholism

John R. Hughes, M.D.

This chapter reviews evidence for the association between smoking and alcoholism, including possible reasons and possible implications. The chapter also reviews evidence on how the cessation of either nicotine or alcohol use affects the use of or cessation of use of the other drug. These topics have been covered previously in several reviews (Istvan and Matarazzo 1984; Bobo 1989; Bien and Burge 1990; Henningfield et al. 1990; Kozlowski et al. 1990; Sobell et al. 1990; Zacny 1990; Johnson and Jennison 1992; Orleans and Hutchinson 1992; Hurt et al. 1993).

INTERPRETING THE ASSOCIATION BETWEEN SMOKING AND ALCOHOLISM

Most studies conducted on smoking and alcoholism have focused on current smoking, although several studies have included data on both exsmoking and never-smoking as well as on the number of cigarettes smoked per day (Istvan and Matarazzo 1984). Alcoholics are more likely to be ever-smokers and current heavy smokers and less likely to be exsmokers compared with the general population (table 1) (also see Sobell et al., chapter 12). This pattern

J.R. Hughes, M.D., is Professor in the Departments of Psychiatry, Psychology, and Family Practice, University of Vermont, 38 Fletcher Place, Burlington, VT 05401–1419.

Table 1. Prevalence of Smoking Status in Alcoholics or Problem Drinkers With Active Problems or in Treatment for Alcohol Problems.

		Prevalence		
		Ever-Smokers		
			Current Smokers	
Population Study	Never-Smokers (%)	Exsmokers (%)	Light[1] Smokers (%)	Heavy Smokers (%)
Alcoholics				
Ayers et al. 1976	–	–	3	90[2]
Burling and Ziff 1988	–	–	44	46[3]
DiFranza and Guerrera 1990	4	5	–	–
Dreher and Fraser 1967, 1968	3	4	18	75[2]
Emirgil et al. 1974	9	18	–	–
Gritz et al. 1985	7	15	–	–
Hendtlass 1979	–	–	–	69[4]
Lyons et al. 1986	15	37	–	–
Moody 1976	11	–	–	38[4]
Sobell et al. 1992	8	33	–	–
Walton 1981	3	–	2	95[3]
Median[5]	8	17	11	72
General population[6]	42	28	21	9[2]

[1]Light smokers smoke less than heavy smokers (heavy smokers are defined below).
[2]Heavy smokers defined as ≥ 20 cigs/d.
[3]Heavy smokers defined as > 25 cigs/d.
[4]Heavy smokers defined as > 20 cigs/d.
[5]Median row does not add to 100% because different studies contributed different rates.
[6]Based on Pierce et al. 1986.

of higher ever-smoking and heavy smoking and lower exsmoking also appears to be true for adolescent alcoholics (Myers and Brown 1994) and for those with other drug dependencies (Budney et al. 1993).

In interpreting the association between smoking and alcoholism, several issues must be addressed. First, most data are derived from studies of alcoholics seeking treatment. The minority of alcoholics who seek treatment are those experiencing more severe disorders (Sobell et al. unpublished data 1994). In the only study of alcoholics in the general population, the rate of smoking among subjects with lifetime histories of severe, moderate, mild, or no alcohol dependence was 56, 39, 21, and 18 percent, respectively (Hale and Hughes in press).

Second, strong historical trends may be occurring. One article reports that from 1965 to 1980, smoking among alcoholic men in treatment only declined from 90 to 86 percent, whereas smoking among men in the general population declined from 60 to 40 percent (Kozlowski et al. 1986). More recent surveys of smoking among alcoholics seeking treatment report much lower smoking rates (e.g., from 55 to 61 percent during 1988–91) (Hurt et al. 1994). Therefore, although the prevalence of smoking among alcoholics is high, it is unclear exactly how prevalent smoking is. Another historical trend also may be occurring: If fewer alcoholics than smokers in the general population stop smoking, a selection bias could occur such that future populations of smokers will primarily consist of alcoholics (Hughes 1993a). In other words, it appears that the association between smoking and alcoholism will become stronger over time.

Third, a distinction must be made between smoking and nicotine dependence. Alcoholism may be associated more strongly with nicotine dependence than with smoking (Breslau et al. 1991; Hale and Hughes in press). For example, in one study, the lifetime prevalence of alcohol dependence was 38 percent in smokers with moderate to severe nicotine dependence but was only 21 percent in smokers with mild dependence (Breslau et al. 1991).

Fourth, the large majority of studies conducted on smoking and alcoholism have only examined the association between current smoking and alcoholism. It would seem to be more insightful to examine the association of alcoholism with ever-smoking and with quitting, because current smoking is the product of ever-smoking and of failure to quit smoking.

Fifth, most studies have failed to report the subjects' ages of onset of cigarette and alcohol use, and no studies have indicated either the subjects' ages of onset of the first indicators of dependence or the subjects' ages when the full criteria for dependence was first met. Since temporal precedence is a criterion for causality, knowing the order of starting or developing dependence on nicotine versus alcohol would be useful.

RECOMMENDATIONS

The epidemiological evidence for the association between smoking and alcoholism has several deficiencies. Further studies are needed that:

- Use general population samples
- Examine ever-smoking and quitting as well as current smoking
- Examine nicotine dependence as well as smoking rate and the like
- Report the relative ages of onset and ages of cessation of use of and dependence on alcohol and tobacco
- Employ longitudinal and repeated cross-sectional surveys to determine historical trends in smoking among alcoholics and whether the association between smoking and alcoholism is becoming stronger.

POSSIBLE REASONS FOR THE ASSOCIATION BETWEEN SMOKING AND ALCOHOLISM

Since the causes of smoking and alcoholism are not known, it is difficult to postulate the causes for the association between the two. The association could be attributed to the effects of one drug on the initiation of use of the other. Adolescents who begin smoking are three times more likely to begin using alcohol and vice versa (U.S. Department of Health and Human Services [USDHHS] 1994). However, in one study, a history of alcohol and other drug dependence did not potentiate the development of nicotine dependence among younger smokers (Breslau et al. 1993). The association between smoking and alcoholism also could be due to the use of one drug (i.e., alcohol or nicotine) affecting the cessation of use of the other. As discussed in more detail later, alcohol use appears to decrease the ability to stop smoking and vice versa (Gritz et al. 1985; DiFranza and Guerrera 1990; Hughes and Oliveto 1993).

The increased initiation or decreased cessation of alcohol or tobacco use could be attributed to a third factor that predisposes a person to both begin and not be able to stop using either drug, rather than the direct effects of one drug on the other (see Flay et al., chapter 3, and Wills and Cleary, chapter 6). For example, initiation of smoking and drinking appears to be part of a "rebellious" lifestyle (USDHHS 1994). In addition, some personality traits (e.g., sensation-seeking behavior or extroversion) are associated with both smoking and drinking (USDHHS 1994). Finally, some of the genetic effects on the initiation of tobacco

and alcohol use are shared (i.e., the genotype that increases the probability of alcoholism also appears to increase the probability of smoking and vice versa) (see Prescott and Kendler, chapter 4, and Carmelli and Swan, chapter 5). Similarly, lower education levels, lower income levels, and being around a smoker or alcoholic are all associated with the inability to stop smoking (USDHHS 1990) and stop drinking (Vaillant 1983; Sobell et al. 1992).

Several possible direct interactions exist between alcohol and tobacco that could explain the association between smoking and alcoholism (Collins 1990; Zacny 1990). In terms of how alcohol use could influence smoking, most available data are from studies of humans. For example, experimental studies have reported that alcohol use prompts smoking, increases ongoing smoking, decreases the ability to stop smoking, and increases relapse to smoking (Collins 1990; Zacny 1990) (see also Shiffman and Balabanis, chapter 2). The only studies conducted on the ways in which alcohol influences nicotine effects in animals have shown a cross-tolerance between the two drugs that is mediated, in part, by genetic factors (Collins 1990; Zacny 1990) (see also Collins and Marks, chapter 7).

Conversely, most studies on how smoking may influence alcohol use have been conducted with animals. In animals, nicotine increases voluntary alcohol consumption, increases alcohol discrimination, and offsets the sedating and motor incoordination effects of alcohol (Collins 1990; Zacny 1990; Dar et al. 1993). Although much less research has been conducted on alcohol-nicotine interactions in humans, some of the findings are intriguing. For example, smoking slows gastric emptying, thereby delaying alcohol absorption (Johnson et al. 1991), and smoking decreases subjective sensations of intoxication (Madden et al. in press). In terms of common mechanisms, a task learned while under the influence of both alcohol and nicotine is best performed when tested while under the influence of both drugs, as opposed to being tested while under the influence of either drug alone (i.e., state-dependent learning occurs) (Zacny 1990). Thus, perhaps some people combine alcohol and nicotine to recreate conditions in which these two drugs were previously paired (e.g., at parties). In addition, both smokers and alcoholics appear to have reduced aldehyde dehydrogenase (Helander 1989) and higher acetaldehyde (Hesselbrock and Shaskan 1985) levels, suggesting that an abnormality in alcohol metabolism is common in the use of both alcohol and tobacco (see Pomerleau, chapter 8). Finally, studies have not consistently found that alcohol changes the elimination of nicotine or vice versa (Zacny 1990).

RECOMMENDATIONS

Most of the mechanism results presented above are each based on a single study; therefore, replication is needed. In addition, laboratory studies in humans are especially needed in the following areas:
- How nicotine changes the subjective and reinforcing effects of alcohol
- Whether nicotine induces a cross-tolerance to alcohol and vice versa
- Whether genetic predisposition to alcoholism changes one's response to nicotine and whether genetic predisposition to nicotine dependence changes one's response to alcohol.

IMPLICATIONS OF THE ASSOCIATION BETWEEN SMOKING AND ALCOHOLISM

One major implication of the association between smoking and alcoholism is that many alcoholics die from smoking-related illnesses. This is especially plausible because not only do more alcoholics smoke cigarettes than do nonalcoholics, but those that smoke appear to smoke more cigarettes per day and to smoke each cigarette more intensely than nonalcoholic smokers (Keenan et al. 1990). Long-term mortality studies indicate that among alcoholics, lung cancer, myocardial infarction, chronic obstructive pulmonary disease, and other smoking-induced disorders are major causes of increased mortality (Hurt et al. 1994). For example, in one study, the relative risk of mortality over 12 years, compared with nonsmoking nonalcoholics, was 11.0 in smoking nonalcoholics, 17.0 in nonsmoking alcoholics, and 26.4 in smoking alcoholics (Rosengren et al. 1988). In addition, in some illnesses, alcohol and tobacco act synergistically to increase the risk of mortality (US-DHHS 1982). In one study, the relative risk of laryngeal cancer, compared with nonsmoking nonalcoholics, was 2.1 in heavy smokers, 2.2 in heavy drinkers, and 8.1 in heavy smokers-heavy drinkers (Hinds et al. 1979). In an important recent followup study of alcoholics in treatment, researchers found that more alcoholics had died of smoking-related illnesses than of alcohol-related illnesses (Hurt in press).

A second implication of the association between smoking and alcoholism is that perhaps smoking could be used as a marker for alcoholism (DiFranza and Guerrera 1990; Vaillant et al. 1991; Hughes 1994b). For example, one study found that 13–15 percent of smokers who currently smoked more than 20 cigarettes per day also were alcohol dependent (Hughes 1994b) (table 2). Thus, perhaps physicians should be encouraged to screen heavy smokers for alcoholism, because, at least in this study, one in six heavy smokers were currently alcohol dependent.

A third implication of the association between smoking and alcoholism is that alcohol use may influence the treatment of smoking and vice versa. In terms of the effect of alcohol on smoking cessation, as mentioned earlier, several studies have found that alcohol use decreases one's chances of stopping smoking and is implicated in many cases of relapse to smoking

(Shiffman 1982; DiFranza and Guerrera 1990; Hughes and Oliveto 1993). Data across six retrospective studies show that a median of 17 percent of ever-smokers with current alcoholism were able to stop smoking (table 1). In comparison, according to USDHHS (1990) data from the same time period, approximately 45 percent of ever-smokers in the general population had quit smoking (USDHHS 1990). However, other retrospective data suggest that past alcohol dependence may not be associated with less likelihood of stopping smoking. Two retrospective studies found that 44 percent and 53 percent, respectively, of recovering alcoholics who had ever smoked had stopped smoking (Tuchfeld 1976; DeSoto et al. 1985), which is comparable to the percentages found in the general population (USDHHS 1990). In addition, recent studies by Sobell and colleagues (see chapter 12) indicate high rates of smoking cessation in recovering alcoholics. Conversely, another study reported that only 27 percent of ever-smoking, recovering alcoholics had quit smoking (Bobo et al. 1987). Finally, a large population-based retrospective survey (Covey et al. 1994) reported that a lifetime history of alcohol dependence was associated with a 30-percent less chance of having stopped smoking than smokers without this history.

Prospective studies also are not consistent. One clinical trial reported that only 7 percent of smokers with a past but not current history of alcohol/drug problems were able to stop smoking, compared with 20 percent of smokers without such history (Hughes 1993*b*). Conversely, a second trial did not find that smokers with higher scores on the Short Alcohol Dependence Data questionnaire had lower cessation rates (Hughes and Hatsukami in press). A third prospective trial reported data consistent with the large survey cited previously (i.e., a history of alcoholism was associated with a decreased chance of stopping smoking); however, in this study, the finding was attributed to the association between alcoholism and depression (Covey et al. 1993).

In terms of the effect of smoking on recovery from alcoholism, again the data are not clear cut. Two studies reported that among recovering alcoholics who smoked, the rate of relapse to drinking was similar to that of nonsmoking alcoholics. However, recovering alcoholics who smoked drank more alcohol when they did re-

lapse (see Monti et al., chapter 11, and Sobell et al., chapter 12).

RECOMMENDATIONS

Because retrospective studies and studies of those in treatment can be biased, researchers need to conduct population-based, longitudinal studies in order to examine the following:

- The relative contribution of alcohol- and tobacco-induced diseases to the increased morbidity and mortality of alcoholics
- Whether physicians could use heavy smoking as a marker of alcohol abuse
- Whether alcoholics who smoke are more alcohol dependent or less likely to stop drinking than alcoholics who do not smoke
- Whether smokers who have past or current alcohol problems are more nicotine dependent or less likely to stop smoking than smokers who do not have past or current alcohol problems.

Table 2. Prevalence of Moderate to Severe Alcohol Dependence by Smoking Status.[1]

Smoking Status	Lifetime Alcohol Dependence[2] (%)	Current Alcohol Dependence[3] (%)
≥ 20 cigs/d	35	13
1–19 cigs/d	20	15
Exsmokers	12	5
Never-smokers	10	5

[1]Adapted from Hughes 1994*b*.
[2]Lifetime alcohol dependence = ever in life.
[3]Current alcohol dependence = in last year.

CESSATION OF SMOKING AND DRINKING

Should those who both smoke and have alcohol problems stop smoking and drinking simultaneously or sequentially? As reported earlier, few active alcoholics are able to stop smoking (table 1). Often the social problems of alcoholism are so imminent and clinically significant that most clinicians have recommended that these patients first stop drinking and then stop smoking. However, two studies found that 38 percent and 26 percent of those with drinking problems reported that they stopped smoking before they stopped drinking (Tuchfeld 1976; Snow et al. 1992) (see also Sobell et al., chapter 11). Those subjects who stopped drinking first were those who had less severe alcohol problems. Therefore, perhaps those with less pressing alcohol problems could stop smoking first, learn from the experience, and then stop drinking.

Clinicians' more common concerns regarding smoking cessation revolve around its effects on patients' efforts to stop drinking. Three concerns are often voiced: (1) that stopping smoking along with or soon after stopping drinking increases chances of relapsing to drinking; (2) that some patients will not find it acceptable to stop drinking and smoking simultaneously; and (3) if drinking and smoking are not stopped simultaneously, one will need to wait quite a while after stopping drinking before stopping smoking.

Among those without alcohol problems, it is unclear whether alcohol use increases after smoking cessation (Hughes et al. 1990; Perkins et al. 1990; Carmelli et al. 1993). In one retrospective study, smoking cessation among recovering alcoholics did not increase the rate of relapse to alcohol use (Miller et al. 1983). Only three prospective studies are available. In these studies, smokers with alcohol problems did not increase their alcohol intake after they stopped smoking (Hughes 1993b; Joseph et al. 1993; Marks et al. 1994); however, in one of these studies, subjects who received an intervention for smoking cessation were somewhat more likely to begin using other drugs (Joseph et al. 1993). Finally, a larger study reported that 18 percent of smokers with past histories of alcoholism relapsed to alcohol use after stopping smoking (Glassman et al. 1993).

Several surveys have found that a high percentage of patients in treatment for alcohol/drug problems are interested in receiving treatment for smoking (Kozlowski et al. 1989) (see Bobo et al., chapter 13). Of those interested in receiving treatment, however, only a minority want to stop smoking along with stopping drinking. Many patients prefer to wait several months after stopping drinking before stopping smoking. Clinicians' interests and attitudes about smoking cessation are generally similar to those of their patients (see Bobo et al., chapter 13).

One could hypothesize that trying to stop smoking soon after resolving alcohol problems would predict either better or worse smoking cessation outcomes. A better outcome might be hypothesized because many of the motivational and relapse prevention skills that a person learns and uses to stop drinking would still be fresh in the person's mind and could be adapted to the smoking cessation process. In addition, stopping smoking might be seen as part of an overall lifestyle change that first began with stopping alcohol use. Conversely, a worse outcome might be hypothesized because quitting two habits at the same time is much too difficult. In fact, when animals are deprived of one drug reinforcer, a second drug reinforcer becomes more efficacious and more resistant to change (Carroll and Meisch 1984). The only human data available relevant to this issue is a retrospective analysis indicating that increased success in stopping smoking was not associated with duration of sobriety (Bobo et al. 1987).

RECOMMENDATIONS

Since much of the data are contradictory, a two-pronged approach to studying the natural history of drinking and smoking cessation and experimental trials is needed. Studies of particular relevance would include the following:

• More longitudinal studies of how many alcoholic smokers stop smoking first, stop drinking first, or stop both together. Among those alcoholic smokers who stop drinking first, how long after they stop drinking do they stop smok-ing? Does the rate of successful cessation of alcohol or tobacco use vary across these patterns?

• A randomized trial of alcoholic smokers that includes those who stop drinking and smoking simultaneously versus those who first stop drinking and then stop smoking. The later experimental group could be further divided into two groups: (1) those who stop smoking soon after they stop drinking and (2) those who stop smoking long after they stop drinking.

TREATING SMOKING AMONG CURRENT OR RECOVERING ALCOHOLICS

Because of the recent revisions of the Joint Commission on Accreditation of Health Care Organizations standards, many inpatient treatment facilities for alcoholism have become smoke-free. Consistent with the literature from other types of medical facilities (USDHHS 1989), simply instituting a "no smoking" rule in an alcoholic treatment center does not substantially increase smoking cessation among recovering alcoholics (Joseph et al. 1990; Hurt et al. 1993, 1994). However, it is difficult to implement a successful smoking cessation program in a facility that allows smoking (Hurt et al. 1993, 1994).

Because the data are inconsistent about whether recovering alcoholic smokers find it more or less difficult to stop smoking than nonalcoholic smokers, it is difficult to argue that alcoholics should automatically receive more intensive treatment. Whether alcoholic smokers should receive a different content therapy is also debatable. For example, many, but not the majority of, alcoholics receive 12-step-based therapy for alcoholism (Sobell et al. unpublished data 1994); therefore, one might hypothesize that a 12-step-based therapy program for smoking would be especially beneficial for treated alcoholics and could be integrated into existing treatment.

Two studies treated smokers who were enrolled in a 12-step-based program for alcoholism with a smoking cessation therapy that included several 12-step elements. The alcoholic smokers were compared with a historical control group (Joseph et al. 1990; Hurt et al. 1994). The long-term smoking cessation rates in both studies were small (i.e., 12 percent and 10 percent, respectively). In one of the studies, only 24 percent of the alcoholics in treatment were willing to enroll in smoking cessation therapy (Hurt et al. 1994). Another randomized trial reported that "cognitive/behavioral intervention incorporating an AA [Alcoholics Anonymous] 12-step model" produced significantly higher smoking cessation than a control group, but this trial did not report actual cessation rates (Martin et al. in press). Programs using only a 12-step model for smoking have been developed (Casey 1987); however, none have been tested empirically in either smokers with or without histories of alcoholism. In summary, the efficacy of 12-step therapy for smoking cessation among recovering alcoholics has not been adequately evaluated.

In the only other controlled study of smoking cessation in alcoholics, homeless veteran smokers with histories of alcohol/drug problems who were in a residential program were assigned to either a nicotine-fading, relapse-prevention or a self-contracting treatment regimen or a wait-list control group (Burling et al. 1991). The active treatments produced no abstinence at 3-month followup.

Alcoholic smokers may be more nicotine dependent and therefore require nicotine replacement therapy. On scales of nicotine dependence, smokers with histories of alcoholism usually (Marks et al. 1994), but not always (Hughes 1993b), score higher than smokers without histories of alcoholism. Whether alcoholic smokers experience more withdrawal or craving symptoms postcessation than smokers without histories of alcoholism is debatable (Hughes 1993b; Marks et al. 1994). One posthoc analysis of a clinical trial reported that smokers with past histories of alcohol/drug problems especially benefited from nicotine replacement (i.e., such smokers did very poorly unless they received nicotine replacement). However, even with nicotine replacement, the cessation rate was low (i.e., 10 percent) (Hughes 1993b).

One potential treatment that researchers have not examined in this population is naltrexone. Naltrexone appears to be effective in treating alcohol dependence (O'Malley et al.

1992; Volpicelli et al. 1992). Perhaps less well known is that most, but not all, studies suggest that naltrexone blocks the reinforcing effects of nicotine and, therefore, might also be useful as a treatment for smoking (Hughes 1994*a*). Unfortunately, the trials of naltrexone in alcoholism treatment did not report data on whether any patients spontaneously stopped smoking as well.

RECOMMENDATIONS

Because so little is known about treating smoking in alcoholics, the following three-pronged approach might be useful:

- Test standard treatments for smoking among alcoholic smokers and compare the results with those in nonalcoholic smokers. Depending on these results, a trial of more intensive versus less intensive treatment might be indicated.
- While doing the above, collect information on possible special needs of alcoholics when they stop smoking.
- Then conduct a trial of a treatment tailored to alcoholic smokers versus a time-matched standard treatment of smoking.

In addition to this three-pronged approach, two other trials should be considered:

- Because a substantial minority of alcoholics have received 12-step therapy, a trial of 12-step versus behavior therapy for smoking should be conducted in alcoholics with and without histories of 12-step therapy.

- Because naltrexone is an effective therapy for alcoholism and also may be effective for smoking, a trial of naltrexone in patients who wish to stop drinking and smoking simultaneously or sequentially is indicated.

ACKNOWLEDGMENTS

This chapter was funded by National Institute on Alcohol Abuse and Alcoholism grant 1 R01–AA09480 and the National Institute on Drug Abuse's Research Scientist Development Award 2 K02–00109.

REFERENCES

Ayers, J.; Ruff, C.F.; and Templer, D.I. Alcoholism, cigarette smoking, coffee drinking and extroversion. *J Stud Alcohol* 37:983–985, 1976.

Bien, T.H., and Burge, R. Smoking and drinking: A review of the literature. *Int J Addict* 25:1429–1454, 1990.

Bobo, J.K. Nicotine dependence and alcoholism epidemiology and treatment. *J Psychoactive Drugs* 21:323–329, 1989.

Bobo, J.K.; Gilchrist, L.D.; Schilling, R.F., II; Noach, B.; and Schinke, S.P. Cigarette smoking cessation attempts by recovering alcoholics. *Addict Behav* 12:209–216, 1987.

Breslau, N.; Kilbey, M.M.; and Andreski, P. Nicotine dependence, major depression, and anxiety in young adults. *Arch Gen Psychiatry* 48:1069–1074, 1991.

Breslau, N.; Kilbey, M.M.; and Andreski, P. Nicotine dependence and major depression: New evidence from a prospective investigation. *Arch Gen Psychiatry* 50:31–35, 1993.

Budney, A.J.; Higgins, S.T.; Hughes, J.R.; and Bickel, W.K. Nicotine and caffeine use in cocaine-dependent individuals. *J Subst Abuse* 5:117–130, 1993.

Burling, T.A., and Ziff, D.C. Tobacco smoking: A comparison between alcohol and drug abuse inpatients. *Addict Behav* 13:185–190, 1988.

Burling, T.A.; Marshall, G.D.; and Seidner, A.L. Smoking cessation for substance abuse inpatients. *J Subst Abuse* 3:269–276, 1991.

Carmelli, D.; Swan, G.E.; and Robinette, D. The relationship between quitting smoking and changes in drinking in World War II veteran twins. *J Subst Abuse* 5:103–116, 1993.

Carroll, M.E., and Meisch, R.A. Increased drug-reinforced behavior due to food deprivation. In: Thompson, T.; Dews, P.B.; Barrett, E., eds. *Advances in Behavioral Pharmacology*. Vol. 4. New York: Academic Press, 1984. pp. 47–88.

Casey, K. *If Only I Could Quit: Recovering From Nicotine Addiction*. Center City, MN: Hazelden Foundation, 1987.

Collins, A.C. Interactions of ethanol and nicotine at the receptor level. In: Galanter, M., ed. *Recent Developments in Alcoholism*. New York: Plenum Press, 1990. pp. 221–231.

Covey, L.S.; Glassman, A.H.; Stetner, F.; and Becker, J. Effect of history of alcoholism or major depression on smoking cessation. *Am J Psychiatry* 150:1546–1547, 1993.

Covey, L.S.; Hughes, D.C.; Glassman, A.H.; Blazer, D.G.; and George, L.K. Ever-smoking, quitting, and psychiatric disorders: Evidence from the Durham, North Carolina, Epidemiologic Catchment Area. *Tobacco Control* 3:222–227, 1994.

Dar, M.S.; Li, C. and Bowman, E.R. Central behavioral interactions between ethanol, (-)-nicotine, and (-)-cotinine in mice. *Brain Res Bull* 32:23–28, 1993.

DeSoto, C.B.; O'Donnell, W.E.; Allred, L.J.; and Lopes, C.E. Symptomatology in alcoholics at various stages of abstinence. *Alcohol Clin Exp Res* 9:505–512, 1985.

DiFranza, J.R., and Guerrera, M.P. Alcoholism and smoking. *J Stud Alcohol* 51:130–135, 1990.

Dreher, K.F., and Fraser, J.G. Smoking habits of alcoholic out-patients. I. *Int J Addict* 2:259–270, 1967.

Dreher, K.F., and Fraser, J.G. Smoking habits of alcoholic out-patients. II. *Int J Addict* 3:65–80, 1968.

Emirgil, C.; Sobol, B.J.; Heymann, B.; and Shibutani, K. Pulmonary function in alcoholics. *Am J Med* 57:69–77, 1974.

Glassman, A.H.; Covey, L.S.; Dalack, G.W.; Stetner, F.; Rivelli, S.K.; Fleiss, J.; and Cooper, T.B. Smoking cessation, clonidine, and vulnerability to nicotine among dependent smokers. *Clin Pharmacol Ther* 54:670–679, 1993.

Gritz, E.R.; Stapleton, J.M.; Hill, M.A.; and Jarvik, M.E. Prevalence of cigarette smoking in VA medical and psychiatric hospitals. *Bull Soc Psychol Addict Behav* 4:151–165, 1985.

Hale, K.L., and Hughes, J.R. The prevalence of caffeine and nicotine use and dependence among alcoholics vs nonalcoholics. In: *Problems of Drug Dependence, 1994*. National Institute on Drug Abuse Research Monograph. Washington,

DC: Supt. of Docs., U.S. Govt. Print. Off., in press.

Helander, A. Reduced blood aldehyde dehydrogenase activity in smokers. *Alcohol Clin Exp Res* 13:144–145, 1989.

Hendtlass, J. Survey of alcoholism treatment in Victoria: Relationship of alcoholic drug use to their use of medical facilities. *Med J Aust* 2:635–636, 1979.

Henningfield, J.E.; Clayton, R.; and Pollin, W. Involvement of tobacco in alcoholism and illicit drug use. *Br J Addict* 85:279–292, 1990.

Hesselbrock, V.M., and Shaskan, E.G. Endogenous breath acetaldehyde levels among alcoholic and non-alcoholic probands: Effect of alcohol use and smoking. *Prog Neuropsychopharmacol Biol Psychiatry* 9:259–265, 1985.

Hinds, M.W.; Thomas, D.B.; and O'Reilly, H.P. Asbestos, dental x-rays, tobacco, and alcohol in the epidemiology of laryngeal cancer. *Cancer* 44:1114–1120, 1979.

Hughes, J.R. Pharmacotherapy for smoking cessation: Unvalidated assumptions and anomalies, and suggestions for further research. *J Consult Clin Psychol* 61:751–760, 1993*a*.

Hughes, J.R. Treatment of smoking cessation in smokers with past alcohol/drug problems. *J Subst Abuse Treat* 10:181–187, 1993*b*.

Hughes, J.R. Non-nicotine pharmacotherapies for smoking cessation. *J of Drug Dev* 6:197–203, 1994*a*.

Hughes, J.R. Smoking and alcoholism. In: Hatsukami, D.K., and Cox, J., eds. *Behavioral Approaches to Addiction.* New York: Cahners, 1994*b*. pp. 1–3.

Hughes, J.R., and Hatsukami, D.K. Past history of alcohol problems and the ability to stop smoking. In: Harris, L.S., ed. *Problems of Drug Dependence,* 1995. Washington, DC: Supt. of Docs., U.S. Govt. Print. Off., in press.

Hughes, J.R., and Oliveto, A.H. Caffeine and alcohol intake as predictors of smoking cessation and tobacco withdrawal. *J Subst Abuse* 5:305–310, 1993.

Hughes, J.R.; Higgins, S.T.; and Hatsukami, D.K. Effects of abstinence from tobacco: A critical review. In: Kozlowski, L.T.; Annis, H.; Cappell, H.D.; Glaser, F.; Goodstadt, M.; Israel, Y.; Kalant, H.; Sellers, E.M.; and Vingilis, J., eds. *Research Advances in Alcohol and Drug Problems.* Vol. 10. New York: Plenum Press, 1990. pp. 317–398.

Hurt, R.D. Do more alcoholics die from tobacco than alcohol? *Addictive Diseases,* in press.

Hurt, R.D.; Eberman, K.M.; Slade, J.; and Karan, L. Treating nicotine addiction in patients with other addictive disorders. In: Orleans, C.T., and Slade, J., eds. *Nicotine Addiction: Principles and Management.* New York: Oxford University Press, 1993. pp. 310–326.

Hurt, R.D.; Eberman, K.M.; Croghan, I.T.; Offord, K.P.; Davis, Jr.; Morse, R.J.; Palmen, M.A.; and Bruce, B.K. Nicotine dependence treatment during inpatient treatment for other addictions: A prospective intervention trial. *Alcohol Clin Exp Res* 18:867–872, 1994.

Istvan, J., and Matarazzo, J.D. Tobacco, alcohol and caffeine use: A review of their interrelationships. *Psychol Bull* 95:301–326, 1984.

Johnson, K.A., and Jennison, K.M. The drinking-smoking syndrome and social context. *Int J Addict* 27:749–792, 1992.

Johnson, R.D.; Horowitz, M.; Maddox, A.F.; Wishart, J.M.; and Shearman, D.J.C. Cigarette smoking and rate of gastric emptying: Effect on alcohol absorption. *BMJ* 302:20–23, 1991.

Joseph, A.M.; Nichol, K.L.; Willenbring, M.L.; Korn, J.E.; and Lysaght, L.S. Beneficial effects of treatment of nicotine dependence during an inpatient substance abuse treatment program. *JAMA* 263: 3043–3046, 1990.

Joseph, A.M.; Nichol, K.L.; and Anderson, H. Effect of treatment for nicotine dependence on alcohol and drug treatment outcomes. *Addict Behav* 18:635–644, 1993.

Keenan, R.M.; Hatsukami, D.K.; Pickens, R.W.; Gust, S.W.; and Strelow, L.J. The relationship between chronic ethanol exposure and cigarette smoking in the laboratory and the natural environment. *Psychopharmacology* 100:77–83, 1990.

Kozlowski, L.T.; Jelinek, L.C.; and Pope, M.A. Cigarette smoking among alcohol abusers: A continuing and neglected problem. *Can J Public Health* 77:205–207, 1986.

Kozlowski, L.T.; Skinner, W.; Kent, C.; and Pope, M.A. Prospects for smoking treatment in individuals seeking treatment for alcohol and other drug problems. *Addict Behav* 14:273–278, 1989.

Kozlowski, L.T.; Ferrence, R.G.; and Corbit, T. Tobacco use: A perspective for alcohol and drug researchers. *Br J Addict* 85:245, 1990.

Lyons, D.J.; Howard, S.V.; Milledge, J.S.; and Peters, T.J. Contribution of ethanol and cigarette smoking to pulmonary dysfunction in chronic alcoholics. *Thorax* 41:197–202, 1986.

Madden, P.A.F.; Heath, A.C.; Starmer, G.A.; Whitfield, J.B.; and Martin, N.G. Alcohol sensitivity and smoking history in men and women. *Alcoholism*, in press.

Marks, J.L.; Hill, E.M.; Pomerleau, C.S.; Mudd, S.A.; and Blow, F.C. DSM–III–R tobacco dependence and withdrawal symptoms in male alcoholic and non-alcoholic ex-smokers. *Ann Behav Med* 16: S113, 1994.

Martin, J.E.; Calfas, K.J.; Polarek, M.S.; Noto, J.; Barrett, L.K.; Beach, D.; Patten, C.; and Hofstetter, R. Preliminary outcome results of a smoking cessation intervention for recovering alcoholic persons: A randomized controlled trial. *Ann Behav Med*, in press.

Miller, W.R.; Hedrick, K.E.; and Taylor, C.A. Addictive behaviors and life problems before and after behavioral treatment of problem drinkers. *Addict Behav* 8:403–412, 1983.

Moody, P.M. Drinking and smoking behavior of hospitalized medical patients. *J Stud Alcohol* 37:1316–1319, 1976.

Myers, M.G., and Brown, S.A. Smoking and health in substance-abusing adolescents: A two-year follow-up. *Pediatrics* 93:561–566, 1994.

O'Malley, S.S.; Jaffe, A.J.; Chang, G.; Schottenfield, R.S.; Meyer, R.E.; and Rounsaville, B. Naltrexone and coping skills therapy for alcohol dependence. *Arch Gen Psychiatry* 49:881–887, 1992.

Orleans, C.T., and Hutchinson, D. Tailoring nicotine addiction treatments for chemical dependency patients. *J Subst Abuse Treat* 9:197–208, 1992.

Perkins, K.A.; Epstein, L.H.; Sexton, J.E.; and Pastor, S. Effects of smoking cessation on consumption of alcohol and sweet, high-fat foods. *J Subst Abuse* 2:287–297, 1990.

Pierce, J.P.; Hatziandreu, E.; Flyer, P.; Hull, J.; Maklan, D.; Morganstein, D.; and Schreiber, G. *Report of the 1986 Adult Use of Tobacco Survey.* Rockville, MD: U.S. Department of Health and Human Services, 1986.

Rosengren, A.; Wilhelmsen, L.; and Wedel, H. Separate and combined effects of smoking and alcohol abuse in middle-aged men. *Acta Med Scand* 223:111–118, 1988.

Shiffman, S.M. Relapse following smoking cessation: A situational analysis. *J Consult Clin Psychol* 50:71–86, 1982.

Snow, M.G.; Prochaska, J.O.; and Rossi, J.S. Stages of change for smoking cessation among former problem drinkers: A cross-sectional analysis. *J Subst Abuse* 4:107–116, 1992.

Sobell, L.C.; Sobell, M.B.; Kozlowski, L.T.; and Toneatto, T. Alcohol or tobacco research versus alcohol and tobacco research. *Br J Addict* 85:263–269, 1990.

Sobell, L.C.; Sobell, M.B.; and Toneatto, T. Recovery from alcohol problems without treatment. In: Heather, N.; Miller, W.R.; and Greeley, J., eds. *Self-control and Addictive Behaviors.* Australia: Maxwell MacMallion, 1992. pp. 198–242.

Tuchfeld, B.S. *Changes in Patterns of Alcohol Use Without the Aid of Formal Treatment: An Exploratory Study of Former Problem Drinkers.* Research Triangle Park, NC: Research Triangle Institute, 1976. As cited by Sobell, L.C.; Sobell, M.B.; and Toneatto, T., in Recovery from alcohol problems without treatment. In: Heather, N.; Miller, W.R.; and Greeley, J., eds. *Self-control and Addictive Behaviors.* Australia: Maxwell MacMallion, 1992. pp. 198–242.

U.S. Department of Health and Human Services. *The Health Consequences of Smoking.* Washington, DC: Supt. of Docs., U.S. Govt. Print. Off., 1982.

U.S. Department of Health and Human Services. *Reducing the Health Consequences of Smoking: 25 Years of Progress. A Report of the U.S. Surgeon General.* Rockville, MD: the Department, 1989.

U.S. Department of Health and Human Services. *Health Consequences of Smoking Cessation. A Report of the U.S. Surgeon General.* Washington, DC: Supt. of Docs., U.S. Govt. Print. Off., 1990.

U.S. Department of Health and Human Services. *Preventing Tobacco Use Among Young People: A Report of the Surgeon General.* Washington, DC: Supt. of Docs., U.S. Govt. Print. Off., 1994.

Vaillant, G.E. *The Natural History of Alcoholism.* Cambridge, MA: Harvard University Press, 1983.

Vaillant, G.E.; Schnurr, P.P.; Baron, J.A.; and Gerber, P.D. A prospective study of the effects of cigarette smoking and alcohol abuse on mortality. *J Gen Intern Med* 6:299–304, 1991.

Volpicelli, J.R.; Alterman, A.I.; Hayashida, M.; and O'Brien, C.P. Naltrexone in the treatment of alcohol dependence. *Arch Gen Psychiatry* 49:876–880, 1992.

Walton, T.G. Smoking and alcoholism: A brief report. *Am J Psychiatry* 11:139–140, 1981.

Zacny, J.P. Behavioral aspects of alcohol-tobacco interactions. In: Galanter, M., ed. *Recent Developments in Alcoholism.* New York: Plenum Press, 1990. pp. 205–219.

Chapter 11

Smoking Among Alcoholics During and After Treatment: Implications for Models, Treatment Strategies, and Policy

Peter M. Monti, Ph.D., Damaris J. Rohsenow, Ph.D.,
Suzanne M. Colby, M.A., and David B. Abrams, Ph.D.

The co-occurrence of alcohol and tobacco consumption is well documented, and the relationship is particularly strong for alcoholics. More alcoholics than nonalcoholics are smokers, with the prevalence rates for alcoholics ranging from 71 to 97 percent (Battjes 1988; Istvan and Matarazzo 1984). There has been no decline in the prevalence of smoking among alcoholics, as has been the case in the general population (Kozlowski et al. 1986). Alcoholics smoke more heavily than nonalcoholic smokers do and frequently report that cigarettes would be harder to quit than alcohol (Kozlowski et al. 1989). Furthermore, as Hughes has suggested in chapter 10, heavy smoking may be a good preliminary screening tool for identifying alcoholics.

P.M. Monti, Ph.D., is an associate career research scientist at the Providence Veterans Affairs Medical Center (VAMC) and a professor of psychiatry and human behavior at Brown University. D.J. Rohsenow, Ph.D., is a research clinical psychologist at Providence VAMC and associate professor (research) of community health at Brown University. S.M. Colby, M.A., is a project director at the Addictive Behavior Research Lab at Brown University. D.B. Abrams, Ph.D., is director of the Division of Behavioral Medicine at The Miriam Hospital and professor of psychiatry and human behavior at Brown University School of Medicine. Drs. Monti and Rohsenow and Ms. Colby can be reached at the Center for Alcohol and Addiction Studies, Box G, Brown University, Providence, RI 02912. Dr. Abrams can be reached at the Division of Behavioral Medicine, RISE Building, The Miriam Hospital, 164 Summit Avenue, Providence, RI 02906.

The correlations between smoking and drinking rates raise many questions about mechanisms and treatment implications. These questions include whether smoking helps alcoholics resist the temptation to drink by coping with reactions to high-risk situations or whether smoking increases the risk of relapse by mechanisms such as neuropsychological changes or associative learning. Other questions include how tobacco-alcohol interactions relate to comorbidity of psychiatric conditions (such as depression) or medical conditions (such as laryngeal cancer). Still other questions involve the role of cognitive processes, such as expectancies about tobacco-alcohol interactions or propositional networks, in mediating the interactions during ongoing use and relapse risk during sobriety from alcohol.

One key question concerning the correlation of smoking with drinking is whether increased smoking occurs during drinking episodes or, alternatively, whether smoking may be lower during drinking episodes but higher on days following a drinking occasion. The former pattern was empirically supported by Shiffman and colleagues (1994) when 57 smokers monitored both their daily smoking and circumstances surrounding their smoking using palm-top computers. Drinking days were associated with increased smoking, and this effect was stronger for heavier drinkers. Interestingly, this relationship was found only in self-monitoring data; retrospective self-reports failed to show a significant relationship between smoking and drinking.

In some earlier research, Mello and colleagues (1980, 1987) studied 6 male and 24 female drinkers who were living in a laboratory. On two 5-day blocks, the subjects could work for alcohol on an operant task. The amount of alcohol consumed varied considerably from day to day, and the daily number of drinks coincided closely with the daily number of cigarettes smoked. Thus, on days that the subjects drank more, they also smoked more. The increased health risks of both smoking and drinking indicate that these interrelationships are an important area to study further.

CONCEPTUAL OVERVIEW

This chapter includes considerations of the following areas of research:
- Several preliminary hypotheses about the effects smoking may have on sobriety
- Controlled laboratory investigations based on these hypotheses
- Data on smoking during followup of alcohol treatment
- Data on alcoholics' expectancies about the effects smoking may have on their treatment or sobriety
- Studies of treatment trials of smoking cessation during treatment for alcoholism
- Implications of results for theory and model development, methodology, and future research.

Our own interest in this area started over a decade ago with two independent but parallel research programs, one studying alcohol and the other tobacco dependence. These programs included research in the following areas:

- High-risk situations were assessed for smokers and alcoholics (Abrams et al. 1987, 1991).
- Role-play measures were developed to assess coping skills for smokers and alcoholics (Monti et al. 1993a; Abrams et al. 1987).
- Strengths and weaknesses were identified for alcoholics and smokers using the role-play measures (Abrams et al. 1987; Monti et al. 1993a). Baseline coping skills discriminated relapse for smokers (Abrams et al. 1988) and the amount of drinking at 6-month followup for alcoholics (Monti et al. 1990).
- Coping skills treatment protocols were developed for smokers and alcoholics. Coping skills treatment was found to be successful for alcoholics (Monti et al. 1989, 1990).
- Cue reactivity assessment protocols were developed for smokers and drinkers to investigate conditioned reactions to the presence of alcohol or cigarettes. (In these paradigms the alcohol or cigarette stimuli are referred to as cues and the reactions as cue reactivity.) Both populations were found to show cue reactivity (e.g., Monti et al. 1987; Abrams et al. 1988).
- Based on these studies, cue exposure treatment protocols were developed for both smokers and alcoholics and are under evaluation. Preliminary investigations have shown positive treatment effects for alcoholics (Monti et al. 1993b; Rohsenow et al. 1995).
- Combined pharmacotherapeutic and behavioral therapies are being investigated in both populations in our labs. For smokers, nicotine replacement treatment is being studied in conjunction with cognitive-behavioral and cue exposure treatment, and medications for comorbid depression, such as fluoxetine, are being studied as an adjunct to smoking treatment. Finally, a large clinical trial of naltrexone treatment with alcoholics is underway in our lab, and we will assess its effects on alcoholics' smoking as well.
- Prevention studies are underway in both populations in our labs. We have conducted several studies with defined populations, such as smokers in the workplace (e.g., Abrams et al. 1994) and are investigating motivational approaches with adolescent drinking and driving.

FROM INVESTIGATING COMMONALITIES TO INTERACTIONS

More recently, the parallel lines of research on alcohol and tobacco dependence have led to studies that more directly address interactions between tobacco and alcohol. We have found a relationship between smoking and drinking rates and between tobacco and alcohol dependence in several data sets (Abrams et al. 1992; Gulliver et al. 1995). The correlations between smoking rate and drinking range from $r = 0.16$ to 0.27, and the correlations between measures of nicotine and alcohol dependence range from $r = 0.20$ to 0.39 across five samples in our lab. These data, in the context of our biopsychosocial approach, have stimulated interest in going beyond the question of commonalities and differences underlying the use of alcohol and tobacco and moving into consideration of the nature of possible interactions and implications for treatment.

Our recent line of research has been driven by our interest in treatment implications for alcoholics. Some treatment programs recommend ceasing smoking at the same time that alcohol treatment begins. More typically, programs advise patients that they should concentrate only on alcohol and other drug (AOD) abuse while in treatment and postpone smoking cessation efforts. However, recommendations are made with insufficient information about mediating mechanisms and the answers to unresolved questions, such as the extent to which smoking during early recovery is harmful or beneficial to alcohol sobriety. Our focal interest has centered on questions about the effects smoking or smoking cessation might have on recovery.

OVERVIEW OF RESEARCH STRATEGIES IN THIS AREA

Before conducting clinical trials of treatment in any area, a series of research steps are commonly undertaken, such as the following:

- Population and naturalistic studies, clinical observations, and single case studies provide correlations, suggesting a degree of association between two behaviors or possible subject characteristics.
- Theory-driven models are developed to hypothesize mechanisms mediating the relationship between the two behaviors and to hypothesize predictions about the effects of changing one behavior on the other.
- Controlled laboratory investigations are done to study parameters of relationships and hypothesized mediating mechanisms between the two behaviors.
- Theories and models are revised and new predictions tested in laboratory investigations.
- Treatment components are designed based on the results of prior investigations.
- Small-scale clinical trials are conducted with short-term followup.
- Definitive large-scale clinical trials compare several parameters of treatment with matching to individual differences among patients.
- Technology transfer or dissemination research studies are undertaken to evaluate the efficacy and cost-effectiveness of treatment in larger populations through channels such as physicians, work sites, and schools.

HYPOTHESIZED MECHANISMS OF TOBACCO'S EFFECTS ON SOBRIETY AFTER ALCOHOL TREATMENT

Other chapters in this monograph discuss models of the interactions of smoking and ongoing alcohol use. However, models of tobacco's influence on aspects of recovery are also important when considering clinical implications. Three types of hypotheses of the effects of smoking on sobriety have guided our work. These hypotheses do not always lead to contrasting predictions, because some aspects may be complementary. These hypotheses, outlined below, are preliminary at this point.

1. *Priming:* Smoking may potentiate urges to drink and risk for drinking during recovery through several possible biobehavioral mechanisms. In this hypothesis, smoking would increase risk of relapse to drinking for alcoholics.

a. *Neurological:* As both smoking and alcohol increase dopamine and endogenous opiate release in the ventral tegmental area and the pathways to the nucleus accumbens (e.g., Wise 1988), smoking may increase craving for alcohol by stimulating common neurological mechanisms.

b. *Associative learning:* As smoking and drinking are highly contiguous among alcoholics, smoking may serve as a conditional stimulus for drinking or the two may be related through any of a variety of associative learning processes (Rohsenow et al. 1990–91).

c. *Propositional network:* Collins and Loftus (1975) proposed a model of semantic memory, extended by Lang (1979) to information processing of emotions, in which any construct is thought to have a network of associations. The co-occurrence of smoking and drinking may lead to associations on a cognitive or construct level. Stimulating one part of the semantic network facilitates activation of other associated parts.

2. *Coping:* Smoking may be used to cope with urges to drink or with situations that pose a high risk for drinking. Here, smoking would decrease risk of relapse to drinking for alcoholics.

a. *Social learning theories:* These indicate that smoking and drinking have some common reinforcement properties, such as stress reduction. Consequently, an alcoholic may smoke instead of drink as a means of coping with stress or attaining some other desired reinforcement properties. To the extent that both smoking and drinking may be used for affect regulation, alcoholics with comorbid primary depression may be particularly likely to substitute tobacco for alcohol. Expectancies about the reinforcement properties of tobacco and alcohol may mediate the observed relationships and are therefore important to study.

b. *Coping as a neuropsychological strategy:* Alcohol craving may involve a depletion of dopamine or endorphins in the ventral tegmental area (Wise 1988). In this case, smoking may satisfy the desire for increased dopamine or endorphin release so that alcohol is not needed to produce that effect, as described by Pomerleau in chapter 8. This effect may be particularly important for alcoholics with comorbid depression as an alternative mechanism to produce enhanced dopaminergic release.

3. *Interaction Only During Use, Not During Sobriety:* It may be that smoking and alcohol use affect each other during ongoing use but that smoking has no effect on urges to drink or on ability to cope with high-risk alcohol situations during sobriety. This hypothesized interaction of smoking with alcohol use has been discussed in detail earlier in this volume (e.g., Pomerleau, chapter 8; Collins, chapter 7); therefore, only two examples will be mentioned here. First, smoking may be a neuropsychological strategy to cope with some of alcohol's effects during intoxication. Nicotine has been found to decrease the attentional deficits that alcohol administration causes (Lyon et al. 1975; Tong et al. 1974). Therefore, people may smoke more while drinking to reduce the resulting cognitive deficit. Second, Collins and colleagues (1988) have shown that nicotine may result in cross-tolerance to the effects of alcohol for some measures. In these cases, smoking may not be needed for a compensatory effect during sobriety.

OVERVIEW OF RESEARCH PRESENTED

To investigate mediating mechanisms, we have conducted a series of theoretically guided studies. These include laboratory studies, investigations of alcoholics' self-reported expectations about the interactions between smoking and alcohol use, measures of change in smoking-related variables as a function of alcohol treatment, and investigations of the role of individual differences.

LABORATORY INVESTIGATIONS

ADVANTAGES OF CAREFULLY CONTROLLED LABORATORY STUDIES

Considerable information is obtained by observing the natural covariation of smoking and drinking or urges to drink among alcoholic smokers. However, specific relationships among mediating mechanisms can best be studied by manipulating one variable and observing its effects on other variables of interest. In order to generalize our results to alcoholics during sobriety, most of our investigations have been conducted with alcoholics in treatment. However, studies involving analog populations of nonproblem drinkers are also of interest, particularly when studying relationships that are presumed to exist for all drinkers during periods of time in which drinking is occurring and when manipulating smoking variables and studying their effects on alcohol consumption under controlled conditions. Some of our investigations are described briefly in this chapter to provide an overview of our findings to date.

EFFECTS OF ALCOHOL CUES ON URGES TO SMOKE

These results include those of Gulliver and colleagues (1995) and replication data not previously reported. Several questions were investigated concerning the effects of exposure to alcohol cues on urges to smoke using a paradigm that has reliably been found to elicit urges to drink in most alcoholics. The first sample was 88 male alcoholic smokers in treatment at the Providence Veterans Affairs Medical Center (VAMC). Some of these results were then replicated in a sample of 144 male and female alcoholics (mostly in private residential or partial hospital treatment) currently in one of our ongoing alcohol treatment studies. In both samples, alcoholic smokers in treatment were assessed for degree of alcohol dependence as measured by the Alcohol Dependence Scale (Skinner and Allen 1982), tobacco dependence as measured by minutes to first cigarette of the day (Fagerstrom and Schneider 1989), and smoking rate (number of cigarettes per day). Alcoholics were then exposed to control cues for 3 minutes, followed by 3 minutes of exposure to the sight and smell of their usual alcoholic beverage. The results replicated in both samples were as follows:

- Those with greater alcohol dependence reported a stronger urge to smoke at baseline, even when controlling for tobacco dependence.
- Exposure to alcohol cues resulted in an increased urge to smoke.
- Smoking rate and dependence were unrelated to the urge to drink in response to alcohol cues.

- The urge to drink positively correlated with the urge to smoke during both control and alcohol trials.

Thus, alcoholics in sobriety experienced increased urges to smoke when exposed to alcohol stimuli, and the urge to smoke was greatest in those with the most alcohol dependence. One possible explanation was that alcoholics may use smoking to cope with urges to drink in high-risk situations. We investigated predictions based on this hypothesis in several of the following studies.

SMOKING TOPOGRAPHY STUDY

The purpose of this study was to investigate whether exposure to alcohol cues results in increased urge to smoke or quantity/intensity of smoking as compared to no exposure (Rohsenow et al. unpublished data 1995). Both the priming and coping hypotheses predict that alcoholic smokers should experience a greater urge to smoke and increased smoking when exposed to alcohol cues. The third hypothesis predicts no relationship. One-half of our sample of alcoholic smokers were exposed to 6 minutes of control cues, followed by 6 minutes of alcohol cues, and the other one-half were exposed to only control cues in both trials. Next, all were asked to look at the same beverage for 20 minutes and were told they were free to smoke during this time. Smoking topography was assessed in terms of latency to first puff, puff duration, interpuff interval, and length of time smoking the first cigarette. Those exposed to alcohol had a significantly higher urge to drink and to smoke during the extended period (p's < 0.05). However, groups did not differ in the topography of their smoking behavior. Thus, although alcohol exposure resulted in increased urge to smoke, even while allowed to smoke a cigarette, alcohol cue exposure did not significantly affect the intensity of smoking.

SMOKING DEPRIVATION'S EFFECTS ON ALCOHOL CUE REACTIVITY AND CONSUMPTION

In one study, we investigated the effect of smoking deprivation on the cue-elicited urge to drink and alcohol consumption. Fifty alcohol-dependent smokers were deprived of tobacco for 4 hours or allowed to smoke. Then one-half of them were exposed to alcohol cues and the other one-half only to control cues. Alcohol exposure reliably increased urge to drink and salivation, and smoking deprivation decreased heart rate and blood pressure (all p's < 0.05). Smoking deprivation, however, had no effect on cue-elicited changes in urge to drink, salivation, blood pressure, or heart rate. Finally, in an unobtrusive measure of alcohol consumption (Higgins and Marlatt 1973), smoking deprivation did not affect the amount of beer consumed.

GENDER DIFFERENCES

In the previously discussed studies, we have investigated degree of alcohol dependence or tobacco dependence as individual difference variables that may affect results.

However, gender is another important individual difference, particularly considering the differential relationship between depression and smoking outcomes for women.

In a study of male and female alcoholic smokers in a clinical trial of alcohol treatment, we matched 2 men to every woman by score on the Alcohol Dependence Scale (ADS) (Skinner and Allen 1982) (n = 74 men, 37 women). No gender differences were found in pretreatment smoking rate (number of cigarettes per day for 30 days pretreatment) or dependence (minutes to first cigarette), but men smoked a higher dose of nicotine per day (M = 30.2 mg men, 24.6 mg women; p < 0.05). No gender differences in smoking or drinking varables were found at 6-month followup in gender-by-time repeated measures analyses of variance. Genders did not differ in urge to smoke after either water or alcohol cues in this matched sample.

After the first alcohol trial, a mood induction was done based on the person's highest ranked drinking trigger. We matched 2 men to each woman on the basis of both the ADS score and the type of negative mood induced (i.e., anger, depression, or anxiety) (n = 54 men, 27 women). Repeated measures analysis found a higher urge to smoke in the alcohol trial after mood induction than in the alcohol trial before mood induction, with no gender differences. However, when only the people whose highest trigger was depression were selected (21 men, 11 women), a gender-by-time interaction effect was found (F [1,30] = 4.95, p < 0.04). The women's urge to smoke was significantly higher after the depression induction than before, whereas the men's urge to smoke did not change as a function of the depression induction.

Thus, the women did not differ in smoking (other than nicotine content) before or after treatment or in urges to smoke in response to alcohol stimuli. However, women may be more affected by the combination of depressed affect and alcohol cues than are men. Women with a history of major depression have a more difficult time quitting smoking than do women without such a history (Glassman et al. 1988), and women smokers have lower self-efficacy about resisting relapse in negative affect situations than do men (Abrams et al. 1987). However, among alcoholics, comorbidity of major depression or recurrent episodes of major depression reduced the probability of successfully quitting smoking among both men and women (Covey et al. 1993). Unfortunately, we were unable to investigate current or past depression as a mediator of our results. We investigated menstrual phase (luteal versus follicular) as a mediator of the effects we observed and failed to find any significant effect.

A final lab study reflects our recent enthusiasm for the influence of attentional processes in cue reactivity (e.g., Rohsenow et al. 1994) and smoking (Lyon et al. 1975). In this study conducted by Tibor Palfai in our lab, we are manipulating attentional processes along lines suggested by Wegner (1994). Heavy-drinking nonalcoholic smokers are asked to either monitor or suppress their reactions to alcohol cues. When released from these instructions, those previously asked to suppress their reactions are predicted to show a rebound effect, unlike those asked to monitor their reactions. Such a rebound has been found as a result of thought suppression (Wegner 1994) and pain suppression (Cioffi and Holloway 1993) in prior studies. Preliminary results showed a significant rebound on urge to drink, urge to smoke, and smoking topography for the suppression group. As no tobacco cue exposure was involved, the rebound on urge to smoke appears to be mediated by the urge to drink.

CONCLUSIONS FROM LABORATORY STUDIES

We have uncovered several relationships between smoking variables and alcohol-related variables among alcoholics in treatment. Some of these vary as a function of individual differences, such as alcohol dependence, gender, and depressed mood. Some results suggest that smoking may not be used as a means to cope with urges to drink, so that quitting smoking may not be removing an important coping tool for alcoholics. However, the fact that alcohol cues increase urges to smoke suggests that smoking cessation may be particularly difficult during alcohol treatment and early recovery when urges to drink may be strongest. Individual differences clearly need to be considered in studying the influence of smoking on the ability to remain sober.

SMOKING DURING FOLLOWUP OF ALCOHOL TREATMENT

As a companion to our laboratory investigations, we have conducted clinical studies of the interrelationships of smoking and drinking outcome measures. In a series of studies, we investigated the relationship of various pretreatment alcohol or smoking measures to alcohol or tobacco use during 6-month followup after treatment.

EFFECTS OF DETOXIFICATION ON SMOKING RATE AND URGES

A common clinical observation is that alcoholics appear to smoke more during detoxification. However, since alcoholics smoke more than nonalcoholics, it is not clear whether detoxification affects alcoholics' own smoking rates or if staff members interpret a normally high smoking rate as a response to detoxification. In a study of 38 alcoholic smokers who were detoxified without medication at the Providence VAMC (described in Monti et al. 1993b), no relationship was found between length of time since last drinking day and number of cigarettes per day ($r = 0.02$). In fact, the number of cigarettes per day was significantly lower during the last 24 hours (M = 27 cigarettes) during the first week of detoxification than during the 30 days before treatment (M = 31 cigarettes, $F[1,36] = 4.26$, $p < 0.05$). Because the patients had

substantial free time and no smoking restrictions at that time, the decrease was not due to restrictions on the unit. Thus, detoxification appears to be associated with decreased smoking rate.

EFFECTS OF TOBACCO DEPENDENCE ON RISK FOR POOR ALCOHOL OUTCOMES

A study reported by Abrams and colleagues (1992) investigated effects of tobacco dependence on responses to alcohol high-risk situations and on outcome while controlling for differences in alcohol dependence. A VA sample ($n = 45$) and a private hospital sample ($n = 163$) of alcoholics in alcohol treatment clinical trials were assessed with the Alcohol Specific Role Play Test (ASRPT) (Monti et al. 1993a) to investigate their urge to drink, self-reported difficulty, anxiety, and observer-rated skillfulness in coping with 10 simulated high-risk situations. They were then followed up 6 months later. Alcoholic smokers with greater tobacco dependence had greater urge to drink and greater difficulty and more anxiety in the role plays of high-risk alcohol situations while controlling for alcohol dependence. This suggested that tobacco dependence could increase risk for alcohol relapse. However, tobacco dependence did not predict alcohol use during followup, as assessed by the mean number of drinks per day or the frequency of drinking in either sample. In the private hospital sample, among those who relapsed to drinking, those with greater tobacco dependence drank more alcohol on days that they drank.

We replicated and extended the followup analyses in a sample of 78 alcoholic smokers in an alcohol treatment trial. Again no relationship was found between tobacco dependence (minutes to first cigarette) or number of cigarettes smoked per day pretreatment and quantity or frequency of drinking or number of drinks per drinking day at followup. Therefore, smoking dependence could increase apparent risk for poor alcohol use outcomes, as indicated by responses to alcohol role plays, but shows no consistent effect on drinking outcomes for alcoholics after alcohol treatment.

In a study of 95 alcoholic smokers, those who at baseline said they often or always smoke to cope with urges to drink smoked more but relapsed to alcohol use at a lower rate a month later than did those who said they never or rarely smoke to cope ($p < 0.05$). These analyses controlled for baseline smoking and drinking rates. Thus, this strategy may be working for many alcoholic smokers. Of interest is the fact that smoking to cope did not have a detrimental effect on motivation to quit smoking at followup: Alcoholics who reported frequently smoking to decrease urges to drink were also significantly more likely to consider quitting smoking at followup ($p < 0.05$).

CHANGE IN MOTIVATION TO QUIT SMOKING AFTER ALCOHOL TREATMENT

One model that is not directly relevant to the hypotheses we have been discussing but that has considerable treatment implications is the transtheoretical model of behavior change (Prochaska and DiClemente 1983). In this model, smokers who are "precontemplators" are not yet even thinking about changing their smoking, but those in the "contemplation" or "action" stages are seriously thinking about or have begun to quit smoking. The transtheoretical model suggests that providing action-oriented treatment to precontemplators will result in very poor treatment impact.

Among alcoholic smokers, we have found that over 70 percent are precontemplators, compared with 42 percent of smokers in Rhode Island health care facilities (Colby et al. 1994). Thus, the majority of alcoholics in treatment are not yet thinking about changing their smoking and may not be receptive to interventions. However, readiness to consider quitting smoking changes during followup to alcohol treatment. We interviewed a sample of 95 alcoholic smokers 1 month after their detoxification, 80 percent of whom were still abstinent. Significantly more alcoholics were contemplating quitting smoking at followup (52 percent) than at baseline (28 percent), with no significant difference by relapse status (figure 1). Thus, even without any smoking intervention, alcoholics become more willing to consider changing smoking after some sobriety. This result has important clinical implications, because it suggests that the period early in recovery may be a window of opportunity for interventions, such as

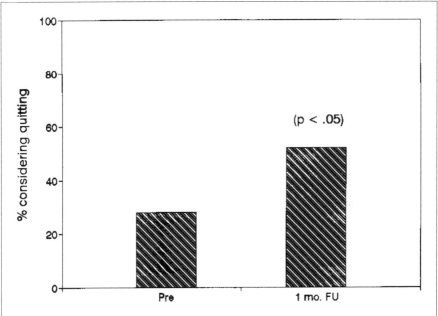

Figure 1. Change in readiness to quit smoking 1 month after alcohol treatment. Note: FU = followup.

motivational interviewing (Miller and Rollnick 1991), to enhance receptivity to quitting smoking.

ALCOHOL AND SMOKING INTERACTION EXPECTANCIES

Expectancies have been an important component of social learning theory. We have recently developed a questionnaire to investigate some of the beliefs alcoholics have about the relationships among smoking and drinking urges and use during drinking periods and during sobriety (Colby et al. 1992, 1994). We also asked about their reactions to the idea of smoking treatment during or after alcohol treatment and the effects on the perceived risk to their sobriety of continuing or of quitting smoking.

About 70 percent of 116 alcoholics sampled said that during sobriety they would smoke more when they had an urge to drink. Therefore, smoking cessation might be particularly difficult early in recovery for some alcoholics. Although only 20 percent expected smoking to decrease their urge to drink, a majority of alcoholics (58 percent) have at times smoked to cope with an urge to drink.

When asked about smoking treatment, about 70 percent said it would be harder to stay sober if they quit smoking during alcohol treatment. Almost 80 percent said it would be harder to quit smoking during alcohol treatment than at a later time. If offered smoking treatment during alcohol treatment, voluntary treatment is more acceptable than mandatory treatment. If voluntary smoking treatment were available, 40 percent said they would probably or definitely refuse it, but 30 percent said they might try it and 30 percent said they would probably try it. However, if smoking treatment were mandatory, 29 percent said they would leave treatment, 30 percent said they would stay but refuse to quit, and 41 percent said they might quit or would quit smoking. While these reports may not accurately predict behavior, they demonstrate the strong resistance many alcoholics feel toward mandatory smoking treatment during alcohol treatment.

Tobacco and alcohol dependence affect responses to some key expectancy items. Those with higher alcohol dependence scores reported stronger urges to drink when they could not smoke and were more likely to say that drinking increases their smoking. This is consistent with Shiffman and colleagues' (1994) results when smokers self-monitored their smoking and drinking behavior using palm-top computers. Alcoholics with greater tobacco dependence were more likely to say they would leave the program if smoking treatment were mandatory ($r = 0.19$), were more likely to say it is harder to quit smoking during alcohol treatment ($r = 0.29$), and were more likely to believe that smoking cessation is a

threat to their sobriety ($r = 0.30$, all p's < 0.01).

Several conclusions may be drawn from this questionnaire study. It may be better to offer smoking intervention as a voluntary—rather than mandatory—treatment, possibly after initial sobriety has been achieved, and possibly to those with less tobacco dependence. Many alcoholics with greater tobacco dependence may use smoking as a means to cope during early sobriety, and this coping strategy may work for many of them. We would like to point out that these results do not conflict with the data presented on natural recovery by Sobell and colleagues in chapter 12, because (1) all their quitters had quit voluntarily and (2) they refer to changes within a 6-month period as simultaneous, whereas we are interested in differences within the 6-month followup period.

EFFECTS OF SMOKING CESSATION TREATMENT ON ALCOHOLICS IN TREATMENT

In general studies of smoking interventions, assessing alcohol use may improve predictions. Hughes (1993) found that of 315 volunteers for nicotine replacement treatment for smoking, the 12 percent with a past history of AOD abuse were less likely to stop smoking and benefited more from nicotine replacement therapy.

A few studies have been published investigating the effects of smoking treatment on sobriety for AOD abusers (see table 1). Burling and colleagues (1991) offered voluntary smoking treatment in a 4-month residential treatment program and randomly assigned 19 alcoholics to smoking treatment and 20 alcoholics to a waiting list. Those offered smoking treatment were more likely to continue in inpatient treatment for 30 more days, and one-third of the treated patients quit smoking during the 10-day contract period. No effects were found on smoking or on AOD use at the 3- and 6-month followups except that treated subjects were using lower nicotine cigarettes. Because the study had a small sample, it may not have had the power to detect differences. The results are generalizable only to volunteers.

Joseph and colleagues (1990, 1993) studied the effects of instituting a no-smoking policy combined with mandatory three-session smoking cessation treatment. They compared 160 people hospitalized during the 5 months before the policy change with 154 people hospitalized during the 5 months after the policy change. Although the early report found no harmful effects of the mandatory treatment, the later report was less optimistic. People in the treated group showed significantly more cocaine use (40 percent of the treated group were improved, compared with 71 percent of the control group) and tended to use more marijuana. No significant effect was found on smoking rates at followup: Seven of the treated group and three of the control group said they were not smoking. Thus, implications from the little research that has been done suggest that it is important to proceed with caution before implementing mandatory smoking cessation programs during AOD abuse treatment.

Martin and colleagues (1993) and Calfas and Martin (1994) investigated

Table 1. Effects of Smoking Treatment for Substance Abusers.

Study	Type of Treatment	Method of Assignment	Results at Followup	
			Smoking	Alcohol and Other Drug Use
Burling et al. 1991	voluntary	random	ns for cigs/d ↓nicotine cigs (6 mo)	ns
Joseph et al. 1990, 1993	mandatory	sequential	ns	↑cocaine ↑marijuana (trend)
Martin et al. 1993	voluntary	random	↓cigs/d (6 mo)	ns
Hurt et al. 1994	voluntary	sequential	abstinence (1 yr)	ns

the effects of smoking cessation after some sobriety has been achieved. Free smoking cessation treatment was offered to members of the Alcoholics Anonymous community who had been sober at least 3 months. At 6-month followup, no harmful effects on AOD use were seen. However, significantly fewer cigarettes were smoked per day at followup than at pretreatment.

Hurt and colleagues (1994) also provided smoking treatment to 51 volunteers from an inpatient addictions unit and compared the results with 50 controls who had been admitted prior to the availability of smoking treatment. At 1-year followup, 12 percent of the treated and none of the untreated smokers were confirmed as abstinent from cigarettes (a significant difference), with no differences in AOD use. One problem Hurt noted was the differential volunteer rate in this study: Only one out of four eligible alcoholics volunteered for the smoking treatment condition, whereas three out of four eligible alcoholics volunteered to participate in the control condition, leading to a confounding of motivation with intervention. This study illustrates the importance of not concluding from studies of voluntary treatment that mandatory smoking treatment would also do no harm.

Several conclusions may be drawn from the above studies. Concurrent smoking cessation treatment has little beneficial effect on smoking, but smoking treatment offered after a period of sobriety has a significant effect

6 months later. Voluntary treatment may produce less harm than mandatory treatment in effects on sobriety. We look to the exciting work being conducted by Hughes and colleagues for guidance with respect to the use of nicotine replacement therapy for alcoholics trying to quit.

IMPLICATIONS FOR HYPOTHESIZED MECHANISMS

Although more research needs to be done, both in the human experimental laboratory and in the context of clinical treatment trials, the series of studies reviewed herein has begun to shed light on the possible mechanisms and interactions of alcohol and tobacco (nicotine). First, little or no support appears for the hypothesis that smoking primes relapse to alcohol in alcoholics. Both Gulliver and colleagues (1995) and Abrams and colleagues (1992) reported that alcohol dependence and alcohol cue exposure produced more urges to smoke but that smoking rate and dependence were unrelated to urges to drink. This is more suggestive of the hypothesized lack of interaction during sobriety than the priming hypothesis. Moreover, in another study we assessed reactions to alcohol cue exposure in drinking smokers, one-half of whom were deprived of cigarettes for 4 hours. Smoking immediately prior to cue exposure had no effect on cue-elicited changes in urge to drink, salivation, or actual drinking on a taste test. Clearly the whole range of definitive parametric studies that manipulate both smoking and drinking have not been completed. Our results require replication and possibly greater refinement of the mechanisms and hypotheses to be tested. Nevertheless, work reported in this chapter illustrates the kind of theory-driven model building that we believe will advance our understanding of alcohol-tobacco interactions.

The treatment outcome studies provide some support for the coping hypothesis. These studies suggest that individual differences and coping may interact so that there is a subset of smokers who do smoke to cope, especially early on in their sobriety, that they find it is helpful, and that they would resist or refuse treatment for smoking cessation. Several studies of alcohol treatment samples provide some support for the idea that smoking may not prime the urge to drink but rather may be a coping tool for some during followup after treatment. Our models, working hypotheses, and studies conducted to date illustrate the advantages of having theory-driven approaches as well as the complex interactions of multiple variables that are possible. We are only beginning to define the boundary conditions needed for more definitive research.

IMPLICATIONS FOR FUTURE RESEARCH

Recommendations for future research are as follows:

- We recommend adding smoking measures to most studies of alcoholics to provide further information about interrelationships between tobacco and alcohol use. Many studies of the family history of tobacco dependence have failed to include measures of drinking history, yet the familial transmission of smoking may be accounted for by familial transmission of drinking. Measures should be standardized across studies. Controlled laboratory studies allow for careful manipulation of smoking- and drinking- related variables, but the laboratory does have its limitations. Shiffman's (1994) methodology of using palm-top computers to assess drinking and smoking behavior has exciting possibilities. Replication is crucial for our understanding, but some findings have failed to be replicated.

- Individual differences may affect response to treatment. For example, our data suggest that it may be advisable to offer smoking interventions only to those alcoholics with lower levels of addiction to tobacco or alcohol. The role of gender differences also needs further investigation, because the treatment needs of alcoholic women smokers may be different from those of men. The understanding of special issues for adolescent populations may be important, as is evident from work being conducted by Mark Myers. In summary, it is likely that a sequential stepped-care approach based on patient-treatment matching will be needed.

- The changing *zeitgeist* provides opportunities to study the effects of treatment policy changes on both smoking cessation and alcohol use outcomes in alcohol treatment centers. However, the evidence suggests that policy changes should not be implemented without careful study of their consequences. Some of our data support long-held concerns of many counselors, and it is of primary importance to do no harm.

- The field is not yet ready for the definitive treatment outcome trial. However, such a trial is likely to involve crossing individual differences with skills-oriented versus motivational approaches, with pharmacologic adjuncts, and with sequencing (i.e., immediate versus after 1 month or more of sobriety has been attained) using a voluntary approach.

IMPLICATIONS FOR POLICY

Suggested implications for policy are as follows:

- Alcoholics who say they smoke to cope with urges to drink are less likely to relapse. In addition, findings indicate that a mandatory smoking intervention results in increased use of other drugs (Joseph et al. 1993).

- Mandatory treatment may result in counter-control efforts by alcoholics, whereas voluntary approaches may result in more alcoholics trying the treatment.

- Smoking interventions may not be beneficial for those with comorbid primary depression, for those high in tobacco dependence, or for those high in alcohol dependence.

- Sequencing smoking interventions after some sobriety has been established may be a more beneficial approach. Alcoholics are more receptive to changing their smoking after some sobriety has been attained, even those who smoke to cope with urges to drink.

- Furthermore, the large proportion of precontemplators may benefit more from approaches designed to increase motivation to change than from skills-training approaches.

ACKNOWLEDGMENTS

This work was supported in part by a Veterans Affairs Merit Review grant awarded to Drs. Rohsenow and Monti; by National Institute on Alcohol Abuse and Alcoholism grants 2R01–AA08734 and 1R01–AA07850 awarded to Dr. Monti; and by National Heart, Lung, and Blood Institute grant HL32318 and National Cancer Institute grants CA38309 and P01 CA50087 awarded to Dr. Abrams. Grateful appreciation is expressed to Drs. Suzy Gulliver, Raymond Niaura, and Alan Sirota for their scientific contributions to the development of some of the studies described herein.

REFERENCES

Abrams, D.B.; Monti, P.M.; Pinto, R.P.; Elder, J.P.; Brown, R.A.; and Jacobus, S.I. Psychosocial stress and coping in smokers who relapse or quit. *Health Psychol* 6:289–303, 1987.

Abrams, D.B.; Monti, P.M.; Carey, K.B.; Pinto, R.P.; and Jacobus, S.I. Reactivity to smoking cues and relapse: Two studies of discriminant validity. *Behav Res Ther* 26:225–233, 1988.

Abrams, D.B.; Binkoff, J.A.; Zwick, W.R.; Liepman, M.R.; Nirenberg, T.D.; Munroe, S.M.; and Monti, P.M. Alcohol abusers' and social drinkers' responses to alcohol-relevant and general situations. *J Stud Alcohol* 52:409–414, 1991.

Abrams, D.B.; Rohsenow, D.J.; Niaura, R.S.; Pedraza, M.; Longabaugh, R.; Beattie, M.C.; Binkoff, J.A.; Noel, N.E.; and Monti, P.M. Smoking and treatment outcome for alcoholics: Effects on coping skills, urge to drink, and drinking rates. *Behav Ther* 23:283–297, 1992.

Abrams, D.B.; Emmons, K.M.; Linnan, L.; Biener, L. Smoking cessation at the workplace: Conceptual and practical considerations. In: Richmond, R., ed. *Smoking Cessation: An International Perspective*. New York: Williams and Wilkins, 1994. pp. 137–169.

Battjes, R.J. Smoking as an issue in alcohol and drug abuse treatment. *Addict Behav* 13:225–230, 1988.

Burling, T.A.; Marshall, G.D.; and Seidner, A.L. Smoking cessation for substance abuse inpatients. *J Subst Abuse* 3: 269–276, 1991.

Calfas, K., and Martin J.E. Smoking cessation in a recovering alcoholic population: A randomized control trial. In: Monti, P.M., and Abrams, D.B., chairs.

"Alcohol and Nicotine Dependence: Biobehavioral Mechanisms, Treatment and Policy Implications." Symposium presented at the annual meeting of the Research Society on Alcoholism, Maui, Hawaii, June 1994.

Cioffi, D., and Holloway, J. Delayed costs of suppressed pain. *J Pers Soc Psychol* 64: 274–282, 1993.

Colby, S.M.; Gulliver, S.B.; Rohsenow, D.J.; Monti, P.M.; Niaura, R.S.; Sirota, A.D.; Rubonis, A.V.; Michalec, E.; and Abrams, D.B. "Impact of Alcohol Cue Reactivity on the Smoking Topography of Alcoholics." Poster presented at the annual meeting of the Association for Advancement of Behavior Therapy, New York, November 1991.

Colby, S. M.; Abrams, D.B.; Gulliver, S.B.; Niaura, R.S.; Monti, P.M.; Rohsenow, D.J.; and Sirota, A.D. "Assessing Alcohol and Smoking Interaction Expectancies in Male Alcoholics." Poster presented at the annual meeting of the Association for Advancement of Behavior Therapy, Boston, November 1992.

Colby, S.M.; Rohsenow, D.J.; Sirota, A.D.; Abrams, D.B.; Niaura, R.S., and Monti, P.M. Alcoholics' beliefs about quitting smoking during alcohol treatment: Do they make a difference? In: Monti, P.M., and Abrams, D.B., chairs. "Alcohol and Nicotine Dependence: Biobehavioral Mechanisms, Treatment and Policy Implications." Symposium presented at the annual meeting of the Research Society on Alcoholism, Maui, Hawaii, June 1994.

Collins, A.M., and Loftus, E.F. A spreading-activation theory of semantic processing. *Psychol Rev* 82:407–428, 1975.

Collins, A.C.; Burch, J.B.; DeFiebre, C.M.; and Marks, M.J. Tolerance to and cross tolerance between ethanol and nicotine. *Pharmacol Biochem Behav* 29: 365–373, 1988.

Covey, L.S.; Glassman, A.H.; Stetner, F.; and Becker, J. Effect of history of alcoholism or major depression on smoking cessation. *Am J Psychiatry* 150:1546–1547, 1993.

Fagerstrom, K.O., and Schneider, N. Measuring nicotine dependence: A review of the Fagerstrom Tolerance Questionnaire. *J Behav Med* 12:159–182, 1989.

Glassman, A.H.; Stetner, F.; Walsh, B.T.; Raizman, P.S.; Fleiss, J.L.; Cooper, T.B.; and Covey, L.S. Heavy smokers, smoking cessation, and clonidine. *JAMA* 259: 2863–2866, 1988.

Gulliver, S.B.; Rohsenow, D.J.; Colby, S.M.; Dey, A.N.; Abrams, D.B.; Niaura, R.S.; and Monti, P.M. Interrelationship of smoking and alcohol dependence, use and urges to use. *J Stud Alcohol* 56:202–206, 1995.

Higgins, R.L., and Marlatt, G.A. Effects of anxiety arousal on the consumption of alcohol by alcoholics and social drinkers. *J Consult Clin Psychol* 41:426–433, 1973.

Hughes, J.R. Treatment of smoking cessation in smokers with past alcohol/drug problems. *J Subst Abuse Treat* 10: 181–187, 1993.

Hurt, R.D.; Eberman, K.M.; Croghan, I.T.; Offord, K.P.; Davis, L.J., Jr.; Morse, R.M.; Palmen, M.A.; and Bruce, B.K. Nicotine dependence treatment during inpatient treatment for other addictions: A prospective intervention trial. *Alcohol Clin Exp Res* 18:867–872, 1994.

Istvan, J., and Matarazzo, J.D. Tobacco, alcohol and caffeine use: A review of their interrelationships. *Psychol Bull* 95:301–326, 1984.

Joseph, A.M.; Nichol, K.L.; Willenbring, M.L.; Korn, J.E.; and Lysaght, L.S. Beneficial effects of treatment of nicotine dependence during an inpatient substance abuse treatment program. *JAMA* 263: 3043–3046, 1990.

Joseph, A.M.; Nichol, K.L.; and Anderson, H. Effect of treatment for nicotine dependence on alcohol and drug treatment outcomes. *Addict Behav* 18: 635–644, 1993.

Kozlowski, L.T.; Jelinek, L.C.; and Pope, M.A. Cigarette smoking among alcohol abusers: A continuing and neglected problem. *Can J Public Health* 77:205–207, 1986.

Kozlowski, L.T.; Skinner, W.; Kent, C.; and Pope, M.A. Prospects for smoking treatment in individuals seeking treatment for alcohol and other drug problems. *Addict Behav* 14:273–278, 1989.

Lang, P.J. A bio-informational theory of emotional imagery. *Psychophysiology* 16: 495–512, 1979.

Lyon, R.J.; Tong, J.E.; Leigh, G.; and Clare, G. The influence of alcohol and tobacco on the components of choice reaction time. *J Stud Alcohol* 36:587–596, 1975.

Martin, J.E.; Calfas, K.; Polarek, M.S.; Hofstetter, R.; Noto, J.; Beach, D.; and Patten, C. Treating smoking in the recovering alcoholic population. In: Hughes, J., chair. "Smoking Cessation in Alcohol/Drug Abuse." Symposium conducted at the Sixth International Conference on Treatment of Addictive Behaviors, Santa Fe, January 1993.

Mello, N.K.; Mendelson, J.H.; Sellers, M.L.; and Kuehnle, J.C. Effect of alcohol and marihuana on tobacco smoking. *Clin Pharmacol Ther* 27:202–209, 1980.

Mello, N.K.; Mendelson, J.H.; and Palmieri, S.L. Cigarette smoking by women: Interactions with alcohol use. *Psychopharmacology* 93:8–15, 1987.

Miller, W.R., and Rollnick, S. *Motivational Interviewing: Preparing People To Change Addictive Behavior.* New York: Guilford, 1991.

Monti, P.M.; Binkoff, J.A.; Abrams, D.B.; Zwick, W.R.; Nirenberg, T.D.; and Liepman, M.R. Reactivity of alcoholics and nonalcoholics to drinking cues. *J Abnorm Psychol* 96:122–126, 1987.

Monti, P.M.; Abrams, D.B.; Kadden, R.M.; and Cooney, N.L. *Treating Alcohol Dependence: A Coping Skills Training Guide.* New York: Guilford, 1989.

Monti, P.M.; Abrams, D.B.; Binkoff, J.A.; Zwick, W.R.; Liepman, M.R.; Nirenberg, T.D., and Rohsenow, D.J. Communication skills training with family and cognitive behavioral mood management training for alcoholics. *J Stud Alcohol* 51:263–270, 1990.

Monti, P.M.; Rohsenow, D.J.; Abrams, D.B.; Zwick, W.R.; Binkoff, J.A.; Munroe, S.M.; Fingeret, A.L.; Nirenberg, T.D.; Liepman, M.R.; Pedraza, M.; Kadden, R.M.; and Cooney, N.L. Development of a behavior analytically derived alcohol-specific role-play assessment instrument. *J Stud Alcohol* 54:710–721, 1993*a*.

Monti, P.M.; Rohsenow, D.J.; Rubonis, A.V.; Niaura, R.S.; Sirota, A.D.; Colby, S.M.; Goddard, P.; and Abrams, D.B. "Cue exposure with coping skills treatment for male alcoholics: A preliminary investigation." *J Consult Clin Psychol* 61:1011–1019, 1993*b*.

Prochaska, J.O., and DiClemente, C.C. Stages and processes of self-change in smoking: Toward an integrative model of change. *J Consult Clin Psychol* 51:390–395, 1983.

Rohsenow, D.J.; Niaura, R.S.; Childress, A.R.; Abrams, D.B.; and Monti, P.M. Cue reactivity in addictive behaviors: Theoretical and treatment implications. *Int J Addict* 25(7A & 8A):957–993, 1990–91.

Rohsenow, D.J.; Monti, P.M.; Rubonis, A.V.; Sirota, A.D.; Niaura, R.S.; Colby, S.M.; Wunschel, S.M.; and Abrams, D.B. Cue reactivity as a predictor of drinking among male alcoholics. *J Consult Clin Psychol* 62:620–626, 1994.

Rohsenow, D.J.; Monti, P.M.; Abrams, D.B.; Gulliver, S.B.; Rubonis, A.V.; and Colby, S.M. "Cue exposure and coping skills treatment for alcohol abuse: Outcome at six and twelve months." Paper presented at the Seventh International Conference on Treatment of Addictive Behaviors, Noordwijkerhout, the Netherlands, May 1995.

Shiffman, S.; Fischer, L.A.; Paty, J.A.; Gnys, M.; Hickcox, M.; and Kassel, J.D. Drinking and smoking: A field study of their association. *Ann Behav Med* 16:203–209, 1994.

Skinner, H.A., and Allen, B.A. Alcohol dependence syndrome: Measurement and validation. *J Abnorm Psychol* 91:199–209, 1982.

Tong, J.E.; Knott, V.J.; McGraw, D.J.; and Leigh, G. Alcohol, visual discrimination and heart rate: Effects of dose, activation and tobacco. *Q J Stud Alcohol* 35:1003–1022, 1974.

Wegner, D.M. Ironic processes of mental control. *Psychol Bull* 101:34–52, 1994.

Wise, R.A. The neurobiology of craving: Implications for the understanding and treatment of addiction. *J Abnorm Psychol* 97:118–132, 1988.

Chapter 12

Dual Recoveries From Alcohol and Smoking Problems

Mark B. Sobell, Ph.D., Linda C. Sobell, Ph.D.,
and Lynn T. Kozlowski, Ph.D.

Alcohol consumption and smoking cigarettes are strongly associated, particularly the heavy use of both drugs (Istvan and Matarazzo 1984; Kozlowski et al. 1986; Bobo 1989; Bien and Burge 1990; Friedman et al. 1991; Kozlowski et al. 1993). Although this relationship suggests possible etiologic linkages between these two behaviors (Addesso 1979; Henningfield et al. 1984; Niaura et al. 1988), an equally important issue is how the relationship affects attempts to recover from smoking or problem drinking. Most information about the effects of alcohol-tobacco interactions derives from studies of persons in alcohol treatment programs (DiFranza and Guerrera 1990; Joseph et al. 1993) or from short-term followups of such programs (Bobo et al. 1986, 1987; Abrams et al. 1992). These studies have examined how changes in smoking affect recovery from alcohol problems. Although there is evidence that concurrent treatment for smoking does not decrease recovery rates from drinking (for a review, see Bien and Burge 1990), less is known about how drinking affects attempts to stop smoking.

M.B. Sobell, Ph.D., is a professor at the Center for Psychological Studies, Nova Southeastern University, Fort Lauderdale, FL 33314. L.C. Sobell, Ph.D., is senior scientist and chief of the Guided Self-Change Unit at the Clinical Research and Treatment Institute, Addiction Research Foundation, 33 Russell Street, Toronto, Ontario, Canada M5S 2S1; she is also professor in the Departments of Psychology, Family and Community Medicine, and Behavioural Science, University of Toronto. L.T. Kozlowski, Ph.D., is professor and head of the Department of Biobehavioral Health, College of Health and Human Development, 208 Health and Human Development East, The Pennsylvania State University, University Park, PA 16802.

This chapter reports data from two studies of individuals who had recovered from alcohol problems without formal help or treatment and who had also stopped smoking. One study was a cross-sectional general survey of the Canadian population; the other study was a longitudinal investigation of individuals who, when first interviewed, had been recovered from an alcohol problem without treatment for a minimum of 1–3 years, and who were scheduled to be reinterviewed 5 years following the first interview. The latter group represents an exceptionally stable set of alcohol recoveries; at the second interview, subjects had been recovered for an average of 13 years. The longitudinal design of the second study provided for a comparative examination of relapse rates from alcohol problems and smoking.

STUDY 1

METHOD

The National Alcohol and Other Drugs Survey (NADS) was conducted by Statistics Canada in March 1989, using a random digit dialing method (Statistics Canada 1990). Telephone interviews were conducted with 11,634 persons 15 years of age or older drawn from the 10 Canadian provinces (the Yukon and Northwest Territories were excluded because many individuals did not have telephones). One respondent was randomly selected per household, and persons living in institutions were not interviewed. All respondents were assured anonymity.

The overall response rate for the survey was 78.7 percent. The final sample was weighted to adjust for several factors (e.g., homes without telephones, census projections for each province). The weighting procedures are described in detail elsewhere (Statistics Canada 1990). Statistical analyses were performed using weighted sample data. However, sample sizes are reported using unweighted data. The present analyses are based on data from 10,796 respondents 20 years of age or older (this age category was closest to the legal drinking age of 19 in Canada) who met the drinking criteria listed for respondents below.

The interview questions allowed for the determination of (a) whether respondents had ever had an alcohol problem (i.e., amount and frequency of drinking, drinking-related problems); (b) whether respondents who had an alcohol problem were recovered at the time of the interview and, if recovered, the length of their recovery; and (c) for recovered respondents, whether their resolution was to abstinence or to moderate drinking, and whether they had ever received any formal services, help, or treatment for an alcohol-related problem. Various background questions (e.g., age, education) were also asked of all respondents.

Although the alcohol field has never had consensus on criteria to define alcohol problems, the criteria applied in this study are consistent with previous research (Klatsky et al. 1981; National Institute on Alcohol Abuse and Alcoholism 1992). Respondents were grouped according to their drinking status at the time of interview. Group designations and the criteria used for assignment to groups are as follows:

- Resolved Abstinent (n = 302): Current abstainers who had been abstinent for ≥ 1 year when interviewed and reported that they had once experienced problems related to their alcohol use (i.e., their drinking had affected their "work, studies, employment opportunities," "physical health," "friendships or social life," or "financial position," or had interfered with their "family or home life").
- Resolved Nonabstinent (n = 144): Current drinkers who reported that they had once experienced alcohol problems, but for ≥1 year they had reduced their drinking to a moderate drinking level as defined by (a) no current (i.e., past 12 months) problems due to their alcohol use and (b) their drinking in the past 12 months (i.e., period covered by the survey) was at levels not considered to constitute a gender-related health risk (Babor et al. 1987; Rimm et al. 1991; Anderson et al. 1993). Moderate drinking was defined as (a) usual drinking of ≤ 3 drinks for males and ≤ 2 drinks for females, (b) no more than 2 days of 5–7 drinks in the past year (to allow for a small amount of celebratory drinking), and (c) no more than 7 drinks

consumed on any single day in the past year.

- Problem Drinkers (n = 1,158): These respondents were current drinkers who drank at least one time per week in the past year and reported experiencing alcohol-related problems or drinking at a level associated with definite health risks. Health risk drinking for males was defined as usually drinking ≥ 7 drinks on a drinking day, and for females as usually drinking ≥ 5 drinks (Kranzler et al. 1990).

Recovered respondents were further classified according to whether they had ever used any of the following treatment services or other types of help for their drinking: Alcoholics Anonymous (AA) or other support groups; psychologist, psychiatrist, or social worker; psychiatric hospital; minister, priest, or rabbi; doctor or nurse; hospital or emergency department; alcohol/drug addiction agency; detoxification center or halfway house. Respondents's smoking status was also assessed during the interview. For respondents to be classified as recovered smokers, they had to have stopped smoking cigarettes for at least 14 months (the closest interval to 1 year that could be derived from the interview data) prior to the interview.

RESULTS

Of those respondents who had recovered from an alcohol problem, 77.5 percent did so without formal help or treatment. Of the 22.5 percent who used help or treatment, the predominant help was AA, which was used in

82.8 percent of cases. Of the total number of recoveries, 62.0 percent were to abstinence and 38.0 percent involved moderate drinking. Further details about the drinking recoveries and respondent characteristics are presented elsewhere (Sobell et al. unpublished data 1995).

Table 1 displays respondents' smoking status when interviewed for the two groups of recovered respondents and for the current problem drinkers from the same survey. Nondaily smokers were excluded from all subsequent analyses for study 1. As shown in table 1, a greater number of respondents in the Resolved Abstinent group had smoked at some time in their lives compared with the other two groups. To provide comparability between groups, table 1 also presents smoking continuation and cessation rates for respondents who had ever been smokers. A 2 x 3 chi-square analysis of these data was statistically significant, $\chi^2(2) = 48.15$, $p < 0.001$. The smoking cessation rate for both groups of recovered respondents was higher than that for current problem drinkers, and the cessation rate for respondents who had resolved to moderate drinking was the highest across all the groups. Although the rate of current smoking was relatively similar between current problem drinkers and respondents who had resolved to abstinence, the difference was statistically significant, $\chi^2(1) = 18.91$, $p < 0.01$. The rate of current smoking was also significantly lower among respondents who had resolved to moderate drinking than among current drinkers, $\chi^2(1) = 45.92$, $p < 0.001$.

Although these cross-sectional survey data cannot reflect temporal

Table 1. Smoking Status for Respondents Who Had an Abstinent Recovery From an Alcohol Problem (Resolved Abstinent), Who Had a Moderate Drinking Recovery From an Alcohol Problem (Resolved Nonabstinent), or Who Were Problem Drinkers When Interviewed.

Smoking Status at Interview	% Resolved Abstinent ($n = 302$)	% Resolved Nonabstinent ($n = 144$)	% Problem Drinkers ($n = 1,158$)
Still smoking	50.2	23.4	49.1
Stopped smoking	28.9	37.8	16.2
Never smoked	14.7	31.5	26.4
Excluding Subjects Who Never Smoked			
	($n = 232$)	($n = 89$)	($n = 785$)
Still smoking	63.5	38.3	75.1
Stopped smoking	36.5	61.7	24.9

Note: Data are from 1989 Canadian National Alcohol and Other Drugs Survey respondents who were ≥ 20 years of age ($n = 10,796$). Figures within groups do not sum to 100% because short-term (≤ 14 months) smoking recoveries and nondaily smokers are excluded.

changes between alcohol and cigarette use, they do allow an examination of smoking status as a function of length of drinking problem recovery. In table 2 recoveries of two lengths are presented: 1–5 years and > 5 years. Although a greater percentage of long-term versus short-term recovered respondents in both recovered groups had never smoked, the never smoked rate among long-term recovered respondents was lower than (17.7 percent for abstinent recoveries) or similar to (25.1 percent for nonabstinent recoveries) that of current problem drinkers (26.4 percent). Table 2 also includes smoking continuation and cessation rates for respondents who had ever smoked. Although there is little difference between the smoking recovery rates for short-term and long-term moderate drinking recoveries, $\chi^2(1) = 0.22$, $p > 0.05$, a significantly greater percentage of short-term than long-term abstinent recoveries were still smoking when interviewed, $\chi^2(1) = 8.22$, $p < 0.01$.

Whereas study 1 explored the prevalence of dual recoveries in a general population survey, study 2 provides a more detailed examination of dual recoveries using a selected sample of individuals who recovered from an alcohol problem on their own.

STUDY 2

METHOD

Study 2 was a longitudinal investigation of natural recoveries from alcohol problems. To conserve space, only features of the study relevant to the issue of dual recoveries are presented

Table 2 Smoking Status at the Time of Interview for Resolved Abstinent and Resolved Nonabstinent Subjects as a Function of Resolution Length (1–5 Years, > 5 Years).

Smoking Status at Interview	% Resolved Abstinent		% Resolved Nonabstinent	
	Length of Recovery			
	1–5 Years ($n = 117$)	> 5 Years ($n = 185$)	1–5 Years ($n = 68$)	> 5 Years ($n = 76$)
Still smoking	62.3	41.6	41.0	23.4
Stopped smoking	19.9	35.2	30.4	44.2
Never smoked	10.4	17.7	21.5	25.1
	Excluding Subjects Who Never Smoked			
	($n = 92$)	($n = 140$)	($n = 39$)	($n = 50$)
Still smoking	75.8	54.1	41.5	36.2
Stopped smoking	24.2	45.9	58.5	63.8

Note: Data are from 1989 Canadian National Alcohol and Other Drugs Survey respondents who were ≥ 20 years of age ($n = 10,796$). Figures within groups do not sum to 100% because short-term (≤ 14 months) smoking recoveries and nondaily smokers are excluded.

here; for subject characteristics and other details, see our other publications on this study (Sobell et al. 1992, 1993*a*, 1993*b*). Subjects were recruited through media advertisements, and collateral informants had to corroborate that subjects had an alcohol problem and that the problem had been resolved. Although not relevant to the present discussion, the study also included a control group of subjects who had current alcohol problems when interviewed. The 120 recovered subjects were classified into three groups:

- Resolved Abstinent (*n* = 71): These subjects had recovered from an alcohol problem through abstinence and had sustained their recovery for at least 3 years when first interviewed. Mean recovery length was approximately 8 years.
- Resolved Nonabstinent (*n* = 21): These subjects had resolved their drinking problem for at least 3 years when first interviewed, and any drinking after their resolution had to have met criteria as nonhazardous and without evidence of problems (Sobell et al. 1992). Mean recovery length was almost 7 years.
- Resolved Abstinent Treatment (*n* = 28): These subjects reported that their recovery was independent of treatment that had occurred sometime in the past. To be included, these subjects had to have a recovery of at least 1 year. Their mean recovery length was approximately 4.5 years.

Because there were no significant differences between groups in terms of subjects' reported reasons for resolution or factors that helped them maintain their resolution, data for the three groups have been combined for this report. The subjects were predominantly male (79.2 percent), and the majority were employed at the time of their recovery (74.3 percent). They had a mean (SD) of 12.0 (2.7) years of education, and most (70.1 percent) were married at the time of their recovery. Subjects reported a mean (SD) of 13.2 (7.8) years of problem drinking and had a mean (SD) Michigan Alcoholism Screening Test (MAST) (Selzer 1971) score of 12.8 (4.3); 98.3 percent met DSM–III–R criteria for an alcohol dependence diagnosis (American Psychiatric Association 1987).

Subjects were scheduled to be reinterviewed 5 years after their initial interview. Reinterviews were conducted with 95.6 percent (109) of the 113 living subjects, and information was available on 2 subjects who were not reinterviewed. The reinterviews allowed for an assessment of the stability of recoveries. Subjects were classified as having a stable recovery or as having relapsed. Stable recoveries included 8 subjects (7.2 percent) who had maintained their recovery but switched recovery type (5 switched from abstinent to nonabstinent; 3 from nonabstinent to abstinent).

RESULTS

Temporal Ordering of Recoveries

At the initial interview, 91.7 percent (110/120) of the subjects reported that they had been smokers at some time in their life. Of these 110, 32.7 percent (36) were still smoking when first interviewed, and 67.3 percent (74) were dually recovered. For this analysis, concurrent recovery was defined as both recoveries occurring within a 1-year period. With respect to temporal ordering of recoveries, no pattern was evident: 48.6 percent (36/74) resolved their alcohol problem before stopping smoking, 40.5 percent (30/74) stopped smoking first, and only 10.8 percent (8/74) had concurrent recoveries. Of those who stopped smoking first, 30 percent (9/30) quit before the onset of their alcohol problem.

Analyses of subject factors associated with recovery patterns indicated that subjects who stopped smoking after or concurrent with recovering from their alcohol problem (a) reported a longer problem drinking history (years), $M(SD) = 14.72(4.42)$ versus $10.33(3.41)$, $t(1) = 4.56$, $p < 0.001$; (b) reported experiencing more alcohol-related consequences, $M(SD) = 9.73(2.71)$ versus $7.93(3.08)$, $t(72) = 2.64$, $p < 0.01$; (c) reported consuming more drinks per drinking day prior to recovery, $M(SD) = 16.32(10.58)$ versus $11.20(5.87)$, $t(72) = 2.41$, $p < 0.02$; (d) had fewer years of education, $M(SD) = 11.45(2.64)$ versus $13.10(3.17)$, $t(72) = -2.43$, $p < 0.02$; and (e) had smoked for a longer number of years, $M(SD) = 32.72(14.34)$ versus $23.07(12.80)$, $t(60) = 2.73$, $p < 0.01$. These findings suggest that individuals who had more severe alcohol and smoking problems tended to

recover from their drinking problem before stopping smoking. Snow and colleagues (1992) also reported that individuals who resolved their drinking problem prior to smoking had more severe drinking problems than those who stopped smoking first.

The perceived relative difficulty of recovering from the two disorders was probed with these subjects. Although other studies (e.g., Kozlowski et al. 1989) have explored this question, heretofore this has not been examined with individuals who have achieved successful dual recoveries, particularly a long-term recovery from alcohol problems. Reinterviews with 57 subjects who had experienced both problems concurrently (i.e., those who had quit smoking before developing an alcohol problem were excluded) were asked to rate whether smoking or drinking problems were more difficult to resolve. Consistent with previous research, 40.4 percent rated smoking as more difficult, 28.1 percent rated alcohol problems as more difficult, and 31.6 percent reported no difference. Related to the difficulty of recovering, subjects were also asked how many "serious" attempts they had made. Data from 59 subjects who had achieved dual recoveries indicated that they had made a mean (SD) of 2.20 (3.43) previous serious attempts (median = 1.0) prior to stopping smoking and a mean (SD) of 2.49 (9.27) previous serious quit attempts (median = 1.0) prior to recovering from their alcohol problem. The difference between the alcohol and smoking is not statistically significant,

$t(58) = 0.22$, $p > 0.05$. It is likely that subjects in this study reported fewer attempts to stop smoking than Schachter's (1982) subjects because the question in the present study was qualified by asking about "truly serious" attempts versus any attempts.

Temporal Stability of Recoveries

Longitudinal data for individuals who have recovered from an alcohol problem and have also stopped smoking permit the comparison of relapse rates for the two disorders. Information for 111 of the subjects who had been recovered from an alcohol problem at the first interview indicated that 17 (15.3 percent) relapsed over the 5-year interval. Likewise, longitudinal data were available for 63 subjects who had stopped smoking by the first interview. Of these, 4 relapsed between interviews, yielding a relapse rate of 6.3 percent, less than half the relapse rate for alcohol. Statistical comparisons between these rates would be inappropriate because of the overlap in subjects.

Another important issue was the stability of smoking status across interviews. For the 107 subjects reinterviewed (smoking data were unavailable for 2 subjects), 97 (90.7 percent) maintained their smoking status across interviews (10 were never smokers, 28 remained smokers, and 59 remained quitters). Of the 34 smokers at the initial interview, 6 (17.6 percent) quit smoking by the second interview, whereas 4 (6.3 percent) of the 63 subjects who had quit by the first interview had relapsed by the second interview. Excluding

subjects who never smoked, the between-interviews quit rate for smoking was significantly greater than the relapse rate, $\chi^2(1) = 54.31$, $p < 0.001$. It is notable that by the second interview 67.0 percent (65/97) of all subjects who had ever smoked had stopped.

The interaction between alcohol and cigarette use over time can be explored by examining the stability of one behavior as a function of the other. A total of 111 cases were available for an analysis of drinking status at the second interview (all subjects were recovered from an alcohol problem at the first interview) as a function of smoking status at the first interview. Excluding the 10 subjects who had never smoked, it was found that subjects were significantly more likely to have relapsed to drinking if they were smokers at the first interview (11/38, 28.9 percent) than if they had quit smoking by the first interview (5/63, 7.9 percent), $\chi^2(1) = 6.35$, $p < 0.05$. This suggests that continued smoking increases the risk of relapse for recovered alcohol abusers.

Table 3 presents a more detailed analysis of the relationship between smoking status and drinking status across interviews. Although the number of cases in critical cells is small, the data suggest that the risk of relapse to drinking may be very high for individuals who relapse to smoking. A Fisher's Exact test indicated that subjects with a dual recovery at the first interview had a significantly greater likelihood of relapse to drinking if they relapsed to smoking, and only a

Table 3. Relationship Between Relapse to Smoking and Relapse to Drinking for 109 Subjects Recovered From a Drinking Problem at Interview 1.

Smoking Status		Drinking Status at Interview 2		
Interview 1	Interview 2	Still Recovered	Relapsed	Relapse Rate
Quitter	Smoker	2	2	50.0%
Quitter	Quitter	56	3	5.1%
Smoker	Smoker	21	7	25.0%
Smoker	Quitter	6	2	25.0%
Never smoked	Never smoked	9	1	10.0%

small likelihood of relapse to drinking if they did not relapse to smoking ($p = 0.029$).

Ways of Maintaining Recoveries

Approximately half (52.3 percent) of the subjects who had quit smoking by interview 1 and slightly less than half (47.7 percent) of those who had recovered from a drinking problem reported having experienced urges to drink or smoke during the first 6 months following their recovery. The proportion of subjects experiencing no urges is somewhat higher than that reported by Carmody and colleagues (1986) in a study of recovered smokers (about 25 percent of their subjects reported having experienced no urges).

Subjects who reported urges for smoking and/or drinking were asked how they coped with the urges. Table 4 presents a comparison of methods used to cope with urges. Subjects responded to the question "What did you do to cope with these desires and thoughts?" by endorsing possible strategies derived from the literature (Carmody et al. 1986; Garvey et al. 1989). Subjects' reports of other methods not on the list were also recorded. For each drug the most frequent coping strategies were cognitive in nature and included thinking about negative consequences of use, thinking about positive consequences of not using, and toughing it out. As shown in table 4, with the exception of the strategy of eating, a greater percentage of subjects reported using coping strategies to deal with drinking urges than with smoking urges. Also, a small but not insubstantial proportion of subjects reported smoking to cope with drinking urges and vice versa (18.9 percent and 12.1 percent, respectively).

At the second interview, recovered subjects were also asked about their reasons for not relapsing to smoking and drinking: "You have been resolved for __ years now. Why wouldn't you go back to problem drinking (smoking)?" Their responses to these two open-ended questions were independently grouped into categories by two trained raters, with disagreements settled by discussion between the raters. Subjects' grouped responses are shown in table 5 for the 94 subjects who were still recovered from a drinking problem at the second interview and the 65 subjects who were recovered from smoking. In this case there were clear differences between the behaviors. The most frequently stated reason for not relapsing to drinking or smoking was a desire to avoid negative consequences, and particularly health consequences for smoking. This finding for smokers is consistent with results reported by Carmody and colleagues (1986).

Based on the literature, a final matter of interest with regard to the

Table 4 Strategies Used by Subjects Who Experienced Urges To Drink ($n = 53$) or To Smoke ($n = 33$) To Deal With Urges Within the First 6 Months Following Recovery.

Strategy	% Who Used Strategies To Deal With Urges To	
	Drink ($n = 53$)	Smoke ($n = 33$)
Thought about the negative consequences if drank/smoked	71.7	45.5
Tried to just tough it out using will power	60.4	48.5
Thought about the positive consequences of not drinking/smoking	52.8	36.4
Drank nonalcoholic beverages	45.3	33.3
Tried to distract self	41.5	18.2
Ate something sweet	26.4	24.2
Light physical activity	26.4	21.2
Made use of other people	22.6	9.1
Ate food	18.9	30.3
Smoked cigarettes	18.9	n.a.
Tried not to think about the desire	17.0	18.2
Tried to relax	17.0	6.1
Drank alcohol	n.a.	12.1

maintenance of recoveries involves changes in other appetitive behaviors, body weight, or activities related to changes in drinking or smoking (Carmody et al. 1986; Garvey et al. 1989; Carmody 1990). As shown in table 6, which presents data for 65 subjects who had dual recoveries, multiple changes in activities were reported as associated with both types of recoveries. Of those subjects who reported changes in weight, 91.4 percent said they gained weight following recovery from smoking, whereas 63.9 percent reported a weight loss associated with recovery from drinking. Table 6 also shows that subjects generally reported an increase in many appetitive behaviors associated with their recovery from drinking, although the percentage who reported any changes varied greatly from behavior to behavior. A somewhat smaller proportion of subjects reported changes associated with their recovery from smoking. In both cases the predominant direction of change was toward increased use. Although some subjects reported increased alcohol use associated with their stopping smoking, this study did not assess whether increased smoking was associated with recovery from drinking.

GENERAL DISCUSSION

The findings reported in this chapter are consistent with other studies in the literature showing a high rate of co-occurrence of smoking and heavy drinking. A striking finding in study 2 was the exceptionally high stability of long-term recoveries from both smoking and alcohol problems. Although the relapse rates of 6.3 percent for smoking and 15.3 percent for drinking are well below those typical in the literature (Marlatt and Gordon 1985), that literature derives

Table 5. Reasons for Not Relapsing as Reported at the Second Interview by Subjects Still Recovered From Drinking ($n = 94$) and/or Smoking ($n = 65$).

Reasons for Not Relapsing to Problem Drinking	%	Reasons for Not Relapsing to Smoking	%
Costs/negative effects	68.1	Health	70.8
No need/no desire	33.0	Smell/taste/dirty	32.2
Feeling better	26.6	Costs	30.8
Loss of control	20.2	No desire/stupid	24.6
Effect of family/friends	13.8	Bad habit	15.4
		Socially unacceptable	12.3

Table 6. Changes Reported During the First 6 Months After Resolving an Alcohol Problem or Stopping Smoking for 65 Subjects With Dual Recoveries.

Change In	After Smoking Resolution			After Drinking Resolution		
	% Yes	% Increase	% Decrease	% Yes	% Increase	% Decrease
Weight	53.8	91.4	8.6	55.4	36.1	63.9
Use of coffee	20.3	46.2	46.2	42.9	88.9	11.1
Exercise	18.5	100.0	0.0	29.2	94.7	5.3
Diet	35.4	82.6	13.0	50.8	87.9	12.1
Use of alcohol	15.4	90.0	10.0	—	—	—
Use of decaffeinated beverages	6.3	100.0	0.0	55.4	80.0	16.0
Use of caffeinated soft drinks	4.7	100.0	0.0	24.6	93.8	6.3
Use of prescription drugs	—	—	—	12.3	50.0	50.0

Note: The percent increase or decrease refers only to those individuals who experienced change. Percent change does not always sum to 100 because some subjects reported their change was bidirectional.

mostly from studies of short-term recoveries of treated clients (i.e., < 1 year). For example, a study by Carmody and colleagues (1986) that examined the stability of long-term recoveries from smoking found that for ex-smokers who had maintained their recovery for approximately 9 years, only 9 percent relapsed over a subsequent 5-year period, a finding similar to the high stability of recoveries reported in study 2 in this chapter. Likewise, De Soto and colleagues (1989) reported low relapse rates among AA members who had maintained abstinence for at least 3 years.

Study 2 also provided evidence suggesting that for recovered alcohol abusers, continued smoking may increase the risk of relapse. However, because these findings are correlational, it is possible that both continued smoking and relapse to drinking result from another factor (e.g., life stress). The possible role of alcohol consumption in relapse to smoking has been suggested by laboratory studies (see Shiffman 1982) and clinical studies (Brandon et al. 1986). The results of studies 1 and 2 showing that substantial numbers of alcohol abusers who had successful moderate drinking recoveries had also stopped smoking demonstrate that, at least for some, continued drinking at low levels does not constitute a serious risk for relapse to alcohol abuse. This is because the smoking relapse rate across 5 years was quite low.

An important caveat that applies to both studies is that, by virtue of the criteria imposed for recovery, the studies reported on selected samples. Also, with regard to study 2, it is possible that persons who recover without treatment differ from those who seek treatment.

ISSUES CONCERNING DUAL RECOVERIES

With regard to the timing of dual recoveries, only a small percentage (10.8 percent) of cases in study 2 resolved both problems within a 12-month period, and individuals with more severe drinking problems tended to stop their smoking after they had resolved their alcohol problem. However, those who continued to smoke after resolving their alcohol problem appeared at greater risk of relapse to problem drinking. These data, unfortunately, shed no light on the advantages or limitations of attempting to recover from both problems simultaneously.

It is possible that no general recommendation about treatment timing will be supported when the issues are carefully considered. In particular, the specific nature of the association between drinking and smoking has not been defined by existing research. The nature of the covariation could range from fully independent behaviors that occur coincidentally, to functionally interdependent behaviors where the onset of one behavior signals the onset of the other or vice versa. Further, it is conceivable that a range of interdependency will best describe smokers who are also heavy drinkers and that these individual differences will suggest different treatment strategies. For example, to the extent that the two behaviors are independent, the timing of interventions would probably be unimportant. Conversely, if the behaviors are highly interdependent, concurrent treatment may offer the best chance of recovery from both problems. One occasion when concurrent treatment may be unwise is during detoxification for severely dependent alcohol abusers. The elicitation of a nicotine withdrawal syndrome simultaneously with an alcohol withdrawal syndrome could potentiate agitation and interfere with alcohol detoxification.

Irrespective of timing, another important issue is treatment content. For example, Hughes (1993) suggested that nicotine replacement therapy may be especially helpful for individuals who are severely dependent on alcohol. Given the similarities between smoking and excessive drinking, it can be hypothesized that it would be beneficial for the same treatment rationale to be used for both behaviors. In sequential treatment, the increased self-efficacy associated with overcoming one problem might generalize more readily to dealing with the other problem if clients view the problems as having analogous etiologies.

Another issue concerning concurrent treatments is whether treatments should be independent or a specially designed conjoint treatment. Although a conjoint treatment would seem to have obvious cost savings, reports of combined treatments have yet to be published. Besides a shared rationale, a conjoint treatment might emphasize the linkage between smoking and drinking in terms of mutual cues and how such cues trigger both behaviors (e.g., at a party). It might also be important to consider differences in the behaviors. For example, except in severe cases, heavy drinking typically is not constant throughout the waking cycle, something characteristic of nicotine dependence.

Issues of treatment content become complicated when one considers that in studies 1 and 2 there were multiple cases of persons who had a stable, moderate drinking recovery yet continued to smoke (i.e., smoking did not lead to a relapse to problem drinking), and who had a stable, moderate drinking recovery but had stopped smoking (i.e., alcohol use did not occasion a relapse to smoking). Moderate drinking recoveries with or without smoking suggest that individual differences may be important in determining how best to achieve dual recoveries. In particular, to the extent that the two behaviors are strongly linked, independent (rather than concurrent) recoveries may be difficult unless the individual has quit smoking. Dependence severity for each

substance may also be important. Research more precisely defining the relationship between smoking and heavy drinking is greatly needed.

There are many other individual difference factors that could similarly affect how dual recoveries could be best achieved. For example, if individuals view both their drinking and smoking as reflecting compulsive personality traits or as being ways of coping with problems, there might be benefit to treating the problems simultaneously and, in the latter case, establishing alternative behaviors to replace the functions of both behaviors. Given the large population of persons who both smoke and drink heavily, it seems highly unlikely that any single treatment formulation will be suitable for all cases. Rather, individual differences will likely be the key to effective treatment planning.

IMPLICATIONS FOR RELAPSE PREVENTION

The data in this report, although from selected samples, suggest that continued smoking may increase the risk of relapse to drinking for some individuals. However, these data speak only to the occurrence and not the severity of relapse. It is also possible that, rather than smoking directly cuing alcohol use, continued smoking and relapse to drinking reflect a third factor (e.g., motivation or life stress). In study 1 a sizable number of respondents in each recovery group were still smoking at the time they were interviewed. For these individuals continued smoking clearly had not triggered a relapse to excessive drinking. Also, the highest rates of smoking cessation in study 1 were for respondents who had achieved moderate drinking recoveries. For these respondents, continued moderate drinking even for longer than 5 years had not led them to relapse to smoking. Demographic variables found to distinguish between abstinent and moderate drinking recoveries could also account for differences in smoking status. Moderate drinking recoveries, compared with abstinent recoveries, were more likely to involve better educated, younger females who had higher incomes and white-collar jobs (Sobell et al. unpublished data 1995).

Conceptually, because smoking occurs frequently and throughout the day, drinking might be more likely to cue relapse to smoking than vice versa, particularly for less severe problem drinkers. However, for heavy drinkers whose heavy drinking is regularly associated with smoking, the discriminative stimulus value of drinking for smoking may be strong and could lead to relapse to smoking. Finally, individual difference variables may be important in determining risk of relapse.

RESEARCH RECOMMENDATIONS

Based on the two studies described in this chapter as well as a broader consideration of the issues involved in concurrent alcohol and smoking disorders, the following research recommendations are offered:

- Prospective studies of dual recoveries are necessary to understand the processes antecedent and consequent to such outcomes and factors that precipitate relapses.
- More sensitive measures of the strength of the association between smoking and drinking in individual subjects may be important for explaining different patterns of change.
- Treatment trials need to assess the outcome of concurrent treatment for alcohol problems and smoking. Ideally, such studies would be structured to evaluate the influence of subject variables (e.g., severity of dependence, strength of association between smoking and excessive drinking, compulsivity) on outcomes.
- Given the high co-occurrence of smoking among alcohol abusers in treatment and vice versa, a large amount of data on the relationship between drinking and smoking could be generated if agencies funding alcohol and smoking treatment studies were to require that treatment outcome evaluations gather data on the use of both drugs.
- Studies similar to those reported here but focusing on a population identified as having recovered from smoking, and examining not just excessive drinking but any alcohol consumption, would provide valuable information on the effect of drinking on the maintenance of smoking recoveries.

- Individuals who achieve a dual recovery and then relapse to one or both drugs could be compared with those who sustain their recovery with respect to previous use patterns and perhaps their conditioned responses to stimulus cues for both drugs.

In conclusion, knowledge of the relationship between recovering from and relapsing to smoking and drinking problems could have substantial clinical implications. Alcohol abuse and nicotine abuse are both diagnosable disorders (American Psychiatric Association 1994). The costs to society of abusing either drug are substantial (U.S. Department of Health and Human Services 1988; National Institute on Alcohol Abuse and Alcoholism 1993), but their combined use makes such costs synergistic. Thus, it is time that serious attention be paid to this topic.

ACKNOWLEDGMENTS

This chapter was prepared with support from National Institute on Alcohol Abuse and Alcoholism grant AA–08593. Dr. John Cunningham and Ms. Sangeeta Agrawal assisted with statistical analyses, and Ms. Joanne Jackson assisted with typing.

REFERENCES

Abrams, D.B.; Rohsenow, D.J.; Niaura, R.S.; Pedraza, M.; Longabaugh, R.; Beattie, M.C.; Binkoff, J.A.; Noel, N.E.; and Monti, P.M. Smoking and treatment outcome for alcoholics: Effects on coping skills, urge to drink, and drinking rates. *Behav Ther* 23:283–2297, 1992.

Addesso, V.J. Some correlates between cigarette smoking and alcohol use. *Addict Behav* 4:269–273, 1979.

Anderson, P.; Cremona, A.; Paton, A.; Turner, C.; and Wallace, P. The risk of alcohol. *Addiction* 88:1493–1508, 1993.

American Psychiatric Association. *Diagnostic and Statistical Manual of Mental Disorders, Third Edition, Revised.* Washington, DC: the Association, 1987.

American Psychiatric Association. *Diagnostic and Statistical Manual of Mental Disorders, Fourth Edition.* Washington, DC: the Association, 1994.

Babor, T.F.; Kranzler, H.R.; and Lauerman, R.J. Social drinking as a health and psychosocial risk factor: Anstie's limit revisited. In: Galanter, M., ed. *Recent Developments in Alcoholism.* Vol. 5. New York: Plenum, 1987. pp. 373–402.

Bien, T.H., and Burge, R. Smoking and drinking: A review of the literature. *Int J Addict* 25:1429–1454, 1990.

Bobo, J.K. Nicotine dependence and alcoholism epidemiology and treatment. *J Psychoactive Drugs* 21:323–329, 1989.

Bobo, J.K.; Schilling, R.F.; Gilchrist, L.D.; and Schinke, S.P. The double triumph: Sustained sobriety and successful cigarette smoking cessation. *J Subst Abuse Treat* 3: 21–25, 1986.

Bobo, J.K.; Gilchrist, L.D.; Schilling, R.F.I.; Noach, B.; and Schinke, S.P. Cigarette smoking cessation attempts by recovering alcoholics. *Addict Behav* 7:209–215, 1987.

Brandon, T.H.; Tiffany, S.T.; and Baker, T.B. The process of smoking relapse. In: Tims, F.M., and Leukefeld, C.G., eds.

Relapse and Recovery in Drug Abuse. National Institute on Drug Abuse Research Monograph No. 72. Rockville, MD: the Institute, 1986. pp. 104–117.

Carmody, T.P. Preventing relapse in the treatment of nicotine addiction: Current issues and future directions. *J Psychoactive Drugs* 22:211–238, 1990.

Carmody, T.P.; Brischetto, C.S.; Pierce, D.K.; Matarazzo, J.D.; and Connor, W.E. A prospective five-year follow-up of smokers who quit on their own. *Health Educ Res* 1:101–109, 1986.

De Soto, C.B.; O'Donnell, W.E.; and De Soto, J.L. Long-term recovery in alcoholics. *Alcohol Clin Exp Res* 13:693–697, 1989.

DiFranza, J.R., and Guerrera, M.P. Alcoholism and smoking. *J Stud Alcohol* 51:130–135, 1990.

Friedman, G.D.; Tekawa, I.; Klatsky, A.L.; Sidney, S.; and Armstrong, M.A. Alcohol drinking and cigarette smoking: An exploration of the association in middle-aged men and women. *Drug Alcohol Depend* 27:283–290, 1991.

Garvey, A.J.; Heinold, J.W.; and Rosner, B. Self-help approaches to smoking cessation: A report from the normative aging study. *Addict Behav* 14:23–33, 1989.

Henningfield, J.E.; Chait, L.D.; and Griffiths, R.R. Effects of ethanol on cigarette smoking by volunteers without histories of alcoholism. *Psychopharmacology* 82:1–5, 1984.

Hughes, J.R. Treatment of smoking cessation in smokers with past alcohol drug problems. *J Subst Abuse Treat* 10:181–187, 1993.

Istvan, J., and Matarazzo, J.D. Tobacco, alcohol, and caffeine use: A review of their interrelationships. *Psychol Bull* 95:301–326, 1984.

Joseph, A.M.; Nichol, K.L.; and Anderson, H. Effect of treatment for nicotine dependence on alcohol and drug treatment outcomes. *Addict Behav* 18:635–644, 1993.

Klatsky, A.L.; Friedman, G.D.; and Siegelaub, A.B. Alcohol and mortality: A ten-year Kaiser-Permanente experience. *Ann Intern Med* 95:139–145, 1981.

Kozlowski, L.T.; Jelinek, L.C.; and Pope, M.A. Cigarette smoking among alcohol abusers: Continuing and neglected problem. *Can J Public Health* 77:205–207, 1986.

Kozlowski, L.T.; Skinner, W.; Kent, C.; and Pope, M. Prospects for smoking treatment in individuals seeking treatment for alcohol and other drug problems. *Addict Behav* 14:273–279, 1989.

Kozlowski, L.T.; Henningfield, J.E.; Keenan, R.M.; Lei, H.; Leigh, G.; Jelinek, L.C.; Pope, M.A.; and Haertzen, C.A. Patterns of alcohol, cigarette, and caffeine and other drug use in 2 drug abusing populations. *J Subst Abuse Treat* 10:171–179, 1993.

Kranzler, H.R.; Babor, T.F.; and Lauerman, R.J. Problems associated with average alcohol consumption and frequency of intoxication in a medical population. *Alcohol Clin and Exp Res* 14:119–126, 1990.

Marlatt, G.A., and Gordon, J.R. *Relapse Prevention.* New York: Guilford, 1985.

National Institute on Alcohol Abuse and Alcoholism. *Alcohol Alert No 16: Moderate Drinking.* PH 315. Rockville, MD: the Institute, 1992.

National Institute on Alcohol Abuse and Alcoholism. *Eighth Special Report to the U.S. Congress on Alcohol and Health.* National Institutes of Health Publication No. 94–3699. Washington, DC: U.S. Government Printing Office, 1993.

Niaura, R.S.; Rohsenow, D.J.; Binkoff, J.A.; Monti, P.M.; Abrams, D.B.; and Pedraza, M. Relevance of cue reactivity to understanding alcohol and smoking relapse. *J Abnorm Psychol* 97:133–152, 1988.

Rimm, R.B.; Giovannucci, E.L.; Willett, W.C.; Colditz, G.A.; Ascherio, W.C.; Rosner, B.; and Stampfer, M.J. Prospective study of alcohol consumption and risk of coronary disease in men. *Lancet* 338:464–468, 1991.

Schachter, S. Recidivism and self-cure of smoking and obesity. *Am Psychol* 37:436–444, 1982.

Selzer, M.L. The Michigan Alcoholism Screening Test: The quest for a new diagnostics instrument. *Am J Psychiatry* 127:89–94, 1971.

Shiffman, S.M. Relapse following smoking cessation: A situational analysis. *J Clin Consult Psychol* 50:71–86, 1982.

Snow, M.G.; Prochaska, J.O.; and Rossi, J.S. Stages of change for smoking cessation among former problem drinkers: A cross-sectional analysis. *J Subst Abuse* 4:107–116, 1992.

Sobell, L.C.; Sobell, M.B.; and Toneatto, T. Recovery from alcohol problems without treatment. In: Heather, N.; Miller, W.R.; and Greeley, J., eds. *Self-Control and the Addictive Behaviours.* New York: Maxwell MacMillan, 1992. pp. 198–242.

Sobell, L.C.; Cunningham, J.A.; Sobell, M.B.; and Toneatto, T. A life span perspective on natural recovery (self-change) from alcohol problems. In: Baer, J.S.; Marlatt, G.A.; and McMahon, R.J., eds. *Addictive Behaviors Across the Lifespan: Prevention, Treatment, and Policy Issues.* Beverly Hills, CA: Sage, 1993a. pp. 34–66.

Sobell, L.C.; Sobell, M.B.; Toneatto, T.; and Leo, G.I. What triggers the resolution of alcohol problems without treatment? *Alcohol Clin Exp Res* 17:217–224, 1993b.

Statistics Canada. *National Alcohol and Other Drugs Survey: Microdata Documentation and Users Guide.* Ottawa: Statistics Canada, 1990.

U.S. Department of Health and Human Services. *The Health Consequences of Smoking: Nicotine Addiction. A Report of the Surgeon General.* DHHS Publication No. 88–8406. Washington, DC: U.S. Government Printing Office, 1988.

Chapter 13

Enhancing Alcohol Control With Counseling on Nicotine Dependence: Pilot Study Findings and Treatment Implications

Janet Kay Bobo, Ph.D., R. Dale Walker, M.D.,
Harry A. Lando, Ph.D., and Helen E. McIlvain, Ph.D.

Tobacco use among alcoholics, recovering alcoholics, and problem drinkers is a major public health problem. The health effects of a history of combined heavy drinking and smoking are substantial (Bobo 1989; Hurt et al. 1994), and the size of the affected population is large. An indication of the magnitude of the population can be obtained by coupling data on the prevalence of people in the United States meeting diagnostic criteria for alcohol abuse or alcoholism *within the past year* with estimates of the proportions of such persons who are likely to be smokers. Grant and colleagues (1991) analyzed data from a 1988 national probability sample of adults in the United States and estimated that 8.63 percent of the population, or approximately 15.3 million people, met the criteria

J.K. Bobo, Ph.D., is an associate professor and epidemiology section chief in the Department of Preventive and Societal Medicine, University of Nebraska Medical Center, 600 South 42d Street, Omaha, NE 68198–4350. R.D. Walker, M.D., is a professor in the Department of Psychiatry and Behavioral Sciences, University of Washington and Chief, Addictions Research Center (116 ATC), Seattle Veterans Affairs Medical Center, 1600 South Columbian Way, Seattle, WA 98108. H.A. Lando, Ph.D., is a professor in the Department of Epidemiology, University of Minnesota, 1300 South 2d Street, Suite 300, Minneapolis, MN 55454–1015. H.E. McIlvain, Ph.D., is an associate professor in the Department of Family Practice, University of Nebraska Medical Center, 600 South 42d Street, Omaha, NE 68198–4350.

as designated by the *Diagnostic and Statistical Manual of Mental Disorders, Third Edition, Revised* (DSM–III–R) for alcohol dependence and abuse during the prior year. To date, most studies of nicotine use in recovering alcoholics have reported rates exceeding 80 percent (Dreher and Fraser 1968; Ashley et al. 1981; Kozlowski et al. 1986; Burling and Ziff 1988), a finding that suggests that as many as 12.2 million adults routinely combine smoking with heavy use of alcohol.

Another compelling argument for studying tobacco use in this population rests on a small group of studies that have suggested that quitting smoking may actually enhance, not threaten, the process of alcohol recovery. At least four research teams have reported evidence of better drinking outcomes among smokers who quit smoking than among those who continued to smoke (Miller et al. 1983; Bobo 1989; De Soto et al. 1989; Sobell and Sobell 1993). Unfortunately, none of these studies were designed specifically to address the possible effects of quitting smoking on alcohol recovery and may thus be biased in ways that are difficult to detect or interpret. Furthermore, studies of the effects of smoking cessation on levels of alcohol use in samples of the general population of moderate drinkers have been much less consistent (Zimmerman et al. 1990; Carmelli et al. 1993; Nothwehr et al. 1995).

For these reasons, we designed a pair of consecutive, randomized community intervention trials to evaluate the safety and efficacy of urging recovering alcoholics in treatment to consider quitting smoking and to assess the impact of any serious attempts to quit on rates of relapse to drinking or using other drugs. Findings from the first of these two trials are reported here. The first study was a pilot investigation that took place in four residential alcohol treatment centers in central and western Nebraska and enrolled 90 recovering alcoholic patients for 6 months of followup. The second, full-scale replication study has enrolled about 600 patients from 12 residential treatment facilities in Iowa, Kansas, and Nebraska for 18 months of followup, but it will not be completed until 1997. Pilot study facilities and all participating alcohol patients from those facilities were excluded from participation in the replication study.

PILOT STUDY METHODS

To further limit any intermingling of pilot and replication study processes, all pilot study activities took place in rural communities of central and western Nebraska. Of the six residential alcohol treatment facilities in that part of the State, two were excluded from participation, because they either did not serve a representative cross-section of the population or were not well organized administratively. The remaining four programs were first ranked by data obtained from a 1992 survey (Bobo and Davis 1993) on staff attitudes toward treatment of nicotine dependence in alcohol patients and then matched and randomly assigned to the intervention or control condition. After randomization, staff at each site were asked to recruit 30 patients who were (1) at least 18 years old, (2) currently receiving intensive treatment for their problems with alcohol, (3) regularly smoking at least one cigarette per day, and (4) willing to sign a consent form and comply with study protocol during the 6 months of followup. To encourage enrollment, a $10.00 incentive was offered to eligible patients for completion of each of the two followup questionnaires. Demographic data on eligible patients who declined to participate were collected to assess enrollment bias.

In the intervention centers, registered nurses or social workers with graduate degrees used a protocol developed by the investigators to provide 15 minutes of counseling about nicotine dependence and quitting smoking to each participant shortly before he or she was scheduled for discharge from treatment. Several hours of intensive training were provided on use of the intervention protocol, and two of the investigators provided backup telephone consultation as needed. The counseling protocol was based on the stages of change approach to smoking cessation (DiClemente et al. 1991; Prochaska and Goldstein 1991; Prochaska and DiClemente 1993) and explicitly discouraged staff from trying to set an immediate quit date for patients in the precontemplation

and contemplation stages. Intervention site staff were asked to complete a counseling session summary form for each participating subject that included their assessment of the patient's current stage of change. Staff also were given copies of several National Cancer Institute pamphlets (*How to quit smoking...and quit for keeps* and *Why do you smoke?*) to distribute to interested participants.

Intervention and control patients were asked to complete an identical series of three self-administered questionnaires. The first was completed at study enrollment and included a detailed demographic battery; the Self-Administered Alcohol Screening Test, usually referred to as the SAAST (Hurt et al. 1980; Davis et al. 1987); a 30-day timeline followback drinking calendar (Sobell et al. 1988; Sobell and Sobell 1992); a series of questions on use of illicit drugs in the prior year; several items to assess current and historical tobacco use, such as the Fagerstrom Test for Nicotine Dependence, also known as the FTND (Fagerstrom et al. 1990); and the Center for Epidemiologic Studies–Depression Scale (CES–D), which is a widely used depression screening inventory (Radloff 1977; Weissman et al. 1977; Anda et al. 1990).

The second and third questionnaires were mailed to participants 1 and 6 months, respectively, after their date of discharge from residential treatment. These brief assessments used a series of items to measure alcohol, tobacco, and other illicit drug use since leaving the treatment center. A typical item from the 1-month questionnaire read as follows:

> About one (1) month ago, you were discharged from an intensive, residential treatment program for alcohol/drug dependency. Concerning your alcohol use since you were discharged from the center, have you: Drank heavily for at least 1-2 days? (Yes/No) Had several drinks on one occasion? Had more than one alcoholic drink? Had even one alcoholic drink?

Saliva cotinine samples were requested from participants who reported no longer smoking at followup, but technical difficulties with storage of the first set of samples limited the interpretation of physiologic data from the pilot study.

Data analysis used chi square and *t*-test statistics to compare the two groups of patients at enrollment and to identify predictors of outcome that could confound study findings. To control for the design effect of condition assignment, outcome analyses used logistic regression models that included a term for study site (Breslow and Day 1987). A parallel series of analyses also were undertaken using generalized estimating equation (GEE) methods, which explicitly account for the type of nested data obtained in this study (Zeger et al. 1988; Donner and Klar 1994). Because point estimates derived from our standard logistic regression models were nearly identical to those obtained with GEE methods, only results from the former are presented here.

PILOT STUDY RESULTS

During the 13-month enrollment period (February 1, 1993, to February 28, 1994), both control sites successfully enrolled the required total of 30 patients each. One intervention site was closed by its parent company after the first 10 patients were enrolled. The other intervention site also experienced an unexpected drop in census and enrolled only 20 patients during the allotted timeframe. Overall, 93 percent of all patients approached about study participation across the four sites signed a consent form and completed the enrollment questionnaire. Patients who declined did not differ from those who consented by gender, age, or ethnicity.

Completed counseling session summary forms were obtained for 100 percent of all intervention patients. Stages of change data derived from the counseling forms and from the participant questionnaires will be reported elsewhere.

Intervention and control participants were comparable on most demographic, mental health, and drug abuse variables. Seventy percent of the intervention group and 77 percent of the control group were male; 7 and 10 percent, respectively, were nonwhite. The mean age in the intervention group was 38 years, compared to a control group mean of 34. The mean number of years of formal education in the two groups were 12.7 and 12.1, respectively.

Limited data were collected on three mental health indicators. About

48 percent of the intervention group and 53 percent of the control group reported having seen a mental health counselor or a physician for feelings of depression, anxiety (i.e., fearfulness), or anger. Corresponding percentages of intervention patients and controls who reported having been advised by a doctor to take medication for *depression* were 33 and 40 percent, respectively; for *anxiety*, 21 and 16 percent; for *sleeplessness*, 26 and 19 percent; and for *schizophrenia*, 0 and 4 percent). Using the standard CES–D cut-point of 16, 71 percent of the intervention patients and 76 percent of the controls met screening criteria for depression in the prior week. None of these differences was clinically or statistically significant.

Most intervention and control participants scored above the SAAST cut-point of 7 (100 and 97 percent, respectively); 97 and 93 percent had scores of 10 or more. (Scores of 7 through 9 are usually interpreted as suggesting possible alcoholism, and scores of 10 or higher as denoting probable alcoholism [Hurt et al. 1980].) Over 44 percent reported the current admission as at least the second time they had entered a residential alcohol treatment facility. Both groups reported an average of 1.9 intensive treatment efforts. The intervention patients reported drinking on 22 of the 30 days before their last drink, with an average number of 12 drinks per drinking day. The controls drank on 19 of the 30 days and averaged 9 drinks per drinking day. The number of drinks per drinking day was the only enrollment item that significantly distinguished the two groups ($t = -2.13$, $p < 0.05$). About 60 percent of the intervention group and 62 percent of the control group used one or more illicit drugs during the prior year.

Tobacco use histories were also comparable. The average number of cigarettes smoked per day in both groups was 22. The mean FTND scores for intervention and control participants were 6.3 and 5.6, respectively. Both values exceed the mean of 5.15 reported for a sample of 1,447 smokers attending a low-cost smoking cessation program in Ontario, Canada, in the late 1980's (Fagerstrom et al. 1990).

Overall, 87 percent of all 1-month and 90 percent of all 6-month followup assessments were completed. The mean number of days between the mailing of the 1-month followup questionnaires and receipt of the completed measures in the research office was 36 for the intervention group and 35 for the control group. Corresponding means for the 6-month questionnaires were 23 and 18 days, respectively. Table 1 displays drinking relapse rates, recent use of illicit drugs, and tobacco use data from both followups. For all alcohol and illicit drug use indicators, relapse rates in the intervention sites were about one-half as great as those observed in the control sites. Intervention participants were somewhat more likely than controls to report having quit smoking for 48 hours or more and to be current nonsmokers at the

Table 1. Both 1- and 6-Month Alcohol and Tobacco Use Followup Data on Study Participants, Including Number in Group and Percentage, Nebraska, 1993–94.

Item	1-Month Followup		6-Month Followup	
	Intervention	Control	Intervention	Control
No. returned (% returned)	28 (93)	50 (83)	29 (97)	52 (87)
Had at least 1 alcoholic drink*	3 (11)	13 (26)	5 (17)	18 (35)
Drank heavily ≥ 1 day*	2 (7)	6 (12)	2 (7)	9 (17)
Any use of illicit drugs*	1 (4)	4 (8)	3 (10)	13 (25)
Mean no. cigs/d [sd] during prior 7 days	22 [12]	24 [13]	20 [12]	21 [13]
Nonsmoker ≥ 48 hours*	8 (29)	11 (22)	8 (27)	15 (29)
Nonsmoker at followup	2 (7)	0 (0)	1 (3)	4 (8)

*Since discharge from the residential alcohol treatment center program.

1-month followup but not at the 6-month assessment.

Table 2 displays findings for several hypothesized predictors of drinking relapse at 6 months. Female gender, nonwhite race, and lower levels of education were associated with higher relapse rates, although not significantly so. Subjects who met screening criteria for depression at the time of study enrollment were more likely than those who did not to report both having had at least 1 drink since leaving treatment (32 versus 25 percent) and having drank heavily for 1 or more days (16 versus 10 percent). Participants 20 years of age or younger were significantly more likely than older participants to report having had at least one drink since leaving treatment ($p < 0.05$). Relapse rates were also significantly higher among those who had previously undergone intensive alcohol treatment before entering the program they were attending at the time of study enrollment ($p < 0.01$).

Relapse rates measured by the "had even 1 drink" variable were slightly higher for those who had tried to quit smoking by the 1-month followup than for those who had not (33 versus 29 percent) but were slightly lower for the more intensive indicator of several days of heavy drinking (11 versus 16 percent). All relapses to drinking among those who tried to quit smoking during their first month after discharge occurred among control site patients.

The lower relapse rates for intervention patients were confirmed by multivariate analyses using logistic regression models that controlled for study site plus patient age, gender, education, depression, prior use of illicit

Table 2. Predictors of Drinking Relapse at 6-Month Followup by Demographic, Mental Health, and Chemical Dependency Indicators, Nebraska, 1993–94.[1]

Variable	% Reporting Even One Drink Since Treatment Discharge	% Reporting ≥ 1 Day of Heavy Drinking Since Treatment Discharge
Gender		
Male	26	12
Female	35	17
Race		
White	27	14
Nonwhite	50	17
Age (years)		
≤ 20[2]	75	25
21–34	27	15
35–49	20	10
≥ 50	22	11
Education (years)		
< 12	39	23
12	30	16
> 12	21	4
Prior alcohol treatment		
Yes[3]	50	27
No	13	4
Used illicit drugs in prior year		
Yes	35	17
No	19	9
Depressed at enrollment		
Yes	32	16
No	25	10
Tried to quit smoking within 1 month of discharge		
Yes	33	11
No	29	16

[1]For 81 of 90 study participants (90%).
[2]For "had even 1 drink," $\chi^2 = 9.20$, $p < 0.05$.
[3]For "had even 1 drink," $\chi^2 = 12.62$, $p < 0.001$; for "drank heavily," $\chi^2 = 7.84$, $p < 0.01$.

drugs, and prior intensive alcohol treatment. Intervention patients were significantly less likely than control patients to report having had at least one drink during the 6-month interval since completing treatment (odds ratio: 0.15; 95-percent confidence intervals: 0.02, 0.89). Similarly, at 6-month followup, intervention patients were less likely to report 1 or more days of heavy drinking, but the confidence interval included the null value (odds ratio: 0.17; 95-percent confidence intervals: 0.01, 1.95). Intervention and control patients were about equally likely to have quit smoking for 48 hours or longer (odds ratio: 0.73; 95-percent confidence intervals: 0.24, 2.25).

DISCUSSION AND RECOMMENDATIONS FOR FUTURE RESEARCH

The pilot study investigation resulted in four primary findings. *First*, multivariate analyses suggest a positive effect of tobacco counseling on alcohol recovery and use of other illicit drugs. In the small sample of recovering alcoholics reported here, relapse rates among intervention group patients were less than one-half of those observed among controls. *Second*, participants who reported having quit smoking for 48 hours or longer by the 1-month followup were less likely to have relapsed to 1 or more days of heavy drinking by the 6-month assessment, an observation which is consistent with other research in this area.

Third, the stages of change counseling approach for quitting smoking appears feasible and workable for use in residential alcohol treatment centers. Treatment staff in both intervention sites reported that they found the approach easy to use and consistent with other aspects of their therapeutic milieu. But *fourth*, the ef-

fects of the counseling on short-term quit rates are weak, a finding that is also consistent with other studies of minimal smoking cessation interventions (Demers et al. 1990; Gritz et al. 1992).

Selection bias, loss to followup, and differential recall are not likely explanations for the observed findings. Most alcohol patients approached about study participation consented to enrollment, and the intervention and control groups were comparable on almost all demographic and chemical dependency indicators. Loss to followup was minimal in both groups. Note that even if all controls with missing 6-month followup data had had perfect records of abstinence, our findings would still favor the intervention group. Differential recall is also not likely, because the number of lapsed days before return of the completed followup questionnaires was essentially equal for the two groups of participants.

Nevertheless, any generalization of study findings must be tempered by limitations inherent in the study design, including the small sample size, the limited followup period, and our reliance on self-report data. Pilot studies necessarily operate under constraints such as these. The replication study will correct the above limitations through use of a larger sample with longer followup and collection of physiologic and collateral contact data to verify self-reports. The full-scale study is also testing a more powerful smoking cessation intervention in which telephone counseling sessions at 8, 12, and 16 weeks post-treatment discharge have been added to bolster the effectiveness of the 15 minutes of counseling received while still in residential treatment.

Findings from table 2 on predictors of drinking relapse highlight areas in which more research is warranted. In this sample of smokers, women, young adults, and ethnic/racial minorities had higher relapse rates on both 6-month drinking indicators. To date, white, adult males (Bobo et al. 1987; Burling et al. 1991; Joseph et al. 1993) have been the focus of most clinical research on quitting use of both alcohol and tobacco. Full-scale "special population" cohort studies are urgently needed to complement this initial research on men.

The significant increase in risk we observed for those who had completed a prior course of alcohol treatment suggests that severity of alcohol use history is also important. Another study of tobacco quit ratios in a sample of alcohol treatment staff who self-identified either as problem drinkers or as recovering alcoholics found significantly greater success rates among the problem drinkers, who presumably had less severe alcohol use histories (Bobo and Davis 1993). Replication of this finding in more representative samples of problem drinkers and recovering alcoholics is needed. Consistent with recommendations from the 1990 Institute of Medicine (IOM) report on the future of alcohol treatment (IOM 1990), we believe the broad spectrum of people with a history of alcohol problems should be included in studies of nicotine dependence.

Higher relapse rates among those with CES–D scores of 16 or more indicate the need for additional research on possible "third-factor" variables, such as depression and anxiety. Recovering alcoholics in our sample who met screening criteria for depression at enrollment were 28 percent more likely to report having had at least one alcoholic drink by the 6-month followup and 60 percent were more likely to have had 1 or more days of heavy drinking than those who did not appear to be depressed. An important caveat is that the CES–D is a screening inventory, not a diagnostic tool. Future research in this arena would benefit from use of a more comprehensive depression measure, such as the Composite International Diagnostic Interview developed by Robins and colleagues to cover 40 DSM–III categories (Robins et al. 1988).

Findings from other studies of depression and alcohol recovery have been mixed. Some investigators have reported evidence suggesting that depression increases alcohol use, particularly among women (Aneshensel and Huba 1983; Ellis and McClure 1992), but others have failed to show significant differences in relapse rates between depressed and nondepressed alcoholics (Merikangas and Gelernter 1990). At least one group of researchers has found that alcoholic women, but not men, with a history of major depression were less likely to relapse than those lacking a similar history (Rounsaville et al. 1987).

The issue of gender differences is a recurrent theme in the depression literature. Consistent with data from population studies (Helzer and Pryzbeck 1988; Schoenborn and Horm 1993; Kessler et al. 1994), we found higher proportions of women than men meeting our depression screening criteria (87 versus 70 percent). The female mean score significantly exceeded the corresponding mean for males (female mean: 32.5, male mean: 22.1, $t = -3.24$, $p < 0.01$). The observed distribution of scores by gender is shown in figure 1.

A relationship between depression and tobacco use has been reported for a variety of female and male populations, including adolescents (Kandel and Davis 1986; Covey and Tam 1990), a sample of young adults from a Michigan health maintenance organization (Breslau et al. 1991; Breslau et al. 1992; Breslau et al. 1993), placebo subjects in a smoking cessation study (Covey et al. 1990), participants in the St. Louis Epidemiologic Catchment Area Study (Glassman et al. 1990), female co-twins from the Virginia Twin Registry (Kendler et al. 1993), and participants in the first National Health and Nutrition Examination Survey (NHANES I) (Anda et al. 1990). The female co-twin study by Kendler and colleagues (1993) looked prospectively at new episodes of major depression during a 1-year followup and found a consistent increase in rate as a function of daily

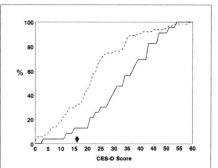

Figure 1. Center for Epidemiologic Studies–Depression Scale (CES–D) scores by gender for 23 female and 67 male recovering alcoholic patients in Nebraska from 1993 to 1994. The solid line indicates female scores, and the broken line indicates male scores. The arrow marks the standard cut-point of 16 for distinguishing depressed from nondepressed patients.

smoking ranging from 6.4 percent in nonsmokers to 20.7 percent in those consuming more than 20 cigarettes per day. Using a probability sample of the U.S. population, NHANES I collected data on smoking habits and used the CES–D to assess depression status. After 9 years of followup, findings indicated that depressed smokers were 40 percent less likely to have quit smoking than nondepressed smokers. Other investigators have reported data suggesting that some people with a prior history of depression who try to quit smoking may be more likely to experience a new episode of major depression (Flanagan and Maany 1982; Covey et al. 1990; Glassman et al. 1990).

In summary, the observed relationships between and among the variables of depression, anxiety, alcohol use, and smoking pose many complex questions. How strong and how consistent are the relationships? Do they vary with sociodemographic attributes? Does a history of major depression alter the effects of quitting smoking on alcohol recovery? If nicotine is an effective antidepressant for some women and if continued problems with depression compromise the maintenance of sobriety in some people, are there recovering alcoholics who require nicotine replacement therapy when they try to quit smoking?

The urgent need for further work in the laboratory, in the clinical environment, and in the community is clear. Laboratory studies are needed to pin down biological processes that might explain the above findings. As other researchers have noted, the various neurotransmitters may prove to be particularly important (Hall et al. 1993; Jarvik and Henningfield 1993). Clinical studies are critical to assess immediate behavioral manifestations of changes in tobacco use—for example, on affective status and desire for alcohol. Some exciting work has already been done in this area by the group at Brown University (Abrams et al. 1992; Gulliver et al. 1995). Finally, epidemiologic studies in the community are the most appropriate vehicle for observing interaction patterns in the natural environment and for addressing the broad spectrum of people with a history of alcohol problems. Our hope is that the pilot study findings reported here stimulate additional work in each of these research environments.

ACKNOWLEDGMENTS

This chapter was prepared with support from National Institute on Alcohol Abuse and Alcoholism grant AA–09233. James R. Anderson, Ph.D., assisted in analyzing the study data. Amber Leed-Kelly, Gennus Miller, and Karen Svoboda provided essential field support during data collection.

REFERENCES

Abrams, D.B.; Rohsenow, D.J.; Niaura, R.S.; Pedraza, M.; Longabaugh, R.; Beattie, M.C.; Binkoff, J.A.; Noel, N.E.; and Monti, P.M. Smoking and treatment outcome for alcoholics: Effects on coping skills, urge to drink, and drinking rates. *Behav Ther* 23:283–297, 1992.

Anda, R.F.; Williamson, D.F.; Escobedo, L.G.; Mast, E.E.; Glovino, G.A.; and Remington, P.L. Depression and the dynamics of smoking. *JAMA* 264:1541–1545, 1990.

Aneshensel, C.S., and Huba, G.J. Depression, alcohol use and smoking over one year: A four-wave longitudinal causal model. *J Abnorm Psychol* 92:134–150, 1983.

Ashley, M.; Olin, J.; le Riche, W.; Kornaczewski, A.; Schmidt, W.; and Rankin, J. Morbidity patterns in hazardous drinkers: Relevance of demographic, sociologic, drinking, and drug use characteristics. *Int J Addict* 16:593–625, 1981.

Bobo, J.K. Nicotine dependence and alcoholism: Epidemiology and treatment. *J Psychoactive Drugs* 21:323–329, 1989.

Bobo, J.K., and Davis, C.M. Cigarette smoking cessation and alcohol treatment. *Addiction* 88:405–412, 1993.

Bobo, J.K.; Gilchrist, L.D.; Schilling, R.F., II; Noach, B.; and Schinke, S.P. Cigarette smoking cessation attempts by recovering alcoholics. *Addict Behav* 12: 209–215, 1987.

Breslau, N.; Kilbey, M.M.; and Andreski, P. Nicotine dependence, major depression, and anxiety in young adults. *Arch Gen Psychiatry* 48:1069–1074, 1991.

Breslau, N.; Kilbey, M.M.; and Andreski, P. Nicotine withdrawal symptoms and psychiatric disorders: Findings from an epidemiologic study of young adults. *Am J Psychiatry* 149:464–469, 1992.

Breslau, N.; Kilbey, M.M.; and Andreski, P. Nicotine dependence and major depression. *Arch Gen Psychiatry* 50:31–35, 1993.

Breslow, N.E., and Day, N.E. *Statistical Methods in Cancer Research.* Vol. I. Lyon, France: International Agency for Research on Cancer, 1987.

Burling, T.A., and Ziff, D.C. Tobacco smoking: A comparison between alcohol and drug abuse inpatients. *Addict Behav* 13:185–190, 1988.

Burling, T.A.; Marshall, G.D.; and Seidner, A.L. Smoking cessation for substance abuse inpatients. *J Subst Abuse* 3:269–276, 1991.

Carmelli, D.; Swan, G.E.; and Robinette, D. The relationship between quitting smoking and changes in drinking in World War II veteran twins. *J Subst Abuse* 5:103–116, 1993.

Covey, L.S., and Tam, D. Depressive mood, the single-parent home and adolescent cigarette smoking. *Am J Public Health* 80:1330–1333, 1990.

Covey, L.S.; Glassman, A.H.; and Stetner, F. Depression and depressive symptoms in smoking cessation. *Compr Psychiatry* 31: 350–354, 1990.

Davis, L.J.; Hurt, R.D.; Morse, R.M.; and O'Brien, P.C. Discriminant analysis of the self-administered alcoholism screening test. *Alcohol Clin Exp Res* 11:269–273, 1987.

De Soto, C.B.; O'Donnell, W.E.; and De Soto, J.L. Long-term recovery in alcoholics. *Alcohol Clin Exp Res* 13:693–697, 1989.

Demers, R.Y.; Neale, A.V.; Adams, R.; Trembath, C.; and Herman, S.C. The impact of physicians' brief smoking cessation counseling: A MIRNET study. *J Fam Pract* 31:625–629, 1990.

DiClemente, C.C.; Prochaska, J.O.; Fairhurst, S.K.; Velicer, W.F.; Velasquez, M.M.; and Rosse, J.S. The process of smoking cessation: An analysis of precontemplation, contemplation, and preparation stages of change. *J Consult Clin Psychol* 59:295–304, 1991.

Donner, A., and Klar, N. Methods for comparing event rates in intervention studies when the unit of allocation is a cluster. *Am J Epidemiol* 140:279–289, 1994.

Dreher, K.F., and Fraser, J.G. Smoking habits of alcoholic out-patients. II. *Int J Addict* 3:65–80, 1968.

Ellis, D., and McClure, J. In-patient treatment of alcohol problems—predicting and preventing relapse. *Alcohol Alcohol* 27:449–456, 1992.

Fagerstrom, K.O.; Heatherton, T.F.; and Kozlowski, L.T. Nicotine addiction and its assessment. *Ear Nose Throat J* 69: 763–768, 1990.

Flanagan, J., and Maany, I. Smoking and depression (Letter). *Am J Psychiatry* 139:54, 1982.

Glassman, A.H.; Helzer, J.E.; Cottler, L.B.; Stetner, F.; Tipp, J.E.; and Johnson, J. Smoking, smoking cessation, and major depression. *JAMA* 264:1546–1549, 1990.

Grant, B.F.; Harford, T.C.; Chou, P.; Pickering, R.; Dawson, D.A.; Stinson, F.S.; and Noble, J. Prevalence of DSM-III-R alcohol abuse and dependence. *Alcohol Health Res World* 15:91–96, 1991.

Gritz, E.R.; Berman, B.A.; Bastani, R.; and Wu, M. A randomized trial of a self-help smoking cessation intervention in a nonvolunteer female population: Testing the limits of the Public Health Model. *Health Psychol* 11:280–289, 1992.

Gulliver, S.B.; Rohsenow, D.J.; Colby, S.M.; Dey, A.N.; Abrams, D.B.; Niaura, R.; and Monti, P.M. Interrelationship of smoking and alcohol dependence, use and urges to use. *J Stud Alcohol* 56:202–206, 1995.

Hall, S.M.; Munoz, R.F.; Reus, V.I.; and Sees, K.L. Nicotine, negative affect and depression. *J Consult Clin Psychol* 61: 761–767, 1993.

Helzer, J.E., and Pryzbeck, T.R. The co-occurrence of alcoholism with other psychiatric disorders in the general population and its impact on treatment. *J Stud Alcohol* 49:219–224, 1988.

Hurt, R.D.; Morse, R.M.; and Swenson, W.M. Diagnosis of alcoholism with a self-administered alcoholism screening test: Results with 1,002 consecutive patients receiving general examinations. *Mayo Clin Proc* 55:365–370, 1980.

Hurt, R.D.; Eberman, K.M.; Slade, J.; and Karan, L. Treating nicotine addiction in patients with other addictive diseases. In: Orleans, C.T., and Slade, J., eds. *Nicotine Addiction: Principles and Management.* New York: Oxford University Press, 1994. pp. 310–326.

Institute of Medicine. *Broadening the Base of Treatment for Alcohol Problems.* Washington, DC: National Academy Press, 1990.

Jarvik, M.E., and Henningfield, J.E. Pharmacological adjuncts for the treatment of tobacco dependence. In: Orleans, C.T., and Slade, J., eds. *Nicotine Addiction, Principles and Management.* New York: Oxford University Press, 1993. pp. 245–261.

Joseph, A.M.; Nichol, K.L.; and Anderson, H. Effect of treatment for nicotine dependence on alcohol and drug treatment outcomes. *Addict Behav* 18: 635–644, 1993.

Kandel, D.B., and Davis, M. Adult sequelae of adolescent depressive symptoms. *Arch Gen Psychiatry* 43:255–262, 1986.

Kendler, K.S.; Neale, M.C.; MacLean, C.J.; Heath, A.C.; Eaves, L.J.; and Kessler, R.C. Smoking and major depression. *Arch Gen Psychiatry* 50:36–43, 1993.

Kessler, R.C.; McGonagle, K.A.; Zhao, S.; Nelson, C.B.; Hughes, M.; Eshleman, S.; Wittchen, H.U.; and Kendler, K.S. Lifetime and 12-month prevalence of DSM–III–R psychiatric disorders in the United States. *Arch Gen Psychiatry* 51: 8–19, 1994.

Kozlowski, L.T.; Jelinek, L.C.; and Pope, M.A. Cigarette smoking among alcohol abusers: A continuing and neglected problem. *Can J Public Health* 77:205–207, 1986.

Merikangas, K.R., and Gelernter, C.S. Comorbidity for alcoholism and depression. *Psychiatr Clin North Am* 13:613–632, 1990.

Miller, W.R.; Hedrick, K.E.; and Taylor, C.A. Addictive behaviors and life problems before and after behavioral treatment of problem drinkers. *Addict Behav* 8:403–412, 1983.

Nothwehr, F.; Lando, H.A.; and Bobo, J.K. Alcohol and tobacco use in the Minnesota Heart Health Program. *Addict Behav*, 20:463–470, 1995.

Prochaska, J.O., and DiClemente, C.C. Standardized, individualized, interactive and personalized self-help programs for smoking cessation. *Health Psychol* 12:399–405, 1993.

Prochaska, J.O., and Goldstein, M.G. Process of smoking cessation: Implications for clinicians. *Clin Chest Med* 12:727–735, 1991.

Radloff, L.S. The CES-D Scale: A self-report depression scale for research in the general population. *Appl Psychol Measurement* 1:385–401, 1977.

Robins, L.N.; Wing, J.; Wittchen, H.U.; Helzer, J.E.; Babor, T.F.; Burke, J.; Farmer, A.; Jablenski, J.; Pickens, R.W.; Regier, D.A.; Sartorius, N.; and Towle, L.H. The composite international diagnostic interview. *Arch Gen Psychiatry* 45:1069–1077, 1988.

Rounsaville, B.J.; Dolinsky, Z.S.; Babor, T.F.; and Meyer, R.E. Psychopathology as a predictor of treatment outcome in alcoholics. *Arch Gen Psychiatry* 44:505–513, 1987.

Schoenborn, C.A., and Horm, J. Negative moods as correlates of smoking and heavier drinking: Implications for health promotion. *Advanced Data* 236:1–13, 1993.

Sobell, L.C., and Sobell, M.B. Timeline follow-back: A technique for assessing self-reported alcohol consumption. In: Litten, R.Z., and Allen, J.P., eds. *Measuring Alcohol Consumption: Psychosocial and Biochemical Methods.* Totowa, NJ: Humana Press, 1992. pp. 41–72.

Sobell, M.B., and Sobell, L.C. "A Longitudinal Study of Dual Recoveries From Smoking and Alcohol Problems." Paper presented at the annual meeting of the Association for the Advancement of Behavior Therapy, Atlanta, November 1993.

Sobell, L.C.; Sobell, M.B.; Leo, G.I.; and Cancilla, A. Reliability of a timeline method: Assessing normal drinkers' reports of recent drinking and a comparative evaluation across several populations. *Br J Addict* 83:393–402, 1988.

Weissman, M.M.; Sholomskas, D.; Pottenger, M.; Prusoff, B.A.; and Locke, B.Z. Assessing depressive symptoms in five psychiatric populations: A validation study. *Am J Epidemiol* 106:203–214, 1977.

Zeger, S.L.; Liang, K.Y.; and Albert, P.S. Models for longitudinal data: A generalized estimating equation approach. *Biometrics* 44:1049–1060, 1988.

Zimmerman, R.S.; Warheit, G.J.; Ulbrich, P.M.; and Auth, J.B. The relationship between alcohol use and attempts and success at smoking cessation. *Addict Behav* 15:197–207, 1990.

Chapter 14

Identification of Subgroups With Differential Rates of Relapse After Smoking Cessation: Applications to Alcohol Research

Gary E. Swan, Ph.D., Marcia M. Ward, Ph.D., Dorit Carmelli, Ph.D., and Lisa M. Jack, M.A.

Our research group has been working in the area of relapse following smoking cessation for about 14 years. During that time we, along with a number of other researchers, have participated in the search for a better understanding of the relapse problem using both traditional (Swan et al. 1988) and newer analytic methods (Swan and Denk 1987; Swan et al. 1993*a*, 1993*c*, 1995*b*) to identify predictors, in the hope that this information could be translated to improved treatment programs. This search has, at times, been frustrating and disappointing.

On the other hand, the challenge provided by this problem has led us to rethink the entire question of why relapse prediction is typically so difficult, regardless of whether cessation has occurred as a result of participation in a program, quitting on one's own, or the use of nicotine replacement. The answer to this question is not that we have not yet identified the "magic bullet"; we have plenty of candidate variables. Rather, the answer lies with the fact that smokers are heterogeneous with regard to how, why, and when they relapse. This heterogeneity makes it extremely

G.E. Swan, Ph.D., is director of the Health Sciences Program, Stanford Research Institute, 333 Ravenswood Ave., Menlo Park, CA 94025. M.M. Ward, Ph.D., is a senior health care consultant, D. Carmelli, Ph.D., is a senior biostatistician, and L.M. Jack, M.A., is a programmer/analyst II in the Health Sciences Program at Stanford Research Institute.

difficult to conduct traditional prediction efforts for an entire sample of smokers because of the large amount of between-subject variation that cannot be completely accounted for.

We have identified an approach to help explore this issue in a way that will increase the odds of finding more compelling predictors of relapse. In this chapter we present a rationale, describe the method, show how we have applied the method to smoking relapse in two separate studies, and describe how the approach may be helpful to investigators in the field of alcohol research.

UNDERSTANDING RELAPSE

The heterogeneity of alcoholics and smokers is of great interest to researchers in their respective fields. Investigators in alcoholism from the 19th century on have attempted to reduce the heterogeneity seen in alcoholics by creating typologies (Babor 1994). A similar history, though perhaps not as long, can be described for smoking research (Shumaker and Grunberg 1986). As table 1 shows, there is a fair amount of overlap in the factors contributing to heterogeneity in users of both substances.

Several models to explain relapse in alcoholics and smokers have been described. In alcoholics, they range from short- and long-term homeostatic dysregulation and conditioned craving and drug effects, to cognitive-behavioral and social learning factors (Meyer 1994). The overlap with current models in smoking relapse is striking (table 2). As is the case for relapse theories concerning smoking, it is not clear how the various theories of relapse in alcoholics relate to simple subgroupings based on demographics such as gender, socioeconomic status, or age (Del Boca 1994). The heterogeneity of the population vis-à-vis relapse and the maintenance of abstinence is an issue to be dealt with for both fields.

Implicit in the use of conventional models to identify predictors of relapse is the necessity to conclude that once a significant risk factor for relapse has been identified, it is a risk factor for everyone. If a significant p value is found attached to a regression coefficient for perceived stress, for example, all too often a treatment program built around stress management will be designed for everyone. In this way the problem of appropriate targeting of treatment is compounded because, though stress may be a risk factor for enough of the particular sample under study for it to achieve statistical significance, stress is not necessarily a significant risk factor for everyone.

The interesting problem from the standpoint of the prediction of relapse is how to describe the heterogeneity among those who use alcohol, tobacco, and other drugs (ATOD's) while maintaining the ability to describe and model the dynamic nature of relapse. In other words, the issue of the prediction of relapse can be reframed from "What are the risk factors for relapse?" to "Who relapses, and

Table 1. Factors Contributing to Heterogeneity Among Alcoholics and Smokers.

Alcoholics	Smokers
Health status	Health status
Neuropsychological status	Nicotine dependence
Alcohol dependence	Personality traits
Psychological disability	Prior quit attempts
Personality traits	Psychological disability (e.g., depression)
Family history of alcoholism	Reasons for smoking
Psychopathology	
Previous treatment	
Presenting symptoms	

Note: Data are from Meyer (1994) for alcoholics and from Shumaker and Grunberg (1986) for smokers.

when do they relapse?" When we say, for example, that stress is a predictor of relapse, we should ask the question differently: "For whom is stress a predictor of relapse, and when are they most at risk?"

At this point, the state of relapse theory and research can be summarized along the following lines. First, available theories of relapse were not designed to be specific to a particular group of ATOD users. Second, the problem of assumed maximum generalizability of relapse theory results from a mismatch with the heterogeneity of ATOD users and the factors that promote relapse. Third, it is entirely possible that factors from the biological, social, cognitive, and behavioral realms interact simultaneously to promote relapse and may do

so in a nonlinear fashion for different subgroups of ATOD users. Fourth, relapse is a time-dependent process. The rate at which people relapse is not uniform over time; different people relapse at different rates, and the underlying processes of relapse themselves vary in time. Fifth, we need methods to study relapse that permit a higher fidelity to the heterogeneity in ATOD users and in the processes involved in their relapse.

TREE-STRUCTURED SURVIVAL ANALYSIS

A methodology known as classification and regression tree analysis (Breiman et al. 1984) has been used for some time in branches of medicine such as rheumatology and oncology

Table 2. Similarities in Models of Relapse Among Alcoholics and Smokers.

Alcohol	Smoking
Conditioning, craving, and withdrawal	Conditioning, craving, and withdrawal
Marlatt's cognitive-behavioral model	Marlatt's cognitive-behavioral model
Self-efficacy	Self-efficacy
Homeostatic dysregulation	Shiffman's situational model

Note: Data are from Meyer (1994) for alcohol and from Sutton (1989) for smoking.

to identify subgroups of patients with differing prognoses (Gilpin et al. 1983; Ciampi et al. 1988; Kwak et al. 1990). The extension of this methodology to include time-based outcomes is referred to as tree-structured survival analysis (TSSA) (Gordon and Olshen 1985). The method is non-parametric and makes no assumptions about the underlying distribution of the variables involved. It is also computer-intensive, relying on the full power of the computer to conduct repeated passes through the data to find the most accurate and reliable classification structure.

Nonlinear interactions among the classification variables can be identified by this method, along with the cut-points used to define subgroups with differing rates of relapse. These cut-points are more readily translated to the clinical setting than are the risk ratios and parameter estimates generated from conventional methods used to model relapse.

We have applied TSSA to relapse in smokers from cessation programs (Swan et al. 1993a) including nicotine replacement (Swan et al. 1995b),

as well as to the issue of all-cause and disease-specific mortality in older adults (Carmelli et al. 1991; Swan et al. 1995a), another area in which subject heterogeneity plays an important role. We have published or have in press four papers that have used TSSA, and, judging by the reactions from the reviewers of these papers, the approach has been well received.

TSSA was applied to construct distinct relapse risk groups for several reasons. First, approaches to forming strata that are model based (e.g., logistic regression) require the specification of the joint probability distribution of predictors and class membership, the nature of which is generally unknown. Second, since the relationships among predictors, class membership, and time to relapse are complex and difficult to model, a nonparametric approach is most applicable. Third, TSSA has shown promise in other areas of clinical research involving survival data and therefore seemed an appropriate tool for examining relapse rates after smoking cessation.

The recursive partitioning paradigm involves a set of predictors and the response variable, time to relapse. The process can be visualized as a procedure involving the selection of sequences of questions in which the range of the predictors is successively partitioned into regions or "boxes." Specifically, the task is to find yes-no questions concerning the classification variables so as to optimally separate subjects by class or to divide subjects into a "yes" group (those above a certain cut-point for a continuously distributed variable) and a "no" group (those below a certain cut-point). This process of splitting corresponds to the construction of a binary tree and the boxes generated to its branching nodes. The procedure essentially generates the minimum number of cells needed to capture all the information in the covariates as they relate to relapse. Best splits in the current algorithms are compared with the log-rank statistic, which compares the Kaplan-Meier relapse curves of the two resulting groups at each node (Kaplan and Meier 1958).

Because the splitting rules do not initially specify the size or structure of the tree, a large tree is constructed first and is then subjected to a stringent cross-validation procedure in which a randomly chosen part of the data is repeatedly set aside and sorted down to test the tree. Only those portions of the tree that are able to improve the correct classification rate of the independent data survive the test (Barnes et al. 1991). This cross-validation procedure is known as pruning the tree. The output of this computer-intensive, nonparametric approach to survival analysis is a set of survival functions, estimated by the Kaplan-Meier method, corresponding to each terminal node of the retained pruned tree.

The relapse experience of the entire cohort and each of the identified subgroups is described by Kaplan-Meier survival curves over the entire duration of followup using SAS LIFETEST (SAS Institute 1987) and then plotted using EGRET software (Statistics and Epidemiology Research Corporation 1991). SAS LIFETEST allows pairwise comparisons of the terminal node groups by the log-rank test procedure. After the final groups are identified, we continue their characterization on other individual characteristics of relevance to the investigators. Chi-square or one-way analysis of variance tests are used to detect the presence of an effect due to terminal node group membership on each of a set of characterization variables.

The findings presented in the following examples are based on a published paper (Swan et al. 1993a) and two presented papers (Swan et al. 1993b, 1995b); these papers present more details on the samples, methods, results, and their interpretation.

EXAMPLE 1: RELAPSE IN SMOKING CESSATION PROGRAM PARTICIPANTS

The overall goal of this study was to determine the extent to which background variables (i.e., smoking history, demographics, and smoking-related psychological traits) and psychophysiological changes associated with the process of quitting itself were predictive of relapse in a cohort followed for 1 year (see Swan et al. 1993*a* for more details of this study). The final study group for which complete and validated data were available consisted of 265 smokers (74 percent of those who volunteered and met eligibility criteria); of these, 158 (59.6 percent) were females and 107 (40.4 percent) were males, with an average age of 42.6 years (range = 20–65 years). At intake into this study, the group reported smoking an average of 26 cigarettes per day (range = 10–80 cigarettes) and had smoked for an average of 25 years (range = 5–50 years). Mean reported nicotine content of their usual cigarette was 0.72 mg (range = 0.10–1.40). Consistent with the reported level of smoking, saliva cotinine before cessation averaged 352.2 ng/mL (range = 34.0–996.0 ng/mL).

DEFINITION OF RELAPSE

An important requirement for studies employing survival analysis is the collection of good time-to-relapse data. The followup phase of this study consisted of diaries beginning on the quit day and continuing biweekly for one year. On each diary form, subjects reported whether or not they had smoked on each of the 14 days in the reporting period. By arranging all forms in chronological order, we identified the first occurrence of smoking and determined the number of days to the earliest relapse. If an individual did not relapse by the end of followup, he or she was considered to be "censored" and given a value of 365 days.

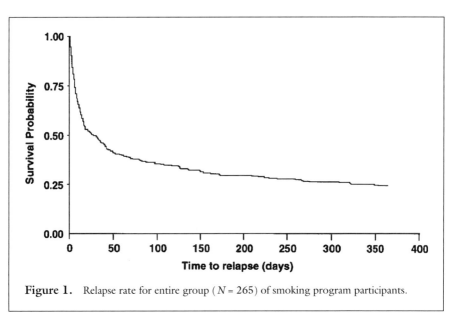

Figure 1. Relapse rate for entire group ($N = 265$) of smoking program participants.

We used thiocyanate and/or cotinine levels to verify the subject's self-report in order to determine a time-to-relapse value for each subject.

RESULTS

The overall proportion of subjects who relapsed over the 1-year followup for the entire study group was 76 percent. The time-dependent relapse experience is shown in figure 1.

Using age, gender, amount smoked, family history of smoking, and precessation cotinine, recursive partitioning identified five terminal node groups that differed reliably with respect to rates of relapse. Three of the five individual characteristics included in the analysis (cotinine, gender, and age) contributed to the identification of these groups. The remaining two variables, number of cigarettes smoked prior to cessation and family history of smoking, did not contribute to the classification of subjects and were subsequently pruned from the final tree. The variable splits and node groups are summarized in figure 2.

The first major split in the tree occurred for cotinine, separating out a small group of individuals with exceptionally low cotinine (≤ 129 ng/mL) who showed a particularly low percentage of relapse. No further splits occurred for this group; they are

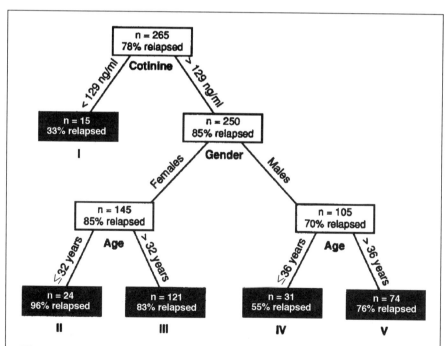

Figure 2. Classification tree for entire group ($N = 265$) of smoking program participants. Terminal nodes are identified by Roman numerals.

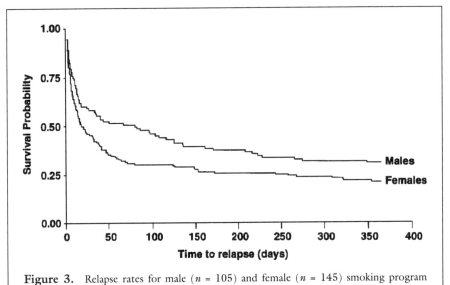

Figure 3. Relapse rates for male ($n = 105$) and female ($n = 145$) smoking program participants.

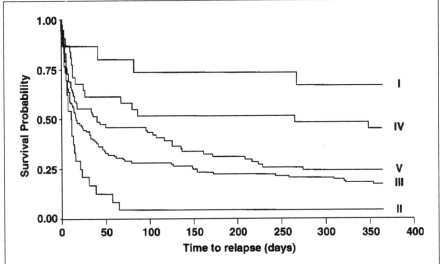

Figure 4. Relapse rates for all five subgroups of smoking program participants identified by tree-structured survival analysis.

Table 3. Relapse Rates and Descriptive Statistics for the Five Terminal Node Groups.

	Terminal Node Groups				
	I (*n* = 15)	II (*n* = 24)	III (*n* = 121)	IV (*n* = 31)	V (*n* = 74)
Relapse events (*n*, %)	5 (33%)	23 (96%)	100 (83%)	17 (55%)	56 (76%)
Mean survival (days)	269.7	30.5	98.9	196.7	130.2
Gender (% female)	87	100	100	0	0
Age (range)	40.5 (20–57)	27.9 (23–32)	45.9 (33–65)	30.5 (22–36)	47.6 (37–65)
Cotinine, precessation (ng/mL) (range)	84.5 (34–129)	376.8 (132–628)	354.7 (135–989)	367.9 (133–996)	391.0 (133–899)
Amount smoked (cigarettes/day) (range)	19.0 (10–50)	22.0 (10–40)	25.8 (10–60)	24.5 (12–50)	29.8 (10–80)
Family history of smoking (% of family) (range)	54.6 (0–100)	50.9 (0–100)	64.1 (0–100)	60.1 (0–100)	68.8 (0–100)

identified as terminal node group I. Further partitioning then divided the other node on gender. As shown in figure 2, relapse occurred in 85 percent of females (123/145) and in 70 percent of males (73/105). The relapse experiences of these two groups are shown in figure 3. The log-rank test indicated a significant difference between these relapse curves, $\chi^2(1) = 10.96$, $p < 0.001$.

Final splits in the tree occurred within each gender on age. In females, two groups with different relapse experiences were identified at a cut-point of 32 years of age. Women 32 years old or younger showed 96 percent relapse, whereas women over 32 fared somewhat better with 83 percent relapse. In males, those 36 years old or younger showed a 55 percent relapse, compared with 76 percent relapse in those over 36. Survival curves for each of the terminal node groups are presented in figure 4. The log-rank test revealed a highly significant difference between these curves, $\chi^2(1) = 31.56$, $p < 0.0001$.

DESCRIPTION OF THE TERMINAL NODE GROUPS

To understand better the characteristics of these five terminal node groups, we completed descriptive analyses. Values of the variables used for classification are given in table 3 for each of the groups. To facilitate further characterization of the groups, smoking history and background characteristics are presented

Table 4. Background and Smoking History Characteristics of the Five Terminal Node Groups.

	Terminal Node Groups					
	I	II	III	IV	V	Group Effect
Income	5.8	4.1	5.6	5.4	6.6	$F(4,237)=$
(M, SD)	(2.6)	(1.8)	(2.2)	(1.9)	(1.9)	$6.22****$
Education	4.3	4.3	4.9	4.9	5.4	$F(4,251)=$
(M, SD)	(1.5)	(1.3)	(1.5)	(1.4)	(1.4)	$3.16**$
Marital status						$\chi^2(4)=$
(% married)	57.1	21.7	43.7	45.1	59.4	$11.31**$
Age started	18.7	14.9	17.9	16.7	16.6	$F(4,260)=$
smoking (M, SD)	(5.2)	(2.7)	(3.7)	(2.3)	(3.6)	$4.97****$
Years smoked	22.1	12.7	27.3	13.5	30.7	$F(4,260)=$
(M, SD)	(11.3)	(3.7)	(9.7)	(3.7)	(8.0)	$38.33****$
Nicotine content						
of cigarette (mg)	0.61	0.74	0.66	0.84	0.78	$F(4,252)=$
(M, SD)	(0.27)	(0.26)	(0.30)	(0.22)	(0.32)	$3.73***$
Fagerstrom score	4.7	5.4	6.1	6.0	6.3	$F(4,242)=$
(M, SD)	(1.4)	(1.9)	(1.6)	(2.1)	(1.7)	$3.29**$
First cigarette ≤ 30						
minutes after						$\chi^2(4)=$
waking (% yes)	40.0	62.5	80.0	58.1	68.9	$15.04***$
Reasons for Smoking Scale						
Pharmacologic	1.5	1.3	1.7	1.2	1.5	$F(4,259)=$
(M, SD)	(0.5)	(0.4)	(0.5)	(0.5)	(0.5)	$7.58****$
Nonpharmacologic	1.1	1.0	0.9	0.9	1.0	$F(4,259)=$
(M, SD)	(0.3)	(0.4)	(0.4)	(0.3)	(0.3)	0.96, n.s.
Perceived Stress	28.1	24.7	24.9	21.1	23.4	$F(4,258)=$
Scale (M, SD)	(4.4)	(6.2)	(7.2)	(4.0)	(5.5)	$4.04***$
Previous reasons for relapse						
after quit attempt (%)						
High desire						$\chi^2(4)=$
for cigarettes	72.7	81.3	83.0	88.5	73.2	3.71, n.s
Enjoyed smoking						$\chi^2(4)=$
too much	45.5	62.5	69.2	46.2	55.4	6.88, n.s.
Pressure on job	45.5	37.5	42.6	42.3	63.6	$\chi^2(4)=7.58*$
Weight gain	36.4	50.0	43.6	11.5	21.4	$\chi^2(4)=$ $15.61***$

$*p < 0.10.$
$**p < 0.05.$
$***p < 0.01.$
$****p < 0.001.$

in table 4, and biological, physical, and health characteristics are given in table 5.

Terminal Node Group I

This group consisted of 15 subjects who abstained an average of 270 days; only 5 of the 15 subjects relapsed. Thirteen of the 15 members of this group were female; mean age was 40.5 years. The group is most strikingly different from the other terminal node groups with respect to precessation cotinine levels; the average concentration was 84.5 ng/mL, approximately one-fourth the levels in any of the other identified groups. Although this group also smoked fewer cigarettes per day (19.0) than any of the other groups, the difference in average consumption can account only partly for the large difference noted for cotinine. The relapse curve for this group, when compared by the log-rank test with that for all remaining subjects combined, was highly significant, $\chi^2(1) = 9.87$, $p < 0.002$.

This group of smokers had the second highest frequency of marriage among the groups. Of the five groups, they were the oldest when they began smoking, were the least likely to smoke within 30 minutes of waking, and smoked cigarettes with the lowest nicotine content; their corresponding Fagerstrom Tolerance scores (Fagerstrom 1978) were the lowest of all five groups. These individuals were the least likely to give "high desire" and "enjoyed smoking" as reasons for relapse in the past. They smoked 5.7 fewer cigarettes than their typical amount in the 24 hours prior to their first examination, the largest decrease in consumption of all the groups. Before cessation, this group of smokers had the lowest heart rate levels. The measured decline in heart rate pre- to postcessation was also the lowest of all five groups. Surprisingly, they had the highest score on the Perceived Stress Scale (Cohen et al. 1983), as well as the highest craving score on the Shiffman-Jarvik Withdrawal Scale (Shiffman and Jarvik 1976).

Terminal Node Group II

This group consisted entirely of younger women (mean age = 27.9 years, $n = 24$) who relapsed at an extraordinarily high rate (mean abstinence time = 30.5 days). Figure 4 indicates that 100 percent of the relapse events for this group had occurred by 65 days. Although this group tended toward lighter smoking (mean cigarettes per day = 22.0), they had one of the higher average cotinine levels (376.8 ng/mL) at precessation.

These women reported the lowest income and educational levels of all five groups, and they were the least likely to be married. They began smoking at a younger age than any of the other groups and were more likely to give "weight gain" as a reason for relapsing in the past. Interestingly, they had the smallest percentage of first-degree relatives who smoked. Prior to cessation, this group had the highest resting heart rate level. They were the most active of all five groups in terms of reported miles walked daily.

Terminal Node Group III

This group consisted of the majority of the women ($n = 121$) in the study. They were older (mean age = 45.9 years) and were heavier smokers (mean cigarettes per day = 25.8) than their group II counterparts. Their abstinence curve was significantly differ-

Table 5. Biological, Physical, and Health Characteristics of the Five Terminal Node Groups.

			Terminal Node Groups			
	I	II	III	IV	V	Group Effect
Cigarettes smoked in the 24 hours prior to first exam (M, SD)	13.3 (10.9)	20.6 (9.5)	22.6 (11.3)	22.0 (10.0)	24.8 (11.8)	$F_{(4,259)}=$ 3.53**
Precessation HR (bpm)[a] (M, SE)	73.8 (2.4)	80.4 (2.2)	74.4 (0.9)	75.8 (1.9)	76.3 (1.1)	$F_{(5,258)}=$ 2.26*
Pre- to postcessation ΔHR (bpm)[a] (M, SE)	4.1 (2.3)	10.1 (2.2)	9.0 (0.9)	6.2 (1.9)	10.2 (1.1)	$F_{(5,212)}=$ 1.62, n.s.
Withdrawal symptoms Craving (M, SD)	5.3 (1.0)	4.8 (1.5)	5.1 (1.4)	4.3 (1.5)	4.5 (1.7)	$F_{(4,243)}=$ 3.00*
Appetite (M, SD)	1.1 (0.8)	1.0 (0.7)	0.9 (0.8)	0.8 (0.8)	1.0 (0.8)	$F_{(4,243)}=$ 0.76, n.s.
Psychological (M, SD)	5.1 (1.0)	4.8 (1.6)	4.8 (1.4)	4.2 (1.6)	4.8 (1.2)	$F_{(4,242)}=$ 1.54, n.s.
Physical (M, SD)	1.1 (1.4)	1.3 (1.6)	1.0 (1.1)	1.1 (1.2)	1.0 (1.0)	$F_{(4,242)}=$ 0.39, n.s.
Arousal (M, SD)	3.8 (1.7)	2.8 (2.4)	2.7 (2.0)	2.9 (2.1)	3.1 (1.8)	$F_{(4,243)}=$ 1.23, n.s.
Body mass index[a] (kg/m^2) (M, SE)	23.6 (0.9)	22.6 (0.8)	23.7 (0.3)	25.8 (0.7)	25.6 (0.4)	$F_{(5,251)}=$ 7.30***
Weight change Exam 1 to exam 2 (M, SD)	1.0 (1.1)	1.2 (2.2)	0.9 (1.7)	1.3 (3.4)	1.6 (1.7)	$F_{(4,177)}=$ 0.83, n.s.
Exam 1 to exam 3 (M, SD)	1.9 (2.1)	1.8 (3.3)	3.0 (2.7)	2.6 (4.2)	3.1 (3.3)	$F_{(4,150)}=$ 0.78, n.s.
Activity (miles walked daily) (M, SD)	2.3 (1.8)	4.4 (5.6)	1.4 (1.7)	1.8 (1.7)	2.1 (2.4)	$F_{(4,113)}=$ 3.18*

[a]Age-adjusted values. Heart rate (HR) is expressed as beats per minute.
*$p < 0.05$.
**$p < 0.01$.
***$p < 0.001$.

ent from that of the younger group of females, log-rank $\chi^2(1) = 5.43$, $p < 0.02$, with members of group III abstaining for an average of 98.9 days.

Members of group III had higher income and education levels and were more likely to be married than members of group II. This older group of female smokers had Fagerstrom Tolerance scores comparable to those found in the male terminal node groups and had the highest percentage of members reporting that they smoked their first cigarette within 30 minutes of awakening. They scored the highest of all five groups on the Pharmacologic Subscale of the Reasons for Smoking Scale. Compared with their younger counterparts, they were less likely to give "weight gain" as a reason for previous relapse. In comparison with the younger women, these women were heavier and reported less activity before cessation.

Terminal Node Group IV

This group consisted of 31 young male subjects (mean age = 30.5 years) who abstained for an average of 196.7 days. They smoked an average of 24.5 cigarettes per day before cessation and reported the highest cigarette nicotine content. Whereas these smokers gave "high desire" for a cigarette as a reason for previous relapse more frequently than any of the other smoker groups, they gave "weight gain" in relation to previous relapse less frequently than any of the other groups. Of the five groups, this group scored the lowest on the Perceived Stress Scale. These younger men reported

the least degree of craving and appetite symptoms after cessation.

Terminal Node Group V

Members of this group ($n = 74$) were older men (mean age = 47.6 years) who abstained an average of 130.2 days, 67 days less than their group IV counterparts. They were the heaviest smokers of the five groups (mean cigarettes per day = 29.8) and showed the highest average cotinine level (391.0 ng/mL). The relapse behaviors of groups IV and V were significantly different, log-rank $\chi^2(1) = 3.63$, $p < 0.05$.

Group V had the highest income and education levels of all the groups and the highest percentage of married subjects. They also reported the highest percentage of first-degree relatives who smoked (68.8 percent). They had the highest Fagerstrom Tolerance scores, and this was reflected in the comparatively high nicotine content of the usual cigarette and the relatively high frequency of smoking the first cigarette within 30 minutes of awakening. Members of this group were most likely to indicate "pressure on the job" as a reason for previous relapse. The log-rank test revealed that group III (older women) and group V (older men) were not different from each other with respect to their relapse history.

PREDICTORS OF RELAPSE

Having identified the terminal node groups, we then wanted to test the proposition that the creation of homogeneous subgroups of smokers would lead to improved prediction of relapse. We hypothesized that a set of weight-related variables would be especially predictive of relapse in the subgroup with the highest relapse rate, which consisted entirely of younger women.

We examined the relationship between these variables and time to relapse using Cox regression analysis. The prediction model was tested in the entire group and for each of the five subgroups.

In the sample as a whole, none of the weight-related variables was associated with time to relapse (see table 6). Among the five subgroups, however, weight-related variables were associated with time to relapse only for the subgroup of younger women (terminal node group II). We found "weight gain as a reason for prior relapse," body mass index prior to cessation, and family history of obesity to be associated significantly with the rate of relapse for this subgroup.

In this analysis, weight-related variables appear to have particular relevance to relapse in younger women of lower socioeconomic status; these women have an especially high rate of relapse and may need relapse prevention programs that emphasize the management of concerns about weight and weight gain. These findings suggest that using a method such as TSSA to sort smokers into homogeneous subgroups based on their relapse experience could lead to improved relapse models and more tightly focused intervention programs.

EXAMPLE 2: RELAPSE IN USERS OF TRANSDERMAL NICOTINE

The efficacy of transdermal nicotine for smoking cessation has been determined in several clinical trials, with nicotine patches producing end-of-treatment cessation rates ranging from 18 to 77 percent, rates that are approximately double those found for subjects treated with placebo patches. Nicotine patches result in 6-month abstinence rates of 22 to 42 percent, whereas placebo patches result in abstinence rates of 5 to 28 percent. The patches appear to reduce some withdrawal symptoms (e.g., craving and negative moods) but not others (e.g., hunger and weight gain) (Fiore et al. 1992; Hughes 1993).

Despite the enormous popularity of transdermal nicotine, relatively little is known about the characteristics of smokers for whom the patch is more or less effective. The few prescription guidelines provided to physicians for assigning initial treatment indicate that smokers with coronary heart disease or who weigh less than 100 pounds or who smoke fewer than 10 cigarettes per day should receive the smaller dose patch initially for safety reasons. The use of transdermal nicotine is contraindicated in smokers with hypersensitivity or allergy to nicotine (Physicians' Desk Reference 1993).

Guidelines published in the scientific literature suggest that highly dependent smokers (defined as high scores on the Fagerstrom Tolerance

Questionnaire, smoking 20 or more cigarettes per day, smoking the first cigarette of the day within 30 minutes of rising, or a history of strong craving after prior quit attempts) and smokers who are highly motivated to quit (Fiore et al. 1992) are especially good candidates for transdermal nicotine therapy. Unfortunately, there is little evidence to support these recommendations. For example, a high level of nicotine dependency does not consistently predict better response to transdermal nicotine (Hughes 1993), and in at least one study a trend was reported for higher abstinence rates in smokers with lower nicotine dependency scores (Norregaard et al. 1993). The most sophisticated study to date reported that none of the assessed demographic or smoking history variables (including Fagerstrom Tolerance score and baseline cigarette use) interacted with treatment response or the dose-response relationship (Transdermal Nicotine Study Group 1991).

The lack of information concerning which smokers do better or worse with transdermal nicotine may contribute to the dilution of its overall effectiveness. The prescription of the patch as if all smokers are the same may lead to less effective medical treatment of nicotine addiction (Sachs and Leischow 1991). Although this assumption of homogeneity among patients may be unusual in medicine, it is not at all unusual in the behavioral change therapies in general and in the treatment of smoking cessation more specifically (Shiffman 1993). Thus, there is a need for both empirical and theoretical approaches to matching patients to treatments so as to maximize therapeutic effectiveness of the patch, as well as other forms of treatment of tobacco addiction.

Using data from the Transdermal Nicotine Study Group (1991), we

Table 6. Weight-Related Variables in Relation to the Rate of Relapse.

Weight-Related Variable	Entire Group (N = 265)		Subgroup II (n = 24)	
	Beta	p value	Beta	p value
Prior weight gain	0.026	0.412	-0.494	0.015
Appetite	-0.001	0.491	0.011	0.477
Body mass index (kg/m^2)	0.005	0.372	0.077	0.035
Change in weight	-0.011	0.359	-0.059	0.170
Family obesity	0.463	0.106	1.341	0.023

summarize here the use of TSSA to identify patient characteristics that are related differentially to outcome after treatment with the patch (see Swan et al. 1995*b* for more details). The original study used a 6-week randomized, double-blind, placebo-controlled, parallel-group design to evaluate the efficacy of Nicoderm®, a transdermal nicotine delivery system that delivers nicotine at rates of 7, 14, or 21 mg over a period of 24 hours. Successful abstainers from both parallel groups were then enrolled in a trial for blinded downtitration from medication (6 weeks) and subsequent off-drug followup for an additional 12 weeks. Group counseling sessions were provided to all participants. Rates of continuous abstinence from smoking were determined during 6 weeks of full-dose treatment, a 6-week weaning period, and a 3-month followup. Abstinence was defined by patient diary reports of no smoking during the designated peri-

Table 7. Descriptive Statistics for All Subjects ($N = 935$) Included in the Transdermal Nicotine Study Group Evaluation of Nicoderm®.

Characteristic	M	SD	Range
Age (years)	42.6	10.3	21–67
Body mass index (kg/m^2)	25.2	4.4	15.0–47.6
Cigarettes per day	30.7	10.2	12–90
Carbon monoxide (ppm)	35.2	13.8	5–95
Fagerstrom score	7.1	1.7	2–11
Number of previous quits	4.1	4.2	1–50
Motivation to quit	8.4	1.5	1–10
Height (cm)	169.2	9.4	143.5–202.7
Weight (kg)	72.4	15.9	42.5–154.7
Years smoked	24.1	10.1	1–59
Gender (% female)	60		
Ethnic origin (%)			
Caucasian	95.2		
Black	3.1		
Hispanic	0.9		
Native American	0.6		
Asian	0.2		

ods, confirmed by expired-breath carbon monoxide levels of 8 parts per million (ppm) or lower.

The participating centers enrolled 935 subjects with the following numbers randomized to the 21-mg, 14-mg, 7-mg, and placebo groups, respectively: 262, 275, 127, and 271. All subjects were included in the previously published analyses except for the excluded members of couples ($n = 49$) and 9 patients with major protocol violations (Transdermal Nicotine Study Group 1991). This resulted in 254, 249, and 253 subjects available for analysis of outcome in the 14-mg, 21-mg, and placebo groups, respectively. At all time points, the 21-mg group did significantly better than the 14-mg group ($p = 0.031$). Multiple logistic regression analysis revealed that none of the demographic or smoking history variables (including Fagerstrom Tolerance score and baseline cigarette use) interacted with treatment-response or dose-response relationship. All transdermal nicotine doses significantly decreased the severity of nicotine withdrawal symptoms and significantly reduced cigarette use in patients who did not stop smoking.

The data included the following characteristics measured at the beginning of the trial: age, body mass index, number of cigarettes per day typically smoked, expired-breath carbon monoxide, initial nicotine dose, ethnic origin, Fagerstrom Tolerance score, height, weight, self-rated motivation to quit, gender, years smoked, and the number of previous quit attempts. Descriptive statistics for all 935 subjects entered into the study are presented in table 7.

TIME TO RELAPSE

After receipt of the data from Marion Merrell Dow, we calculated relapse time for each subject (beginning at week 3) as the number of days until the subject first smoked or until the patient withdrew from the study, whichever was smaller. Mean times to relapse for the 21-mg, 14-mg, and placebo groups were 79.6 days (SD = 62.3), 62.7 days (SD = 57.3), and 44.7 days (SD = 53.2), respectively. Comparison of the relapse curves using the log-rank statistic from SAS LIFETEST confirmed the previously reported superiority of the 21-mg and 14-mg treatments relative to placebo with respect to subsequent relapse rates (Transdermal Nicotine Study Group 1991) (see figure 5). Using EGRET software, we then plotted the relapse curves for the 21-mg, 14-mg, and placebo groups and compared them with the published relapse curves (see figure 2 in Transdermal Nicotine Study Group 1991). Allowing for slight differences in presentation, the curves were virtually identical.

SELECTION OF THE CLASSIFICATION VARIABLES

Since one of our goals with this analysis was to develop a classification of patch users that is clinically relevant, the selection of variables for inclusion in the TSSA was critical. Our experience has been that using a total of five to seven variables in a data set this size is optimal in the sense that

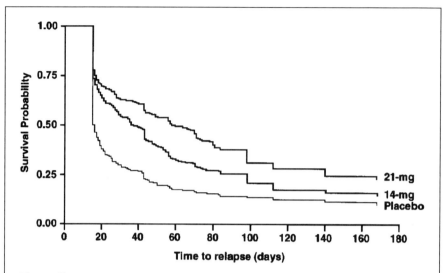

Figure 5. Relapse rates for the 14-mg (*n* = 254), 21-mg (*n* = 249), and placebo (*n* = 253) patch groups in the transdermal nicotine trial. Sample size shown for each group after exclusion of members of couples and those subjects with protocol violations.

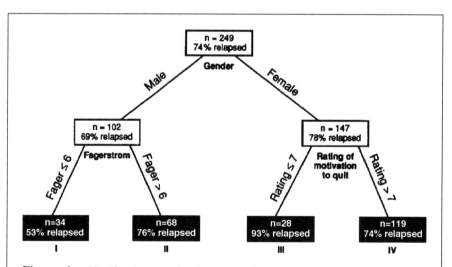

Figure 6. Classification tree for the group administered the 21-mg patch in the transdermal nicotine trial. The entire 21-mg sample is shown in the top box. Terminal nodes are identified by Roman numerals.

tree complexity remains manageable and interpretable. Furthermore, variables selected for inclusion in the TSSA should be easy to assess and should have either an empirical or theoretical basis for selection. On the basis of these considerations, we selected the following six variables:

- *Age.* This characteristic contributed to the classification of subgroups in our previous recursive partitioning analysis of relapse (Swan et al. 1993*a*).
- *Gender.* This characteristic also contributed to the classification of subgroups in our previous analysis of relapse (Swan et al. 1993*a*) and may influence both the pharmacokinetics of nicotine (Prather et al. 1993) and success with transdermal nicotine (Norregaard et al. 1993).
- *Fagerstrom Tolerance score.* This variable is proposed as a selection criterion for treatment with transdermal nicotine (Fiore et al. 1992; Miller and Corcores 1993) and may be related to success with the patch (Norregaard et al. 1993).
- *Rating of motivation to quit.* This variable is considered by some to be an essential element in the clinical decision to prescribe the patch for smoking cessation (Fiore et al. 1992).
- *Number of cigarettes smoked.* This variable is used as a criterion (e.g., 20 or more cigarettes per day) for determining appropriateness for nicotine patch therapy (Fiore et al. 1992).
- *Body mass index.* This variable is derived from standard measure-

ment of height and weight, a routine element of any office visit with a physician, and it may influence the pharmacokinetics of transdermal nicotine in obese individuals (Prather et al. 1993).

RESULTS

We elected to focus our efforts on the survival experience of the 21-mg patch group because of the demonstrated superiority of that dose with respect to treatment effectiveness. TSSA identified four subgroups within the larger 21-mg patch group, with two of the subgroups consisting entirely of males and the other two subgroups consisting entirely of females. The tree diagram for these groups is presented in figure 6, with the corresponding Kaplan-Meier curves following in figure 7.

In this analysis, males had significantly better survival with the 21-mg patch than did females, log-rank $\chi^2(1) = 4.50$, $p < 0.04$. Among males, those who were less dependent (identified by TSSA as having a score of 6 or lower on the Fagerstrom Tolerance Questionnaire) did significantly better (mean time to relapse = 106.6 days, 53 percent relapse) than did those men who were more dependent (mean time to relapse = 82.5 days, 76 percent relapse), log-rank $\chi^2(1) = 4.48$, $p < 0.04$. Among females, women with a higher rating of motivation to quit (identified by TSSA as a rating of greater than 7) did better (mean time to relapse 75.5 days, 74 percent relapse) with the 21-mg patch than did those women with

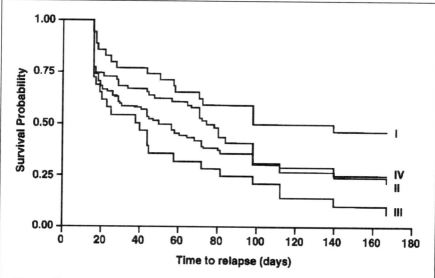

Figure 7. Relapse rates for the four subgroups of 21-mg patch users identified by tree-structured survival analysis.

lower motivation to quit (mean time to relapse = 57.1 days, 93 percent relapse), log-rank $\chi^2(1)$ = 3.53, $p < 0.06$.

Table 8 presents the baseline characteristics for all four subgroups identified for the 21-mg treatment group. Overall, compared with men who did not fare as well on the patch (group II), males who did better with the 21-mg patch (group I) were lighter smokers (M = 26.5 cigarettes per day, SD = 8.4), had lower levels of baseline carbon monoxide (M = 31.1 ppm, SD = 15.8), and had lower Fagerstrom Tolerance scores (M = 5.1, SD = 1.0)—all characteristics indicative of less dependency. Compared with women who did worse on the patch (group III), those who did better with the 21-mg patch (group IV) were somewhat older (M = 42.2 years, SD = 10.0), had higher body mass index (M = 24.9 kg/m², SD = 4.9), and had a much higher motivation to quit (M = 9.0, SD = 0.9).

ADVANTAGES OF TSSA

The relapse experience after followup of the samples of smokers used in both examples is consistent with previous observations. However, the present analyses go a step farther by showing that the overall relapse curves actually consist of several distinct relapse curves corresponding to subgroups of smokers. Using a relatively small number of personal characteristics as covariates, we identified five subgroups of quitters in the first analysis and four subgroups in the second.

Table 8. Characteristics of the Subgroups Found Using TSSA for the 21-mg Patch.

	Terminal Node Groups				
	I (n = 34)	II (n = 68)	III (n = 28)	IV (n = 119)	Group Effect
Relapse events (n, %)	18 (53%)	52 (76%)	26 (93%)	88 (74%)	$\chi^2(3)=$ 13.2**
Mean survival (days) (M, SD)	106.6 (64.7)	82.5 (59.6)	57.1 (52.6)	75.5 (63.0)	$F(3,245)=$ 3.7*
Gender (% female)	0	0	100	100	$\chi^2(3)=$ 249.0***
Age (M, SD)	44.6 (10.8)	44.0 (11.1)	40.6 (8.8)	42.2 (10.0)	$F(3,245)=$ 1.2, n.s
Weight (kg) (M, SD)	85.2 (14.6)	82.4 (13.2)	62.4 (10.6)	67.5 (15.1)	$F(3,245)=$ 29.8***
Body mass index (kg/m²) (M, SD)	27.1 (4.0)	26.0 (3.8)	23.4 (3.9)	24.9 (4.9)	$F(3,244)=$ 4.8**
Amount smoked (cigarettes/day) (M, SD)	26.5 (8.4)	34.2 (10.2)	28.4 (14.3)	31.0 (9.3)	$F(3,245)=$ 5.1**
Years smoked (M, SD)	26.0 (12.3)	26.3 (10.5)	23.2 (7.0)	23.9 (10.2)	$F(3,245)=$ 1.2, n.s.
Number of previous quits (M, SD)	4.8 (5.8)	4.7 (4.4)	3.7 (2.3)	4.4 (4.1)	$F(3,242)=$ 0.4, n.s.
Baseline carbon monoxide (ppm) (M, SD)	31.1 (15.8)	38.1 (14.3)	32.6 (14.5)	35.3 (13.4)	$F(3,245)=$ 2.2, n.s.
Fagerstrom score (M, SD)	5.1 (1.0)	8.2 (1.0)	6.8 (1.6)	7.3 (1.7)	$F(3,245)=$ 35.8***
Rating of motivation to quit (M, SD)	8.2 (1.7)	8.4 (1.6)	6.0 (1.1)	9.0 (0.9)	$F(3,245)=$ 43.9***

*$p < 0.05$.
**$p < 0.01$.
***$p < 0.001$.

In both analyses, gender was clearly a major contributor to the ability to remain off cigarettes. Women relapsed more quickly and more completely than did men. There is increasing interest in the role of gender differences in the use of tobacco (Grunberg et al. 1991). Previous research has suggested, but not confirmed, that women are at a significant disadvantage with respect to maintaining abstinence (Hammond and Garfinkle 1961; Eisinger 1971; Gritz 1979; Blair et al. 1980; U.S. Department of Health and Human Services 1980; Grunberg et al. 1991). The nature of the difference is unknown. Speculation as to the basis for the gender difference has focused on both psychosocial (e.g., perceived desirability of smoking, extent of social disapproval encountered, and perceived risks versus benefits) and biological (e.g., nicotine sensitivity, metabolism, and distribution) explanations (Grunberg et al. 1991).

Even though the previously reported analysis of Nicoderm® failed to find significant interactions between subject characteristics and dose (Transdermal Nicotine Study Group 1991), it is important to remember that the underlying methodology for TSSA can identify complex, nonlinear interactions in a way that linear models are unable to do. By so doing, TSSA has an important side benefit: the identification of cut-points on continuously scored variables that result in maximum discrimination between individuals who are more or less successful with the patch. For example, the Transdermal Nicotine Study Group (1991) reported that smokers with less self-rated motivation to quit were less successful, regardless of treatment. The translation of this finding into meaningful information for clinical decisionmaking is unclear (e.g., how much motivation is enough?). TSSA, on the other hand, can tell us where on the 11-point motivation scale maximum separation occurs for more or less successful patch users. The cut-point is easily translatable into guidelines for the effective prescription of the patch.

Should this approach be successful in identifying meaningful subgroups of smokers who are more or less successful with transdermal nicotine, we will have demonstrated its feasibility for use in the context of a clinical trial. We then would be in a position to apply it to other currently available clinical trial data sets that use time to relapse as an outcome variable. These data sets need not be limited to clinical evaluations of transdermal nicotine but also could include data from trials of nicotine polacrilex, as well as trials of behavioral approaches.

APPLICATIONS TO ALCOHOL RESEARCH

TSSA of outcome data from alcohol treatment programs may offer unique opportunities to further understand the heterogeneity of relapse in alcoholics. One way to proceed would be to start with a set of classification variables that are essentially demographic. After the subgroups have been identified on the basis of relapse experience, the frequency of each of the various alcoholic subtypes (as described in Babor 1994) could be determined for each of the identified terminal node subgroups. This might give us some clues as to how the various alcoholic typologies relate to demographically determined relapse subgroups, a need identified by Del Boca (1994).

A more theoretical way to proceed would be to incorporate key variables thought to be markers of the various typologies into the classification set (Allen et al. 1994; Gordis and Allen 1994). The characteristics of the resulting subgroups (determined by differences in relapse rates) could be compared with those of the known alcoholic typologies (Brown et al. 1994) and would give us some idea of the importance of the indicator variables in determining relapse subgroups.

After the creation of homogeneous subgroups, prediction of relapse with theoretically relevant variables also might be more powerful. For example, for a subgroup with an extremely high rate of relapse, markers of the homeostatic dysregulation described by Meyer (1994) (e.g., anxiety, depression, cognitive dysfunction) might be especially predictive of time to relapse. For a subgroup with a longer time to relapse, the number of drinking situations, conditioned environmental cues, or stress might be related especially strongly to the rate of relapse.

The ultimate payoff will come, of course, if it can be shown that identification of relapse subgroups leads to more informed patient-treatment matching. The method could be used to identify patient-treatment interactions that otherwise might go undetected. We think TSSA will be of assistance to alcohol researchers concerned with the heterogeneity problem and relapse.

ACKNOWLEDGMENTS

This research was supported by grant HL39225 from the National Heart, Lung, and Blood Institute and funds provided by the Cigarette and Tobacco Surtax Fund of the State of California through the Tobacco-Related Disease Research Program of the University of California, grant 3RT376.

The authors wish to thank Marion Merrell Dow and the Transdermal Nicotine Study Group for making this data available for analysis.

REFERENCES

Allen, J.P.; Fertig, J.B.; and Mattson, M.E. Personality-based subtypes of chemically dependent patients. *Ann NY Acad Sci* 708:7–22, 1994.

Babor, T.F. Introduction: Method and theory in the classification of alcoholics. *Ann NY Acad Sci* 708:1–6, 1994.

Barnes, G.M.; Welte, J.W.; and Dintcheff, B. Drinking among subgroups in the adult population of New York State: A classification analysis using CART. *J Stud Alcohol* 52:338–344, 1991.

Blair, A.; Blair, S.N.; Howe, H.G.; et al. Physical, psychological, and sociodemographic differences among smokers, ex-smokers, and nonsmokers in a working population. *Prev Med* 9:747–759,1980.

Breiman, L.; Friedman, J.H.; Olshen, R.A.; and Stone, C.J. *Classification and Regression Trees.* Belmont, CA: Wadsworth, 1984.

Brown, J.; Babor, T.F.; Litt, M.D.; and Kranzler, H.R. The Type A/Type B distinction: Subtyping alcoholics according to indicators of vulnerability and severity. *Ann NY Acad Sci* 708:23–33, 1994.

Carmelli, D.; Halpern, J.; Swan, G.E.; et al. 27-year mortality in the Western Collaborative Group Study: Construction of risk groups by recursive partitioning. *J Clin Epidemiol* 44:1341–1351, 1991.

Ciampi, A.; Lawless, J.F.; McKinney, S.M.; and Singhal, K. Regression and recursive partition strategies in the analysis of medical and survival data. *J Clin Epidemiol* 41:737–748, 1988.

Cohen, S.; Kamarck, T.; and Mermelstein, R. A global measure of perceived stress. *J Health Soc Behav* 24:385–396, 1983.

Del Boca, F.K. Sex, gender, and alcoholic typologies. *Ann NY Acad Sci* 708:34–48, 1994.

Eisinger, R.A. Psychosocial predictors of smoking recidivism. *J Health Soc Behav* 12:355–362, 1971.

Fagerstrom, K.O. Measuring degree of physical dependence to tobacco smoking with reference to individualization of treatment. *Addict Behav* 3:235–241, 1978.

Fiore, M.C.; Jorenby, D.E.; Baker, T.B.; and Kenford, S.L. Tobacco dependence and the nicotine patch: Clinical guidelines for effective use. *JAMA* 268:2687–2694, 1992.

Gilpin, E.; Olshen, R.; Henning, H.; and Ross, J. Prediction after myocardial infarction: Comparison of three multivariate methodologies. *Cardiology* 70:73–84, 1983.

Gordis, E., and Allen, J.P. Research opportunities in typology and genetics of alcoholism. *Ann NY Acad Sci* 708:214–217, 1994.

Gordon, L., and Olshen, R.A. Tree-structured survival analyses (with discussion). *Cancer Treat Rep* 69:1065–1069, 1985.

Gritz, E.R. Women and smoking: A realistic appraisal. In Schwartz, J.L., ed. *Progress in Smoking Cessation: Proceedings of the International Conference on Smoking Cessation*. New York: American Cancer Society, 1979.

Grunberg, N.E.; Winders, S.E.; and Wewers, M.E. Gender differences in tobacco use. *Health Psychol* 10:143–153, 1991.

Hammond, G., and Garfinkle, L. Smoking habits of men and women. *J Natl Cancer Inst* 27:419–442, 1961.

Hughes, J.R. Pharmacotherapy for smoking cessation: Unvalidated assumptions, anomalies, and suggestions for future research. *J Consult Clin Psychol* 61:751–760, 1993.

Kaplan, E.L., and Meier, P. Non-parametric estimation from incomplete observation. *J Am Stat Assoc* 53:457–481, 1958.

Kwak, L.W.; Halpern, J.; Olshen, R.A.; and Horning, S.J. Prognostic significance of actual dose intensity in diffuse large cell lymphoma: Results of a tree-structured survival analysis. *J Clin Oncol* 8:963–977, 1990.

Meyer, R.E. Toward a comprehensive theory of alcoholism. *Ann NY Acad Sci* 708:238–250, 1994.

Miller, N.S., and Corcores, J.A. Nicotine dependence: Diagnosis, chemistry, and pharmacologic treatments. *Pediatr Rev* 14:275–279, 1993.

Norregaard, J.; Tonnesen, P.; and Petersen, L. Predictors and reasons for relapse in smoking cessation with nicotine and placebo patches. *Prev Med* 22:261–271, 1993.

Physicians' Desk Reference. Oradell, NJ: Medical Economics Company, 1993.

Prather, R.D.; Tu, T.G.; Rolf, C.N.; and Gorsline, J. Nicotine pharmacokinetics of Nicoderm (Nicotine Transdermal System) in women and obese men compared with normal-sized men. *J Clin Pharmacol* 33:644–649, 1993.

Sachs, D.P., and Leischow, S.J. Pharmacologic approaches to smoking cessation. *Clin Chest Med* 12:769–791, 1991.

SAS Institute. *SAS/STAT Guide Version 6 Edition*. Cary, NC: SAS Institute, 1987.

Shiffman, S.A. Assessing smoking patterns and motives. *J Consult Clin Psychol* 61: 732–742, 1993.

Shiffman, S.A., and Jarvik, M.E. Trends in withdrawal symptoms in abstinence from cigarette smoking. *Psychopharmacology* 50:35–39, 1976.

Shumaker, S.A., and Grunberg, N.E., eds. Proceedings of the National Working Conference on Smoking Relapse. *Health Psychol* 5 (Suppl):1–99, 1986.

Statistics and Epidemiology Research Corporation. *EGRET Version 0.26.04*. Seattle: Statistics and Epidemiology Research Corporation, 1991.

Sutton, S. Relapse following smoking cessation: A critical review of current theory and research. In: Gossop, M., ed. *Relapse and Addictive Behaviour*. London: Routledge, 1989. pp. 41–72.

Swan, G.E., and Denk, C.E. Dynamic models for the maintenance of smoking cessation: Event history analysis of late relapse. *J Behav Med* 10:527–554, 1987.

Swan, G.E.; Denk, C.E.; Parker, S.D.; Carmelli, D.; Furze, C.T.; and Rosenman, R.H. Risk factors for late relapse in male and female ex-smokers. *Addict Behav* 13: 253–266, 1988.

Swan, G.E.; Ward, M.M.; Carmelli, D.; and Jack, L.M. Differential rates of relapse in subgroups of male and female ex-smokers. *J Clin Epidemiol* 46:1041–1053, 1993a.

Swan, G.E.; Ward, M.M.; Jack, L.M.; and Carmelli, D. Weight-related factors as predictors of a high rate of relapse. Paper presented to the Annual Meeting of the Society of Behavioral Medicine, San Francisco, CA, March 1993. *Ann Behav Med* 15 (Suppl):S134 (abstract), 1993b.

Swan, G.E.; Ward, M.M.; Jack, L.M.; and Javitz, H. Cardiovascular reactivity as a predictor of relapse in male and female smokers. *Health Psychol* 12:451–458, 1993c.

Swan, G.E.; Carmelli, D.; LaRue, A.; and McElroy, M.R. Performance on the Digit Symbol Substitution Test and 5-year mortality in the Western Collaborative Group Study. *Am J Epidemiol* 141:32– 40, 1995a.

Swan, G.E.; Jack, L.M.; and Ward, M.M. Subgroups of smokers with different success rates after use of transdermal nicotine. Paper presented to the Annual Meeting of the Society for Research on Nicotine and Tobacco, San Diego, CA, March 1995b.

Transdermal Nicotine Study Group. Transdermal nicotine for smoking cessation. *JAMA* 266:3133–3138, 1991.

U.S. Department of Health and Human Services. *The Health Consequences of Smoking for Women. A Report of the Surgeon General*. Washington, DC: U.S. Department of Health and Human Services, Public Health Service, Office of the Assistant Secretary for Health, Office on Smoking and Health, 1980.

Chapter 15

Secondary Prevention of Alcohol and Tobacco Use With Heavy Drinking College Students

John S. Baer, Ph.D.

This chapter draws from research on secondary prevention of alcohol use to suggest directions for research and to make recommendations for the development of integrated programming to prevent tobacco and alcohol use. Secondary prevention makes sense for those who have already initiated experimentation or regular use of alcohol, tobacco, and other drugs (ATOD's). Assuming a fairly high concordance of smoking and drinking among young people, secondary prevention efforts for alcohol and smoking might be combined from a "wellness" or "general health" model. Such a combination could be made at an individual level, that is, the information or content of preventive interventions, as well as at a more macro level, by supporting programs and policies for reduction of use of both drugs. However, secondary preventive efforts are argued to be most effective when tailored to a specific population and specific ATOD use risk. Ultimately, research is necessary to identify the critical processes associated with the transition from experimentation to regular use for both alcohol and tobacco. Preliminary epidemiological data suggest some similarities in the natural history of the use of these two drugs but also reveal lower rates of concordance for young people compared with older populations.

The first section of this chapter describes the nature of heavy drinking among young people. Specific developmental and psychological features of this population and their drinking

_____

J.S. Baer, Ph.D., is a research associate professor in the Department of Psychology, Box 351525, University of Washington, Seattle, WA 98195–1525.

lead to the use of specific preventive approaches. An example of a research program utilizing a brief, motivational intervention for college student drinkers is described, and extension of this kind of secondary prevention to smoking prevention is discussed. Similarities, differences, and issues of integration for prevention of both smoking and alcohol in this population are reviewed.

HEAVY DRINKING AMONG COLLEGE STUDENTS

Experimentation and at least occasional heavy use of alcohol among young people can be viewed as a normative activity. For example, Johnston and colleagues (1994), summarizing the latest followup in the Monitoring the Future Project, reported that 67 percent of 8th graders and 87 percent of 12th graders have tried alcohol. The researchers also reported widespread occasions of heavy drinking. Binge drinking in the previous month, defined as consumption of five or more drinks in a row, was reported by 14 percent of 8th graders and 28 percent of 12th graders.

Even though most students are under the age of 21, drinking on college campuses is even more extreme than that of high school seniors (Johnston et al. 1994; Wechsler et al. 1994). Between 80 and 90 percent of college students drink alcohol at least monthly, and most surveys suggest that 15–25 percent of students drink in such a way as to interfere with their social, educational, or physical functioning

(Saltz and Elandt 1986). Many problems on college campuses, including date rape, vandalism, accidents, and academic failure, are associated with alcohol use (Berkowitz and Perkins 1986). Drinking typically follows a binge pattern, with consumption of several drinks in a short period of time on weekend evenings (Rabow and Neuman 1984). Johnston and colleagues (1994) reported that 40 percent of college students acknowledge drinking five or more drinks in a row in the previous month.

Two developmental/social processes are critical for understanding heavy drinking in the student population. First, the practice is surprisingly normative and socially accepted and is not often thought to be a problem by those who engage in it (Perkins and Berkowitz 1986; Baer and Carney 1993). Heavy drinking is seen as being part of the "party scene" in college and is associated with fun, entertainment, and sexuality (Larimer unpublished data 1992). For example, in the movie "Animal House," the heavy-drinking fraternity is presented as fun loving, in contrast to the serious, studious, boring fraternity. Who would want to be a part of the boring social scene? Drinking is a central or key aspect of the social system these young people live in. To challenge this norm is to challenge the very social fabric that so strongly affects social life.

The second critical developmental/ social process is the change in drinking pattern as people age. Most students see heavy drinking as a temporary activity that will pass when they move on to more important things. Fortunately for the larger society, this is true. Perhaps two-thirds of heavy-drinking young people will moderate their drinking as they age through their middle and late twenties (Cahalan and Room 1974; Fillmore 1988). For example, the incidence of binge drinking peaks at ages 21–22 at 40 percent, declines to 35 percent by ages 23–24, and further declines to 25 percent by ages 29–30 (Johnston et al. 1994). The late teens and early twenties, then, can be considered as a developmental phase or a window of risk for many, if not most.

Who is at the most risk and, therefore, might be targeted for prevention programs? To answer this question, we must first consider the issue of near-term versus long-term risk. *Near-term risk* refers to accidents and problems in the immediate future, whereas *long-term risk* refers to the development of long-standing dependence on alcohol. Predictions of risk are difficult. Change in drinking patterns over time may be more the rule than continuity, and much more research is needed to link late adolescent drinking with drinking problems experienced later in life (Fillmore 1988). Nevertheless, a host of biological, personality, psychological, and social variables have been associated with young people's drinking, and some are hypothesized as risk factors for long-term problems (Baer 1993).

To review briefly, the best predictor of drinking among young people is the drinking of their friends. Young people appear both to select associates who drink in similar fashion and to influence each other to drink more (cf. Kandel 1986). General social contexts, like living in a group setting (e.g., dormitories) or belonging to clubs and societies that have traditions of heavy drinking (e.g., fraternities), clearly influence drinking rates and associated problems (Baer et al. 1995). These social context factors are presumably important for near-term risks; their relationship to long-term dependency problems remains generally untested. Psychological factors, such as expectancies about alcohol effects, have also been associated with earlier initiation and heavier drinking patterns (Christiansen et al. 1989; Sher et al. 1991). Genetic factors, such as being the child of an alcoholic, place young people at increased risk of developing dependency over the long term, although samples studied from college campuses do not generally reflect heightened risk for children of alcoholics in the near term (Alterman et al. 1989). Personality features of impulsivity and conduct disorder are associated with greater alcohol problems in both the near and long term (Jessor and Jessor 1977; Baer et al. 1995). A smaller subgroup of young people may also display drinking problems as part of comorbidity with depression and anxiety-related disorders (Lewinsohn et al. 1993).

In summary, drinking among young people, and drinking among college students more specifically, is argued to be both risky and determined by multiple factors. Although alcohol problems for young people are not nearly as systematic or predictable as those of older populations (Fillmore 1988; Baer 1991), they nonetheless constitute an enormous social problem (Cahalan and Room 1974). Developmental factors appear to be crucial in understanding this window of risk. Young people want to feel autonomous and are generally resistant to adult messages to avoid alcohol. To date it is not clear what factors are associated with individual differences in longer term risk, that is, for the development of dependency at midlife, although both genetic and personality factors are likely candidates. Near-term risks seem best predicted from the social context of drinking.

RATIONALE FOR A SECONDARY PREVENTION APPROACH

Secondary prevention approaches follow logically from the natural history and psychology of heavy drinking on college campuses. First, because the vast majority of students have initiated use, primary prevention programs have difficulty gaining audience. Informational campaigns to minimize risk, although reasonable from an educational mission, have shown little success in changing drinking behavior (Kraft 1984). Likewise, broad policy changes are often ineffective and sometimes create unwanted negative side effects (George et al. 1989).

Second, formal treatment programs assume a well-developed pattern of drug dependency and the self-identity of an "alcoholic." As stat-ed earlier, many of the problems associated with drinking on campus do not come from those who are addicted in the traditional sense, but rather from those who drink heavily and to intoxication intermittently. These individuals will not accept the label of "alcoholic" and do not feel that their lives have become "unmanageable."

Finally, some individuals are indeed at higher risk than others. A secondary prevention approach that targets only those at highest risk for problems can be more effective and more efficient than programs targeted to all individuals.

The targeting of individuals for secondary prevention can, of course, be difficult both conceptually and practically. Selection of targets for secondary prevention can be based on aspects of the individual, such as showing early signs of a disorder or showing risk factors that increase the likelihood of a disorder. Alternatively, targets can be selected based on broad social or environmental features that place entire subgroups at risk. On the college campus one could select those drinking at risky levels, those with early problems, those living in settings where problems are common, or those with elevated risk of problems based on previous conduct or family history issues. Once selected, these individuals must be engaged to receive prevention programming. A model program is described in the next section; the design and content of the program reflect some possible solutions to these operational issues.

THE LIFESTYLES '94 PROJECT

The Lifestyles '94 Project at the University of Washington was designed to test a secondary prevention approach for the minimization of alcohol problems in college students. It is presented here as an example of one carefully controlled secondary prevention program. Additional details of the research appear in other publications (Baer 1993; Marlatt et al. 1995). Before detailing the secondary prevention approach, some description of the research design is necessary. Clearly, application of all these research procedures is not necessary for all prevention programming.

The design of the longitudinal study involved three groups of subjects. The incoming class to the University of Washington was screened for alcohol risk factors while still in their senior year of high school. Those students defined as "high-risk" were then randomly assigned to either an intervention condition or a no-treatment (assessment only) control group. In addition, a third group was randomly selected from the entire screening pool to serve as a normative comparison of college students drinkers (at all levels of risk).

The screening questionnaire was mailed in the spring of 1990 to all students who (1) were accepted and had indicated an intention to enroll at the University of Washington the following fall term, (2) were matriculating from high school, and (3) were not over 19 years of age. Return of the questionnaires was awarded with $5 and entrance into a prize drawing. Of 4,000 questionnaires sent, 2,179 (54 percent) completed forms were returned. Of these 2,179, 2,041 students (94 percent) provided usable questionnaires and indicated a willingness to be contacted for future rsearch.

Within the screening pool, students were considered as high risk if they (a) reported drinking at least monthly and consuming at least five to six drinks on one drinking occasion in the past month, or (b) reported the experience of three alcohol-related problems on three to five occasions in the past 3 years on the Rutgers Alcohol Problem Inventory (RAPI) (White and LaBouvie 1989). These selection criteria identified the top quartile of the screening sample (n = 508). An additional normative comparison sample was randomly selected from the pool of 2,041 responders (n = 151); because this sample was selected to represent normative practices, it included subjects at all risk levels (including those previously screened as high risk).

Upon arrival on campus for the fall term, students identified as high risk or selected for the normative comparison group were sent a personal letter inviting them to participate in a 4-year longitudinal study of alcohol use and other lifestyle behaviors. The students were asked if they would be willing to (1) complete a baseline interview and fill out questionnaires and (2) provide the names and addresses of two "collateral" reporters who could be called to confirm the subjects' drinking practices. Subjects were compensated for their participation in the study. Students in the high-risk group agreed to be randomly assigned to participate in the intervention program or to the no-treatment control condition. Of the 508 high-risk students invited, 348 (68.5 percent) were recruited for the intervention study; 115 of 151 (76.2 percent) normative comparison subjects were similarly recruited.

At the baseline interview, structured assessments measured family history of alcohol problems, history of conduct disorder, and personal drinking history. At the baseline and each followup assessment, subjects also completed a questionnaire packet containing measures of drinking and drug use, problems associated with alcohol abuse and dependence, and a variety of psychosocial measures (life events, perceived drinking norms, alcohol expectancies, sexual behavior). Followup assessment occurred first at 6 months postbaseline (approximately 3 months postintervention) and then annually each subsequent fall term.

Description of this sample's drinking during high school and the transition into college have been described elsewhere (Baer et al. 1995). High-risk subjects increased their drinking significantly upon entry into college. Increases in drinking were primarily found among men, and were more extreme when the subject reported a history of conduct problems or residence in a fraternity.

At baseline, prior to randomization, the sample of high-risk drinkers (188 females and 160 males) reported drinking about twice a week, consuming over 11 drinks a week. High-risk subjects reported reaching an average estimated peak blood alcohol concentration (BAC) of 0.12 percent weekly. The high-risk sample on average met almost one and one-half of nine DSM–III–R alcohol dependence criteria (American Psychiatric Association 1987). In contrast, the random comparison group, representing the freshman norm, reported drinking once a week, less than six drinks each week, and lower estimated typical peak BAC's (0.08 percent). Few DSM–III–R dependence criteria were met by the random comparison group (M = 0.54). Using the RAPI, the high-risk sample reported an average of 7.49 (SD = 5.86) alcohol-related problems as having occurred at least once over the 6 months prior to the first-year fall assessment.

MOTIVATIONAL INTERVENTION

First Winter Term

The motivational intervention provided in the winter term (January-March) of the first year of college was based on our prior research with brief interventions with college students (Baer et al. 1992b) and on motivational interviewing more generally (Miller and Rollnick 1991). Students assigned to receive the intervention were contacted first by phone and subsequently by mail to schedule an appointment for a feedback interview (based on the data obtained the previous fall term). Students were provided with alcohol consumption monitoring cards and asked to keep track of their drinking on a daily basis for 2 weeks prior to their scheduled interview.

The interviewers consisted of two doctoral-level clinical psychologists, two postdoctoral-level clinical psychologists, and four advanced graduate students in clinical psychology. In the feedback session, interviewers met individually with students, reviewed their alcohol self-monitoring cards, and gave them concrete individualized feedback about their drinking patterns, risks, and beliefs about alcohol effects. Subjects' self-reported drinking rates were compared to college averages, and risks for current and future problems (e.g., grades, blackouts, and accidents) were identified. Beliefs about real and imagined alcohol effects were addressed through discussions of placebo effects and the nonspecific effects of alcohol on social behavior. Biphasic effects of alcohol (stimulant followed by depressive effects) were described, and the students were encouraged to question the "more alcohol is better" assumption. Suggestions for risk reduction were outlined.

The style of the interview was based on techniques of motivational interviewing (Miller and Rollnick 1991). Confrontational communications, such as "you have a problem and you are in denial" (thought to create a defensive response in the client) were specifically avoided. Instead, interviewers simply placed the available evidence in front of the student and avoided moralistic judgments and arguments. Interviewers

sought to allow students to evaluate their situation and to begin contemplation of the possibility of change. "What do you make of this?" and "Are you surprised?" were common questions raised in an effort to facilitate conversations about risk and the possibility of behavior change. The technique is quite flexible. Issues of high-risk residential setting (life in a fraternity), peer use, prior conduct difficulties, and family history were addressed where applicable. Risk factors, such as family history of alcohol problems or conduct disorder, were explored with students to determine their own experience and impressions of risk. The existence of increased risk based on family history or conduct history was acknowledged, but each student was encouraged to reflect about how that risk might manifest in his or her own life.

Motivational techniques assume that college-student drinkers are in a natural state of ambivalence and must come to their own conclusions regarding the need to change behavior and reduce risks. Thus, the specific goals of behavior change were left to the student and not directed or demanded by the interviewer. Each student left the interview with a "personalized summary feedback sheet" (comparing his or her responses with college norms and listing reported problems and risk factors), along with a generic "tips" page describing biphasic responses to alcohol, placebo effects, and suggestions for techniques of reduced risk drinking. Students were encouraged to contact the Lifestyles '94 Project if they had any further questions or were interested in any additional services throughout college.

Second Winter Term

During the winter term of the second year of the study (1 year after the individual feedback interviews), members of the motivational intervention group were mailed graphic feedback pertaining to their reports of drinking at baseline and at 6- and 12-month followups. Each feedback sheet contained individualized bar graphs depicting baseline and subsequent levels of drinking quantity, drinking frequency, and alcohol-related problems (RAPI items). Based on two variables at the 12-month followup, the report of peak drinking experiences and the number of reported alcohol-related problems, intervention subjects were categorized into four risk categories: low (neither elevated), medium (one elevated), high (both elevated), and extreme (both elevated and RAPI problems greater than 10).

In a summary paragraph, each intervention subject was given individualized feedback about his or her level of risk and was encouraged to seek assistance if so desired. Subjects in the high (n = 40) and extreme (n = 16) risk categories were also contacted by phone to offer assistance and encouragement to reduce their risks associated with alcohol use. If the student was interested, an additional followup interview was scheduled.

OUTCOME

Results from the Lifestyles '94 Project have been reported in varying degrees of detail (Baer et al. 1992a; Baer 1993; Baer et al. 1994; Baer 1994; Marlatt et al. 1995). A complete report of the study is currently in preparation. Because this chapter is concerned primarily with the design and content of the secondary prevention program, only general results are described.

Summarizing through 2-year followup assessments, students who received the motivational intervention and followup graphic feedback reported significantly less drinking quantity, less drinking frequency, and fewer alcohol-related problems at each assessment compared with those in the control condition. The magnitude of the effects is not large but is consistent over time. The effects on alcohol-related problems and dependence scores reveal the largest changes. For example, at the 2-year followup, those who completed the motivational interview in their freshman year reported on average 3.3 (SD = 3.5) problems on the RAPI in the previous 6 months, compared with 4.7 (SD = 4.4) problems for the high-risk control group. This represents a standardized effect size of 0.32. In comparison, the normative control group reported an average 2.4 (SD = 3.5) problems at the 2-year assessment. Similar effects were noted with a measure of alcohol dependence, the Alcohol Dependence Scale (Skinner and Horn 1984). Using a cutoff score of 11 on this scale (Ross et al. 1990), only 16 of 145 (11.0 percent) of those in the motivational intervention group were classified as showing mild dependence at the 2-year assessment, compared with 42 of 156 (26.9 percent) of those in the control group.

Different patterns of risk were evident among these young people. In particular, men with a history of conduct problems or those living in fraternities, compared with those without conduct histories or those living elsewhere, showed greater drinking rates, more drinking problems, and less natural reduction in risk over time. A history of conduct problems and living in a fraternity, did not, however, interact with or moderate treatment effects.

The motivational intervention was designed to facilitate contemplation and action in self-change, as well as challenge perceptions of normative use of alcohol and expected positive effects of alcohol. Treatment subjects who received the motivational intervention reported consistently higher motivation to change their drinking over time ("action" subscale scores from the University of Rhode Island Change Assessment [URICA] [McConnaughy et al. 1983]) than did members of the control group. Perceived general norms for alcohol use (ratings of the typical quantity and frequency of drinking of a "typical college student" [Baer et al. 1991]) also declined significantly over time and showed differences based on motivational intervention. Consistent with treatment impact on subject drinking, the magnitude of treatment

effects on perceived norms is statistically significant but small.

Ongoing followup of this sample will assess the impact of the intervention throughout the college years. Preliminary data analysis of 3-year followup suggests continued benefits for the treatment group (Quigley et al. 1994). Analysis of 4-year outcomes is just beginning.

RECOMMENDATIONS FOR SECONDARY PREVENTION OF TOBACCO AND ALCOHOL USE

The research described in this chapter illustrates several themes that are important when considering the development of secondary prevention programs generally, and the integration of secondary prevention of both alcohol and tobacco use more specifically. First, the techniques and style of motivational interviewing provide a clinical model for intervention with young people. A number of features of our preventive work with college students are noteworthy. We assume that students do not want to change their behavior and are not seeking help. Therefore, we attempt to talk with young people in a manner that does not heighten resistance but rather facilitates reflection. We do not confront "denial" and insist that the individual accept that he or she has a problem. We also assume considerable heterogeneity in risk status. Only those issues that are pertinent to the student are raised. In this manner the prevention is both tailored and efficient. In addition, we support the autonomy of developing young adults. Plans and goals for change, if any, are developed in tandem with the student. These features of our secondary prevention program seem critical for any intervention targeted to young people, be it for tobacco use alone or for tobacco and alcohol use combined.

Second, a more general "wellness" model works well as a frame for alcohol use and could be easily generalized to include messages about smoking. In fact, motivational interviewing has been used in a variety of contexts for a variety of health behaviors (Baker and Dixon 1991; Garland and Dougher 1991). The benefits of the technique, such as flexibility and individual goal setting, are not specific to the topic. Health risks about smoking can be detailed in a nonconfrontational fashion as described above for alcohol. Further, we find that discussion of alcohol use is best placed in a broad context of wellness. Students have an easier time evaluating the choices they make about their lifestyle (hence the project name) than they do evaluating alcohol in isolation. In fact, the link between alcohol and lifestyle choices is likely a true reflection of both the young person's experience and prevalence data for smoking and drinking. Young people consider smoking and drinking as choices, often with considerable knowledge of health risks.

Third, access to students who either smoke or drink (and thus might be targets for prevention) remains a challenge. Note that identification of an "at-risk" population is necessary for secondary prevention programs. In the Lifestyles '94 Project we specifically targeted high-risk drinkers based on drinking during high school and invited them into a long-term study where they might occasionally make money. This technique may not be easily transferred to less research-based programs. Nevertheless, our payments are not large, and our results suggest that students are willing to participate in long-term studies and evaluate their risks due to drinking for relatively small external incentives. Some incentive may be required to gain access to young people who are at most risk.

We are currently experimenting with providing secondary prevention to entire groups of students identified as high risk based on social context factors (i.e., living in fraternities and sororities). With this strategy, large numbers of the heaviest drinkers can participate in a secondary prevention program as long as the organization is supportive (usually as represented by its leaders). Because members of these organizations do not specifically request programs on alcohol, information about a variety of health risk behaviors (like smoking) could be incorporated relatively easily.

Our model of motivational interviewing and the provision of feedback might also provide an outline for adaptation to primary care settings where health professionals regularly encounter individuals experimenting with alcohol and tobacco. The critical issue, of course, is the efficacy of such an intervention in a very brief form. Health care professionals may have only a few minutes to provide secondary prevention programming. One of our students, Linda Dimeff, is currently developing a project evaluating the efficacy of training physicians and nurses at a local student health center to provide motivational feedback. She is also planning to integrate computer-based feedback to save time. The primary care setting is an area where smoking risks, as well as multiple lifestyle risks, could easily be incorporated into secondary interventions.

Of course, effective combined programming for alcohol and tobacco use assumes concordance between the two behavior patterns—that individuals who use one drug are likely to use the other. Among college students the concordance between smoking and drinking is moderate but does not come close to the 90 percent concordance found in treatment populations (DiFranza and Guerrera 1990). One reason for this is that base rates for smoking among college students are not high. For example, in the Monitoring the Future data, daily smoking among college students is significantly less common (15 percent) than among same-age peers who do not attend college (27 percent) (Johnston et al. 1994).

A current study of heavy-drinking college seniors, the Transitions Project, allows some examination of concordance among students who are fairly heavy drinkers (Baer 1995). To qualify for this study, subjects must report binge drinking (to an estimated BAC of 0.12 percent) twice monthly. Of the first 197 subjects, 12.2 percent reported that they smoked every day, another 7.1 percent smoked at least weekly, and 26.4 percent smoked occasionally (less than weekly). Thus, 45.7 percent (90 of 197) described themselves as smoking at least occasionally; this statistic is somewhat higher than that estimated for college students generally, but it is accounted for primarily by occasional smoking. Recruitment and targeting individuals who use one drug would therefore yield some increased number of those also using the other drug but would not capture most individuals who use only alcohol or only tobacco.

Further, it is not clear that alcohol use and tobacco use follow similar developmental paths or are based on similar psychological and developmental issues. An understanding of these issues, including etiologic risk factors, as they relate to tobacco use is necessary for the design of an integrated secondary prevention program.

Longitudinal data reveal both similarities and differences in the natural history of tobacco and alcohol use. Experimentation with both alcohol and tobacco begins in early adolescence (Johnston et al. 1994; Chen and Kandel 1995), with very little initiation in young adulthood. Also, the same risk factors during adolescence are associated with tobacco and alcohol use (Clayton 1992). Efforts to prevent the acquisition of smoking and drinking are thus appropriately placed at younger age groups (e.g., junior high schools) and completed simultaneously.

Trends for use of alcohol and tobacco in late adolescence and young adulthood, however, reveal different patterns. Johnston and colleagues (1994) suggested that smoking habits are consolidated in the twenties. They stated that "relatively few new people are recruited to smoking after high-school. On the other hand, smoking at heavier levels—such as smoking daily or smoking a half-a-pack daily—is considerably higher among the older age groups, reflecting the fact that many previous moderate smokers move into a pattern of heavier consumption during their twenties" (p. 40). The developmental pattern for alcohol use is somewhat different than that for regular smoking, with the numbers of binge drinkers in the Monitoring the Future panels steadily declining throughout the twenties (but with small gains in the numbers of daily drinkers). Chen and Kandel (1995) described similar patterns in a longitudinal study. High-frequency tobacco use is stable or increasing through the twenties, whereas high-frequency use of alcohol and other drugs declines.

Of course, these trends are averages across large groups. Perhaps a small subgroup of individuals continues to both drink heavily and gradually smoke more. Are the processes of smoking consolidation and continuity of binge drinking related? Data from the Transitions Project can be used illustratively. Examination of followup data 1 year after college graduation reveals the different developmental trends noted above. Large reductions in drinking were observed once young people left the college environment. For example, the self-reported average number of drinks per drinking day declined from 6.23 (SD = 2.66) to 4.11 (SD = 1.97; $F(1, 196) = 76.51$, $p < 0.001$). In contrast, changes in smoking practices were common but inconsistent in direction. Forty-two percent of the sample continued to smoke at least occasionally. Thirty-one subjects reduced smoking rates, whereas 20 subjects increased smoking rates. Three previously occasional smokers reported daily smoking 1 year after college, but 8 previously daily smokers now smoked occasionally or less (2 quit completely). Of particular importance for this chapter, however, is the fact that, among these subjects, changes in drinking were not accompanied by changes in smoking status. No significant associations were noted between changes in smoking status and changes in drinking quantity, drinking frequency, or alcohol-related problems. Changes in these two lifestyle habits seem to occur independently.

The Transitions Project is a small sample to address epidemiological questions. It nevertheless exemplifies the issues that are necessary for the development of secondary preventive programming. To the extent that tobacco and alcohol use are associated with different developmental processes, it may be necessary to develop different preventive messages targeted to different individuals. For example, for young "party animals," the psychological issues associated with alcohol use are autonomy, individuation, and sexuality. An epidemiological view suggests that this is a distinct and time-limited window of risk or vulnerability. A motivation-based, moderate-use, "risk reduction" approach has much to offer these young people in terms of drinking behavior. Because of the different nature of nicotine and typical smoking habits, however, a similar message for smoking may have considerable limitations. It is not clear what the nature or content of feedback for smokers of college age might be. Nor is it clear that occasional smoking is risky in the short or long term for these young people. Are young people worried about getting hooked? Do they see such behavior as normative? Is smoking associated with other specific risk factors?

There is ample room to develop research programs and theories to address transitions from occasional smoking and binge drinking to regular use in later years. It is often thought that drinking declines when young people adopt adult roles, because regular intoxication interferes with family and employment responsibilities. Nicotine does not create the same interference. Perhaps those who find that cigarettes help them with job performance find their way into regular smoking as they age into their twenties. Although alcohol and tobacco use may both be supported by young adult socializing, they may be differentially supported by demands of the daily working world. This speculative theory is only one of many that could be addressed with longitudinal studies, and, if supported, would lead to different kinds of preventive messages, perhaps targeted to different individuals at different points in time.

CONCLUSIONS

Secondary prevention should be more than information. It should be personalized and sensitive to the motivational state of the recipient, and it should be specific to particular behaviors, habits, and environments. The research described herein summarizes one program tailored to heavy drinking college students. Considerable research is needed to facilitate the development of secondary prevention programs for both smoking and drinking. Such programs might include the following components:

- Examination of the transitions from experimentation with tobacco to regular use, particularly among those of college age. Predictive factors of this consolidation process from the biological, psychological, and contextual domains need to be illuminated.

- Studies of the concurrent use of alcohol and tobacco in social and work settings by young adults. Although we know that many of those who use alcohol also tend to smoke, we must know how the two drugs are used separately and in combination for specific desired effects.

- Development and evaluation of motivation-based secondary prevention programs for college-age individuals who smoke. What kind of feedback might move college students to consider reduction or elimination of smoking? Can the rates of regular smoking be reduced through this type of intervention?
- Evaluation of secondary prevention approaches that combine messages for reductions in health risks from both alcohol and tobacco (as well as other lifestyle issues). These trials could be developed at university health services, where students have regular contact with health care professionals. Quite brief forms of prevention must be developed and tested for efficacy.

ACKNOWLEDGMENTS

This research is supported by National Institute on Alcohol Abuse and Alcoholism grants AA05591 and AA08632. The efforts of Kristine Luce, Connie Fillis, and Andrew Hummel-Schluger are gratefully acknowledged for preparation of this manuscript. Dan Kivlahan provided helpful feedback on an earlier draft.

REFERENCES

Alterman, A.I.; Searles, J.S.; and Hall, J.G. Failure to find differences in drinking behavior as a function of familial risk for alcoholism: A replication. *J Abnorm Psychol* 98:50–53, 1989.

American Psychiatric Association. *Diagnostic and Statistical Manual of Mental Disorders, Third Edition, Revised.* Washington, DC: the Association, 1987.

Baer, J.S. Implications for early intervention from a biopsychosocial perspective on addiction. *Behav Change* 8:51–59, 1991.

Baer, J.S. Etiology and secondary prevention of alcohol problems with young adults. In: Baer, J.S.; Marlatt, G.A.; and McMahnon, R.J., eds. *Addictive Behaviors Across the Lifespan*. Newbury Park, CA: Sage Publications, 1993. pp. 111–137.

Baer, J.S. Effects of college residence on perceived norms for alcohol consumption: An examination of the first year in college. *Psychol Addict Behav* 8(1):43–50, 1994.

Baer, J.S. Continuity of heavy drinking after college graduation: Preliminary prospective analyses. *Alcohol Clin Exp Res* 19(2):40A, 1995.

Baer, J.S., and Carney, M.M. Biases in the perceptions of the consequences of alcohol use among college students. *J Stud Alcohol* 54:54–60, 1993.

Baer, J.S.; Stacy, A.; and Larimer, M. Biases in the perception of drinking norms among college students. *J Stud Alcohol* 52(6):580–586, 1991.

Baer, J.S.; Kivlahan, D.R.; and Marlatt, G.A. Feedback and advice with high-risk college freshmen reduces drinking rates at three-month follow-up. *Alcohol Clin Exp Res* 16:403, 1992a.

Baer, J.S.; Marlatt, G.A.; Kivlahan, D.R.; Fromme, K., Larimer, M.; and Williams, E. An experimental test of three methods of alcohol risk reduction with young adults. *J Consult Clin Psychol* 60:974–979, 1992b.

Baer, J.S.; Kivlahan, D.R.; and Marlatt, G.A. Drinking risk reduction based on feedback and advice with college students: Two-year follow-up. *Alcohol Clin Exp Res* 18(2):466, 1994.

Baer, J.S.; Kivlahan, D.R.; and Marlatt, G.A. High-risk drinking across the transition from high school to college. *Alcohol Clin Exp Res* 19(1):54–61, 1995.

Baker, A., and Dixon, J. Motivational interviewing for HIV risk reduction. In: Miller, W.R., and Rollnick, S., eds. *Motivational Interviewing: Preparing People To Change Addictive Behavior.* New York: Guilford Press, 1991. pp. 293–302.

Berkowitz, A.D., and Perkins, H.W. Problem drinking among college students: A review of recent research. *J Am Coll Health* 35:21–28, 1986.

Cahalan, D., and Room, R. *Problem Drinking Among American Men.* New Brunswick, NJ: Rutgers Center of Alcohol Studies, 1974.

Chen, K., and Kandel, D.B. The natural history of drug use from adolescence to the mid-thirties in a general population sample. *Am J Public Health* 85(1):48–54, 1995.

Christiansen, B.A.; Smith, G.T.; Roehling, P.V.; and Goldman, M.S. Using alcohol expectancies to predict adolescent drinking behavior after one year. *J Consult Clin Psychol* 57:93–99, 1989.

Clayton, R.R. Transitions in drug use: Risk and protective factors. In: Glanz, M., and Pickens, R., eds. *Vulnerability to Drug Abuse.* Washington, DC: American Psychological Association, 1992.

DiFranza, J.R., and Guerrera, M.P. Alcoholism and smoking. *J Stud Alcohol* 51(2):130–135, 1990.

Fillmore, K.M. *Alcohol Use Across the Life Course.* Toronto: Alcoholism and Drug Addiction Research Foundation, 1988.

Garland, R.J., and Dougher, M.J. Motivational intervention in the treatment of sex offenders. In: Miller, W.R., and Rollnick, S., eds. *Motivational Interviewing: Preparing People To Change Addictive Behavior.* New York: Guilford Press, 1991. pp. 293–302.

George, W.H.; Crowe, L.C.; Abwender, D.; and Skinner, J.B. Effects of raising the drinking age to 21 years in New York State on self-reported consumption by college students. *J Appl Soc Psychol* 19: 623–635, 1989.

Jessor, R., and Jessor, S.L. *Problem Behavior and Psychosocial Development: A Longitudinal Study of Youth.* New York: Academic Press, 1977.

Johnston, L.D.; O'Malley, P.M.; and Bachman, J.G. *National Survey Results on Drug Use From the Monitoring the Future Study, 1975–1993.* NIH Pub. No. 94–3810. Rockville, MD: National Institutes of Health, National Institute on Drug Abuse, 1994.

Kandel, D.B. Processes of peer influences in adolescence. In: Silbereisen, R.K., ed. *Development as Action in Context.* Berlin: Springer-Verlag, 1986.

Kraft, D.P. A comprehensive prevention program for college students. In: Miller, P.M., and Nirenberg, T.D., eds. *Prevention of Alcohol Abuse.* New York: Plenum, 1984. pp. 327–370.

Lewinsohn, P.M.; Hyman, H.; Roberts, R.E.; Seeley, J.R.; and Andrews, J.A. Adolescent psychopathology: I. Prevalence and incidence of depression and other DSM–III–R disorders in high school students. *J Abnorm Psychol* 102(1): 133–144, 1993.

Marlatt, G.A.; Baer, J.S.; and Larimer, M.E. Preventing alcohol abuse in college students: A harm-reduction approach. In: Boyd, G.M.; Howard, J.; and Zucker, R., eds. *Alcohol Problems Among Adolescents: Current Directions in Prevention Research.* Northvale, NJ: Lawrence Erlbaum, 1995. pp. 147–172.

McConnaughy, E.A.; Prochaska, J.O.; and Velicer, W.F. Stages of change in psychotherapy: Measurement and profiles. *Psychotherapy* 20(3):368–375, 1983.

Miller, W.R., and Rollnick, S. *Motivational Interviewing: Preparing People To Change Addictive Behavior.* New York: Guilford Press, 1991.

Perkins, H.W., and Berkowitz, A.D. Perceiving the community norms of alcohol use among students: Some research implications for campus alcohol education programming. *Int J Addict* 21:961–976, 1986.

Quigley, L.A.; Baer, J.S.; and Marlatt, G.A. The Lifestyles '94 Project: Three year outcome for alcohol risk reduction among high risk college students. Paper presented at the 28th Annual Association for the Advancement of Behavior Therapy Convention, San Diego, CA, 1994.

Rabow, J., and Neuman, C.A. Saturday night live: Chronicity of alcohol consumption among college students. *Subst Alcohol Actions/Misuse* 5(1):1–7, 1984.

Ross, H.E.; Douglas, R.G.; and Skinner, H.A. Diagnostic validity of the MAST and the alcohol dependence scale in the assessment of DSM–III alcohol disorders. *J Stud Alcohol* 51:506–513, 1990.

Saltz, R., and Elandt, D. College student drinking studies 1976–1985. *Contemp Drug Prob* 13:117–159, 1986.

Sher, K.J.; Walitzer, K.S.; Wood, P.K.; and Brent, E.E. Characteristics of children of alcoholics: Putative risk factors, substance use and abuse, and psychopathology. *J Abnorm Psychol* 100(4):427–448, 1991.

Skinner, H.A., and Horn, J.L. *Alcohol Dependence Scale (ADS).* Toronto, Canada: Addiction Research Foundation, 1984.

Wechsler, H.; Davenport, A.; Dowdall, G.; Moeykens, B.; and Castillo, S. Health and behavioral consequences of binge drinking in college. A national survey of students at 140 campuses. *JAMA* 272(21):1672–1677, 1994.

White, H.R., and LaBouvie, E.W. Towards the assessment of adolescent problem drinking. *J Stud Alcohol* 50:30–37, 1989.

Chapter 16

Screening and Intervention for Smoking and Alcohol Use in Primary Care Settings: Similarities, Differences, Gaps, and Challenges

Judith K. Ockene, Ph.D., and Abigail Adams, M.D.

Smokers often present with multiple behavioral risk factors for health problems and engage in unhealthy behaviors significantly more often than nonsmokers or former smokers (see tables 1 and 2). Consequently, smokers represent a large percentage of the preventable health care cost burden. Studies have demonstrated unhealthy eating patterns among smokers compared with nonsmokers (Schoenborn and Benson 1988; Larkin et al. 1990) and a strong relationship between smoking and alcohol use (Zacny 1990; Tillotson et al. in press). For example, in the Multiple Risk Factor Intervention Trial—a study conducted of "healthy" men, ages 35–57, who were in the top 10-percent risk group for coronary heart disease for their age and sex—those who were smokers exhibited significantly less favorable dietary patterns at baseline than those who were nonsmokers (table 3). Heavy smokers (i.e., those who smoked more than 20 cigarettes per day) consumed more alcohol and calories, proportional to the number of cigarettes they smoked per day, and also consumed a greater percentage of kilocalories from total fat and

J.K. Ockene, Ph.D., is a professor and the director of the Division of Preventive and Behavioral Medicine, Room 57–755, University of Massachusetts Medical School, 55 Lake Avenue, North, Worcester, MA 01655. A. Adams, M.D., is an assistant professor of medicine and the director of the Adult Primary Care Center, Benedict Building, University of Massachusetts Medical School, 55 Lake Avenue, North, Worcester, MA 01655.

Table 1. Summary of 1985 National Health Interview Survey Data on Behaviors of Men (Never-, Former, and Current Smokers) Age 20 and Older.

	Male Subjects		
Behavior	Never-Smokers (%)	Former Smokers (%)	Current Smokers (%)
Alcohol consumption			
Heavier drinker ($\geq 2/d$)	7.9	12.7	18.9
≥ 5 drinks/episode ($\geq 10/yr$)	13.8	21.2	28.7
Weight, diet, and exercise			
Never eats breakfast	18.9	22.3	33.3
Sedentary	46.6	47.7	57.2
Overweight (1.2.I.W.[1])	28.1	30.0	21.2
Other			
Sleeps ≤ 6 h	21.5	22.5	24.9

[1]1.2.I.W. = 1.2 times ideal weight.
Source: Reprinted from Schoenborn, C., and Benson, V. Relationships between smoking and other unhealthy habits: United States, 1985. In: U.S. Department of Health and Human Services, Public Health Service. *Vital Health Statistics No. 154.* DHHS Pub. No. (PHS)88–1250. Washington, DC: Supt. of Docs., U.S. Govt. Print. Off., 1988.

Table 2. Summary of 1985 National Health Interview Survey Data on Behaviors of Women (Never-, Former, and Current Smokers) Age 20 and Older.

	Female Subjects		
Behavior	Never-Smokers (%)	Former Smokers (%)	Current Smokers (%)
Alcohol consumption			
Heavier drinker ($\geq 2/d$)	1.1	3.7	6.1
≥ 5 drinks/episode ($\geq 10/yr$)	2.2	5.0	8.5
Weight, diet, and exercise			
Never eats breakfast	17.7	19.8	37.6
Sedentary	61.1	58.5	64.3
Overweight (1.2.I.W.[1])	24.9	23.0	17.9
Other			
Sleeps ≤ 6 h	20.4	19.9	24.4

[1]1.2.I.W. = 1.2 times ideal weight.
Source: Reprinted from Schoenborn, C., and Benson, V. Relationships between smoking and other unhealthy habits: United States, 1985. In: U.S. Department of Health and Human Services, Public Health Service. *Vital Health Statistics No. 154.* DHHS Pub. No. (PHS)88–1250. Washington, DC: Supt. of Docs., U.S. Govt. Print. Off., 1988.

Table 3. Adjusted[1] Mean Nutrient Levels at Baseline by Number of Cigarettes Smoked per Day for Men in the Multiple Risk Factor Intervention Trial.

| | Cigarettes/Day | | | | Test: Smokers vs. Nonsmokers | |
Nutrient	0	1–19	20–39	> 40	p Value	p Value
Kilocalories	2,345.5	2,317.8	2,406.5	2,559.4	< 0.001	< 0.001
Cholesterol (mg)	421.6	444.9	451.4	478.7	< 0.001	< 0.001
Keys score	47.6	49.5	49.9	50.4	< 0.001	< 0.001
Total fiber (gm)	14.2	13.6	13.1	13.5	0.002	< 0.001
Alcohol (% kcal)	6.8	6.5	7.2	7.8	< 0.001	0.003
Caffeine (mg)	496.2	541.6	701.5	864.1	< 0.001	< 0.001

[1]Means were adjusted for age, race, education, marital status, diastolic blood pressure, serum cholesterol, special diet status, meals eaten away from home, alcoholic beverages consumed per week, Jenkins Activity Survey score, number of life events, body mass index, and antihypertensive medication status.
Source: Reprinted with permission from Tillotson, J.; Bartsch, G.; and Gorder, D. Food group and nutrient intake at baseline. *Am J Clin Nutr*, in press.

saturated fat, as compared with the nonsmokers and lighter smokers.

The co-occurrence of risk factors for health problems among smokers is of considerable concern in a primary care setting, because patients with multiple risk factors require much of a primary care provider's time and energy. Consequently, primary care providers need to identify such patients early and intervene before problems arise.

Data from the Project Health Study funded by the National Institute on Alcohol Abuse and Alcoholism (NIAAA) (figures 1 and 2) demonstrate the range of alcohol problems seen in a primary care setting. In that study, a short health habits survey is administered to all patients seen in a primary care, general medicine clinic. Survey findings indicate that 22 percent of the patients in the primary care clinic smoke and 10 percent consume "at-risk" or greater levels of alcohol (figure 1). ("At risk" is defined conservatively here, at 10 or more drinks per week for women and at 13 or more drinks per week for men.) According to gender-specific patient data, 14 percent of the male patients and 6 percent of the female patients consume alcohol at at-risk levels (data not shown). In addition, 3.5 percent of the patients both smoke and consume at least at-risk levels of alcohol.

These figures, however, are probably conservative, because only 50 percent of the patients in this sample completed and returned the survey. Furthermore, it is likely that the heavier drinkers were less apt to return it. In addition, the data do not capture binge drinkers (i.e., people who consume five or more drinks per occasion), although they comprise a high-risk drinking group. We are working on retrieving surveys from at least 80 percent of the patients.

As shown in figure 2, of those patients who fall into the categories of drinking either 10 to 12 or 20 or more drinks per week, fewer than 30 percent smoke. However, approximately 40 percent of the patients who fall into the category of drinking 13 to 19 drinks per week smoke: 35 percent of the male patients who drink 13 to 19 drinks per week smoke, and almost 60 percent of the female patients who drink 13 to 19 drinks per week smoke.

THE CLINICAL AND THE PUBLIC HEALTH PERSPECTIVE: A COMPREHENSIVE APPROACH

In the past, approaches to managing alcoholism favored expensive and resource-intensive medical and social rehabilitation for alcohol-dependent patients rather than early intervention for patients engaged in high-risk or harmful alcohol use. Likewise, medical care settings were quicker to respond to smokers who already had developed smoking-related illnesses than to smokers who were still considered healthy. In addition, the already ill smoker and the healthier smoker received more attention from the subspecialty or ancillary clinical

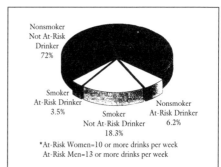

Figure 1. Prevalence of smoking and drinking in the primary care population at the University of Massachusetts Medical Center (*n* = 1,961).*

domain (e.g., psychologists, cardiologists, pulmonologists) than from the primary care setting.

However, in the last decade, there has been a shift from the intensive, more expensive, multisession clinical approach of both smoking treatment and inpatient alcoholism treatment to a public health approach that emphasizes screening and brief intervention. The primary care setting is important for screening patients and for delivering such intervention, as indicated in table 4 (Ockene and Ockene 1992). Brief intervention, when compared with the intensive clinical interventions traditionally provided, is more population focused and thus can reach more of the at-risk population. Because the at-risk population includes a greater percentage of people than the alcoholic population, brief intervention may have a greater overall impact on reducing morbidity and mortality.

This shift to include minimal or brief intervention in the primary care

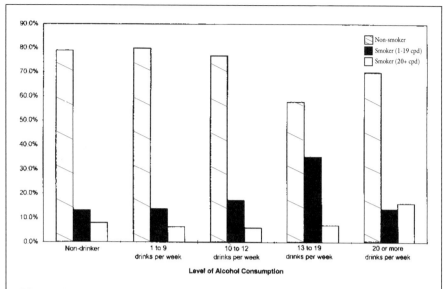

Figure 2. The distribution of smoking status by level of alcohol consumption in the primary care population at the University of Massachusetts Medical Center (*n* = 2,074). cpd = cigarettes per day.

setting makes it essential that primary care providers implement intervention for behaviors such as smoking and problem drinking by identifying patients at risk for health and social consequences earlier, using effective brief screening instruments, before the consequences become clinically evident. Once patients with problem or harmful alcohol use are identified, the primary care provider can potentially offer brief intervention that is implementable, generalizable, and cost-efficient, along with adjunctive materials, such as self-help pamphlets and videos, to help the patient reduce his or her risk for illness or dependence (Babor et al. 1990). Because heavy and regular alcohol use increases the likelihood that a person will develop alcohol-related problems and alcohol dependence,

primary care providers also can use brief intervention to work with patients after disease symptoms develop or after treatment for medical illness has begun (Sanchez-Craig 1986; Babor et al. 1990).

The focus on a public health approach does not remove the need for more intensive clinical interventions, as they are an important part of a comprehensive "stepped-care" approach or a continuum of available interventions and an important resource for highly dependent alcohol users and smokers. A comprehensive stepped-care approach, in which the primary care physician or nurse works with smokers who are less physiologically dependent and refers the more "difficult" smokers to specialized help, provides smokers with a continuum of interventions in a cost-efficient manner (Abrams et al. 1991; Orleans 1993).

A comprehensive approach also has been suggested and used in treating alcohol problems (Skinner 1990). Unfortunately, this approach has not been tested using a randomized trial design for either smoking or drinking cessation.

Challenge: To date there has been no randomized trial assessing a comprehensive model for either smoking or drinking cessation. Both need to be tested. In addition, a major challenge is the development and testing of a comprehensive model for the patient who has both smoking and alcohol problems.

SMOKING, ALCOHOL USE, AND THE PRIMARY CARE SETTING: TOPICS TO BE CONSIDERED

Several topics need to be considered when appraising the current status of interventions for alcohol and tobacco use and the alcohol-tobacco interface in the primary care setting. This section addresses the following topics:

- The at-risk–disease continuum
- Development and efficacy of brief intervention
- Training of providers to conduct brief intervention
- Sequencing of interventions.

THE AT-RISK–DISEASE CONTINUUM

The bias toward a disease model of alcoholism by many providers has been a major barrier both to patients receiving early intervention and to teaching providers how to conduct brief intervention. Although patients are told not to smoke, physicians and other health care providers focus minimal attention on advising patients about safe alcohol consumption levels. Several factors contribute to this lack of advice, as summarized by Bradley and colleagues in their 1993 article (Bradley et al. 1993) (see table 5).

First, unlike cigarette smoking, the relationship between alcohol use and adverse consequences is complex and not consistent across alcohol-related problems. For example, alcohol-related trauma is linked directly to the effects of intoxication, and the risk of trauma increases exponentially with the level of alcohol consumed. However, because the risk relationship of coronary artery disease with alcohol intake is U-shaped, one or two drinks daily may be beneficial.

Second, the limitations of currently available epidemiologic data have made it somewhat difficult to define safe drinking limits (Camargo 1989; Turner 1990). Studies have differed in their definitions of "standard drinks," thereby leading to a range of recommendations. Safe drinking limits based on the current data appear to be 14 drinks per week for men and 11 drinks per week for women. Alcohol consumption for 1 day should be limited to four drinks per day for men and three drinks per day for women (in which one drink equals 12.8 grams of alcohol) (Sanchez-Craig 1986; Babor et al. 1990). These limits apply to healthy

Table 4. The Importance of Primary Care Providers for the Delivery of Smoking and Alcohol Interventions.

- Primary care providers have contact with at least 75% of adults each year.

- High-risk patients frequently use the primary care setting.

- The general public perceives primary care providers as credible and reliable sources of health information and advice.

- Patients do not consider primary care a "special program."

- Primary care is part of the "natural environment" of adult smokers and excessive alcohol users.

- Patients think more seriously about their health when in the health care setting.

- Primary care providers offer continuity of care and potential reinforcement of health messages.

Source: Reprinted with permission from Ockene, I., and Ockene, J. *Prevention of Coronary Heart Disease*. Boston: Little, Brown and Company, 1992.

Table 5. Factors Contributing to the Lack of an At-Risk–Disease Continuum for Alcohol.

- The relationship between alcohol use and adverse consequences is complex.

- Conflicting epidemiological data make it difficult to define safe drinking limits.

- Strict interpretation of the disease model of alcoholism may deter the focus on safe drinking limits, because one is considered to be either an alcoholic or a nonalcoholic.

Source: Adapted from Bradley, K.; Donovan, D.; and Larson, E. How much is too much? Advising patients about safe levels of alcohol consumption. *Arch Intern Med* 153(24):2734–2740, 1993.

men and women for whom there is no medical contraindication for alcohol use (e.g., pregnancy, high blood pressure, use of medications, or alcohol dependence).

Finally, the strict interpretation of the disease model of alcoholism may deter the focus on safe drinking limits. Using that perspective, you either are an alcoholic and should not drink or you are nonalcoholic and your drinking, at any level, poses no risk and therefore requires no intervention or counseling (Bradley et al. 1993). This is especially disconcerting, because research indicates that heavy alcohol use by nonalcoholics increases their risk of adverse medical consequences and their development of alcohol dependency over time (Sanchez-Craig 1986; Babor et al. 1990). Babor and colleagues (1990) have suggested that screening for high-risk drinking can be conducted simultaneously with screening for alcohol dependence and that one does not need to exclude the other.

Because all smoking is high-risk smoking, there is really no safe level of smoking. Therefore, such a level cannot be advised by health care providers. In many ways this minimizes the confusion experienced by providers and patients involved in alcohol intervention. In addition, the 1988 Surgeon General's report on smoking focused on nicotine addiction (U.S. Department of Health and Human Services 1988), resulting in an emphasis by some researchers and clinicians on medicalizing smoking and focusing on it as an addiction. This approach to nicotine dependence mirrors the disease model of alcoholism. Other practitioners, as noted earlier, have approached smoking using a comprehensive or stepped-care approach, which assumes a continuum of addiction to smoking. Both the nondependent and dependent smoker are targeted, representing a range of difficulty with quitting, which, in turn, influences the assigning of patients to different intensities of intervention.

DEVELOPMENT AND EFFICACY OF BRIEF INTERVENTION

When developing and evaluating the efficacy of brief (i.e., 5–10 minutes) intervention in the primary care setting, several points should be noted. For example, brief intervention usually is considered as an early intervention

with nondependent alcohol users. The efficacy of brief intervention for physiologically dependent drinkers has not been reported in the literature to date. The majority of patients in a primary care setting who are high-risk or problem drinkers do not meet the criteria determined by the *Diagnostic and Statistical Manual of Mental Disorders, Fourth Edition* (DSM–IV) (American Psychiatric Association 1994) for dependence and do not require more intensive interventions, such as referral to alcohol counselors. In fact, many drinkers are likely to resist referrals to traditional substance abuse counselors or programs.

Research conducted by Wallace and colleagues (1988) provides evidence that socially stable, nondependent, high-risk drinkers will respond to less intensive intervention strategies, or brief intervention, when delivered by their primary care physician. This British study found a twofold reduction in alcohol use, fewer episodes of binge drinking, and a decrease in gamma-glutamyltransferase levels at the 12-month followup evaluation.

Currently, three NIAAA-funded projects are studying the effectiveness of brief intervention delivered by health care providers for changing the drinking behaviors of nondependent, high-risk, or problem drinkers. The intervention taking place at the University of Massachusetts Medical Center is based on evidence that brief patient-centered counseling delivered by physicians can be efficacious in helping smokers stop smoking. The algorithm developed and demonstrated to be efficacious is illustrated in figure 3 (Ockene et al. 1991).

The efficacious, patient-centered smoking-intervention model from which the alcohol intervention was adapted emphasizes the role of the

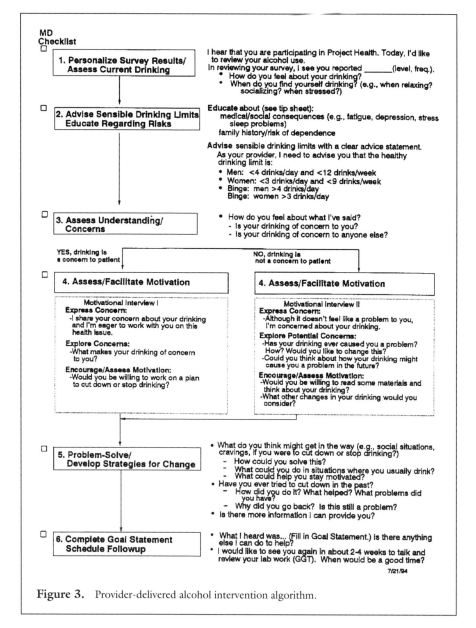

Figure 3. Provider-delivered alcohol intervention algorithm.

patient as an important information source for developing a plan for change. The model uses a theoretical foundation that includes social learning theory (Bandura 1969), the health belief model (Rosenstock 1990), and a stages of change model (Prochaska et al. 1988). It stresses the importance of questioning and incorporates behavioral, cognitive, and psychosocial principles. The results from the Physician-Delivered Smoking Intervention Project demonstrate the efficacy of such a model (Ockene et al. 1991).

For a patient who is ambivalent about changing his or her smoking behavior, the most effective strategies focus on increasing that patient's motivation to change. For example, when a physician provides a patient with information about the negative consequences of smoking, advice to the patient to quit can be effective. If the physician also links smoking cessation with other benefits and elicits from the patient how he or she proposes to cope with barriers to quitting using problem-solving skills, a positive self-efficacy can be facilitated to move the patient toward change.

Developing an algorithm for early alcohol intervention was a more complex endeavor than developing an algorithm for smoking, because an alcohol-intervention algorithm must take into account the following:

- Sensible drinking limits
- Less acceptance by problem drinkers and providers of the harm that alcohol causes and of the need to change drinking behavior

- An often weaker motivation to change drinking behavior than to change smoking behavior
- Possibly fewer opportunities for recalling past experiences with change.

Taking into account the above considerations, an alcohol intervention algorithm was developed and tested in several focus groups of providers. This algorithm (figure 4) currently is being tested with primary care patients who have been screened and identified as high-risk alcohol users or as having alcohol problems.

Challenge: An even greater challenge than developing an algorithm for either drinking or smoking behavior alone will be to develop and test an algorithm for primary care patients who both smoke and use alcohol excessively.

Although studies currently in progress are likely to find that brief provider-delivered alcohol intervention for nondependent drinkers are efficacious, several questions remain unanswered, including the following:

- Which health care providers should deliver a brief alcohol intervention (e.g., nurse practitioners, nurses, or physicians)?
- Because nondependent drinkers comprise a mixed group of patients in terms of other variables, how will patient gender, readiness or stage of change, psychosocial profile, and other variables affect the efficacy of a brief intervention?
- How do health care providers tailor brief intervention and plan subsequent followup interventions to best meet the varying needs of these patients?

TRAINING OF PROVIDERS TO CONDUCT BRIEF INTERVENTION

An essential component for facilitating patient-centered intervention to be delivered by providers is the training of providers. We have trained over 1,000 physicians and nurses to implement brief smoking interventions and

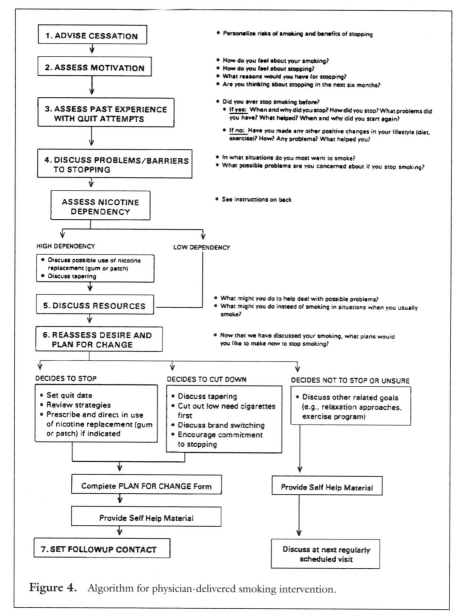

Figure 4. Algorithm for physician-delivered smoking intervention.

approximately 100 physicians and nurses to conduct alcohol interventions. Providing training in alcohol intervention is more complex and time consuming. Table 6 compares some of the different characteristics of providers conducting smoking intervention versus alcohol intervention. Interfacing the interventions for alcohol use and smoking will increase both the time and complexity of the intervention.

In addition to teaching providers how to implement brief intervention, we found that a comprehensive approach in which the primary care provider implements brief counseling requires (1) that office-based systems be developed to cue providers and (2) that administrative and institutional support for providers exist that enable them to take time to conduct such interventions. Each of these elements must be attended to if intervention is to occur with patients who smoke, have alcohol problems, or both.

SEQUENCING OF INTERVENTIONS

Several intervention approaches are possible for patients who are both smokers and high-risk drinkers. These approaches are as follows:

- Start with one behavior, then focus on another after the first behavior is under control
- Work equally on all behaviors simultaneously
- Focus on one behavior and make small changes in others.

Several theoretical models exist that can serve as information models for both strategies and priorities for working with patients with multiple behavioral risk factors. For example, social learning theory emphasizes beginning with behaviors that the patient feels most capable of changing (i.e., he has a high self-efficacy). Similarly, stages of change theory focuses on starting with behaviors for which an individual is at least contemplating a change or preparing to take action. Social support theory also indicates the need to provide strong social support for people who are targeting several risk factors for change. From a medical perspective, the health risks of each behavior must be considered as part of the negotiation and decision about behavior change.

Challenge: To date, there are no studies available indicating whether sequentially changing behaviors or simultaneously changing them is most effective, for whom it is effective, and whether the best outcomes occur when targeting single behaviors or multiple behaviors. When considering the patient who is both a smoker and a high-risk or problem drinker, an important challenge for the research agenda is to determine how to sequence the interventions.

SUMMARY AND CONCLUSIONS

Much research still needs to be conducted to further determine how to best intervene in a primary care setting with patients who both smoke and have alcohol problems. A major challenge is for scientists, clinicians, and the different Institutes within

Table 6. Differences in Characteristics of Providers Conducting Interventions for Smoking Versus Alcohol Use.

Provider Characterization	Smoking	Alcohol Use
Awareness of need to intervene	High	Need consciousness raising
Motivation to intervene	Higher	Low • Perceived as being judgmental • Seen as more personal
Stage of readiness to intervene	Ready for action	• Often precontemplator • See as alcoholic or nonalcoholic
Education needed	How to treat for addiction	• Sensible drinking limits • Reasons for early intervention • At risk versus alcoholic
Self-efficacy (i.e., confidence to intervene)	High	Low

the National Institutes of Health to reach consensus regarding the definition of at-risk drinking. A challenging research agenda should include the following:

- Development and testing of a comprehensive approach to intervention for patients in the primary care setting who both smoke and have alcohol problems
- Development and testing of a tailored intervention for different groups of smokers and non-dependent drinkers (e.g., low-income pregnant women)
- An algorithm for the sequencing of interventions for patients who both smoke and have alcohol problems
- A prospective study of the smoking and drinking behaviors of high-risk or problem drinkers in a

primary care setting, followed over 5–20 years.

ACKNOWLEDGMENTS

This work was supported in part by the National Institute on Alcohol Abuse and Alcoholism grant 1–R01–AA09153–01A1.

REFERENCES

Abrams, D.B.; Emmons, K.M.; Niaura, R.S.; Goldstein, M.G., and Sherman, C.B. Tobacco dependence: An integration of individual and public health perspectives. In: Nathan, P.; McGrady, B.; Langenbucher, J.; Frankenstein, W., eds. *Annual Review of Addictions Treatment and Research.* Vol. 1. New York: Pergamon Press, 1991. pp. 331–396.

American Psychiatric Association. *Diagnostic and Statistical Manual of Mental Disorders, Fourth Edition.* Washington, DC: the Association, 1994.

Babor, T.F.; Mayfield, J.; and Grady, M. Alcohol and substance abuse in primary care settings. In: *Primary Care Research: An Agenda for the 90s.* Washington, DC: U.S. Department of Health and Human Services, 1990. pp. 113–124.

Bandura, A. *Principles of Behavior Modification.* New York: Holt, Rinehart, and Winston, 1969.

Bradley, K.; Donovan, D.; and Larson, E. How much is too much? Advising patients about safe levels of alcohol consumption. *Arch Intern Med* 153(24): 2734–2740, 1993.

Camargo, C. Moderate alcohol consumption and stroke: The epidemiologic evidence. *Stroke* 20:1611–1626, 1989.

Larkin, F.; Basiotis, P.; and Riddick, H. Dietary patterns of women smokers and nonsmokers. *J Am Diet Assoc* 90:230–237, 1990.

Ockene, I., and Ockene, J. *Prevention of Coronary Heart Disease.* Boston: Little, Brown and Company, 1992.

Ockene, J.; Kristeller, J.; and Goldberg, R. Increasing the efficacy of physician-delivered smoking intervention: A randomized clinical trial. *J Gen Intern Med* 6:1–8, 1991.

Orleans, C.T. Treating nicotine dependence in medical settings: A stepped-care model. In: Orleans, C.T., and Slade, J., eds. *Nicotine Addiction: Principles and Management.* New York: Oxford University Press, 1993. pp. 145–161.

Prochaska, J.; Velicer, W.; and DiClemente, C. Measuring processes of change: Applications to the cessation of smoking. *J Consult Clin Psychol* 56:520–528, 1988.

Rosenstock, I. The health belief model: Explaining health behavior through expectancies. In: Glanz, K.; Lewis, F.M.; and Rimer, B.K., eds. *Health Behavior and Health Education: Theory, Research, and Practice.* San Francisco: Jossey Bass, 1990.

Sanchez-Craig, M. How much is too much? Estimates of hazardous drinking based on clients' self-reports. *Br J Addict* 81:251–256, 1986.

Schoenborn, C., and Benson, V. Relationships between smoking and other unhealthy habits: United States, 1985. In: U.S. Department of Health and Human Services, Public Health Service. *Vital Health Statistics No. 154.* DHHS Publication (PHS)88–1250. Washington, DC: Supt. of Docs., U.S. Govt. Print. Off., 1988.

Skinner, H. Spectrum of drinkers and intervention opportunities. *Can Med Assoc J* 143(10):1054–1059, 1990.

Tillotson, J.; Bartsch, G.; and Gorder, D. Food group and nutrient intake at baseline. *Am J Clin Nutr,* in press.

Turner, C. How much alcohol is in a standard drink? An analysis of 125 studies. *Br J Addict* 85:1171–1175, 1990.

U.S. Department of Health and Human Services. *The Health Consequences Of Smoking: Nicotine Addiction. A Report of the U.S. Surgeon General.* Washington, DC: Supt. of Docs., U.S. Govt. Print. Off., 1988.

Wallace, P.; Cutler, S.; and Haines, A. Randomized controlled trial of general practitioner intervention in patients with excessive drinking consumption. *BMJ* 197:663–668, 1988.

Zacny, J. Behavioral aspects of alcohol-related interactions. *Recent Dev Alcohol* 8:205–219, 1990.

Chapter 17

Tobacco and Alcohol Interventions in Health Maintenance Organizations: Principles and Challenges From a Public Health Perspective

Susan J. Curry, Ph.D., and Evette J. Ludman, Ph.D.

This chapter describes some of the principles and challenges inherent in developing and integrating tobacco and alcohol interventions in a health maintenance organization (HMO). Although the frame of reference is the HMO, we encourage the reader to think about an HMO as a microcommunity. Thus, the principles and challenges proposed here pertain to a broad range of public health and organizational settings.

Throughout this chapter, alcohol interventions within a public health context refer specifically to secondary prevention or to interventions that are targeted at those who are not alcoholic but whose drinking patterns place them at risk for negative health and psychosocial consequences. Using the drinking spectrum outlined in the Institute of Medicine (IOM) Report (1990) and by Skinner (1990), we are targeting moderate to heavy, nondependent drinkers, as opposed to alcohol-dependent drinkers.

The chapter covers four main topics. First, we will elaborate the distinctions between the clinical and public health perspectives. Second, we will present principles for intervention development that cut across the tobacco and alcohol domains. Third, using the current state of the art in tobacco interventions as a reference point, we will discuss three key

---

S.J. Curry, Ph.D., is a scientific investigator and E.J. Ludman, Ph.D., is a research associate for the Center for Health Studies, Group Health Cooperative of Puget Sound, 1730 Minor Avenue, Suite 1600, Seattle, WA 98101.

challenges in developing alcohol interventions from a public health perspective: (1) building consensus, (2) understanding the target population, and (3) developing and integrating appropriate treatment paradigms. The chapter concludes with a brief overview of a research agenda for future work in this area.

CLINICAL VERSUS PUBLIC HEALTH PERSPECTIVE

Generally, in the arena of health behavior change, the public health perspective has been defined with reference to the clinical perspective. Lichtenstein and Glasgow (1992), in their assessment of the state of the art in tobacco research, summarize the implications of a public health versus a clinical perspective. In a public health perspective, the target population is neither self-referred nor recruited but includes all people who smoke or engage in at-risk drinking practices regardless of their motivation to change their behavior. Interventions must be delivered in natural settings, and the providers of interventions will not necessarily be specialists in the particular area targeted for behavior change. Finally, in a public health perspective, the interventions should be brief and low cost in order to reach the largest potential proportion of the target population.

There is one aspect of the public health perspective that can be missed by defining it with reference to the clinical perspective; that is, there are multiple levels of intervention. Using the HMO setting as an example, there are interventions at the level of the health care organization, including policies (e.g., regarding benefits or coverage of intervention services), resource allocation, and community outreach or involvement in community initiatives outside the organization. There are also interventions at the practice level, which encompass provider behavior, practice guidelines, and automated office-based systems for identifying and tracking the target population that supports the provider. And, of course, there are the more familiar individual-level interventions that include the array of resources available to help people make and maintain behavior changes. These include classes, self-help materials, and outreach telephone counseling. In a viable public health model, there is a great deal of interaction among these levels; in many ways, each of these levels is necessary, but none alone is sufficient to promote large-scale changes at the population level.

COMMON PRINCIPLES FOR INTERVENTION DEVELOPMENT

There is a rich collection of research and practical experience that can be distilled into common principles for developing interventions at the levels of the health care organization, the practice, and the individual. The underlying principles for intervention development at each of these levels are consistent, whether the focus is alcohol and tobacco interventions or some other focus. Here we will briefly review them.

ORGANIZATIONAL-LEVEL PRINCIPLES

At the organizational level, it is necessary to develop consensus about the health behavior targets among key divisions of the delivery system. Consensus development entails coordinated planning and implementation of activities across divisions, shared allocation of resources, and broad "citizen involvement." By citizen involvement we mean input from administrators, providers, HMO consumers (or members of the patient population), and researchers or people with substantive expertise in these areas. Most often this type of consensus building occurs through an organization's committee structure.

PRACTICE-LEVEL PRINCIPLES

At the practice level, it is necessary to develop defined roles for all practice team members and to provide role-relevant training for each team member. Information and tracking systems need to be created. Equally important are proactive plans for system maintenance (such as specifying who makes sure that enough self-help brochures are provided in physicians' exam rooms), state-of-the-art supportive materials, and guidelines to ensure systematic and consistent practice.

INDIVIDUAL-LEVEL PRINCIPLES

At the individual level, interventions must address different stages of readiness to change; include messages that emphasize positive results and avoid high-threat communications; and provide specific behavioral skills, meaningful supports, and opportunities for individual tailoring.

Although these principles are being applied in the development of public health or population-based interventions for tobacco and alcohol, we are not aware of many instances in which these efforts have been integrated. Indeed, the basic premise of the rest of this chapter is that the application of organizational-, practice-, and individual-level principles is further advanced for early intervention for tobacco use than for secondary prevention of alcohol problems. A potent illustration is a recent full-page advertisement paid for by the R.J. Reynolds (tobacco) company that states the following: "Today, it is cigarettes. Tomorrow....will it be alcohol, caffeine or high-fat foods?" When we are at the point of tobacco companies paying for advertisements that appeal to Americans' civil liberties, we have indeed crossed a threshold in the widespread diffusion of integrated public health efforts regarding tobacco use.

KEY CHALLENGES IN DEVELOPING ALCOHOL INTERVENTIONS

We propose that three main challenges exist for moving ahead with alcohol interventions, to which we as researchers can contribute. These are the challenges inherent in consensus building, understanding the target population, and providing appropriate interventions. We would like to examine these challenges by providing an encapsulated and subjective critique of the current research base. Although our main focus is on alcohol, we will be bringing in the tobacco literature as a reference point. We acknowledge that we are not experts in all these areas and thus would be happy to find out that indeed the data are "in hand" and we have just missed them!

THE CHALLENGE OF CONSENSUS BUILDING

Two different avenues to facilitate consensus building at the organizational level are as follows: (1) obtaining hard data regarding the costs of a behavior and (2) having grass-roots provider initiatives to change current practice. It is often the "movers and shakers" within organizations who can launch action toward addressing a problem. However, the best way to convince people in an organization to make a particular behavior a high priority is to have high-quality, compelling data on the medical, social, and economic costs associated with that behavior. The overwhelming data on the economic and medical costs associated with tobacco use have helped to make it a major focus of many HMO's prevention initiatives. What kind of data are out there with regard to alcohol? In October 1993 the Institute for Health Policy at Brandeis University, with funding from the Robert Wood Johnson Foundation, published a document entitled *Substance Abuse: The Nation's Number One Health Problem. Key Indicators for Policy* (Institute for Health Policy 1993). The interesting statistics in this report include estimates that the total costs of alcohol abuse in 1990 were $99 billion, which is actually higher than a preliminary estimate of total costs of smoking at $72 billion. Although alcohol abuse costs more money, cigarette smoking accounts for over four times as many deaths.

Although these data are compelling, by including medical conditions and economic costs associated with the apex of the drinking continuum (i.e., alcohol dependence), it is not clear how much of these costs and consequences are associated with at-risk drinking, which is the target of secondary prevention efforts. Data specific to at-risk or problem drinking patterns are important to the degree that we are seeking to create treatment models that are distinct from the tertiary prevention or alcoholism treatment programs.

Consensus building must occur at the practice level as well. We have found with our tobacco efforts that even when the organization has made tobacco use the number-one prevention priority (as has been the case at Group Health Cooperative in 1993), that priority does not automatically transfer to the attitudes and practices of providers. What do we know about providers' attitudes and practices with regard to prevention of alcohol problems? We venture to say, not as much as we should. There is a survey of primary care practitioners in Massachusetts that was conducted in 1981 and published in the *New England Journal of Medicine* in 1983 (Wechsler et al. 1983) that has some interesting data on practices across a variety of health behaviors, including smoking and drinking. Across six health behavior/lifestyle issues (i.e., smoking, alcohol, other drugs, diet, exercise, and stress), smoking and alcohol were the most commonly assessed. Ninety percent of all physicians said that they routinely asked their patients about smoking, and 85 percent routinely asked about alcohol use. There were some differences in rates of assessment across different specialties; internists were the most likely to ask about both smoking and alcohol use, and family practitioners and general practitioners were least likely. However, a different picture emerged with regard to the perceived importance of different health-promoting behaviors among the surveyed physicians. Ninety-three percent of all physicians agreed that eliminating cigarette smoking was very important for the average person; only 46 percent agreed that drinking alcohol moderately or not at all was very important. Thus, reducing alcohol consumption was included among the top 10 most important health-promoting behaviors but not among the top 5.

There may have been some changes with regard to prevention of alcohol problems during the past decade. A more recent survey of U.S.

internist attitudes and practices regarding primary and secondary prevention of alcohol problems found some interesting practice patterns (Bradley et al. in press). In this survey, 94 percent of the respondents said that they had a responsibility to advise "all nonalcoholic patients about safe levels of alcohol consumption," but only 30 percent reported that they often or always did so. Although 80 percent of the respondents reported that they often/always advised patients who drank three or more drinks daily about safe levels of alcohol consumption, nearly one-half (45 percent) did not routinely ask patients how much they drank daily. However, the majority of respondents (90 percent) said that they would be more likely to advise patients about safe levels of alcohol consumption if they "thought such advice would decrease alcohol-related morbidity," echoing the need for morbidity data specific to at-risk drinking patterns.

UNDERSTANDING THE TARGET POPULATION

Understanding the target population is a key factor for all three of the intervention levels that we have been considering. For example, at the organizational level, it is important to be able to gauge demand for intervention services when setting benefit policies and allocating resources. At the practice level, we need to know the most efficient ways to identify the target population—for example, by seeing whether the target population has a distinct pattern of service utilization. At the individual level, we want to know how receptive the target population is to changing their behavior. Each of these types of information requires obtaining data, not just from self-selected, motivated treatment participants, but from the broader population base.

With regard to tobacco use, we have found that fewer than 10 percent of smokers in a defined population will participate in smoking cessation programs (Wagner et al. 1990; Klesges et al. 1986; Curry 1993). Studies of health care utilization of smokers show that smokers use more hospital days (20 percent more days per 1,000 person years) and fewer outpatient preventive services than nonsmokers and former smokers, but there is no relationship between use of medical care services and number of cigarettes smoked per day (Vogt and Schweitzer 1985). With regard to level and type of motivation for smoking cessation, we have consistent estimates from different population-based surveys that the vast majority of smokers are not ready to initiate smoking cessation attempts. In both our own and others' research, we have found that approximately 40 percent of smokers stage as precontemplators, 40 percent as in contemplation, and only 20 percent as preparing to quit in the next month. In our work on type of motivation for quitting smoking (Curry et al. 1990, 1991), which builds on an intrinsic/extrinsic motivation model, we are finding higher levels of intrinsic versus extrinsic motivation to be a consistent predictor both of future smoking cessation and of current stage of readiness to quit.

We need these types of data for at-risk drinkers as well. Most of the information we have about at-risk drinkers is from recruited samples of self-labeled problem drinkers. We have begun to look at some of these issues in our research program. Using respondents to a population-based health risk survey, we have been comparing the presenting complaints and utilization patterns of at-risk drinkers to an age-gender matched sample of not-at-risk drinkers (Louie et al. 1994). At-risk drinkers were those whose survey responses indicated one or more of the following drinking patterns: an average of two or more drinks per day during the past 30 days, two or more occasions of drinking five or more drinks in the past 30 days, or one or more occasions of driving after drinking more than two drinks. We abstracted inpatient and outpatient medical records for a 4-year period (2 years before and 2 years after their survey). We coded presenting complaints with the National Ambulatory Medical Care Survey's "reasons for visit" classification and coded diagnoses with the ninth revision of the *International Classification of Diseases Clinical Modifications* classification system.

We found expected differences in the utilization patterns of patients specifically labeled in their medical charts as problem drinkers. These people had more clinic visits, more "no shows," more injury-related visits, and more mentions of domestic violence. Otherwise, there was little evidence that people with at-risk drinking patterns use the health care system differently. We found no differences in the average number of office visits, the number of emergency room or mental health visits, the types of providers seen, or the proportion of charts with mentions of personal or social problems. At-risk and non-at-risk drinkers did not differ on the proportion of visits with injuries or preventive care as the major reason for the visit; however, at-risk drinkers did have significantly more visits related to somatic problems.

We also have data on stage-of-readiness-to-change drinking patterns among a sample of at-risk drinkers who were identified in a pilot study conducted for an investigation that we are just beginning on the treatment of at-risk drinkers through primary care. The sample size is small (only 27 at-risk drinkers), but the distribution across stages is interesting. In this sample, 46 percent were not considering changing their drinking patterns (precontemplative), 19 percent were contemplating changing their drinking patterns but were not confident that they would do so in the next month, and 35 percent were in a preparation stage (defined as seriously considering changing their drinking patterns and confident that they would do so in the next month). It is interesting to note that although the prevalence of cigarette smoking was significantly higher among at-risk drinkers (33 versus 16 percent), we still found that the majority of at-risk drinkers were nonsmokers. Unfortunately, we did not have enough at-risk drinkers who smoked in our sample to give any reliable data on the interactions between stage of readiness to quit smoking and stage of readiness to change drinking patterns.

INTEGRATING DIFFERENT TREATMENT PARADIGMS

Integrating different treatment orientations is a challenge that HMO's and other health care organizations struggle with regularly, not only in the realm of addictive behaviors. Examples include decisions about coverage for chiropractic care as well as physical therapy for people with back pain and pharmacotherapy versus cognitive behavioral treatments for depression. Integration of minimal to intensive smoking cessation services in HMO's and other settings is generally straightforward, although this challenge often takes the form of debate about combining behavioral and pharmacologic interventions. At the organizational level in particular, a decision has to be made whether to cover pharmacotherapies alone or to require concurrent participation in a behavioral program.

Stepped-care intervention approaches involve a continuum of treatments, ranging from very intensive to more minimal interventions. The underlying treatment goals and philosophies for smoking cessation interventions are at least consistent across the treatment continuum. On the other hand, secondary interventions for prevention of alcohol problems, which fall into the minimal intervention range of the treatment continuum, have different treatment goals and underlying models than tertiary prevention programs, which are often already in place. Problems arise when these underlying treatment models differ and are seen as irreconcilable.

The current literature provides useful conceptual models for characterizing these paradigm clashes but not an accompanying research base to guide our integration efforts. Brickman's model of helping and coping, summarized in the IOM report (1990) provides a useful heuristic framework for understanding some fundamental differences between tertiary and secondary prevention treatment orientations. In Brickman's model, treatments are characterized in a 2-by-2 matrix according to whether the person is perceived to be responsible for the problem and by whether the person is responsible for the solution. At the risk of oversimplification, tertiary prevention programs can be characterized as fitting the "medical model," in that neither the development of the problem nor its resolution is seen as the patient's responsibility. Often these programs include mandatory participation in Alcoholics Anonymous, which has been used as an example of an "enlightenment model," with its emphasis on the importance of a "Higher Power" that is responsible for the solution. In contrast, the minimal interventions for secondary prevention programs have what is

called a "compensatory orientation," with a cognitive-behavioral focus on having people learn new skills and strategies to alter their drinking patterns. As pointed out in the IOM report (1990), universal agreement on these categorizations has not been reached, nor has there been much empirical work to operationally define and measure treatment orientation among providers and patients. This leaves several questions to be addressed: Are there individual differences or preferences for treatment orientation? How important is it to match patient and program orientations? To what degree is continuity of treatment orientation important as patients move between treatment models, which is likely to happen in a stepped-care paradigm?

RESEARCH AGENDA

Our wish list of brief recommendations to guide further research in alcohol-tobacco interactions has three parts. The first is a recapitulation of some points made thus far. From the standpoint of moving ahead with secondary prevention initiatives at the health care organization level, it would be helpful to have the following: (1) additional data on the medical, psychosocial, and economic costs associated with at-risk drinking; (2) better understanding of provider attitudes and practices, including their treatment orientation; and (3) better understanding of the motivational characteristics of the general population of at-risk drinkers.

The historical insularity between the alcohol and tobacco research fields contributes to the second part of our wish list: basic methodological needs for future research on interactions between tobacco use and at-risk drinking. First, we need consensus in the research arena on definitions of key constructs that facilitate cross-substance comparisons. Discussed in this chapter alone are three good examples: at-risk drinking, stage of readiness to change, and treatment orientation.

Once we have agreement on these key constructs, we need a core set of behavioral measures for determining smoking status and patterns of alcohol consumption. If every contributor to this volume used a similar set of items on their research surveys, we would have a wealth of information on tobacco and alcohol interactions. Even those of us with interests in both areas do not always get useful information on both behaviors in singly focused studies. We were embarrassed and humbled to find, when preparing this chapter, that we did not have sufficient questions on alcohol consumption patterns on a population-based health survey of over 5,000 adults, conducted as part of a smoking cessation study, to look for alcohol-tobacco interactions in key constructs.

We would like to close by posing three rhetorical questions that we think the general field of public health minimal interventions faces and which we certainly will be facing as we move toward more integration of alcohol and tobacco research. First, do we need new conceptual models? There is remarkable consensus in the major conceptual models that have been guiding behavioral intervention research in alcohol and tobacco. For example, at the individual level, we have such models as expectancy value theories, social learning theory, and the transtheoretical model. From a public health perspective, we do not think we need more basic theories as much as we need better integrative conceptual frameworks. What is not clear is the degree to which understanding alcohol and tobacco interactions requires more sophisticated conceptual models and, if so, what those models might be.

The second question asks whether higher technological intervention formats will result in better outcomes. Although our conceptual models remain constant, there is increasing attention to taking intervention components derived from these models and repackaging them into more "high-tech" models of presentation, such as interactive videodiscs and computer-based expert systems. Many of these approaches are considerably more expensive than "lower tech" versions and may be less accessible to the highest risk populations. One recommendation is to be sure that we are demanding in our outcome evaluations of these innovative intervention formats and that we include appropriate comparison groups in our research designs.

Third, can minimal interventions outpace secular trends? We now have at least three randomized trials of minimal interventions for smoking cessation with population-based, non-volunteer samples of smoking that are finding impressive quit rates in untreated control groups that are not significantly different from intervention group quit rates (Gritz et al. 1992; Lando et al. 1992; Curry, McBride, Grothaus, Louie, and Wagner in press). This may reflect a strong secular trend toward smoking cessation in response to media coverage, government and business policies, and so forth. We do not think this trend is unique to smoking cessation. The implication of this is that we will be challenged to direct our population-based, minimal interventions to people who are most resistant to, or unaffected by, secular trends.

ACKNOWLEDGMENTS

This chapter was prepared with support from National Institute on Alcohol Abuse and Alcoholism grant AA–09175 and National Heart, Lung, and Blood Institute grant HL–48121.

REFERENCES

Bradley, K.A.; Curry, S.J.; Koepsell, T.D.; and Larson, E.B. Primary and secondary prevention of alcohol problems. *J Gen Intern Med*, in press.

Curry, S.J. Self-help interventions for smoking cessation. *J Consult Clin Psychol* 61(5):790–803, 1993.

Curry, S.J.; Wagner, E.H.; and Grothaus, L.C. Intrinsic and extrinsic motivation for smoking cessation. *J Consult Clin Psychol* 58(3):310–316, 1990.

Curry, S.J.; Wagner, E.H.; and Grothaus, L.C. Evaluation of intrinsic and extrinsic motivation interventions with a self-help smoking cessation program. *J Consult Clin Psychol* 59(2):318–324, 1991.

Curry, S.J.; McBride, C.; Grothaus, L.C.; Louie, D.; and Wagner, E. A randomized trial of self-help materials, personalized feedback and telephone counseling with nonvolunteer smokers. *J Consult Clin Psychol*, in press.

Gritz, E.R.; Berman, B.A.; Bastani R.; Wu, M. A randomized trial of a self-help smoking cessation intervention in a non-volunteer female population: Testing the limits of the public health model. *Health Psychol* 11:280–289, 1992.

Institute for Health Policy, Brandeis University. *Substance Abuse: The Nation's Number One Health Problem. Key Indicators for Policy*. Princeton, NJ: The Robert Wood Johnson Foundation, 1993.

Institute of Medicine. *Broadening the Base of Treatment for Alcohol Problems: A Report of a Study by a Committee of the Institute of Medicine, Division of Mental Health and Behavioral Medicine*. Washington, DC: National Academy Press, 1990.

Klesges, R.C.; Vasey, M.M.; and Glasgow, R.E. A worksite smoking modification competition: Potential for public health impact. *Am J Public Health* 76:198–200, 1986.

Lando, H.A.; Hellerstedt, W.L.; Pirie, P.L.; and McGovern, P.G. Brief supportive telephone counseling as a recruitment and intervention strategy for smoking cessation. *Am J Public Health* 82:41–46, 1992.

Lichtenstein, E., and Glasgow, R.E. Smoking cessation: What have we learned over the past decade? *J Consult Clin Psychol* 60:518–527, 1992.

Louie, D.; McBride, C.; Curry, S.J.; Grothaus, L.; and Wagner, E.H. Randomized trial of self-help programs, written feedback and telephone counseling with non-volunteer smokers. *Ann Behav Med* 16(Supp):S064, 1994.

Skinner, H. Spectrum of drinkers and intervention opportunities. *Can Med Assoc J* 143:1054–1059, 1990.

Vogt, T.M., and Schweitzer, S.O. Medical costs of cigarette smoking in a health maintenance organization. *Am J Epidemiol* 122(6):1060–1066, 1985.

Wagner, E.; Schoenbach, V., Orleans, T.; Grothaus, L.; Saunders, K.; Curry, S.; and Pearson, D. Participation in a smoking cessation program: A population-based perspective. *Am J Prev Med* 6(5):258–266, 1990.

Wechsler, H.; Levine, S.; Idelson, R.K.; Rohman, M.; and Taylor, J.O. The physician's role in health promotion—A survey of primary care practitioners. *N Engl J Med* 308(2):97–100, 1983.

Chapter 18

Overview of Section II: Treatment, Early Intervention, and Policy

David B. Abrams, Ph.D., G. Alan Marlatt, Ph.D., and Mark B. Sobell, Ph.D.

Few meaningful data have been reported on the efficacy of treatments that integrate an understanding of alcohol-tobacco interactions. The increasing interest in comorbidity of (a) affective disorder and alcohol and (b) affective disorder and nicotine dependence suggests that the commonalities among all three factors should be examined. There is value in shedding light on the basic biobehavioral mechanisms involved in this three-way interaction. Moreover, the main justification for combining treatments should be that the combined treatments, when applied either to a broad defined population or to a specific subgroup (via screening and matching), will demonstrate some superiority over separate treatments (or no matching).

It is important to begin to look for interrelationships beyond alcohol-tobacco interactions, despite our bias toward a reductionistic or molecular perspective. Some of the lifestyle risk behaviors involve addictive substances, but gambling, excessive exercise, and compulsive eating (to cite a few examples) are also high-risk behaviors. In clinical populations, it is rare to find the simple alcoholic; usually, patients present with polydrug use and other behavioral risk factors. Thus, treatments for alcohol and tobacco use should include a component that encourages other health-promoting behaviors; for example, improving nutritional balance and increasing physical activity are important goals, because alcohol abusers and smokers tend to have poorer

D.B. Abrams, Ph.D., is a professor and director of the Division of Behavioral and Preventive Medicine, Brown University School of Medicine, RISE Building, The Miriam Hospital, 164 Summit Avenue, Providence, RI 02906. G.A. Marlatt, Ph.D., is a professor in the Department of Psychology, Addictive Behavior Research Center NI–25, University of Washington, Seattle, WA 98195. M.B. Sobell, Ph.D., is a professor at the Center for Psychological Studies, Nova Southeastern University, Fort Lauderdale, FL 33314.

diets and be more sedentary than those who do not abuse alcohol or smoke (Emmons et al. 1994*b*; Marcus et al. 1995).

Cognitive-behavioral mediating mechanisms also need to be studied in relation to the interaction of alcohol and tobacco rather than for each drug separately. A cognitive-social learning theory framework has guided much of the research in this area. For example, data presented by the Brown University research group illustrated the importance of research on alcohol and tobacco interaction expectancies (Colby et al. 1993). Research on reactivity to psychosocial stressors and cue reactivity to alcohol and tobacco stimuli can help elucidate the ways tobacco and alcohol interact. We know that alcohol potentiates tobacco consumption, but little is known about the reverse.

Zacny (1990) recommended some research questions to consider for alcohol-tobacco interactions:

- How specifically is the relationship between alcohol and tobacco mediated and what are the treatment implications?
- Does chronic use of one drug produce cross-tolerance leading to higher consumption of both drugs?
- How do alcohol and tobacco interact around measures of performance? The performance-impairing effects of alcohol could be counteracted by the performance-enhancing effects of tobacco, and this could have policy implications (e.g., related to driving impairment).

- Does drug use to enhance performance relate to the findings concerning personality (e.g., sociopathy) and neuropsychological syndromes, including attention deficit disorders and impulse control?

Both similarities and differences between alcohol and tobacco need to be examined to identify boundary conditions (a) *between* these two addictions, (b) *across* other addictions and (c) *within* the specific addiction, where subgroups or clusters of individuals may point to differential etiology, treatments, and prevention strategies. An excellent conceptual and methodological analysis of similarities and differences between eating disorders and addictive disorders illustrates the value of examining differences (Wilson 1995). Binge eating shares many similarities with alcohol and tobacco addiction: strong cravings; a sense of loss of control; being used to regulate emotions and to cope with stress; exhibiting preoccupation with the substance; repeated efforts to stop; inability to stop despite negative medical, psychological, and social consequences; and co-occurrence. Wilson (1995) believes that these commonalities may be superficial and may obscure fundamentally important differences. Research is needed to examine these assumptions. For example, as in eating disorders, researchers have questioned whether tobacco dependence meets all the usual criteria for addiction—tolerance, physical dependence, withdrawal, and loss of control. Wilson (1995) cautions that "an addiction model [of eating disorders] is an in-stance of the seemingly endless exten-sion of the concept to explain any form of habitual behavior including work, sex and TV" (p. 166).

A critical analysis of differences, boundary conditions, and subtypes is more than semantics—it has signifi-cant implications for treatment, pre-vention, and policy. Although the evidence for comorbidity of eating and addictive disorders is mixed in true community samples, there is a higher prevalence of eating disorders among alcoholics in clinical samples of women alcoholics (11 percent). The known use of tobacco to regulate weight and negative moods and to control appetite provides an intrigu-ing connection worthy of research at-tention. Moreover, eating disorders go largely undetected by treatment staff and also tend to precede the de-velopment of alcohol, tobacco, and other drug (ATOD) abuse, suggest-ing that they may be a risk factor for ATOD abuse.

In terms of health risk, many alco-holic individuals actually may suc-cumb to cancers and tobacco-related morbidities or mortalities. It is more than ironic; indeed, it is tragic that treatment for alcoholism ignores to-bacco abuse. Both smoking and al-cohol abuse are risk factors for cardiovascular disease, and they are synergistic for cancers of the mouth, pharynx, and larynx (Flanders and Rothman 1982; Brownson and Chang 1987; Rosengren et al. 1988). At the Mayo Clinic, Dr. Richard Hurt has developed a model program that integrates various drugs of abuse, in-cluding alcohol and tobacco, and of-fers a range of pharmacological and behavioral treatments. The intensity of treatment varies from brief counseling by subdoctoral providers up to and in-cluding inpatient treatment for nico-tine dependence (Hurt et al. 1992).

It has been suggested that research should go beyond simply looking at the issue of what happens when smok-ing treatment is added to alcohol treatment. We often forget how im-portant the sample characteristics are to research; consider, for example, the differences between individuals who have relatively low levels of drug de-pendence and high social support and those who present the opposite pro-file. Measures can be developed that relate the specific intensity and types of treatment. The research strategies recommended by Dr. Swan and col-leagues (chapter 14) concerning the use of nonlinear effects relating to the classification of subjects represent an important statistical development that can aid future research.

More consideration should be given to the transition from the ideal small-scale randomized research trial at the individual level, exemplified by the research conducted by Dr. Monti, Dr. Abrams, and colleagues at Brown University (see chapter 11), to the real-world variability in subjects, set-tings, and treatment delivery. There continues to be a tension between re-searchers conducting treatment out-come studies, where matching patients and selected treatment samples can be tightly controlled, and those studying community populations, where there is less control over both treatment quality and patient characteristics (Abrams et al. 1991). More communication is needed between researchers and practitioners.

SERVICE DELIVERY, POLICY, AND SOCIAL CONTEXT IN TREATMENT RESEARCH

An important challenge for treatment is how to create integrated health care delivery systems and the infrastructure to ensure that comprehensive and complete treatment is given to the whole population on an ongoing basis until the chronic addictive behaviors are resolved or successfully maintained. Data are needed on health care utilization and the long- and short-term costs and savings to the health care system of various treatment models. These data are vital in order to create incentives for insurance and Medicare reimbursement of tobacco treatment on an equal footing with other preventive medicine practices (such as those for hypertension and hypercholesterolemia) and with ATOD treatment.

Policies and the provision of different types of programs can produce market segmentation due to client self-selection. If there are two alcohol treatment programs available and one forbids smoking while the other permits it, then there will be selection factors that determine the population attending each clinic. Relevant issues include cognitive-behavioral mechanisms such as expectations, self-

efficacy, and intrinsic versus extrinsic motivation (Curry et al. 1990) and whether treatment is mandated or involves personal choice.

In considering possible sampling biases produced by self-selection, it is important to note that many people give up smoking and drinking on their own. Studies of natural recovery involve a different sample from those found in clinics or recruited into research studies. Treatment delivery channels also produce sampling biases: for example, Veterans Affairs hospitals versus private hospitals and work-site programs versus physician office-based contacts.

Historical records and epidemiological studies can provide useful information. The *British Medical Journal* published results of a 40-year followup of 35,000 British physicians that included questions about smoking and longevity. Standardized assessment questions of both alcohol and tobacco would be valuable in future longitudinal epidemiological surveys. Survey research is invaluable in that it can shed light on the potential sampling biases inherent in clinical treatment samples, studies of natural recovery, or other samples of convenience.

The importance of cultural norms and changing values over time should not be underestimated in terms of setting the stage for acceptance of specific treatment models and policies. At the turn of the century, several clinics treated ATOD use in a comprehensive all-addictions model. However, during Prohibition, tobacco advertising took advantage of the ban on alcohol by suggesting that tobacco was a legal and viable alternative to alcohol consumption. There was rapid expansion of cigarette consumption between 1919 and 1933. Later, physicians were used as role models in smoking advertising campaigns. More recently, women and minorities have been targeted by the tobacco industry.

As was pointed out by Dr. Bobo and colleagues in chapter 13, when the staff of a chemical dependency unit are recovered alcoholics who continue to smoke, it is difficult to treat their tobacco dependence and implement smoking policy restrictions. Furthermore, research is needed on the impact of staff training concerning nicotine issues, myths about the role of tobacco in alcohol treatment, and how best to assist with treatment. The context and role modeling of professionals or counselors can have an important influence on the attitudes of the clients, and beliefs and attributions can affect self-efficacy and outcome expectations.

HARM REDUCTION PERSPECTIVE

Although the harm reduction approach has been resisted in the United States except for methadone maintenance for heroin addiction, the cultural context may be changing sufficiently for this approach to receive increased attention. Harm reduction can help unify and integrate a number of areas and bring together behavioral scientists, public policy experts, and consumers, including the addicts themselves, to participate in the planning,

implementation, and evaluation of innovative approaches to treatment and prevention (Marlatt and Tapert 1993).

Harm reduction can integrate philosophies like methadone maintenance with those of nicotine replacement, controlled drinking, and other flexible alternatives for the whole population. This approach is in contrast to an extreme model of zero tolerance and total abstinence targeted at the hardcore group of severe abusers. Harm reduction can include abstinence as the ideal end state, but it also embraces a wider range of behavior change. It is a realistic and pragmatic approach rather than the criminal justice or disease model philosophy. Harm reduction emphasizes low-threshold treatments and the removal of barriers to treatment to encourage repeated contact and early access to harm-reducing options.

From a public health perspective, harm reduction encourages a community-based approach that can reach more individuals by meeting them where they are and first helping them meet their own needs. For example, mobile clinics could provide medical, nutritional, or referral services to shelters for those living on the streets without insisting on detoxification as a prerequisite. At some point, small changes toward improving health can be made, and it may be hoped that these changes will lead to abstinence; but harm reduction programs recognize that not everybody will be able to abstain.

Research could begin to evaluate the underlying assumptions of the harm reduction approach and whether it can be successful. One interesting possibility is the provision of nicotine replacement therapy for those with advanced medical illness who might be unable to stop smoking. Clearly, changing the route of administration from smoke inhalation to absorption through the skin or mucosa can significantly reduce the harm due to the more than 4,700 by-products of tobacco as well as reduce some of the powerful reinforcing effects of the cigarette delivery system. As Mark Twain said, "Habit is habit, and not to be flung out of the window by any man, but coaxed downstairs a step at a time."

Several testable research ideas can flow logically from a harm reduction perspective, as illustrated in chapters 15, 16, and 17. For primary care physicians who may be screening individuals for alcohol and tobacco problems, a harm reduction approach helps expand the flexibility and alternatives that can be offered by destigmatizing addictions.

Like motivational interviewing (Miller and Rollnick 1991), a harm reduction philosophy is client or patient centered. One tries to understand what patients are willing to do first and what their priorities are. They are active participants in deciding what habit to change first—smoking or drinking—or whether to change both simultaneously.

A harm reduction approach provides a range of treatment options for individuals who are not alcohol dependent but have intermittent drinking-related problems, such as weekend binges, that may result in alcohol-impaired driving or other risk-taking behavior. In this way a much broader continuum of the population can be treated earlier than otherwise would be the case.

A harm reduction approach also allows for the evaluation of comprehensive treatment programs that incorporate lifestyle and quality of life behaviors, so that stress management, exercise, nutrition, and addictive behaviors can be examined simultaneously. Not only does this provide greater flexibility of alternative healthy lifestyle skills training, but it also destigmatizes the drug abuse aspect of the client's problem. It allows us to combine traditionally insulated treatment philosophies, such as risk factor clinics, work-site wellness and employee assistance programs, rehabilitation programs, and health promotion programs.

A harm reduction approach could be tested to see if it prevents people from giving up and dropping out of treatment. This approach should encourage more rapid recycling following a slip or a relapse. It provides a flexible array of options to keep in contact with the people whom we are trying to help.

It should also be pointed out that related medical complications can be reduced with a harm reduction approach. For example, in a University of Memphis study of a controlled drinking program with men who had hypertension, it was hypothesized that reductions in drinking would lead to improvements in diastolic blood pressure and better hypertension management (Cushman unpublished manuscript 1995). Another study examined the effects of smoking cessation on lung function and found improvements and reduced demand for acute medical care among subjects with existing chronic obstructive pulmonary disease (Connett et al. 1993). A harm reduction approach would greatly facilitate the integrated management of chronic disease. Many of these ideas can be translated into research proposals for either early intervention/prevention or treatment/rehabilitation programs.

EARLY INTERVENTION AND PUBLIC POLICY

From directly changing individual knowledge, attitudes, and behaviors, we shift now to a focus on public health and policy. The research options related to public health and policy include interventions working with proximal social networks such as families, peers, and coworkers; working with organizations and communities; and considering the use of State and Federal regulations for policy change (Abrams et al. 1991). In order to make research contributions in this domain, several criteria should be kept in mind.

First, the problem should be important enough to society. There is no question that the documented biomedical and psychosocial consequences of alcohol and tobacco abuse are important. However, there are more and less visible consequences of abuse that receive attention. For example, alcohol-related crashes are more publicly visible and dramatic than the insidious damaging consequences of secondhand tobacco smoke exposure. In a national study of anti-drug coalition activity (Brandeis University 1993), the percentage of community coalitions addressing alcohol and illicit drugs ranged from 47 to 70 percent, whereas the percentage for coalitions addressing tobacco ranged from 12 to 23 percent.

Second, there should be data showing that a legal or policy intervention will be effective. Research can focus on such questions as whether a specific policy (e.g., raising the drinking age or restricting smoking in public places or work sites) is efficacious or what effect it has on the targeted behavior. Do factors such as lowering the outlet density make a difference? Innovative research on the sale of tobacco products to minors is a good example of research in this area (Altman et al. 1989).

Third, policy interventions should be minimally intrusive but maximally visible. There should be no equally effective but less intrusive alternative to the final policy that is implemented.

More research should also be devoted to the impact of abusive behaviors on others, including traffic accidents, violence, environmental tobacco exposure, and HIV infection. One pivotal point in the tobacco area was clearly the study of the impact of environmental tobacco smoke exposure. The effects of this exposure on pregnancy, early childhood development, and pediatric health care are of particular concern (Emmons et al. 1992, 1994*a*). Research that integrates tobacco and alcohol concerns in pregnancy with routine prenatal care could receive more attention (Brooke et al. 1989; Fingerhut et al. 1990; Mayer et al. 1990). This research area is of particular concern with respect to underserved and low-income groups.

Research should include common measures for alcohol and tobacco interactions. When the drinking age in all States was raised to 21 in the 1980's, there were declines in traffic fatalities; nearly 1,000 teenage deaths were prevented. However, other unintentional injuries, including drownings and pedestrian deaths, were also found to coincide with drinking-age increases. Studies on violence show mixed results in relation to drinking age. Related factors such as tobacco use and sexual behavior were not studied when the drinking age was increased, so the impact of these factors is unknown.

Research attention should be paid not only to the outcomes of policy changes, but also to the study of the process and passage of policy implementation. It is not sufficient to simply pass laws or obtain regulatory guidelines for services. Issues concerning education, enforcement, and compliance are important. There needs to be greater integration of service providers, legislators, policymakers, and health educators to ensure that all aspects of prevention and pol-

icy initiatives are being addressed to maximize the intended outcomes. It is important to study the qualitative and naturalistic tracking of coalition building. What are the mediating mechanisms and the environmental conditions that facilitate or attenuate the rapid adoption of advocacy and legislative initiatives?

Often, there are loopholes in legislation for both underage drinking and underage smoking. It is illegal in most States to *sell* alcohol to minors, but it is not illegal for minors to attempt to *purchase* alcohol in 19 States. Consumption is not illegal in 18 States, and there is no law against misrepresenting one's age in 14 States. Cigarette vending machines are legal in every State, even though it is illegal to sell tobacco products to anyone under 18. Researchers should look at similarities and differences in the alcohol and tobacco arenas with regard to youth access laws, health education in the schools, and related issues.

Although the comorbidity of heavy drinking and heavy smoking has been well described, research has not added a great deal to our knowledge of the underlying mediators and what to do about this association. This points to the importance of focusing on more applied and preventive research, where there is a greater opportunity to have an impact on the public health of communities and populations. Much of the research on early detection and early intervention has been organized around target groups at high risk such as underserved and minority groups, college students, primary care patients, or those in the emergency room of the hospital. Research has also been organized around channels of delivery or applied settings such as health management organizations, obstetrics/gynecology practices, and work sites, and more research is needed in applied settings.

Research is also needed on the extent to which interventions could be improved. Computer technology could be used for better individual tailoring as well as to provide ideographic feedback within individuals over time. Combinations of interactive computer interventions with brief counselor interventions could be evaluated in a number of settings, including work sites, schools, physicians' offices, and hospitals. The possibility of routine screening to make assessment of tobacco and alcohol abuse a "vital sign," as Fiore and colleagues (1990) have recommended, should be considered.

As we shift from individual to public health interventions, various conceptual, methodological, and practical issues are raised. We need to clearly define the research populations and the factors under investigation. For example, how do we define at-risk drinking and smoking? We have made some progress in measuring the continuum of dependence severity, but we do not have consensus on the diagnostic categories and definitions. How do we define and distinguish between early versus later interventions? Does "early" mean early in the developmental history of a progressive disorder or simply earlier than an intervention would ordinarily occur because of health-damaging consequences of drinking or smoking?

It is also important to distinguish between the goals of the intervention. As we move from rehabilitative and tertiary care treatments to primary care, it is appropriate to consider moderation drinking versus abstinence as a goal. Again, this brings up the interest in harm reduction and reducing not only consumption but also related damaging consequences to self and others. If the goal is to reach a whole population, then a range of treatment options needs to be considered—from least to most intensive, costly, and specialized. We need better definitions of what might be regarded as different levels of intervention or stepped-care treatment, such as a minimal intervention, a moderate or brief intervention, a formal treatment program, or a maximally intensive intervention (Abrams 1993). Research is needed to evaluate whether these distinctions make a difference and, if so, in which segments of the continuum of smokers and drinkers in the population? We need better ways to standardize and define our intervention programs and their active ingredients.

These issues add to the complexity of writing competitive grant proposals. Review committees need to be educated so that the realistic limitations are considered with regard to different research designs and the acceptance of alternative research strategies, including naturalistic and observational studies. In particular, the classic research designs derived from basic and clinical sciences are inappropriate, difficult, or impossible to use in some areas of prevention and policy research.

One way to integrate screening and early identification would be to focus on health risk appraisals. The World Health Organization and others have developed screening and intervention programs that integrate smoking, heavy drinking, depression, anxiety disorders, and a variety of other commonly experienced behavioral and mental problems.

TENSIONS OF RESEARCH DEVELOPMENT

Recognition of the strong association between smoking and heavy drinking is a relatively recent phenomenon. Thus, most research on alcohol-tobacco interactions has been at a very fundamental level, such as descriptive studies, and has examined a wide variety of topics. What is now in order is a sorting-out process to determine the specific factors and research questions that are most important. There is a need to identify the "keepers," so to speak.

The sorting-out process necessarily involves some tensions, because the paths to better understanding of alcohol-tobacco interactions are not readily apparent. One tension is between the need to become more comprehensive (i.e., gain a deeper understanding) and the need to be parsimonious. That is, while recognizing the synergistic and other economies of scale

that may accrue to the integration of previously fragmented research questions, programs, settings, and risk behaviors, there is also a need to simplify and focus on specific processes.

Another tension is between the need to test general concepts and the need to identify important individual difference variables. Individual difference factors are important at a number of levels, including biological differences, differences in cognitive skills, differences in demographic and other background factors, and differences in personality. Individual differences can help to define boundaries that limit generalization and to focus on what interventions are appropriate for particular subgroups. Yet, at the present state of knowledge development, it also is important to focus on global issues such as in what ways the association between smoking and heavy drinking is important, and whether there is any advantage to developing treatments that address both problems simultaneously. At the policy level, it is necessary to support a balance between research on global-level variables and research on individual difference level-variables, although in many cases the latter will follow naturally as a modification of conclusions from global-level research.

A final tension is reflected in the question of how strongly research should be theory driven versus descriptive and observational. Oversimplifications, such as asserting that all research should be theory driven, have a detrimental effect on knowledge generation. In this area as in any other area of research, the appropriateness of a research strategy depends on the questions that are being addressed. For some questions, the randomized clinical trial may be considered the "gold standard" for acceptable research rigor, but other research questions are best answered through naturalistic observation or epidemiological studies. When attempting to determine which of a large number of factors might predict cessation of smoking without treatment, a descriptive approach might be preferred.

Lessons learned from the cardiovascular and cancer prevention programs of the last two decades have provided a wealth of innovative statistical and methodological approaches to large-scale applications and research policy. Researchers conducting applied research need to be comfortable with a broad range of research designs. Studies conducted in community settings typically are not as clean in terms of control for confounds or extraneous variables as they are in laboratory, human analog, or clinical trial research. Yet, it is applications in community settings that often serve as the bottom-line measure of the worth of a research-based approach (i.e., the best research treatment is of little value if it cannot be used in ordinary treatment settings).

Studies of natural recovery (Klingemann 1992; Sobell et al. 1992, 1993a, 1993b) provide an example of the benefits of flexible research methods. Some of the patterns observed in these data have now resulted in the

ability to generate important hypotheses about how smoking cessation may or may not relate to alcohol relapse in this population. The evidence that alcoholics who stop smoking simultaneously with drinking or soon thereafter are less likely to relapse suggests a number of possible causal mechanisms that could be tested in controlled settings for various subgroups of individuals.

EMERGENT RESEARCH TRENDS

Researchers in the field of alcohol-tobacco interactions are beginning to reach the stage at which they have accumulated sufficient descriptive data to generate testable hypotheses. The Brown University research group established by Abrams and Monti 15 years ago is already at this stage. An organizational feature that facilitates research on alcohol-tobacco interactions and that is exemplified by this group is collaboration, both across areas of specialization and across disciplines. In this era of information overload, it is impossible for someone to be a specialist in all of the relevant areas within either alcohol or tobacco studies alone, much less to be a specialist on the interactions between these drugs. A high priority should be placed on establishing critical masses of researchers who can then form centers of research excellence. The Brown University group, for example, includes researchers with expertise in nicotine dependence at the biobehavioral mechanisms, the clinical, and the public health levels and researchers with similar expertise in alcohol studies at all three levels. Funding agencies should consider establishing interdisciplinary centers with sufficient critical mass to derive the incremental and synergistic benefits of this approach.

Another emergent theme is that economic and cost factors may be important determinants of how programs are integrated into the delivery system. Concerns about rising health care costs and managed care seem to be accelerating interest in early interventions and prevention in settings such as primary care offices. Clearly, studies will need to be conducted that track measures such as reductions in health care utilization, reductions in demand for expensive acute and rehabilitation services, and both short- and long-term returns on the invested prevention and treatment dollar. Such studies of health care services and of utilization and costs may be vital in order to encourage the widespread adoption of prevention and secondary intervention programs.

As we move toward a more comprehensive continuum of care, it is possible that public health initiatives will succeed in encouraging those members of the population who have less dependency, greater resources, and less vulnerability to adopt healthier lifestyles with minimal help or self-change interventions. Over time, it is likely that what will be left for the clinical care system will be the truly complicated and difficult cases. Some of these patients will be responsive to brief interventions by generalist practitioners or subdoctoral counselors. However, it can be predicted that eventually we will be left with a significant group of extremely complicated and difficult-to-treat cases: patients who have been through lesser levels of intervention and have not been helped. More research is needed on how to treat these patients, whose cases are likely to involve comorbidity of other medical and psychiatric problems as well as unhealthy behaviors in areas such as nutrition and exercise. Ultimately, treatment of these patients may require more highly specialized, intensive, and expensive services. Research is needed to inform the design, decision rules, and intervention types for this more integrated delivery system, which would combine stepped-care and matching strategies (Abrams 1993).

More research is needed on alcohol-tobacco interactions in lower socioeconomic, underserved, and minority populations. These populations tend to have significant barriers to access to health care and less health-promoting social and environmental supports. Smoking rates in lower socioeconomic groups remain in the 40 to 50 percent range, making improvement of prevention and treatment programs a priority for this population. Problems unique to women have also not received sufficient research attention.

Although there is healthy skepticism about the feasibility and promises of patient-treatment matching, it is still a worthwhile ideal (Shiffman 1993). New insights into how the broader and heterogeneous public health populations differ from those who enter clinical programs may explain some of the difficulty with patient-treatment matching within clinical trials research. Patient-treatment matching may make more sense at the macro (population) level of looking along the whole continuum of dependence and vulnerability, rather than seeking to identify a large number of specific patient-treatment interactions within a clinical sample. This is because of the narrow range of clinic samples and because it is unlikely that clinical service providers will be able to deliver a comprehensive array of specific treatments. At the macro level, one broad area of agreement concerns the importance of motivation.

There is consensus that if an individual is not motivated to change, then an intensive action-oriented prescription or skills-training program will not only be ineffective but could be considered a waste of valuable expensive resources (Miller and Rollnick 1991; Prochaska et al. 1992). It makes sense to match motivational interventions to those who are low in motivation and to match action-oriented skills training to those who are high in motivation. Recommended research goals in this area include learning how to quickly assess motivation and learning how to train generalists, subdoctoral counselors, and primary care physicians in motivational interviewing and barriers counseling (Miller and Rollnick 1991).

Matching is an important element of a stepped-care approach to treatment in that it helps determine the nature of the next level of care (i.e., the next step). Assessment and triage into higher levels of stepped care and matching to several options within each step could be researched for feasibility. Eventually, larger scale rigorous trials to evaluate this new macro-level approach to matching and stepped care could be undertaken.

Another area of common interest and concern involves the relapse model of Marlatt and Gordon (1985) and colleagues. Here again there are similarities and differences across alcohol-tobacco interactions. How does one define slips and relapses? Should one be looking at more sensitive measures of improvement, such as a change in motivational stage (Velicer et al. 1992) or days to first slip using survival analysis, rather than absolute outcome criteria at a fixed time such as 12 months posttreatment? How do cues for tobacco affect alcohol self-efficacy, expectations, and temptations to drink? How are coping responses used to manage mood states? How do mood, tobacco, and alcohol interact? In this arena, there are also important opportunities to cross-fertilize research from basic and animal studies to human laboratory analog and clinical studies.

Reciprocal interactions between animal researchers and human experimental researchers could be facilitated by interdisciplinary research on factors initiating and maintaining ATOD use. For example, studying the mechanisms in human analog research involving biobehavioral reactivity to alcohol and tobacco cues under various levels of deprivation and different mood inductions could inform animal researchers about human mechanisms. Animal research could then attempt to better simulate the actual human consumptive behaviors and mechanisms. Human research on tobacco dependence is quite different from animal research on nicotine self-administration. Researchers in these two areas need to develop common languages and methods to better inform each other about basic mechanisms and their treatment implications.

CONCLUSION

The conference on alcohol-tobacco interactions, from which this monograph is derived, represented the beginning of a more sophisticated approach to addictions involving interactions among drugs of abuse and linking these interactions to the broader context of lifestyle and health behavior. This monograph has pointed out the importance of interdisciplinary research and the need to bridge gaps, not only between scientists, practitioners, health educators, and policy researchers, but also between various levels of scientific discipline—from genetics and neurobiology to biobehavioral mechanisms research, to animal and human experimental laboratory research, to process and clinical outcomes research, to studies of prevention, diffusion, dissemination, policy, cost-effectiveness, and health care utilization.

New statistical and research design methodologies are evolving to keep pace with the need to model complex multivariate processes over time and across levels of measurement and units of analysis. Several of these innovative approaches make the traditional randomized group design only one of the options available to advance knowledge. At the risk of overstating the point, it can be said that simple main effects research is increasingly becoming a "dinosaur." Funding agencies and reviewers need to be open to the whole range of scientific methodologies, including naturalistic, qualitative, and observational research, survey and epidemiological approaches, and health services and program evaluation, as well as the traditional randomized clinical trial. The push for complexity, continuity, and comprehensive integration should be tempered by the need to focus on specific goals with achievable incremental advances in knowledge. How each piece fits into the bigger picture should be borne in mind as we move forward to integrate alcohol, tobacco, and other risk factors across basic, clinical, and public health research arenas.

This monograph has provided an exciting starting point for the next generation of research strategies for addictive behaviors in general and alcohol and tobacco abuse in particular. New innovations and syntheses will require interdisciplinary collaboration in centers that have sufficient critical mass, rather than the simple addition of nicotine dependence interventions to alcohol treatment or the study of the co-occurrence of each addictive behavior. Research must move beyond the more obvious relationships to the study of alcohol-tobacco interactions across the lifespan; among high-risk and underserved populations; across individual, group, organizational, and community structures; and in relation to psychological and medical comorbidities, health care services delivery, health policy, health promotion, and harm reduction. The excess cost to society of alcohol and tobacco abuse is enormous and far surpasses that of AIDS, suicide, and traffic fatalities combined (Brandeis University 1993). The hope is that alcohol-tobacco interaction research will contribute significantly to reducing morbidity, mortality, and health costs and to improving the overall quality of life for all citizens.

ACKNOWLEDGMENTS

This overview incorporates two discussions from the conference on alcohol-tobacco interactions: one by Drs. Richard Hurt, Lynn Kozlowski, and John Slade concerning the papers on treatment implications and outcome, and one by Drs. Ralph Hingson and Thomas Babor on the papers regarding early intervention and public policy. Their insights are gratefully acknowledged.

Support for Dr. Abrams is provided by National Institute on Alcohol Abuse and Alcoholism (NIAAA) grants 2 R01 AA08734 and 1 R01 AA07850; National Heart, Lung, and Blood Institute grant 1 R01 HL 48190; and National Cancer Institute grant P01 CA50087. NIAAA support for Dr. Marlatt is provided by a Research Scientist Award (AA00113) and a merit award grant (AA05591). Dr. Sobell's work is supported in part by NIAAA grant AA08593.

REFERENCES

Abrams, D.B. Treatment issues in tobacco dependence: Towards a stepped-care model. *Tobacco Control* 2 (suppl):S17–S37, 1993.

Abrams, D.B.; Emmons, K.M.; Niaura, R.S.; Goldstein, M.G.; and Sherman, C.E. Tobacco dependence: An integration of individual and public health perspectives. In: Nathan, P.E.; Langenbucher, J.W.; McCrady, B.S.; and Frankenstein, W., eds. *Annual Review of Addictions Treatment and Research*. Vol. I. New York: Pergamon Press, 1991. pp. 391–436.

Altman, D.B.; Foster, V.; Rasenick-Douss, L.; and Tye, J.B. Reducing the illegal sale of cigarettes to minors. *JAMA* 261:80–83, 1989.

Brandeis University, Institute for Health Policy. *Substance Abuse: The Nation's Number One Health Problem. Key Indicators for Policy*. Princeton, NJ: The Robert Wood Johnson Foundation, October 1993.

Brooke, O.G.; Ross, A.H.; Bland, J.M.; Peacock, J.L.; and Stewart, C.M. Effects on birth weight of smoking, alcohol, caffeine, socioeconomic factors and psychosocial stress. *BMJ* 298:795–801, 1989.

Brownson, R.C., and Chang, J.C. Exposure to alcohol and tobacco and the risk of laryngeal cancer. *Arch Environ Health* 42:192–196, 1987.

Colby, S.; Gulliver, S.; Rohsenow, D.; Sirota, A.; Abrams, D.B.; et al. Alcohol and smoking interaction expectancies in patients receiving alcohol treatment. Paper presented at the annual meeting of the Association for Advancement of Behavior Therapy, Atlanta, GA, November 1993.

Connett, J.E.; Kusek, J.W.; Bailey, W.C.; O'Hara, P.; and Wu, M. Design of the lung health study: A randomized clinical trial of early intervention for chronic obstructive pulmonary disease. *Control Clin Trials* 14:3S–19S, 1993.

Curry, S.; Wagner, E.H.; and Grothaus, L.C. Intrinsic and extrinsic motivation for smoking cessation. *J Consult Clin Psychol* 58:310–316, 1990.

Emmons, K.M.; Abrams, D.B.; Marshall, R.J.; Etzel, R.A.; Novotny, T.E.; Marcus, B.H.; and Kane, M.E. Exposure to environmental tobacco smoke in naturalistic settings. *Am J Public Health* 82(1):24–28, 1992.

Emmons, K.M.; Hammond, S.K.; and Abrams, D.B. Smoking at home: The impact of smoking cessation on nonsmokers' exposure to environmental tobacco smoke. *Health Psychol* 13:516–520, 1994a.

Emmons, K.M.; Marcus, B.H.; Linnan, L.; Rossi, J.S.; and Abrams, D.B. Mechanisms in multiple risk factor interventions: Smoking, physical activity, and dietary fat intake among manufacturing workers. *Prev Med* 23:481–489, 1994b.

Fingerhut, L.A.; Kleinman, J.C.; and Kendrick, J.S. Smoking before, during, and after pregnancy. *Am J Public Health* 80(5):541–544, 1990.

Fiore, M.C.; Novotny, T.E.; Pierce, J.P.; Giovino, G.E.; Hatziandreu, E.J.; Newcomb, P.A.; Surawicz, T.S.; and Davis, R.M. Methods used to quit smoking in the United States: Do cessation programs help? *JAMA* 263(20): 2760–2765, 1990.

Flanders, W.W., and Rothman, K.J. Interaction of alcohol and tobacco in laryngeal cancer. *Am J Epidemiol* 115:371–379, 1982.

Hurt, R.D.; Lauger, G.G.; Offord, K.P.; Bruce, B.K.; Dale, L.C.; McClain, F.L.; and Eberman, K.M. An integrated approach to the treatment of nicotine dependence in a medical center setting: Description of the initial experience. *J Gen Intern Med* 7(1):114–116, 1992.

Klingemann, H.K.H. Coping and maintenance strategies of spontaneous remitters from problem use of alcohol and heroin in Switzerland. *Int J Addict* 27:1359–1388, 1992.

Marcus, B.H.; Albrecht, A.E.; Niaura, R.S.; Taylor, E.R.; Simkin, L.R.; Feder, S.I.; Abrams, D.B.; and Thompson, P.D. Exercise enhances the maintenance of smoking cessation in women. *Addict Behav* 20:87–92, 1995.

Marlatt, G.A., and Gordon, J.R. *Relapse Prevention: Maintenance Strategies in Addictive Behavior Change*. New York: Guilford Press, 1985.

Marlatt, G.A., and Tapert, S.F. Harm reduction: Reducing the risks of addictive behaviors. In: Baer, J.S.; Marlatt, G.A.; and McMahon, R., eds. *Addictive Behaviors Across the Lifespan: Prevention, Treatment, and Policy Issues*. Beverly Hills, CA: Sage Publications, 1993. pp. 243–273.

Mayer, J.P.; Hawkins, B.; and Todd, R. A randomized evaluation of a smoking cessation intervention for pregnant women at a WIC clinic. *Am J Public Health* 80(1):76–78, 1990.

Miller, W.R., and Rollnick, S. *Motivational Interviewing: Preparing People to*

Change Addictive Behaviour. New York: Guilford Press, 1991.

Prochaska, J.O.; DiClemente, C.C.; and Norcross, J.C. In search of how people change: Applications to addictive behaviors. *Am Psychol* 47:1102–1114, 1992.

Rosengren, A.; Wilhelmsen, L.; and Wedel, H. Separate and combined effects of smoking and alcohol abuse in middle-aged men. *Acta Med Scand* 223:111–118, 1988.

Shiffman, S. Smoking cessation treatment: Any progress? *J Consult Clin Psychol* 61: 718–722, 1993.

Sobell, L.C.; Sobell, M.B.; and Toneatto, T. Recovery from alcohol problems without treatment. In: Heather, N.; Miller, W.R.; and Greeley, J., eds. *Self-Control and the Addictive Behaviours.* New York: Maxwell MacMillan, 1992. pp. 198–242.

Sobell, L.C.; Cunningham, J.A.; Sobell, M.B.; and Toneatto, T. A life span perspective on natural recovery (self-change) from alcohol problems. In: Baer, J.S.;

Marlatt, G.A.; and McMahon, R.J., eds. *Addictive Behaviors Across the Lifespan: Prevention, Treatment, and Policy Issues.* Beverly Hills, CA: Sage, 1993a. pp. 34–66.

Sobell, L.C.; Sobell, M.B.; Toneatto, T.; and Leo, G.I. What triggers the resolution of alcohol problems without treatment? *Alcohol Clin Exp Res* 17:217–224, 1993b.

Velicer, W.F.; Prochaska, J.O.; Rossi, J.S.; and Snow, M.G. Assessing outcome in smoking cessation studies. *Psychol Bull* 111:23–41, 1992.

Wilson, G.T. Eating disorders and addictive disorders. In: Brownell, K.D., and Fairburn, C.G. *Eating Disorders and Obesity.* New York: Guilford Press, 1995. pp. 165–170.

Zacny, J.P. Behavioral aspects of alcohol-tobacco interactions. In: Galanter, M., ed. *Recent Developments in Alcoholism: Volume 8. Combined Alcohol and Other Drug Dependence.* New York: Plenum Press, 1990. pp. 205–219.